THE SUPERHERO READER

THE SUPERHERO READER

Edited by Charles Hatfield, Jeet Heer,
and Kent Worcester

UNIVERSITY PRESS OF MISSISSIPPI • JACKSON

www.upress.state.ms.us

The University Press of Mississippi is a member of the Association of American University Presses.

Copyright © 2013 by University Press of Mississippi
All rights reserved

First printing 2013

∞

Library of Congress Cataloging-in-Publication Data

The superhero reader / edited by Charles Hatfield, Jeet Heer, and Kent Worcester.
    pages cm
  Includes bibliographical references and index.
  ISBN 978-1-61703-802-0 (cloth : alk. paper) — ISBN 978-1-61703-806-8 (pbk. : alk. paper) — ISBN 978-1-61703-803-7 (ebook) 1. Comic books, strips, etc.—History and criticism. 2. Superheroes in literature. 3. Superheroes. I. Hatfield, Charles, 1965– editor of compilation. II. Heer, Jeet, editor of compilation. III. Worcester, Kent, 1959– editor of compilation.
  PN6710.S87 2013
  741.5'9—dc23   2013004069

British Library Cataloging-in-Publication Data available

CONTENTS

Acknowledgments ix

Introduction xi

I. HISTORICAL CONSIDERATIONS 3

Comics Predecessors 7
PETER COOGAN

Men of Tomorrow 16
GERARD JONES

Gladiator 23
PHILIP WYLIE

The Great Comic Book Heroes 30
JULES FEIFFER

The Comics and the Super State 34
WALTER ONG

The Superman Conceit 46
FREDRIC WERTHAM

The Great Women Superheroes 53
TRINA ROBBINS

Fandom and Authorship 61
WILL BROOKER

II. THEORY AND GENRE 73

Literary Formulas 78
JOHN G. CAWELTI

Crowds of Superheroes 80
ROBERT JEWETT AND JOHN SHELTON LAWRENCE

The Epic Hero and Pop Culture 84
ROGER B. ROLLIN

Masked Heroes 99
RICHARD REYNOLDS

The Revisionary Superhero Narrative 116
GEOFF KLOCK

Jack Kirby and the Marvel Aesthetic 136
CHARLES HATFIELD

Navigating Infinite Earths 155
KARIN KUKKONEN

A Song of the Urban Superhero 170
SCOTT BUKATMAN

III. CULTURE AND IDENTITY 199

Wonder Woman 203
GLORIA STEINEM

Invisible Girl 211
LILLIAN ROBINSON

Love Will Bring You to Your Gift 216
JENNIFER STULLER

Batman, Deviance and Camp 237
ANDY MEDHURST

Color Them Black 252
ADILIFU NAMA

Comic Book Masculinity 269
JEFFREY BROWN

The Punisher as Revisionist Superhero Western   279
LORRIE PALMER

Death-Defying Heroes   295
HENRY JENKINS

List of Contributors   305

Index   309

ACKNOWLEDGMENTS

Our thanks go to our contributors, as well to Bart Beaty, Walter Biggins, Paul Buhle, Jon B. Cooke, Craig Fischer, Ian Gordon, Karen Green, Tom Hart, Dean Haspiel, Gene Kannenberg, Jr., Jude Killroy, Guy Lawley, Andrei Molotiu, Heather Nunnelly, and Julia Worcester. We are pleased to dedicate this book to Michele, Robin, and Amy.

INTRODUCTION

To wrench the human soul from its moorings, to immerse it in terrors, ice, flames, and raptures to such an extent that it is liberated from all petty displeasure, gloom, and depression as by a flash of lightening: what paths lead to this goal? And which of them do so most surely?
   FRIEDRICH NIETZSCHE (1967 [1887]: 139)

For if ever there does appear upon this planet a tightly knit minority of really superior people, it will be the end of all the rest of mankind and mankind knows it, not having come through a billion-odd years of evolutionary struggle for nothing.
   PHILIP WYLIE (1942: 139–40)

COMICS IS AN ART FORM; SUPERHEROES ARE A GENRE. THIS TERSE DISTINCTION lies at the heart of current scholarship on comics.[1] While some readers still conflate comic books and superheroes, the recent emergence of interdisciplinary comics studies presupposes that comics, including their long-form incarnation, graphic novels, can be much more. Indeed, comics can advance myriad storytelling agendas. It is no surprise that, until recently, the most compelling contributions to comics scholarship focused on historical, political, autobiographical, avant-garde, and other "serious minded" comics, for it is precisely these kinds of studies that complicate or upend longstanding suppositions regarding the medium's inherently juvenile and unserious nature.[2] If journalists typically depict the world of comics through the lens of box office receipts and costumed convention goers, it makes sense that academics might concentrate on material that is less likely to be mocked on the evening news, or by colleagues.

   The struggle for professional respectability has had a high cost, however. Even as academic specialists have rightly insisted on the depth and range of comics, some persist in downplaying the superhero genre's expressive potential, metaphoric adaptability, and historical durability. Superhero comics are not the same thing as comics *per se*, but they *are* integral to the development of the American comic book, and therefore to the history of the form. Admittedly, the genre has roots outside of comics: antecedents for the superhero can be traced back through pulp literature to ancient myths and legends, what Joseph Campbell called "the basic images of ritual, mythology, and vision" (18). But superheroes are intertwined with comics history to an extent that is not true of other major multimedia genres such as science fiction, horror, romance, or the western. All of those genres, and more, have been very important to comics, but the superhero stands apart. From the standpoint of English-language comics, at least, the superhero is not just another genre, but one that has made all the difference.

Superheroes have played a central role in the story of comic books almost from their inception. Moreover, despite the genre's relative dormancy from the late 1940s through the late 1950s, superheroes have stood the test of time. Indeed the superhero has been a staple of the medium and, since the sixties, the one overwhelmingly dominant market genre. As a result, the sheer volume of superhero comics that have been published over the years is staggering. Indeed, the major superhero universes constitute one of the most expansive storytelling canvases ever fashioned in any culture. Moreover, the characters inhabiting these fictional universes are immensely influential, having achieved iconic recognition around the world. Their images and adventures have also influenced other art forms, such as film, videogames, and prose fiction.

The porous boundary that separates superhero studies from comics fandom may help explain the discomfort that many academics feel in relation to the genre. While fan-based knowledge is increasingly valued in the academy, fannishness is still regarded as, almost by definition, a symptom of a failure to professionalize. But the forward march of comics studies depends not on resisting genre-based storytelling and its attendant fan culture, but on recognizing what superhero artists and writers bring to the table. As Ben Saunders usefully observes in an essay titled "On the Place of Superhero Studies within Comics Studies":

> It will be better for the future of Comics Studies if we refuse to transform generic distinctions into hierarchical ones. We don't need to have our own version of the fight that some music critics got into back in the 1970s over the merits of rock versus disco (or that a rather earlier generation of literary critics got into over the merits of poetry versus the novel). The discipline we want to create together can surely be big enough to contain appreciative studies of the "spirituality of the superhero," shall we say, alongside accounts of "representations of the self in graphic memoir." (151)

In other words, superhero comics merit considered attention. This is true not only because superheroes have sustained the American comic book industry over a period of several decades, thus enabling comic book stores to carry other kinds of comics, but because superheroes are intrinsically engaging from many angles—cultural, historical, sociological, even literary and aesthetic. As our contributor Scott Bukatman has noted, superheroes "embody social anxiety" as well as our "ambivalent and shifting attitudes towards flesh, self, and society." Stressing the corporeal aspect of the superhero, he cites the work of the anthropologist Mary Douglas, who argued—in a different context, to be sure—that "cultures which frankly develop bodily symbolism may be seen to use it to confront experience with its inevitable pains and losses. By such themes they face the greatest paradoxes of existence." For Bukatman, superheroes are "mysterious, invested with magical abilities and a metamorphic pliability; if they are marginal bodies in the body of literature, this still should not blind us to their importance" (49–51).

Superheroes thus occupy a magical yet marginal position in contemporary popular culture. For the better part of a century they have offered a seemingly inexhaustible resource for commercial artists, publishers, moviemakers, animators, radio and television dramatists, videogame designers, and other cultural entrepreneurs looking for fantastical, larger-than-life archetypes, tropes, scenarios, and what-ifs to entertain readers, listeners, viewers, and players. Indeed, in recent years the border between the superhero genre and other mass entertainment genres has been smudged: many contemporary icons, including high-tech spies, martial artists, detectives, vampire hunters, and adolescent wizards, seem to possess powers similar to those traditionally wielded by costumed superheroes. Emboldened by advances in digital visual effects, major film studios have been keen to tap the superhero revenue stream and also to blur the distinction between the superhero and the merely heroic. Thus the number of big screen franchises derived from intellectual properties controlled by either Marvel (currently owned by Disney) or DC (Time Warner) continues to grow. Superhero parodies, pastiches, and revisionisms are also increasingly popular, on both big and small screens. In one guise or another the "super-empowered individual" (Friedman 5–6) has become ubiquitous.[3]

Yet despite their commercial clout and cross-media reach, superheroes have only recently received sustained scholarly attention. The first critical book in English devoted to the "great comic book heroes" appeared in the mid-1960s, and most of the many secondary texts published since have been aimed at hardcore fan-consumers, with an emphasis on commemoration and imagery rather than analysis.[4] This has only bolstered a received wisdom that insists that superhero comics are of necessity formulaic, masculinist, melodramatic, and morally reductive. The phrase that neatly sums up this perspective is "adolescent male power fantasy," a dismissive coinage that suggests that superhero stories are incapable of conveying meaningful ideas or expressing idiosyncratic visions, and that superheroes are inherently superficial and conformist. The fact that graphic novels like *Maus* (1986–91), *Jimmy Corrigan* (2003), *Persepolis* (2007), and *American Born Chinese* (2008) have earned widespread critical acclaim does not mean that critics, intellectuals, and consumers of alternative or (in fan terms) "non-mainstream" comics have jettisoned their preconceptions. Indeed, some of the harshest critics of the superhero genre are precisely those who have most enthusiastically embraced the literary graphic novel.

In thinking about superheroes, it helps to separate two distinct propositions that are often conflated. The first is that comics is an aesthetic form capable of thoughtful and diverse expression; the second is that superheroes warrant sustained attention. Both of these propositions may be true—we believe they are—but they are not interchangeable, nor is one necessarily the corollary of the other. As a survey of the critical literature readily shows, one may argue the first without conceding the second. Conversely, scholars may take a serious interest in superheroes for reasons unconnected to aesthetic interest in comics. Such a position may now be a minority one, but both academics and public intellectuals—such as Walter Ong, Marshall McLuhan, and Fredric Wertham—have taken superheroes seriously without taking seriously the idea that comics can be art. Their interest in superheroes grew out of social and moral concerns, as did much of the early academic criticism of comics generally. In fact, some critics, for example John Shelton Lawrence and Robert Jewett in *The Myth of the American Superhero* (2002) and *Captain America and the Crusade against Evil* (2003), regard the superhero as a value-laden symbol rather than a codified narrative genre. Such critics tend to be indifferent to the specific qualities of superhero comics as such.

One may study comics from an aesthetic angle without granting pride of place, or indeed any place, to the superhero genre. Vice versa, one may explore what superheroes might mean socially, culturally, or ideologically without making any general claim regarding comics as an art form. This is because there are different kinds of seriousness one may take as a rationale. An ideological seriousness about what superheroes mean is not the same as an artistic seriousness about comics. Superhero studies does not automatically benefit from the proposition that comics is an art form. Different kinds of study demand different warrants, that is, different sorts of justification.

In the wake of cultural studies, the proposition that superheroes merit our attention will probably be granted readily enough. The genre, both on the page and on the screen, is widely understood to be ideologically freighted: a mirror, and perhaps a shaper, of cultural and moral values. The study of such things can take either an adversarial or sympathetic stance, depending on the researcher's perspective. However, the claim that superhero comics can reward close study on formal and aesthetic grounds remains controversial, even among scholars who have committed their careers to the study of comics more generally. A warrant on the grounds of aesthetics, form, or genre poses different questions than one based on sociological and political concerns. A number of prominent cartoonists and comic book writers, notably Art Spiegelman and Harvey Pekar, but also others, have concluded that the superhero genre is essentially fascistic and/or absurd and therefore deserves a pitiless shellacking. This would still be a form of seriousness.

Suffice to say that even in this age of blossoming comics study, the superhero remains a divisive topic. Comics studies has not quite granted the necessity or even fitness of studying superheroes from aesthetic or humanistic perspectives such as the literary or art-historical, even though few academics interested in cultural studies would deny the ripeness of the genre for study on semiotic and ideological grounds. Studies of the superhero remain an outlier within the fast-growing literary discourse on comics. As a result, some comics scholars, despite the field's inroads to legitimacy, still continue to decry what they see as the cultural elitism of the academy. The treatment of the superhero is a ready focus for such complaints. In other words, the hoped-for elevation of comics as a research topic has not happened evenly for all genres, or across all disciplines, and the superhero has certainly not been the main beneficiary of the proposition that comics can be art. There persists, and will probably continue to persist, resistance to superhero comics and superhero analysis on both ideological and aesthetic grounds. This is likely to remain a fault line within the field, and indeed treading along that fault line, examining and questioning its persistence, could be a productive area for future metacritical work.

As our bibliography makes clear, though, there is no shortage of current scholarship about the superhero. A substantial chunk of the work now being done by younger comics scholars in North America takes the superhero, and more broadly the so-called mainstream comic book tradition of which the superhero is the core, as its polestar. Journal articles on superheroes have begun to appear in greater numbers only recently—see, for example, the *Journal of Graphic Novels and Comics*'s 2011 issue on "Superheroes and Gender"—but conference papers on the genre have been commonplace for many years. In addition, much scholarship based in fandom, which lies outside the rules and criteria of academe, continues to orbit around the genre. Superheroes are not exactly underserved by contemporary scholarship, even though the number of cutting-edge publications about the genre does not proportionately match the amount of interest it generates at conferences, online, and within fan culture. Superhero studies has long been a major if not the predominate focus of comics studies that do not reach the threshold of scholarly book publication.

Over the past few years, however, the number of scholarly books on the genre has exploded. Academic monographs that have raised the bar for superhero studies include Matthew Costello's *Secret Identity Crisis: Comic Books and the Unmasking of Cold War America* (2009), Charles Hatfield's *Hand of Fire: The Comics Art of Jack Kirby* (2011); Roz Kaveney's *Superheroes! Capes and Crusaders in Comics and Film* (2008); Adilifu Nama's *Super Black: American Pop Culture and Black Superheroes* (2011); Ben Saunders's *Do the Gods Wear Capes? Spirituality, Fantasy, and Superheroes* (2011); and Marc Singer's *Grant Morrison: Combining the Worlds of Contemporary Comics* (2011). In addition, several noteworthy essay collections have recently appeared, including Angela Ndalianis's *The Contemporary Comic Book Superhero* (2008); Terrence Wandtke's *The Amazing Transforming Superhero!* (2007); and Robert Weiner's *Captain America and the Struggle of the Superhero* (2009). While some of these titles were issued by university presses, many were published by independent houses that are known for supporting popular culture studies, such as Continuum, Routledge, and McFarland. Building on earlier works by Brooker (2000), Pearson and Uricchio (1991), and Reynolds (UK 1992; U.S. 1994), as well as Feiffer (1965), this new critical literature has laid the groundwork for a smarter, less impressionist, and more analytic approach to the superhero genre in particular and genre studies more generally. Although these books vary greatly in agenda, methodology, and tone, the majority focus equally on the social significance of superheroes and the recognition that the genre represents a distinctive aesthetic tradition. Such studies offer a way out, or rather multiple ways out, of the impasse between cultural studies and aesthetic appreciation.

Despite this, not a few scholars still seem bemused, if not outraged, by the recognition that our two propositions—that comics is a serious art form, and that superheroes should be studied seriously—don't quite meet, that these propositions may assume different modes of seriousness and do not necessarily lead in the same direction. Superhero comics and superhero studies alike have sought to capitalize on the first proposition, that comics is an art, often ignoring the specific problems posed by the genre, its commercial history, and its ideological baggage. Yet there are good reasons why superhero comics make some people nervous. Rigorous analyses of the genre need to grapple with those reasons, not simply bewail the fact that the equation Comics = Art does not automatically give the genre a free pass. Questions of political content, gender and eroticism, ability and disability, the depiction and celebration of violence, the worship of power, and the genre's reliance on a spectacular hyperrealism all stand in the way of any easy absorption of our first proposition into the second.

While the best superhero comics are vital and fascinating *as* comics, superhero studies can only proceed on the basis of addressing, rather than eliding, the moral, social, and ideological issues that the genre raises. Alan Moore and

Dave Gibbons certainly understood this when they coauthored the landmark graphic novel *Watchmen* (1986–1987), a powerful deconstruction of the genre that nonetheless remains in and of the genre. (In terms of shifting public perceptions of the genre, *Watchmen* is to the superhero what Art Spiegelman's *Maus* (1996) has been to the comics art form as a whole.) Likewise, Denny O'Neil and Neal Adams understood this when they sought to make *Green Lantern/Green Arrow* responsive to the political debates of its time (the early 1970s), and Harvey Kurtzman, Wallace Wood, and Will Elder understood this when they expertly satirized Superman, Batman, and Wonder Woman in early issues of *Mad* (1953–1954). A number of more recent superhero titles—such as Mark Millar et al.'s *Red Son* (2004), Grant Morrison et al.'s *The Invisibles* (1994–2000), Steven Seagle and Teddy Kristiansen's *It's a Bird* (2004), Warren Ellis and John Cassaday's *Planetary* (2000–), Kurt Busiek et al.'s *Astro City* (1999–), and James Sturm and Guy Davis's *Unstable Molecules* (2003)—similarly challenge superhero-phobia with searching, questioning, at times even subversive content. The history of the genre is packed with, if not built on, contradictions, provocations, creative breakthroughs, and ideological troublemaking.

The recognition that comics is a legitimate and endlessly adaptable art form does not win for the superhero any respite from close critical scrutiny. The kinds of seriousness that will make superhero studies productive must confront a variety of issues, ideological as well as aesthetic; economic, historical, and political as well as formal. While we doubt it will be possible to achieve a harmonious consensus on all such questions, we do expect that a mature field of superhero studies, of the kind that is now starting to emerge, will confront, at last, the old charges about academic elitism. It may not do so in ways that make anything easier, or anyone more comfortable, but the intellectual yield and social relevance of the work will be enough. In the meantime, we recognize that there are valuable scholarly works that embrace both of our propositions at once, as well as important ones that approach the superhero, and comics more generally, from a more skeptical angle. We think that superhero comics can bear up under such scrutiny--and warrant it.

The primary aim of this reader is thus twofold: first, to collect in a single volume a sampling of the most sophisticated or influential commentary on superheroes, and, second, to bring into sharper focus the ways in which superheroes connect with larger social, cultural, literary, aesthetic, and historical concerns. Our book brings together essays, articles, and book excerpts by leading freelance writers and academics. It covers a range of topics, including—but certainly not limited to—the following:

• the definitional boundaries of the superhero
• superheroes and the human body

- superheroes and the modern city
- superheroes and gender
- superheroes and fan culture
- the business of superheroes
- the superhero as modern mythology
- the superhero as futurology
- the political, psychoanalytic, and parodic uses of the superhero

To address these topics we have organized the volume into three sections, each opening with a short introduction. The first section, Historical Considerations, explores the prehistory and early history of the superhero genre, and features both primary sources and secondary readings. The second, Theory and Genre, spotlights the range of approaches that scholars have adopted in discussing superheroes, and genre more generally, from folklore and myth studies to cultural studies and critical theory. The third, Culture and Identity, examines the superhero from the perspective of gender, race, sexuality, cultural patterns, and reader identification.

This format echoes the one we adopted for our previous volume, *A Comics Studies Reader* (2009), and the two texts are intended to complement each other. The potential audience for both books includes not only academic specialists working on comics, film, and popular culture, but also students and scholars from across the humanities and historically-minded social sciences, as well as comics fans and general readers. While it would be unrealistic to expect that every historically significant article or monograph on this multifaceted topic could be collected in a single volume, we have striven to include a fair cross-section of the most salient contributions.

The superhero is a polarizing genre that has generated fierce battles for a host of reasons: political, gender-oriented, psychological, formalist, and aesthetic. Is the genre inherently authoritarian, or does it contain multiple ideological valences? What should we make of the hypermasculinity of superhero comics? Is their highly stylized imagery evidence of sexism, a foregrounding of sexual anxiety, or a vivid display of a queer sensibility that is otherwise culturally suppressed? Is the collaborative mode of production used in the making of most superhero comics a betrayal of auteurist authenticity or a way of creatively synthesizing different artistic talents? Is the superhero an embarrassing offshoot of science fiction or a meta-genre that imaginatively fuses together material from a variety of literary traditions? All of these are hotly debated issues, and the very passion stirred up by these arguments is one of the best reasons for taking both the superhero genre and its critics seriously. The intent of this collection is to highlight these debates and tensions with a view toward pushing the conversation forward.

NOTES

1. An influential formulation of this distinction is given in the first chapter of Scott McCloud's *Understanding Comics*, which depicts the medium as a glass pitcher that can hold an endless variety of "liquids," i.e., stories. Given the lengths to which he goes to disentangle the medium from its best-known genre, it is mildly ironic that many of McCloud's fictional comics deal in superheroes. See Scott McCloud, *Understanding Comics: The Invisible Art* (1993) and *Zot! The Complete Black and White Collection: 1987–1991* (2008).
2. In this context, it is perhaps worth noting that our previous coedited volume, *A Comics Studies Reader* (2009), features only two contributions on superhero comics out of more than two dozen essays. While we did not consciously set out to exclude superhero analyses, we ended up reproducing the field's prevailing unease regarding the genre. Superheroes also receive less attention than might be expected in our first coedited volume, *Arguing Comics: Literary Masters on a Popular Medium* (2004). The present volume will hopefully redress the imbalance and help integrate superhero studies into the study of comics more generally. We have added a third editor, Charles Hatfield, precisely because he is a preeminent comics scholar who has written on both superhero and non-superhero comics, and has taught courses on superheroes at the undergraduate and graduate level.
3. The term "super-empowered individual" was coined by the *New York Times* columnist Thomas Friedman, who uses it to refer to non-state actors who "can increasingly act on the world stage directly, unmediated by a state" (5). While he came up with the phrase in the context of writing about Osama bin Laden, it has a definite superhero studies ring to it.
4. See Feiffer, *The Great Comic Book Heroes* (1965). An excerpt from Feiffer's groundbreaking study is included in this volume, as is an excerpt from Fredric Wertham's *Seduction of the Innocent* (1954), which offers a rather sweeping critique of comic books in general. Other early works include Steranko (1970); Lupoff and Thompson (1970); Thompson and Lupoff (1973); and Jacobs and Jones (1985, confusingly billed as "the first history of modern comic books"). In addition, roughly half of Daniels's *Comix* (1971) is devoted to superheroes. The earliest surveys of comics and cartoons tended to relegate superhero comics to a few paragraphs or a single chapter: see for example Becker (1959), Sheridan (1942), and Waugh (1947).

WORKS CITED AND CONSULTED

Andrea, Thomas, and Mel Gordon. *Siegel and Shuster's Funnyman: The First Jewish Superhero. From the Creators of Superman*. Port Townsend, WA: Feral House, 2010.

Becker, Stephen. *Comic Art in America: A Social History of the Funnies, the Political Cartoons, Magazine Humor, Sporting Cartoons, and Animated Cartoons*. New York: Simon and Schuster, 1959.

Berlatsky, Eric L. *Alan Moore: Conversations*. Jackson, MS: University Press of Mississippi, 2012.

Brooker, Will. *Batman Unmasked: Analyzing a Cultural Icon*. New York: Continuum, 2000.

Brown, Jeffrey A. *Black Superheroes, Milestone Comics, and Their Fans*. Jackson, MS: University Press of Mississippi, 2001.

Bukatman, Scott. "X-Bodies: The Torment of the Mutant Superhero." 1994. Reprinted in Scott Bukatman, *Matters of Gravity: Special Effects and Supermen in the Twentieth Century*. Durham, NC: Duke University Press, 2003.

Busiek, Kurt, Brent E. Anderson, Alex Ross, et al. *Astro City*, Vol. 1: *Life in the Big City*. New York: WildStorm, 1999.

Campbell, Joseph. *The Hero with a Thousand Faces.* 1949. Princeton: Princeton University Press, 1973.
Cawelti, John G. *Adventure, Mystery, and Romance: Formula Stories as Art and Popular Culture.* Chicago: University of Chicago Press, 1976.
Chabon, Michael. *The Amazing Adventures of Kavalier and Clay.* New York: Picador, 2001.
Chute, Hillary. "Comics as Literature? Reading Graphic Narrative." *PMLA,* Vol. 123, no. 4 (March 2008).
Coogan, Peter. *Superhero: The Secret Origin of a Genre.* Austin, TX: MonkeyBrain Books, 2006.
Cooke, Darwyn, et al. *The New Frontier,* Volume One. New York: DC Comics, 2004.
———. *The New Frontier,* Volume Two. New York: DC Comics, 2005.
Costello, Matthew J. *Secret Identity Crisis: Comic Books and the Unmasking of Cold War America.* New York: Continuum, 2009.
Daniels, Les. *Comix: A History of Comic Books in America.* New York: Outerbridge and Dienstfrey, 1971.
Ellis, Warren, John Cassaday, et al. *Planetary, Vol 1: All Over the World and Other Stories.* New York: WildStorm, 2000.
Feiffer, Jules. *The Great Comic Book Heroes.* New York: Dial Press, 1965.
Fingeroth, Danny. *Disguised as Clark Kent: Jews, Comics, and the Creation of the Superhero.* New York: Continuum, 2007.
———. *Superman on the Couch: What Superheroes Really Tell Us about Ourselves and Our Society.* New York: Continuum, 2004.
Friedman, Thomas. *Longitudes and Attitudes: The World in the Age of Terrorism.* New York: Anchor, 2003.
Gabilliet, Jean-Paul. *Of Comics and Men: A Cultural History of American Comic Books.* Translated by Bart Beaty and Nick Nguyen. Jackson. MS: University Press of Mississippi, 2010.
Garrett, Greg. *Holy Superheroes! Exploring the Sacred in Comics, Graphic Novels, and Film.* Louisville, KY: Westminster John Knox Press, 2008.
Grossman, Austin. *Soon I Will Be Invisible: A Novel.* New York: Pantheon, 2007.
Hatfield, Charles. *Alternative Comics: An Emerging Literature.* Jackson, MS: University Press of Mississippi, 2005.
———. *Hand of Fire: The Comics Art of Jack Kirby.* Jackson, MS: University Press of Mississippi, 2011.
Haslem, Wendy, Angela Ndalianis, and Chris Mackie, eds. *Super/Heroes: From Hercules to Superman.* Washington, DC: New Academia Publishing, 2007.
Heer, Jeet, and Kent Worcester, eds. *Arguing Comics: Literary Masters on a Popular Medium.* Jackson, MS: University Press of Mississippi, 2004.
———, eds. *A Comics Studies Reader.* Jackson, MS: University Press of Mississippi, 2009.
Howe, Sean, ed. *Give Our Regards to the Atomsmashers! Writers on Comics.* New York: Pantheon, 2004.
Huxley, David, and Joan Ormrod, eds. "Special Issue on Gender and Superheroes." *Journal of Graphic Novels and Comics,* Vol. 2, no. 1 (2011).
Jacobs, Will, and Gerard Jones, *The Comic Book Heroes: From the Silver Age to the Present.* New York: Crown Publishers, 1985.
Jewett, Robert, and John Shelton Lawrence. *Captain America and the Crusade against Evil: The Dilemma of Zealous Nationalism.* Grand Rapids, MI: Wm. B. Eerdmans Publishing Co., 2003.

Jones, Gerard. *Men of Tomorrow: Geeks, Gangsters and the Birth of the Comic Book.* New York: Basic Books, 2004.
Kaveney, Roz. *Superheroes! Capes and Crusaders in Comics and Films.* London: I. B. Tauris, 2008.
Klock, Geoff. *How to Read Superhero Comics and Why.* New York: Continuum, 2006.
Knowles, Christopher. *Our Gods Wear Spandex: The Secret History of Comic Book Heroes.* San Francisco: Weiser Books, 2007.
Lawrence, John Shelton, and Robert Jewett. *The Myth of the American Superhero.* Grand Rapids, MI: Wm. B. Eerdmans Publishing Co., 2002.
Lethem, Jonathan. *Fortress of Solitude.* New York: Vintage, 2004.
———. *Men and Cartoons.* New York: Vintage, 2005.
Lopes, Paul. *Demanding Respect: The Evolution of the American Comic Book.* Philadelphia, PA: Temple University Press, 2009.
Lupoff, Dick, and Don Thompson, eds. *All in Color for A Dime.* New York: Arlington Books, 1970.
McCloud, Scott. *Understanding Comics: The Invisible Art.* Northampton, MA: Tundra, 1993
———. *Zot! The Complete Black and White Collection: 1987–1991.* New York: Harper Paperbacks, 2008.
Millar, Mark, Dave Johnson, Kilian Plunkett, et al. *Red Son.* New York: DC Comics, 2004.
Moore, Alan, and Dave Gibbons. *Watchmen.* With John Higgins. 1986–1987. New York: DC Comics, 1995.
Morris, Tom, and Matt Morris, eds. *Superheroes and Philosophy: Truth, Justice, and the Socratic Way.* Chicago: Open Court, 2005.
Morrison, Grant. *Supergods: What Masked Vigilantes, Miraculous Mutants, and a Sun God from Smallville Can Teach Us about Being Human.* New York: Spiegel & Grau, 2011.
Morrison, Grant, et al. *The Invisibles Omnibus.* New York: Vertigo, 2012.
Nama, Adilifu. *Super Black: American Pop Culture and Black Superheroes.* Austin. TX: University of Texas Press, 2011.
Ndalianis, Angela, ed. *The Contemporary Comic Book Superhero.* New York: Routledge, 2009.
Nietzsche, Friedrich. *On the Genealogy of Morals.* 1887. New York: Vintage Books, 1967.
———. *Thus Spoke Zarathustra: A Book for All and None.* 1892. New York: Penguin, 1978.
O'Neil, Dennis, and Neal Adams. *Green Lantern/Green Arrow: Hard-Traveling Heroes.* New York: DC Comics, 1992.
———. *Green Lantern/Green Arrow: More Hard-Traveling Heroes.* New York: DC Comics, 1993.
Paik, Peter Y. *From Utopia to Apocalypse: Science Fiction and the Politics of Catastrophe.* Minneapolis: University of Minnesota Press, 2010.
Raphael, Jordan, and Tom Spurgeon. *Stan Lee and the Rise and Fall of the American Comic Book.* Chicago: Chicago Review Press, 2003.
Pearson, Roberta E., and William Uricchio, eds. *The Many Lives of the Batman. Critical Approaches to a Superhero and Its Media.* London: Routledge, 1991.
Reynolds, Richard. *Superheroes: A Modern Mythology.* Jackson, MS: University Press of Mississippi, 1994.
Ro, Ronin. *Tales to Astonish: Jack Kirby, Stan Lee, and the American Comic Book Revolution.* London: Bloomsbury, 2004.
Robinson, Lillian. *Wonder Women: Feminisms and Superheroes.* New York: Routledge, 2004.
Satrapi, Marjane. *The Complete Persepolis.* New York: Pantheon, 2007.
Saunders, Ben. *Do the Gods Wear Capes? Spirituality, Fantasy, and Superheroes.* New York: Continuum, 2011.

Seagle, Steven T., and Kristiansen, Teddy. *It's a Bird*. New York: Vertigo, 2004.
Sheridan, Martin. *Comics and Their Creators: Life Stories of American Cartoonists*. Boston: Hale, Cushman and Flint, 1942.
Singer, Marc. *Grant Morrison: Combining the Worlds of Contemporary Comics*. Jackson, MS: University Press of Mississippi, 2011.
Smith, Matthew J., and Randy Duncan, eds. *Critical Approaches to Comics: Theories and Methods*. New York: Routledge, 2012.
Spiegelman, Art. *The Complete Maus: A Survivor's Tale*. New York: Pantheon, 1996.
Steinem, Gloria, and Phyllis Chesler, *Wonder Woman*. New York: Bonanza Books, 1972.
Steranko, James. *The Steranko History of Comics, Volume 1*. Reading, PA: Supergraphics, 1970.
Sturm, James, Guy Davis, et al. *Unstable Molecules (Fantastic Four Legends Volume 1)*. New York: Marvel Comics, 2003.
Stuller, Jennifer K. *Ink-Stained Amazons and Cinematic Warriors: Superwomen in Modern Mythology*. London: I. B. Tauris, 2010.
Thompson, Don, and Dick Lupoff, eds. *The Comic-Book Book*. New York: Arlington Books, 1973.
Wandtke, Terrence R., ed. *The Amazing Transforming Superhero! Essays on the Revision of Characters in Comic Books, Film and Television*. Jefferson, NC: McFarland, 2007.
Ware, Chris. *Jimmy Corrigan: The Smartest Kid on Earth*. New York: Pantheon, 2003.
Waugh, Coulton. *The Comics*. New York: Macmillan, 1947.
Weiner, Robert G. *Captain America and the Struggle of the Superhero: Critical Essays*. Jefferson, NC: McFarland, 2009.
Wertham, Fredric. *Seduction of the Innocent*. New York: Holt, Reinhart and Wilson, 1954.
Witek, Joseph, ed. *Art Spiegelman: Conversations*. Jackson, MS: University Press of Mississippi, 2007.
Worcester, Kent. "Superman, Philip Wylie, and the New Deal." *Comics Forum*, no. 6 (1994).
Wylie, Philip. *A Generation of Vipers: A Survey of Moral Want and a Philosophical Discourse Suitable Only for the Strong and a Study of American Types and Archetypes and a Signpost on the Two Thoroughfares of Man*. New York: Farrar & Reinhart, 1942.
Yang, Gene Luen. *American Born Chinese*. New York: First Second, 2008.

THE SUPERHERO READER

Section One

HISTORICAL CONSIDERATIONS

ALMOST ALL SUPERHEROES HAVE AN ORIGIN STORY: A BEDROCK ACCOUNT OF the transformative events that set the protagonist apart from ordinary humanity. If not a prerequisite for the superhero genre, the origin story is certainly a prominent and popular trope that recurs so frequently as to offer clues to the nature of this narrative tradition. To read origin stories about destroyed worlds, murdered parents, genetic mutations, and mysterious power-giving wizards is to realize the degree to which the superhero genre is about transformation, about identity, about difference, and about the tension between psychological rigidity and a flexible and fluid sense of human nature.

As Gerard Jones notes, comics historians are "always in quest of origin stories" of a different sort. When surveying the superhero genre, preliminary questions often turn to the problem of roots: What are the origins of the genre? Who was the first superhero? Why did superhero comic books start flourishing in the late 1930s? How did the early cartoonists who worked on the genre see themselves? In what ways did the politics of the era influence superhero comics? What was the audience for superheroes? How did fans interpret the genre? All these questions are taken up in this section focusing on historical considerations.

The search for the origins of the genre has often been frustrated by the murkiness of the genre's definition. One school of thought sees the superhero as rooted in perennial human impulses to create mythological stories. By this logic, ancient gods like Hercules and Zeus should be roped into the superhero genre. Such a broad definition, however, divorces the genre from its historical context and creates a category that is too large to enable precise analysis.

In his book *Superhero: The Secret Origin of a Genre*, Peter Coogan brings a welcome taxonomic rigor to this debate. For Coogan, the superhero is defined by three core constituent elements: mission, powers, and identity. In the classical superhero story, the mission has to be a prosocial one, the powers above those of ordinary humans, and the identity a double one including a private civilian self distinct from the public heroic avatar. Coogan acknowledges that the superhero has precursors in the mystery man genre of popular fiction (with protagonists such as the Scarlett Pimpernel, the Lone Ranger, and the Shadow) as well as the tradition in science fiction of the superpowered post-human. Still, Coogan insists that all the defining features of the superhero genre didn't come together until the creation of Superman by Jerry Siegel and Joe Shuster in the mid-1930s, culminating in the publication of the first Superman story in *Action Comics* #1 (1938).

In the excerpt from his book *Superhero* that begins this section, Coogan looks at precursors to the superhero genre in comic strips and comic books, developing a formalist argument as to why the superhero genre is particularly suited to the comics medium (though also acknowledging that computer-generated imagery has recently enabled the genre to make a more successful transition into film). One might question whether Coogan's quest for an airtight definition of the superhero doesn't have the effect of downplaying the messy borders that always surround genres as social phenomena. The superhero genre didn't just emerge out of the mystery man story and science fiction but also continued to interact with these genres and with many others as well.

In his book *Men of Tomorrow*, Gerard Jones complicates our sense of the genre's origin by placing it in a biographical and social context, highlighting the impact of sometimes overlapping social milieus that include Jewish-American immigration, socialist politics, bodybuilding culture, organized crime, and science fiction fandom. Our excerpt from Jones's book details the fact that, as science fiction fans, Siegel and Shuster were much taken with Philip Wylie's novel *Gladiator* (1930), one of many early twentieth-century cultural expressions of the idea of the superman. However, as Jones emphasizes and as the excerpt we've provided from *Gladiator* makes clear, Wylie had a sour and satirical take on the idea of the superior being. An H. L. Mencken-inspired debunker and skeptic, Wylie posited that any superior being would be thwarted and defeated by the powerful forces of mass stupidity and venality. If Siegel and Shuster borrowed key ideas from *Gladiator*, they also transformed those concepts in significant ways, creating a character that embodied a much more positive view of human possibilities.

The cartoonist Jules Feiffer witnessed firsthand what Siegel and Shuster made possible. An avid reader of the new comic book medium, Feiffer got involved in the comic book industry from early on, and in 1946, while still a teenager, joined the shop of Will Eisner, the master cartoonist behind the noir superhero the Spirit. In our excerpt from his pioneering study *The Great Comic Book Heroes*, Feiffer offers a vivid memoir of the early days of the comic book industry seen from the eyes of a fledgling cartoonist. Like Feiffer, many of the early comic book creators, including Siegel and Shuster, were teens or young adults when they joined the burgeoning industry in the 1930s and 1940s. Feiffer's account brings to life the youthful enthusiasm of this first generation of comic book artists and the excitement of working in a new art form that was developing its own visual language and techniques.

Though the early creators of superhero comics invested the genre with their energy and passion, not every reader was enthusiastic; in fact the genre drew fierce criticism from the very start. The roots of the superhero in the déclassé and vulgar world of pulp fiction automatically made the genre suspect in more genteel circles. One strong critic of the genre was the Jesuit philosopher Walter Ong, one of America's leading Catholic intellectuals, who became interested in popular culture through the influence of his mentor Marshall McLuhan. In his 1945 essay "The Comics and the Superstate," Ong forcefully links the superhero genre with the herd mentality and extrajudicial violence of the totalitarian state. Ong's essay is worth reading not just for his ideas but also to appreciate the hostility that the superhero genre generated in its early days.

Of course Ong was not alone in his ideological critique of the superhero genre. The psychiatrist Fredric Wertham would gain fame in the late 1940s and early 1950s as one of the most prominent critics of all genres of comic books. In his famous and influential 1954 book *Seduction of the Innocent*, Wertham argued that comic books contributed to the moral and intellectual degradation of the children who read them. In the excerpt we have selected from this book, Wertham's ire is directed at the superhero genre in particular, though he sees the superhero as an offshoot of the larger category of crime comics. Wertham was especially concerned about what he saw as the dubious politics of the superhero, seeing the idea of the superpowered vigilante as all too reminiscent of the Nazi ideal of the superman. A leading opponent of American racism during his era, Wertham argued that the superhero often embodied noxious notions of white supremacy.

Wonder Woman, created in 1941 by the psychologist William Moulton Marston, was arguably the first female *super*hero (though preceded by Tarpé Mills's costumed crimefighter *Miss Fury* earlier that year), and is significant for her long popularity and in particular for her appeal to girl and women readers as an emblem of female power. In her essay on Wonder Woman, historian and cartoonist Trina Robbins details the creation of the character and analyzes what she meant to readers in the 1940s. Robbins also disputes what she sees as the tendency of recent fan historians and scholars to denigrate Wonder Woman or to misrepresent her popularity with female readers.

Robbins's essay helpfully introduces the issue of reader response, a crucial question when dealing with the superhero genre because the feedback of fans has strongly influenced the developments of the genre. In his essay "Fandom and Authorship," scholar Will Brooker offers a fascinating case study of the origins and development of superhero fan discourse in the letter pages of comics. As Brooker demonstrates, the letter columns that DC Comics introduced in the early 1960s were designed to be sites of fan-building activity. While early columns focused on relatively narrow questions of authorial identity and the development of connoisseurial expertise in recognizing the hidden hand of uncredited writers and artists, later fan letters were devoted to complex critical explications. Perhaps fittingly, the secret origins of superhero scholarship are to be found in these letter pages.

The essays in this section start with a relatively simple question: What are the origins of the superhero genre? During the course of these investigations, the questions become more complex as scholars try to figure out the meanings of the genre and the impact the genre has on readers. These more complex questions will continue to inform the essays found in the later sections of this book.

Comics Predecessors

PETER COOGAN

Reprinted by permission from *Superhero: The Secret Origin of a Genre* (MonkeyBrain Books, 2006), 165–74.

THOUGH DIME NOVELS, SCIENCE FICTION, ADVENTURE STORIES, AND THE PULPS contain the main predecessors of the superhero genre, the superhero did not spring to life in literature but in comics. Comics—both books and strips—provide the final bit of the prehistory of the superhero.

Essentially unknown today, J. Koerner's [actually William H. D. Koerner's—eds.] *Hugo Hercules* ran in the Chicago *Tribune* from September 7, 1902 to January 11, 1903, and was the first positive presentation of a heroic superman in comics.[1]

Hugo Hercules's introductory episode, a six-panel Sunday strip titled "Hugo Hercules Obliges Beauty in Distress," opens with a young woman attempting to board a speeding streetcar, which does not heed her plea to stop. Hugo—dressed in striped pants, a dark jacket, bow tie, and a hat that seems to be a cross between a fedora and a cowboy hat—replies to her request for aid with "I'm a real stopper." He bounds after the streetcar and jerks it to a halt, sending its passengers flying into disarray. He closes the day's strip with his tagline, "Just as easy."[2] Hugo's adventures follow this pattern. Someone asks for help in a relatively minor matter, and Hercules obliges by using his strength in a humorous way.

Most of the time very little is at stake in any of his adventures, although he occasionally does aid someone in a dangerous situation: he stops a runaway carriage; he catches a falling safe; he escorts a woman to her carriage in the rain by removing the portico from her house and using it as an umbrella; he lifts an elephant so a lady can retrieve her dropped handkerchief, which the elephant is standing upon; he lifts a car so a man can kiss his girlfriend, who is in a window some ten feet up a wall; he carries home a woman and her many bags during a cab strike; he puts a derailed train back on its track; and he carries home a party of iceboaters and their iceboat when the craft crashes.

Twice he defends himself from attackers: the first time he faces down armed muggers by fetching a cannon and threatening to fire it at them; the second time he wrestles and defeats a bear who announces "I'll tear him in two" ("Hugo Hercules Wrestles a Bear"). In two instances his strength both creates and resolves the crises: attempting to kick a football, Hugo misses and sends a house flying, which he catches and returns to its foundations; attempting to break "all bowling records" at a New Year's bowling contest, Hugo hurls his ball through the back of the alley, where it derails a street car and overturns two wagons, one loaded with policemen ("Hugo Hercules at New Year's Bowling Contest"). Hugo Hercules does not seem to have been much of an influence on the superhero, coming and going so quickly as he did.

The next cartoon strongman had considerably more influence in comics and specifically on the superhero.[3] Introduced into *Thimble Theatre* in 1929, Popeye soon took over the long-running strip. While not quite achieving the level of Hugo Hercules's might, Popeye's strength is superior to that of just about any comic strip character since the dapper strongman. Popeye once lifted the corner of a house to demonstrate his strength to Bullo Oxheart, the "strongest man in the world," while in contract negotiations for a prizefight. A few years later another boxer, Curley Gazook, the state champ, has designs on Olive Oyl and wants to prove to her that he is stronger than the sailor. He brings a weight to her house and tells her to come to his place that afternoon and she will see that Popeye cannot lift the weight the boxer carried with ease. Gazook bolts the weight to the floor, which foils Popeye, but the sailor goes down to the basement and lifts the house, with Olive and Curley, over his head. Later that year while out walking with Toar, a monstrous brute of a man who has come for a visit, Popeye encounters a crippled boy on crutches who has to walk a mile to and from school each day. Popeye and Toar take pity on the boy and solve his problem by carrying the school, loaded with children and a teacher, to the boy's backyard. Creator E. C. Segar played Popeye for laughs and social satire, so his feats of strength did not need to conform to a realistic depiction.

A third comic-strip strongman appeared in 1933, the cave man Alley Oop. Like Popeye, Alley Oop was drawn in a cartoony style and his comedic adventures were not tainted with realism. Also like Popeye, Alley Oop's feats of strength are primarily expressed in defeating men and monsters many times his size. Unlike Popeye, Oop's strength, while superior to most of his caveman companions, is not unique. After traveling to the present day via a time machine, Ooola, Oop's girlfriend, saves a G-man from an avalanche by grabbing him and leaping into a tree. Oop is very strong, able to snap steel handcuffs, wrench iron bars out of a window to free himself from jail, and uproot a tree. He is tough, able to survive falls from planes and pterodactyls, but not so invulnerable that he can resist being knocked out by a blow to the head from a stone axe.

Like Popeye, Alley Oop helped to establish comics as a medium in which fantastic feats could be depicted, even though neither strip strove for plausibility.[4] Within the world each cartoonist established, feats of incredible strength fit in well. The comic-strip strongmen resolve the savior/ruler/destroyer conundrum of the SF superman in a way different from the "bigger Indian" solution of Aarn Munro and the Lensmen. The superman's titanic strength can be contained if it is limited in some way. Comics offer a possibility for depicting the superman that was seemingly not available to the prose fiction writers or to the artists working in other narrative media, such as radio or film. Comics can depict the fantastic with equal realism as the mimetic, so things that might not be acceptable or might look ridiculous in another medium do not appear so in comics. In comics, everything—whether a building or a talking tiger—can have the same level of surface realism.

An excellent example of this aspect of comics that is of particular reference to the superhero genre is the depiction of the costume. A costume, no matter how well described, cannot appear as striking when described in words as when it appears in pictures. The costumed nature of the superhero cannot be as constantly signaled in prose as it must be in comics, and hence the superhero cannot stand out from a story's "civilians" as he can in comics form.[5] So comics promote the separation of the superhero and other super-characters from the rest of the character cast. On the other side, the superhero's costume can appear much more normal in comics than it can in the more realistic medium of film or television.[6] Until recently, in live-action films or television shows superhero costumes have looked a bit silly. They never seem to attain the level of equivalent surface realism that they attain routinely in comics (and animation).[7] Because they are made out of the same material (ink, paper, color), Clark Kent's suits and Superman's costume come across with the same level of realism.[8] But on television, even in the relatively successful costuming of *Lois and Clark*, the superhero's costume looks a bit silly.[9] This silliness is even more pronounced in the costumes of supervillains. The live-action *Flash* television show was able to achieve a reasonable hero costume, but the costumed supervillains, such as the Trickster, just looked ridiculous. This point is even more marked when looking at live-action superheroes of the past. The costumes used in the Superman and Batman television shows and movie serials do not make their wearers look more heroic than the civilians in the show.[10]

Perhaps a better example of the effect comics can have in depicting realistic and non-realistic elements equally would be the use of animal characters alongside human characters. Tawky Tawny the talking tiger has the same surface realism as Captain Marvel. Even in a photo-realistic comic book such as *Kingdom Come*, the animal-based characters and the human characters interact easily and neither appears more or less believable than another.

In the last decade film has begun to be able to achieve this effect in movies such as *Jurassic Park*, in which the dinosaurs appear as real as the human beings. These dinosaurs are, of course, animated. As recent superhero movies such as the Spider-Man films show, computer-generated imagery—instead of prostheses, costuming, and makeup to portray the heroes—can achieve a similar level of equivalent realism or believability.[11]

Appearing in the spring of 1935 in Mel Graft's *The Adventures of Patsy*, the short-lived Phantom Magician was the first of several clear precursors of the superhero.[12] Graft introduced the Phantom Magician to pull Patsy and her boy sidekick Thimble out of scrapes in the fairy-tale kingdom of Ods Bodkin. The Phantom Magician's powers include flight and invisibility. He wears a costume of black tights, pirate boots, gloves, a tunic with a double-V-shaped chevron, a cape, and a domino mask. After a few months, Graft and his editor decided that the fantasy elements were not working, and *Patsy* was reworked into a Shirley Temple–style Hollywood strip. The Phantom Magician put on a business suit, turned into Patsy's uncle Phil Cardigan, and abandoned superheroing. While the Phantom Magician does roughly fit the mission-powers-identity triumvirate, the comic strip's fantasy basis kept out the conventions that would have marked it as generically distinct from other fantasy land adventures, like *Alice in Wonderland* or *Little Nemo in Slumberland*. So, while the Phantom Magician could, possibly, be considered the first superhero, he was not the initiator of the superhero genre. Interestingly, Ron Goulart proposes a connection between the Phantom Magician and Superman. He relates, "Graft had once been approached by Jerry Siegel to work on the Superman project. He declined, convinced the public would never take such a character to its heart." Thus Superman might have been the inspiration for the Phantom Magician, further strengthening Superman's position as the progenitor of the superhero genre.

Dr. Occult, a Siegel and Shuster creation, served as a kind of trial run for elements of their later hero Superman.[13] The ghost detective, as he was billed, debuted in *New Fun Comics* #6 (October 1935), running in two-page installments to issue #32 of *More Fun Comics*.[14] The strip began as a horror-detective feature with Dr. Occult fighting vampires and werewolves through issue #13. The next four issues change gears, dropping into a storyline that began in *The Comics Magazine* #1 (May 1936). A masked and caped giant appears out of nowhere over the city skyline. Dr. Occult enlarges himself and "advances upon the other figure poised for battle." Occult removes the giant's mask and discovers his friend Zator, who posed as a menace only because he needed to draw Occult to him quickly. Zator informs Occult of a threat to "the Seven" and they whisk off into the spirit world where they encounter monstrous creatures, servants of Koth who offers Occult and Zator a chance to join him against the Seven. The two men refuse and Koth sics his creatures upon them, but the Seven save them. In the next four issues Occult and Zator fight against and defeat Koth's plan to destroy human civilization as he has done several times in the past. To defeat the evil Koth, Occult, who has come increasingly to resemble Slam Bradley (himself a double for Superman), dons a blue outfit emblazoned with "the Symbol of the Seven"—a triangular emblem encompassing a half-moon symbol—a red cape, and a sword, looking much like John Carter.

This symbol, which Zator also wears, protects them from Koth's ether entities as they travel to the Egyptian tomb to secure "a certain belt of miraculous powers." This belt enables its wearer to fly, to turn people to stone, and conjure an inexhaustible phantom army—all of which Occult does in his victorious battle with Koth. In *More Fun* #18 (February 1937) Dr. Occult is back on Earth facing "The Lord of Life," a villain who kills people, resurrects them, and then blackmails them into stealing for him in return for continued injections of the serum that keeps them alive. Flying and wearing a blue and red costume with a chevron, Dr. Occult is clearly a precursor of Superman.

Another clear precursor to the superhero was the Phantom. Appearing first as a daily on February 17, 1936, and then as a Sunday in May of 1939, the Phantom comes close to being a superhero, but remains a mystery man.[15] The Phantom's mission focuses on fighting piracy. His ancestor, Sir Christopher Standish, while on a trading mission in 1525 to the Far East, is attacked by pirates who take his ship and kill his father. A typhoon in the Bay of Bengal interrupts the pirate raid, and Standish washes up on the coast and is nursed to health by the Bandar pygmy tribe. On the skull of the pirate who killed his father Standish takes an oath of vengeance to fight against the Singh Brotherhood and all pirates and to dedicate his descendants to the same task. Each eldest son since has taken the Phantom identity and continued the fight. The costume is a gray hooded bodysuit with a domino mask, completed by a skull belt and skull ring.[16] The Phantom's skull insignia emblemizes his ancestor's oath on the Singh pirate's skull and hence his own repetition of that oath on the same skull. Although the Phantom is tough, strong, and highly athletic, he does not possess true superpowers. Instead he tricks people into thinking he is immortal through the continuing resurrection of the Phantom identity by the sons of the Phantoms. He also pulls stunts that lead criminals to believe he can turn into smoke or walk through walls. As the first true costumed adventurer[17] with adventures set in America, the Phantom laid important groundwork for the superhero because in his adventures can be found nearly all the elements of the superhero genre.[18]

The Phantom's debut year also saw the striking of the Clock in *Funny Pages* #6 (November 1936). The Clock draws heavily upon pulp heroes with a striking resemblance to the Gray Seal. He is Brian O'Brien, a wealthy socialite, who acts as a Robin Hood by recovering riches stolen from wealthy misers and distributing them to the poor instead of returning them. He has a sanctum sanctorum outfitted with torture devices to get crooks to talk, is in the habit of leaving a calling card in the form of a picture of a clock face with the words "The Clock Strikes" printed on it, and has an additional identity as Snowy Winters. His iconic weaponry includes a cane with a spring-loaded knob and a derby hat specially made to protect him against blows to the head. Besides his boxing skills, he can hypnotize criminals into revealing and confessing their crimes.

Like the Phantom, the Clock fits well into the existing mystery man genre, but by appearing in comics he helped to set the stage for the debut of Superman.

The last comics precursor of the superhero actually overlapped with Superman. Rather than precursor, Will Murray actually identifies Olga Mesmer as "The Superhero before Superman" (1998, 25). He writes, "Superman was not the first superhero. A year before *Action* #1, another super-character, possessing super-strength and X-ray vision, with roots in a super-civilization from another planet, had debuted in comic strip form. And the publisher was no less than the publisher of Superman!"[19] "Olga Mesmer, the Girl with the X-Ray Eyes," ran in *Spicy Mystery Stories* from August 1937 to October 1938. The feature was supplied by Adolphe Barreaux's Majestic Studios, a comics shop that supplied material for Harry Donenfeld, the publisher whose company ultimately became DC Comics. Olga is the daughter of Dr. Hugo Mesmer and the mysterious Margot, whom Mesmer has injected with a soluble X-ray while pregnant. These experiments give their baby superstrength and the added bonus of X-ray vision. Olga's parents die on the day she is born, and she is raised by her godfather, Hugh Rankin, who counsels her to keep her powers secret. She uses them to rescue a young man, Rodney Prescott, from an attacker, but transfers her superstrength to the injured man as part of a blood transfusion to save his life. A series of adventures reveal that Margot is the immortal queen of Venus. On Venus, the superpowered Olga and Rodney put down a revolt and see Margot married to Boris, Prince of Mars, thus bringing peace to the two warring planets. Murray concludes his article, "Olga Mesmer was an original. The first superhero to see print . . . definitely the first superheroic in comics history!"

It is unclear exactly what Murray means by *superhero* here. Olga Mesmer's mission is rather limited. She defends herself from her godfather's attempts to molest her, stops a murder in progress, and helps Queen Margot defeat a revolt. With the exception of the attempted murder of Prescott, Olga is involved in family matters, some of which have a broader effect only due to the position of her mother in Venusian society: this mission is more in line with the science fiction genre than with later superheroes. The only clear superhero convention present in the story is superpowers. But many science fiction superfolk and mythical heroes before Olga had powers equal to or greater than hers, so if she is a superhero, then she is not the first and the superhero genre extends back to the legend of Gilgamesh. As already demonstrated, the superhero genre emerged from a concatenation of conventions in the comic books of the Golden Age. Therefore, there is more to superheroes than superpowers. Further Mesmer lacks the codename and costume aspects of the identity convention. Her tale generically fits within the SF superman (or woman) genre, particularly in the way that she gets her superpowers, seemingly drawing directly on Wylie's *Gladiator* for inspiration, but resembling Siegel and Shuster's earlier villainous superman Bill Dunn.

Olga Mesmer has been long forgotten and was probably forgotten by the November 1938 issue of *Spicy Mystery*. Unlikely to have influenced either Siegel or Shuster, Olga Mesmer merely demonstrates the same point that the other comics precursors to Superman demonstrate, that, like the pulps before them, comic books and comic strips contained all the elements of the superhero—the powers, the mission, the identity—but it took Siegel and Shuster to put them all together into Superman. The best popular culture, whether Homer's epics, Shakespeare's plays, or the televised adventures of Xena or Buffy the Vampire Slayer, combine preexisting elements in new and exciting ways. They follow the dictates for success in formula, balancing convention and invention to create successful, popular, and archetypal stories and characters.

NOTES

1. Bill Blackbeard rediscovered Hugo Hercules and includes examples of two Sunday strips in *The Comic Strip Century: Celebrating 100 Years of an American Art Form* (Northampton, MA: Kitchen Sink Press, 1995).
2. Strangely, Hugo Hercules speaks different in his balloons versus the accompanying caption which runs underneath each panel. His closing comment on September 7, 1902, portrays him as a New York tough, quite in contrast to his generally refined appearance and speech in the panels: "Don't mention it lady. I'm Hugo Hercules, the boy wonder, and stoppin' trolley cars is me long, strong suit." Even more pronounced is the contrast between the balloon speech versus the caption speech on October 26, 1902. The second panel shows Hugo lifting a car so that a young man can kiss his girlfriend who stands at a window placed some feet up the wall. Holding the automobile, Hercules says, "I could do this forever." The caption below reads, "Soy up dere. You'll have to hurry. I could hold dis machine for two years, but I hear somebody's fadder a-comin'. Break away." In the third panel Hugo replies to the young lover's thanks with his catchphrase, "Just as easy," but in the caption below the panel says, "Dat's all rite, young felly. I can raise yer oughterknowbetter a plaguy site better'n I kin raise me rent, and that's no kid, either." The contrast between his relatively refined balloon speech and his rough caption speech is puzzling. The captions were discontinued after November 7, 1902.

3. Jerry Siegel listed the animated Popeye as an influence in his creation of Superman (see Thomas Andrae, "Of Superman and Kids with Dreams: A Rare Interview with the Creators of Superman: Jerry Siegel and Joe Shuster," *Nemo: The Classic Comics Library*, August 1983, 10; Mike Benton, *Comics of the Golden Age: The Illustrated History*. Taylor Publishing, 1992, 12; Les Daniels, *Superman: The Complete History*. Chronicle Books, 1998, 18).
4. In the discussion following, by "comics" I am referring to cartoon-based comics, the traditional pen-and-ink, printed-on-paper comics, not sequential art forms such as fumetti, which use photographs.
5. In superhero novels, the full costumes of the superheroes are rarely described. Instead the picture on the book's cover is relied on to convey the heroes' costumes. Radio has the same limitations in depicting costumes that prose has, and fantastic feats of strength and superpowers are essentially visual, not auditory, experiences and so cannot be duplicated well in sound only, as the Superman radio show demonstrates.
6. A similar point may be made about painting, but comics can be painted and even in painted comics the costumes work in the same way. Because neither cartooning nor painting is capable of achieving the same level of mimetic realism as the photograph, the slight distancing of both these art forms make possible the believability of the superhero costume and fantastic feats that other media do not.
7. The two recent Spider-Man movies directed by Sam Raimi (2002, 2004) and *Batman Begins* are exceptions to this trend. They appear to presage workable superhero costumes in live-action media.
8. The same is true in prose. To accurately describe a superhero's costume would entail describing or specifying the fabric of which it is made, thereby making it seem too particular or artificial and thereby puncturing the suspension of disbelief needed to imagine costumed people who do not look silly. In comics the fabric of the costume need not be specified, so the illusion of a realistic appearance can be maintained.
9. The 1996 Phantom film starring Billy Zane did a similarly good job on the costume, but the costumers were still unable to reach the similarity of costume and clothes achieved in the comics.
10. One difference between the earlier Adam West or George Reeves and Christopher Reeves or Dean Cain is that the latter two actors were in considerably better shape than the former two actors, so they physically resembled the superhero body type to a greater extent, although George Reeves accurately resembled Superman as he was depicted in the comics of the 1950s.
11. In Dave Sim's *Cerebus* the title character, a furry cartoonish aardvark, appears with the same level of surface realism and believability as the other characters. Perhaps an even better example is the character Lord Julius. Julius is "played by" Groucho Marx. That is, the character is based upon the characters played by Groucho in a number of Marx Brothers' films. He attains a level of believability in comics that he could not attain in another medium. In prose, the author could describe him and hope that the reader would understand that the character is Groucho Marx, but if the character Lord Julius were actually identified as looking like Groucho or *as* Groucho, this identification would break the reader out of the imaginary world the author has constructed. If there were ever a filmed version of *Cerebus* and a look-alike actor played Groucho playing Julius, the double removal would similarly break the viewer out of Sim's imaginary world. Perhaps a computer-generated Groucho, using recombined speech or synthesized speech, would be able to achieve the same level of believable illusion as Sim's comics currently do. Groucho-the-actor is Lord-Julius-the-character in a way that cannot be duplicated in prose or film. Perhaps radio could achieve a similar level of

believability realism by employing an actor to duplicate Groucho's voice, but doing so would completely sacrifice the visual element that makes comics so powerful.

12. Rather than preceding Superman, the Phantom Magician might have been inspired by Superman. Mel Graff, Patsy's cartoonist, had once rejected Siegel and Shuster's Superman submission (Ron Goulart, "Leaping Tall Buildings: Falling on Faces," *Nemo: The Classic Comics Library*, August 1983, 30).

13. As did Slam Bradley, a private detective adventurer in the Captain Easy mode. Slam Bradley fit solidly within existing adventure genres with touches of science fiction. Instead of being a place to work out the SF concept that they later employed in Superman, it was where they worked on the technical aspects, particularly the action sequences, that they used in Superman. Slam Bradley was in Siegel's words "a dry run for Superman" and in Shuster's "the forerunner of Superman, because we turned it out with no restriction, complete freedom to do what we wanted" in terms of page and panel layout (Andrae, "Of Superman and Kids with Dreams," 11).

14. *New Fun Comics* changed its name to *More Fun Comics* with issue #7.

15. Even though his first appearance in comic books (*Ace Comics* #11, February 1938) predated Superman's debut in *Action Comics* #1 (June 1938), the Phantom did not exactly inspire an outpouring of similar characters either in comic books or strips. None of the creators of Superman or Batman claim the Phantom as an influence, and he is identified in his stories as a "mystery man" on more than one occasion. He has no superpowers that break the laws of physics. His origin is more of a pulp mystery-man origin than a superheroic one. His skull ring clearly draws on the similar spider ring used by the Spider to mark his foes.

16. The Phantom's trademark purple outfit did not come into use until the Sunday strip began in 1939. On May 7, 1936 his costume is identified as gray: "No one sees a gray-clad arm reach for a parachute."

17. Mandrake the Magician began as a daily strip on June 11, 1934, and as a Sunday strip in February 1935. He started as a magician with supernatural powers and evolved into an ordinary man who is a master of hypnotism and illusion. The comic strip was written by Lee Falk and drawn by Phil Davis. Mandrake does not need to be discussed here because he is neither a superman nor a dual-identity crime fighter.

18. An important difference between the Phantom and the superheroes who followed Superman is the focus on crime. The Phantom's adventures take place in exotic locations and fit in more closely with the adventure strips of the 1930s than they do with the urban crime fighting of the superheroes. Reinhold Reitberger and Wolfgang Fuchs refer to the Phantom as "the forerunner of superheroes" (*Comics: An Anatomy of a Mass Medium*. Little Brown, 1971, 102). They point out the way that reversed the secret identity pattern developed in the Superman stories. Each new Phantom, they write, "divests [him]self of [his] individual personality in order to become a hero and the hero in turn takes on the additional aspect of Mr. Walker (The Ghost Who Walks). Superman, in contrast, is first and foremost a hero, and he dons his second identity (Clark Kent, the reporter) to hide his true 'super' nature from the ordinary mortals among who he works" (102).

19. The extraterrestrial aspects of the Olga Mesmer feature did not appear until after Superman's appearance in *Action Comics* #1 (June 1938). See Will Murray, "The Roots of the Superman!" *Comic Book Marketplace*, October 1998: 19–21.

Men of Tomorrow

GERARD JONES

Copyright © 2005 Gerard Jones. Reprinted from *Men of Tomorrow: Geeks, Gangsters and the Birth of the Comic Book*, 80–88, by permission of Basic Books, a member of the Perseus Books Group.

PHILIP WYLIE WAS THE SON OF A PRESBYTERIAN MINISTER WHO BROKE ANGRILY with his father's God, studied theater at Princeton, dropped out to become a successful advertising writer, lost his career to a dubious paternity suit, decided to write fiction, and sold his first novel, a bombastic indictment of repressed Presbyterians, to Alfred A. Knopf—all before his twenty-sixth birthday. His second novel, the juicily titled *Babes and Sucklings*, was a ravaging of his own angry first marriage and a screed against modern morals, and he welcomed the cries of "indecency" from small-town librarians. His writing tilted and pitched as from one page to the next he'd strain to be Sinclair Lewis or H. L. Mencken or Havelock Ellis or Elinor Glyn. A *New York Times* reviewer said he wrote in "in a manner reminiscent of the vaudeville man who plays an entire orchestra single-handed."

The next year, 1929, Wylie decided it was time to tackle a grand social allegory. He wanted to show how a truly superior man would be loathed and destroyed by our mediocre society: "great deeds were always imminent and none of them could be accomplished because they involved humanity, humanity protecting its diseases, its pettiness its miserable convictions and conventions, with the essence of itself—life. Life not misty and fecund for the future, but life clawing at the dollar in the hour, the security of platitudes . . . the needs of skin, belly, and womb."

His plot was a scientific conceit: a biologist turns his son into "a superchild, an invulnerable man" who grows into a being of incomparable strength and vitality and innate moral superiority. "There, in the forest, beyond the eye of man, he learned that he was superhuman. I'm like a man made out of iron instead of meat." He tries to give the gift of his superiority the world: to the good he would lend his strength; to the corrupt he would lend his embattled antipathy. He would not be one impotent person seeking to dominate, but the agent of uplift. But mankind is too small for him. Bullies pick fights with him, the military presses him into a venal war, women give themselves to him and then run from his power, a little Jew cons him into the boxing racket, Congressmen and lobbyists jockey to exploit him, a money-grubbing Communist calls him, "Fool! Dreamer! Impossible idealist!" He imagines tearing down the Capitol Building like Samson, but knows it will accomplish nothing.

Wylie's use of biological fantasy would later lead science fiction fans to claim *Gladiator* as a product of their beloved genre, but his models were not Hugo Gernsback's pulp stories. Wylie mocked junk culture, mocked yellow journalism and Bernarr MacFadden and narcissistic bodybuilders, and he'd surely have mocked *Amazing Stories* if he'd bothered to notice it. He lifted tricks from the satirical parades of Henry Fielding and William Thackeray, pulled themes from the intellectual allegories of H. G. Wells and Friedrich Nietzsche. Then he fell in love with his hero, his man of "breathtaking symmetry . . . a man vehemently alive, a man with the promise of a young god," and hurled him into scenes of sexual awakening and combat and political melodrama as clotted and superheated as anything on the pages of *Cosmopolitan* or *Collier's*.

The result was a drunken disaster of a novel, dumbest at its most intellectually ambitious and emptiest at its most passionate, in the end lurching wildly into a lamppost of self-pitying nonsense:

> "Now—God—oh, God—if there be a God—tell me! Can I defy You? Can I defy Your world? Is this Your will? Or are You, like all mankind, impotent? Oh, God!" He put his hand to his mouth and called God like a name into the tumult above. Madness was upon him and the bitter irony with which his blood ran black was within him.
>
> A bolt of lighting stabbed earthward. It struck Hugo, outlining him in fire. His hand slipped away from his mouth. His voice was quenched.

Hugo Danner wasn't the only one struck by lightning. So was Jerry Siegel.

When other fans called Jerry's attention to *Gladiator* in 1932, it had already been on the shelves for two years. Wylie had had two more books published and was deep in his first big novel, *Finnley Wren*. He'd have cared nothing for a young science fiction fan's love of *Gladiator* (and would no doubt have been shocked to know that eight years later he'd be preparing to sue that fan for plagiarism). It was, however, the perfect moment for Jerry. Eighteen years old and still in the middle of high school, still without a girlfriend or a plausible career but dreaming of beauties and riches, launching a new magazine but hearing the condescending indulgence of his peers—*Gladiator* must have touched upon everything he wanted and feared to be.

The "superman" was scarcely a new idea, and was in fact a common motif of both high and low culture by the early thirties, the inevitable product of those doctrines of perfectability promoted by everyone from Bernarr MacFadden to Leon Trotsky. The word had descended from Nietzsche's *übermensch* through Bernard Shaw's *Man and Superman*, but it was easily wedded to ideas neither Nietzschean nor Shavian. In Germany, Adolf Hitler was claiming that a whole nation of supermen could be forged through institutionalized racism and militarism, and his popularity was rising steadily. In America, the idea of eugenics was being actively explored at Ivy League universities. Eugenics inspired Wylie's pseudo-scientific plot device in *Gladiator*, and his hero explicitly considered its use to improve mankind.

Even leftists could use the word: a Milwaukee radical named Joseph Firicin argued in his lectures that Socialist production methods would create a "superabundance" of goods and opportunities, would make the citizen of a Socialist future a "veritable superman" by our current standards. He claimed he once gave this lecture at a Cleveland community center in the early 1930s, and in the audience were *two young Jewish men who later* . . . We can complete the anecdote, and surely dismiss it as wishful thinking, but it's a measure of the ubiquity of the symbolic superman.

The idea of the superman was explored in much of the more romantic pulp culture, even if the term wasn't used: Edgar Rice Burroughs's Tarzan and John Carter of Mars were not simply the strongest and noblest of their breed, but were clearly described as of an order apart, beings of such innate and apparent superiority that they rose to command every world they entered. Their ties to the English nobility and the old Confederacy explained their potential for superiority, but that potential was realized only through a miracle that lifted them outside history: Tarzan's return to the evolutionary Eden of the apes, John Carter's unexplained, almost mystical, longevity. In 1929, Jerry's Siegel's old pen pal Jack Williamson wrote a novel, published by Hugo Gernsback, which explained the superbeing in a science-fictional way. It was called *The Girl from Mars*, and it featured a strange visitor from another planet with powers far beyond those of normal men.

Until he encountered Wylie's Hugo Danner, however, Jerry had never seen a superman whose feats were set so vividly against a familiar and constraining reality: "I can do things, Dad. It kind of scares me. I can jump higher'n a house. I can run faster'n a train." Hugo transforms clichéd scenes of trench warfare in France when he learns that a bullet can't pierce his skin, and even a bursting shell only knocks him down. And he'd never seen a human portrait of the superman that encompassed his flounderings, his frustrations, his isolation, his pain. Hugo Danner displays his super-strength as a child and frightens the timid townsfolk. His father draws him aside to explain that he must use his strength for "a good and noble purpose" to keep people from hating him; indeed, when men first see his full strength they call him "a demon." Hugo withdraws from the world "to become acquainted with his powers" and builds a solitary fortress in the woods. When he brings his greatness to the world he knows moments of triumph, but each one only deepens his isolation. He's taken to bed by an Ivy League beauty:

> Half goddess, half animal . . . the vanguard of emancipated American womanhood. But only once, for she learned something, too, she never came back to Hugo, and kept the longing for him as a sort of memory which she made hallowed in a shorn soul. It was, for her, a single asceticism in a rather selfish life.

The capsule review of *Gladiator* in Siegel's fanzine hints at none of the impact it must have had on a lonely, angry boy. But his story in the next issue of *Science Fiction*, dated January 1933, suggested that it was working its way into his imagination.

"The Reign of the Superman" by "Herbert S. Fine" (a nod to his cousins) is framed by Joe Shuster's illustrations. Joe's work was coming along: the snarling villain and the futuristic city of skyscrapers, drawn in a clear-line style based on the cylinders and circles of industrial design, show that he was well attuned to the iconography of his moment. Then the nine densely typed pages of Jerry's story begin:

> The bread-line! Its row of downcast, disillusioned men; unlucky creatures who have found that life holds nothing but bitterness for them. The bread-line! Last resort of the starving vagrant.
>
> With a contemptuous sneer on his face, Professor Smalley watched the wretched unfortunates file past him. To him, who had come of rich parents and had never been forced to face the rigors of life, the miserableness of these men seemed deserved. It appeared to him that if they had the slightest ambition at all, they could lift themselves from their terrible rut.

Professor Smalley selects a vagrant as a human guinea pig and injects him with a mysterious element he's discovered in a meteor from another planet. His subject escapes and discovers that the element has given him superhuman powers. He can hear the thoughts of strangers like words in the air: "Brains is what this gang needs and brains is what it ain't got." "I gotta have that dough, Ma. I gotta have it!" "He's just a kid, Mame. Why don't you let him alone?" "To hell with the anarchists!" "I'd starve before I go back to that brute." "I wish he'd keep on his own feet. A helluva nerve he has askin' a swell dancer like me to fox trot with a palooka like him." "Look here, punk, you may be the star reporter on this rag but unless you turn in your copy by three o'clock you'll be out in the street peddling shoelaces."

The character now called "the Superman" goes to the library to read "Einstein's Expanding Universe." "Trash! Bosh!" he cries. When the librarian tells him to be quiet, the Superman hisses, "If I had a ray-tube within reach, I'd blast you out of existence!"

Late 1932 was a politically electrical moment, and most bright eighteen-year-olds, especially in a left-leaning Jewish milieu, could have waxed fairly eloquent about unemployment and class agendas; but Jerry went not an inch beyond the most common Hollywood tropes. The people of his world thought in bad Warner Brothers dialogue. And he obviously had no more interest in science than he had in social reality or character, a fact that sheds some light on his inability to get himself taken seriously by the fans of *Amazing Stories*. He raced impatiently past every detail that would have made his story more convincing to get to the one long sequence that seemed to excite his passion: the angry struggle for control between the Superman and his maker.

One passage leaps out to the reader who knows about Jerry Siegel's later life:

> [Smalley] secured pencil and paper and began to write a long, heated letter. He told how he had taken Dunn from the breadline to make him the noble subject of the greatest experiment of the century. He told of how the chemical had been administered and Dunn's subsequent vanishing. "And," he concluded, "unless this creature is snared and shot dead like a beast, he will grow, his powers will strengthen, increase, until he will hold the fate of the world in the palm of his hand!" When the letter was completed he placed it in an envelope, addressed it to the City Editor of the largest newspaper, then left the laboratory and mailed it.

Maybe it's only an accidental foreshadowing of the long, heated letters that Siegel would later use in his fight to regain control of Superman; but it is the one moment when a character stumbles out of the strictures of plot and behaves in an oddly small and human way. It may be that even before he had a real property to fight over, Jerry was already waging wars of entitlement in his head.

Smalley decides to partake of the meteorite himself and replace Dunn as the Superman. But the Superman murders him first. He's now learned to master others with his mind, and plans to achieve world domination by sending "the armies of the earth to total annihilation against each other." "The

International Conciliatory Council was in session . . . Chinaman and Jap, Frenchman and Englishman. American and Mexican, all smiled genially at each other." The Superman broadcasts "thoughts of hate which would plunge the earth into a living hell." The delegates begin "attacking each other like mad hate-filled wolves."

But a reporter reads Smalley's letter and confronts the Superman. (The reporter's name is Forrest Ackerman; for the fan, the in-joke is always more real than the drama.) The end comes in a scene of religiosity and shouting echoing the lightning-bolt finish of *Gladiator*. "In this moment of dread and terror the reporter sent a silent prayer up to the Creator of the threatened world. He beseeched the Omnipotent One to blot out this blaspheming devil. Was it true that Forrest saw the look of hate swept from the Superman's face and terror replace it, or was it mere fancy?" "No!" shouts the Superman to the empty air. He realizes that the drug is wearing off. "The arrogant, confident figure had departed. Instead, there now stood, a drooping, disillusioned man . . . 'I see, now, how wrong I was. If I had worked for the good of humanity, my name would have gone down in history with a blessing—instead of a curse.'"

Jerry Siegel was not a religious kid. "I don't think he ever went to the synagogue in his life," said Jerry Fine. The Omnipotent One entered via Wylie. Jerry was uninterested in grappling with Wylie's idea that a man could be good and yet still be unable to make a difference, preferring the reassurance of genre fiction that we can all choose whether history will bless us or curse us, but he was playing with the question raised by *Gladiator*: what can and should a superman do in a world of real troubles?

Just a few weeks after he'd mailed out that issue of *Science Fiction* his questioning took a new turn. He was flipping through the issue of *The Shadow* that hit the stands in February 1933, when the boldface word jumped out at him: "SUPERMAN." Beneath it was a picture of a he-man wrestling with a gunman, and the legend, "Doc Savage—man of Master Mind and Body." It was the first ad for Street and Smith's new "superhero."

Doc Savage may also have owed something to Wylie, too. Like Hugo Danner, Doc had been cultivated to human perfection by science, and he had a Fortress of Solitude where he went to think. His name and appearance—a muscular giant with mahogany skin, bronze hair, and gemlike eyes—may have come from a more recent Wylie novel, *The Savage Gentleman* (1932). He shared the Shadow's network of operatives, but instead of fighting urban crime he was a globetrotting rescuer of innocents in peril. Before it had hit the stands, Jerry and Joe knew they would be fans.

Then came another turn. As spring melted the Cleveland snows and the nation waited to see what Franklin D. Roosevelt would do as President and Jerry and Joe waited to see what Doc Savage would be like, a cheesy, tabloid-sized, cardboard-covered magazine called *Detective Dan* appeared on the newsstands. In the wake of *Dick Tracy*, hundreds of young cartoonists had whipped out their own tough-cop comic strips to peddle to the syndicates. A low-end publisher in Chicago, calling itself both the Humor Publishing Company and the Consolidated Publishing Company, decided to print a few of those in black and white and put them on the newsstands to see what happened. They weren't distributed well and probably didn't pay back even their printing costs. *Detective Ace King* and *Bob Scully, Two-Fisted Hick Detective*, disappeared almost without trace, but *Detective Dan* found its way to Cleveland. They were what future comic book historians, always in quest of origin stories, would come to call the "first modern single-character original content comic books." Jerry Siegel, with those quivering pop-culture antennae that enabled him to be the first creator of a science fiction fanzine and one of the original subscribers to *The Time Traveller*, was one of the few people who would ever recall having actually seen one on the stands—and apparently the only one who made an important career decision because of it.

Jerry bought *Detective Dan* and brought it to Joe. Joe thought it wasn't *Dick Tracy* by a longshot but it was pretty good. Jerry said that wasn't the point. The point was that it wasn't much better than what he and Joe could do—but it was in print. And its publication didn't depend on the distant and indifferent world of newspaper syndication but on what was, in Jerry's mind at least, the far more familiar world of cheap magazines. "We can *do* this!" he said.

In his mind it may already have been real: they'd write and draw a comic strip based on an action hero of their own creation and sell it to Humor Publications. To make it stand out they wouldn't copy *Dick Tracy* or any other strip but take their inspiration. Like *Buck Rogers* and *Tarzan*, from another medium. They'd do a pulp-style hero for comics. He even had an idea, springing from *Gladiator* and from the ads for the new *Doc Savage*. They'd create a pulpy adventure about a brawling do-gooder of extraordinary strength.

They'd call it *The Superman*.

Gladiator

PHILIP WYLIE

Reprinted by permission of Harold Ober Associates, Incorporated from *Gladiator* (Manor Books, 1976 [1930]), 240–250.

HUGO HAD THREE HOURS TO WAIT FOR A CHICAGO TRAIN. HIS WAGES PURchased his ticket and left him in possession of twenty dollars. His clothing was nondescript; he had no baggage. He did not go outside the Grand Central Terminal, but sat patiently in the smoking-room, waiting for the time to pass. A guard came up to him and asked to see his ticket. Hugo did not remonstrate and produced it mechanically; he would undoubtedly be mistaken for a tramp amid the sleek travellers and commuters.

When the train started, his fit of perplexed lethargy had not abated. His hands and feet were cold and his heart beat slowly. Life had accustomed him to frustration and to disappointment, yet it was agonizing to assimilate this new cudgeling at the hands of fate. The old green house in the Connecticut hills had been a refuge; Roseanne had been a refuge. They were, both of them, peaceful and whimsical and they had seemed innocent of the capacity for great anguish. Every man dreams of the season-changed countryside as an escape; every man dreams of a woman on whose broad breast he may rest, beneath whose tumbling hair and moth-like hands he may discover forgetfulness and freedom. Some men are successful in a quest for those anodynes. Hugo could understand the sharp contours of one fact: because he was himself, such a quest would always end in failure. No woman lived who could assuage him; his fires would not yield to any temporal powers.

He was barren of desire to investigate deeper into the philosophy of himself. All people turned aside by fate fall into the same morass. Except in his strength, Hugo was pitifully like all people: wounds could easily be opened in his sensitiveness; his moral courage could be taxed to the fringe of dilemma; he looked upon his fellow men sometimes with awe at the variety of high places they attained in spite of the heavy handicap of being human—he looked upon them again with repugnance—and very rarely, as he grew older, did such inspections of his kind include a study of the difference between them and him made by his singular gift. When that thought entered his mind, it gave rise to peculiar speculations.

He approached thirty, he thought, and still the world had not re-echoed with his name; the trumps, banners, and cavalcade of his glory had been only shadows in the sky, dust at sunset that made evanescent and intangible colors. Again, he thought, the very perfection of his prowess was responsible for its inapplicability; if he but had an Achilles' heel so that his might could taste the occasional tonic of inadequacy, then he could meet the challenge of possible failure with successful effort. More frequently he condemned his mind and spirit for not being great enough to conceive a mission for his thews. Then he would fall into a reverie, trying to invent a creation that would be as magnificent as the destructions he could so easily envision.

In such a painful and painstaking mood he was carried over the Alleghenies and out on the Western plains. He changed trains at Chicago without having slept, and all he could remember of the journey was a protracted sorrow, a stabbing consciousness of Roseanne, dulled by his last picture of her, and a hopeless guessing of what she thought about him now.

Hugo's mother met him at the station. She was unaltered, everything was unaltered. The last few instants in the vestibule of the train had been a series of quick remembrances; the whole countryside was like a long-deserted house to which he had returned. The mountains took on a familiar aspect, then the houses, then the dingy red station. Lastly his mother, upright and uncompromisingly grim, dressed in her perpetual mourning of black silk. Her recognition of Hugo produced only the slightest flurry and immediately she became mundane.

"Whatever made you come in those clothes?"

"I was working outdoors, mother. I got right on a train. How is father?"

"Sinking slowly."

"I'm glad I'm in time."

"It's God's will." She gazed at him. "You've changed a little, son."

"I'm older." He felt diffident. A vast gulf had risen between this vigorous, religious woman and himself.

She opened a new topic. "Whatever in the world made you send us all that money?"

Hugo smiled. "Why—I didn't need it, mother. And I thought it would make you and father happy."

"Perhaps. Perhaps. It has done some good. I've sent four missionaries out in the field and I am thinking of sending two more. I had a new addition put on the church, for the drunkards and the fallen. And we put a bathroom in the house. Your father wanted two, but I wouldn't hear of it."

"Have you got a car?"

"Car? I couldn't use one of those inventions of Satan. Your father made me hire this one to meet you. There's Anna Blake's house. She married that fellow she was flirting with when you went away. And there's our house. It was painted last month."

Now all the years had dropped away and Hugo was a child again, an adolescent again. The car stopped.

"You can go right up. He's in the front room. I'll get lunch."

Hugo's father was lying on the bed watching the door. A little wizened old man with a big head and thin yellow hands. Illness had made his eyes rheumy, but they lighted up when his son entered, and he half raised himself.

"Hello, father."

"Hugo! You've come back."

"Yes, father."

"I've waited for you. Sit down here on the bed. Move me over a little. Now close the door. Is it cold out? I was afraid you might not get here. I was afraid you might get sick on the train. Old people are like that, Hugo." He shaded his eyes. "You aren't a very big man, son. Somehow I always remembered you as big. But—I suppose"—his voice thinned—"I suppose you don't want to talk about yourself."

"Anything you want to hear, father."

"I can't believe you came back." He ruminated, "There were a thousand things I wanted to ask you, son—but they've all gone from my mind. I'm not so easy in your presence as I was when you were a little shaver."

Hugo knew what those questions would be. Here, on his deathbed, his father was still a scientist. His soul flinched from giving its account. He saw suddenly that he could never tell his father the truth; pity, kindredship, kindness, moved him. "I know what you wanted to ask, father. Am I still strong?" It took courage to suggest that. But he was rewarded. The old man sighed ecstatically.

"That's it, Hugo, my son."

"Then—father, I am. I grew constantly stronger when I left you. In college I was strong. At sea I was strong. In the war. First I wanted to be mighty in games and I was. Then I wanted to do services. And I did, because I could."

The head nodded on its feeble neck. "You found things to do? I—I hoped you would. But I always worried about you. Every day, son, every day for all these years, I picked up the papers and looked at them with misgivings. 'Suppose,' I said to myself, 'suppose my boy lost his temper last night. Suppose someone wronged him and he undertook to avenge himself.' I trusted you, Hugo. I could not quite trust—the other thing. I've even blamed myself and hated myself." He smiled. "But it's all right—all right. So I am glad. Then, tell me—what—what—"

"What have I done?"

"Do you mind? It's been so long and you were so far away."

"Well—" Hugo swept his memory back over his career—"so many things, father. It's hard to recite one's own—"

"I know. But I'm your father, and my ears ache to hear."

"I saved a man pinned under a wagon. I saved a man from a shark. I pulled open a safe in which a man was smothering. Many things like that. Then—there was the war."

"I know. I know. When you wrote that you had gone to war, I was frightened—and happy. Try as I might, I could not think of a great constructive cause for you to enter. I had to satisfy myself by thinking that you could find such a cause. Then the war came. And you wrote that you were in it. I was happy. I am old, Hugo, and perhaps my nationalism and my patriotism are dead. Sides in a war did not seem to matter. But peace mattered to me, and I thought—I hoped that you could hasten peace. Four years, Hugo. Your letters said nothing. Four years. And then it stopped. And I understood. War is property fighting property, not David fighting Goliath. The greatest David would be unavailing now. Even you could do little enough."

"Perhaps not so little, father."

"There were things, then?"

Hugo could not disappoint his father with the whole formidable truth. "Yes." He lied with a steady gaze. "I stopped the war."

"You!"

"After four years I perceived the truth of what you have just said. War is a mistake. It is not sides that matter. The object of war is to make peace. On a dark night, father, I went alone into the enemy lines. For one hundred miles that night I upset every gun, I wrecked every ammunition train, I blew up every dump—every arsenal that is. Alone I did it. The next day they asked for peace. Remember the false armistice? Somehow it leaked out that there would be victory and surrender the next night—because of me. Only the truth about me was never known. And a day later—it came."

The weak old man was transported. He raised himself up on his elbows. "You did that! Then all my work was not in vain. My dream and my prayer were justified! Oh, Hugo, you can never know how glad I am you came and told me this. How glad."

He repeated his expression of joy until his tongue was weary; then he fell back. Hugo sat with shining eyes during the silence that followed. His father at length groped for a glass of water. Strength returned to him. "I could ask for no more, son. And yet we are petulant, insatiable creatures. What is doing now? The world is wicked. Yet it tries half-heartedly to rebuild itself. One great deed is not enough—or are you tired?"

Hugo smiled. "Am I ever tired, father? Am I vulnerable?"

"I had forgotten. It is so hard for the finite mind to think beyond itself. Not tired. Not vulnerable. No. There was Samson—the cat." He was embarrassed. "I hurt you?"

"No, father." He repeated it. Every gentle fall of the word "father" from his lips and every mention of "son" by his father was rare privilege, unfamiliar elixir to the old man. His new lie took its cue from Abednego Danner's expressions. "My work goes on. Now it is with America. I expect to go to Washington soon to right the wrongs of politics and government. Vicious and selfish men I shall force from their high places. I shall secure the idealistic and the courageous." It was a theory he had never considered, a possible practice born of necessity. "The pressure I shall bring against them will be physical and mental. Here a man will be driven from his house mysteriously. There a man will slip into the limbo. Yonder an inconspicuous person will suddenly be braced by a new courage; his enemies will be gone and his work will progress unhampered. I shall be an invisible agent of right—right as best I can see it. You understand, father?"

Abednego smiled like a happy child. "I do, son. To be you must be splendid."

"The most splendid thing on earth! And I have you to thank, you and your genius to tender gratitude to. I am merely the agent. It is you that created and the whole world that benefits."

Abednego's face was serene—not smug, but transfigured. "I yearned as you now perform. It is strange that one cloistered mortal can become inspired with the toil and lament of the universe. Yet there is a danger of false pride in that, too. I am apt to fall into the pit because my cup is so full here at the last. And the greatest problem of all is not settled."

"What problem?" Hugo asked in surprise.

"Why, the problem that up until now has been with me day and night. Shall there be made more men like you—and women like you?"

The idea staggered Hugo. It paralyzed him and he heard his father's voice come from a great distance. "Up in the attic in the black trunk are six notebooks wrapped in oilpaper. They were written in pencil, but I went over them carefully in ink. That is my life-work, Hugo. It is the secret—of you. Given those books, a good laboratory worker could go through all my experiments and repeat each with the same success. I tried a little myself. I found out things—for example, the effect of the process is not inherited by the future generations. It must be done over each time. It has seemed to me that those six little books—you could slip them all into your coat pocket—are a terrible explosive. They can rip the world apart and wipe humanity from it. In malicious hands they would end life. Sometimes, when I became nervous waiting for the newspapers, waiting for a letter from you, I have been sorely tempted to destroy them. But now—"

"Now?" Hugo echoed huskily.

"Now I understand. There is no better keeping for them than your own. I give them to you."

"Me!"

"You, son. You must take them, and the burden must be yours. You have grown to manhood now and I am proud of you. More than proud. If I were not, I myself would destroy the books here on this bed. Matilda would bring them and I would watch them burn so that the danger would go with—" he cleared his throat—"my dream."

"But—"

"You cannot deny me. It is my wish. You can see what it means. A world grown suddenly—as you are."

"I, father—"

"You have not avoided responsibility. You will not avoid this, the greatest of your responsibilities. Since the days when I made those notes—what days!—biology has made great strides. For a time I was anxious. For a time I thought that my research might be rediscovered. But it cannot be. Theory has swung in a different direction." He smiled with inner amusement. "The opticians have decided that the microscope I made is impossible. The biochemists, moving through the secretions of such things as hippuric acid in the epithelial cells, to enzymes, to hormones, to chromosomes, have put a false construction on everything. It will take hundreds, thousands of years to see the light. The darkness is so intense and the error so plausible that they may never see again exactly as I saw. The fact of you, at best, may remain always no more than a theory. This is not vanity. My findings were a combination of accidents almost outside the bounds of mathematical probability. It is you who must bear the light."

Hugo felt that now, indeed, circumstance had closed around him and left him without succor or recourse. He bowed his head. "I will do it, father."

"Now I can die in peace—in joy."

With an almost visible wrench Hugo brought himself back to his surroundings. "Nonsense, father. You'll probably get well."

"No, son. I've studied the progress of this disease in the lower orders—when I saw it imminent. I shall die—not in pain, but in sleep. But I shall not be dead—because of you." He held out his hand for Hugo.

Some time later the old professor fell asleep and Hugo tiptoed from the room. Food was sizzling downstairs in the kitchen, but he ignored it, going out into the sharp air by the front door. He hastened along the streets and soon came to the road that led up the mountain. He climbed rapidly, and when he dared, he discarded the tedious little steps of all mankind. He reached the side of the quarry where he had built the stone fort, and seated himself on a ledge that hung over it. Trees, creepers, and underbrush had grown over the place, but through the October-stripped barricade of their branches he could see a heap of stones that was his dolmen, on which the hieroglyph of him was inscribed.

Two tears scalded his cheeks; he trembled with the welter of his emotions. He had failed his father, failed his trust, failed the world; and in the abyss of that grief he could catch no sight of promise or hope. Having done his best, he had still done nothing, and it was necessary for him to lie to put the thoughts of a dying man to rest. The pity of that lie! The folly of the picture he had painted of himself—Hugo Danner the scourge of God, Hugo Danner the destroying angel, Hugo Danner the hero of a quick love-affair that turned brown and dead like a plucked flower, the sentimental soldier, the involuntary misanthrope.

"I must do it!" he whispered fiercely. The ruined stones echoed the sound of his voice with a remote demoniac jeer. Do what? What, strong man? What?

The Great Comic Book Heroes

JULES FEIFFER

Reprinted by permission of the author from *The Great Comic Book Superheroes* (Bonanza Books, 1965), section nine.

HAD I ONLY BEEN SIX YEARS OLDER I COULD HAVE BEEN IN COMIC BOOKS FROM almost the beginning: carting my sample case in the spring of 1939 instead of 1945; a black cardboard folio with inside overlapping side sheets, secured tight with black bows on its three unbound corners, containing 14 x 22 pages of Bristol board on which could be drawn typical adventure swipes of the day, inked with as slick a Caniff line as one could evoke at sixteen—a series of thick and thin brush strokes wafted onto the paper with the lightest, most characterless of touches. Draftsmanship was not the point here—this was *technique*!

Going the rounds then: checking the inside glossy covers of comic books for names and addresses, riding the subway out of the Bronx in the morning rush, my portfolio on the deck, squeezed tightly between my legs so that the crowd could not bruise it, nor art thieves steal it. The bigger houses—so official looking—would have scared me, and then dismissed me for lack of experience. How are you supposed to get experience when no one will give you experience? The answer: to begin low—at one of the countless schlock houses grinding out the junk in small, brutal-looking offices all over town. These, the cheapie houses, were where one got the first breaks. Not being worth anything, no one else worth anything would hire you. But the schlock houses operated as way stations for both the beginners and the talentless.

Artists sat lumped in crowded rooms, knocking it out for the page rate. Penciling, inking, lettering in the balloons for $10 a page, sometime less; working from yellow typescripts that on the left described the action, on the right gave the dialogue. A decaying old radio, wallpapered with dirty humor, talked race results by the hour. Half-finished coffee containers turned old and petrified. The "editor," who'd be in one office that week, another the next, working for companies that changed names as often as he changed jobs, sat at a desk or a drawing table—an always beefy man who, if he drew, did not do it well, making it that much more galling when he corrected your work and you knew he was right. His job was to check copy, check art, hand out assignments, pay the artists money when he had it, promise the artists money when he didn't. Everyone got paid if he didn't mind going back week after week. Everyone got paid if he didn't mind occasionally pleading.

The schlock houses were the art schools of the business. Working blind but furiously, working from swipes, working from the advice of others who drew better because they were in the business two weeks longer, one, suddenly, learned how to draw. It happened in spurts. Nothing for a while: not being able to catch on, not being able to foreshorten correctly, or get perspectives straight or get the blacks to look right. Then suddenly: a breakthrough. One morning you can draw forty per cent better than you could when you quit the night before. Then, again you coast. Your critical abilities improve but your talent won't. Nothing works. Despair. Then another breakthrough. Magically, it keeps happening. Soon it stops being magic, just becomes education.

I'd have met, in those early days, other young cartoonists. We'd talk nothing but shop. A new world; new superheroes, new arch-villains. We'd compare swipes—and then, as our work improved, we'd disdain swipes. We'd joke about those who claimed no longer to use them but, secretly, still did. Sometimes, secretly, we still did too. Some of us would pair off, find rooms together—moving our drawing tables away from the family into the world of commercial togetherness. Eighteen hours a day of work. Sandwiches for breakfast, lunch, and dinner. An occasional beer, but not too often. And nothing any stronger. One dare not slow up.

We were a *generation*. We thought of ourselves the way the men who began movies must have. We were out to be splendid—somehow. In the meantime, we talked at our drawing tables about Caniff, Raymond, Foster. We argued over the importance of detail. Must every button on a suit be shown? Some argued yes. The magic realists of the business. Others argued no; what one wanted, after all, was *effect*. The expressionists of the business. Experiments in the use of angle shots were carried on. Arguments raged: Should angle shots be used for their own sake or for the sake of furthering the story? Everyone went back to study *Citizen Kane*. Rumors spread that Welles, himself, had read and learned from comic books! What a great business!

The work was relentless. Some men worked in bullpens during the day free-lanced at night—a hard job to quit work at five-thirty, go home and freelance till four in the morning, get up at eight and go to a job. And the weekends were the worst. A friend would call for help: He had contracted to put together a sixty-four page package over the weekend—a new book with new titles, new heroes—to be conceived, written, drawn, and delivered to the engraver between six o'clock Friday night and eight-thirty Monday morning. The presses were reserved for nine.

Business was booming. New titles coming out by the day, too many of them drawn over a two-day weekend. Cartoonists throughout the city took their pencils, pens, brushes, and breadboards to apartments already crowded with drawing tables, fluorescent lamps, folding chairs, and crippling networks of extension cords. Writers banged out the scripts, handed them by the page to an available artist—one who was not penciling or inking his own page, or assisting on backgrounds on someone else's job, were divided and sub-divided—or sometimes, not divided at all. An artist might not work from a script, but write his own story, in which case it would be planned in pencil right on the finished page. Some artists penciled only the figures, leaving the backgrounds for another artist who then passed the page to a lettering man who then passed the page to an inker who then might ink only the figures, or sometimes only the heads, passing the work, then, to another inker who finished the bodies and the backgrounds. Everybody worked on everybody else's jobs. The artist who contracted the job would usually take the lead feature. Other features were parceled out indiscriminately. No one cared too much. No one was competitive. They were all too busy.

If the place being used had a kitchen, black coffee was made and remade. If not, coffee and sandwiches were sent for—no matter the hour. In mid-town Manhattan something always had to be open. Except on Sundays. A man could look for hours before he found an open delicatessen. The other artists sat working, starving: some dozing over their breadboards, others stretching out for a nap on the floor, their empty fingers twitching to the rhythm of the brush.

During heavy snow storms stores that stayed open were hard to find. A food forager I know of returned to the loft rented for the occasion, a loft devoid of kitchen, stove, hot plate, utensils, plates or can opener, with two dozen eggs and a can of beans. Desperate with rage and hunger and the need to get back to the job, the artists scraped tiles off the bathroom wall, built the tiles into a small oven, set fire to old scripts, heated the beans in the can (which was opened by hammering door keys into it with the edge of a T-square) and fried the eggs on the hot tiles. They used cold tiles for plates.

This was the birth of a new art form! A lot of talk about that: how to design better, draw better, animate a little better—so that it would jump, magically, off the page. Movies on paper—the final dream!

But even before the war the dream began to dissipate. The war finished the job. The best men went into the service. Hacks sprouted everywhere—and, with sales to armed forces booming, Hack houses also sprouted, declared bankruptcy in order to not pay their bills, then re-sprouted under new names. The page rates went up to $15 a page for penciling, $10 for inking, $2 for lettering. Scripts got $5 to $7 a page—few artists wrote their own any more. Few cared.

The business stopped being thought of as a life's work and became a steppingstone. Five years in it at best, then on to better things: a daily strip, or illustrating for the *Saturday Evening Post* or getting a job with an advertising firm. If you weren't in it for the buck, there wasn't a single other reason.

Talk was no longer about work. The men were too old, too bored for that. It was about wives, baseball, kids, broads—or about what a son of a bitch the guy you were working for was: office gas. The same as in any office anywhere, not a means of communication but a ritualistic discharge. The same release could be achieved through clowning: joke phone calls, joke run-around-errands for the office patsy, joke disappearances of the new man's art work. Everyone passed it off as good fun in order not to be marked as a bad sport. By the end of the war the men who had been in charge of our childhood fantasies had become archetypes of the grownup who made us need to have fantasies in the first place.

The Comics and the Super State

WALTER ONG

Reprinted by permission from *Arizona Quarterly*, Vol. 1, no. 3 (Autumn 1945), 34–48. © The Arizona Board of Regents.

IN THE 25,000,000 COMIC BOOKS THAT ARE PRODUCED IN THIS COUNTRY PER month, each to be read by an average of four or five individuals, and in the 6,000,000,000 comic strips that appear every month in U.S. newspapers, there is at work a squirming mass of psychological forces. What all these forces are, no one knows. Nor many people care. We know only that they have been found most effective for attracting men, women, and children in huge numbers.

Unidentified, unlabeled, these forces have been brought together in comic books and newspapers by the trial and error method which fixes its attention squarely on profit and obliquely, not to say ruefully, on a few of the decencies, often pared to or beyond a scant minimum.

Attention to profits in this case means attention to easy reading. With every brief snatch of text locked into position by a picture, the full reaction is made as available to children as to anyone else. Reading habits at a low level of awareness are being indulged more universally now than was ever possible before.

Even if we knew fully the psychological factors in the comic equation, we would be unable to predict the multiple effect of these forces when set loose in a vehicle with the cruising range of the comics, for the area of the reading public over which the comics roll is more extensive than we often like to believe. It is not composed entirely of juveniles. Newspaper comic readers are estimated at between 60,000,000 and 70,000,000; comic book readers at 70,000,000. *Time* magazine last December printed the estimate that one out of every five adults in the United States is an avid comic book addict. At Army post exchanges, comic books outsell by ten to one *Life*, *Reader's Digest*, and the *Saturday Evening Post* combined.

Among the most significant forces at large beneath the surface of life today are those which assert themselves in totalitarian, super state ideologies. These forces are available for exploitation, and in America, too. If no one has completely identified the forces which the comics exploit, we do know that, fishing about in the murky depths of mass reactions, one is sure to encounter strong movements of those often unconscious impulses which have powered the various new orders.

This examination is concerned with intangibles, attitudes, and tendencies. I propose these for what they are and no more, but with the reminder that the preparation of a people to accept whole new ideologies is a long and psychologically involved process, which in many corners of the mind eludes observation: Hence the potential importance of movements which we commonly do not bother to observe.

We do not have to look far in the present comic field to discover a strong crosscurrent of those forces which the German, and other, super states have found useful. The general drift toward unmasked and pretentious sensationalism is perhaps the most evident component, but various less obtrusive trends are even more pointedly indicative.

Among these trends those exhibited by Superman are perhaps most representative, because back of the dozens of comics exploiting "hero" characters, he stands as the raw, elemental prototype, constructed on a monumentally primitive pattern. And the hero comics for which he stands have been the most spectacular development in picture strip history.

The civilization of the new order is in great part a herdist phenomenon. Its subjects are, ideally, standardized men, men *en bloc*, men acting and controlled in the mass on the infra-rational plane. The plan of the monolithic super state depends on there being a maneuverable mass of homogeneous beings that acts automatically. This is the herd. Its members must act, not via their intelligences, but from the impulse to be like the next man, the impulse to conformity. In the herd, differentiation is regarded with terror. Those differences that cannot be leveled—on some occasions racial, on other occasions party differences—are purged. To focus the impulse to conformity, everything is centered on one man—the leader, the hero, the *duce*, the *Fuhrer*. Herd responses not being on the rational level, this hero does not appeal by argument. He does not explain; he puts on a show. He builds on the herd's dreams: he hypnotizes. Thus did Hitler and Mussolini.

So it happens that the notion of a "superman" is part of the herdist economy of the Nazi Third Reich. The very title "superman"—as well as its earlier and unsuccessful form, "overman"—is an importation brought into English by George Bernard Shaw out of Nietzsche, the herald of Nazism and the new order, who had seen in his *übermensch* the salvation of mankind. The Superman of the cartoons is true to his sources. He is not another Horatio Alger hero or a Nick Carter; he is a super state type of hero, with definite interest in the ideologies of herdist politics.

The creature familiar as Superman is the leader of a swarm of satellites separated from him only by a copyright. Scores of comic books feature similar characters—for example, Catman, Bullet Man, The Human Torch, Captain Midnight, Captain Marvel, Black Terror, Blue Beetle, Green Lama, Yankee Boy, and Bogey Man—which follow the Superman pattern of a "hero" who overcomes all obstacles with machine-like precision. Often, victory comes from frankly preternatural powers. These are mostly powers of propulsion and X-ray vision: these heroes' bull necks are often a pretty fair index of their intellectual prowess.

The cult of the hero and the peculiar manifestations connected with it in this literature have overflowed the bounds of sex. The companion female-hero piece that has recently appeared is in a way more symptomatic than Superman himself. Its calculated conception in the mind of an American educational psychologist as an ideal comic strip shows the fertility of the superman ideology outside Germany. It is indicative that the new piece is called Wonder Woman, not, as one might expect, Superwoman (although the Superman-Wonder Woman publishers have run a few strips by this name to secure the copyright for themselves, just in case). For the heroine of the strip is really a female superman, preaching the cult of force spiked, by means of her pretentiously scanty "working" attire, with a little commercial sex. (Force-and-sex is apparently an approved formula of the super state, which baits its hooks with promises of considerable freedom in the use of both.)

Indeed, although he says she is designed to counteract the "bloodcurdling masculinity" of the other comics and to introduce "love" into the comic field, Wonder Woman is dubbed by her enthusiastic creator an Amazon, while the ambit of her activities excludes the life that most normal women might desire. The name she wears in ordinary civil life—she only takes to the woods as Wonder Woman when occasion demands, as it indeed seems to do most of the time—displays a curt and colorful masculinity: "Diana Prince." She is no Cinderella, and the clang of the huntress's name against the mannish cognomen is the kind of note she likes to hear struck. When not in her outré "working" clothes, she habitually wears a suit coat and tie among the jeweled guests at luncheon parties and at formal evening affairs.

However, strange psychological twitches are perhaps to be expected in one with such an errant genealogy: "beautiful as Aphrodite," her publishers never tire of describing her, "wise as Athena, stronger than Hercules, and swifter than Mercury." This is strict, if confused, old-pagan syncretism, which, especially with the fine scorn for gender which it manifests, is fitting enough for a professed Amazon, who swears "By Zeus!" and works as one of Aphrodite's commandos. She takes the bawdy goddess seriously. When things go hell (you can bet they always do, eventually), "Thank Aphrodite," she prays in dead earnest.

Reincarnated in a woman, the present hero ideal reveals its full *bizarrerie*. Like Superman, Wonder Woman is a somewhat strange educational genius to set working on children, consciously or subconsciously. They are shown a world bullied into subjection by the crude instincts of the subnormal male. Men in such a world is bad enough off. But woman's lot is even worse.

The economy of herdism, John Stuart Campbell maintains in *The Menace of the Herd*, demands a mechanistic identification of man and woman, and the woman in the home in the Third Reich was really there in exile because she did not "make good" elsewhere [Ong has here misidentified the author, Frances Stuart Campbell, which was a pen name for Erik Ritter von Kuehnelt-Leddihn—*eds*.]. Well, no exile for Wonder Woman. Once in a while she feels the impulse to live by genuine womanly ideals, but she inevitably gains control of herself and returns resolutely to the world of force peopled by her fellow traveler Superman and his cronies.

She is incapable of sustaining womanly standards in the face of the demand for total leveling in the monolithic state ideology. She therefore exists entirely by the standards of males, supplying on the score of her womanhood only the sexiness which the herd of males demands. This is, of course, not a healthy sex directed toward marriage and family life, but an anti-social sex, sex made as alluring as possible while its normal term in marriage is barred by the ground rules from the start. Wonder Woman, it may be said, is not a pioneer in the field of sex exploitation, where she follows rather than leads other comics.

In view of the political bearing of the present hero ideologies, it is particularly interesting that in this strong-arm division of the comics there is a marked tendency to project the cult of exuberant violence and muscularity onto the field of government, and often onto the full field of world or even cosmic politics. The tendency is plain, for example, in *Captain America*, *Wonderman*, *Wonder Boy*, *Blue Beetle*, *Black Terror*—even to some extent in the case Tarzan as well as of Buck Rogers and other interplanetary hitchhikers.

There are the titles like *Captain America* that tie up the destinies of our country with those of a hero. And Superman's publishers like to circulate testimonials that represent him as the incarnation of an ideal for the whole nation. "As Clark Kent, a typical American," one of these testimonials reads (Clark Kent is Superman's name when he wears his tie and glasses), "Superman represents all that modern American youth ever hoped to be, physically, mentally, morally, and spiritually." An elaborate commercial hocus-pocus circulates this essentially silly but dangerous claptrap in what is calculated to be a serious-minded brochure, fitted with some elaborate educational trappings to give it weight.

Representatives of the ideology of the new order are thus given *Lebensraum* on American soil and by a slick sleight-of-hand even disguised as native citizens: Superman's backers do not hesitate to label him the "Champion of Democracy." The comics' habit of tinkering with the notion of the hero as the emotional correlative of the whole nation marches exactly the technique of Hitler, who was the prototype and hero of those who wanted to be "typical Germans."

Emotionalism in these comics dreams metapolitical dreams. And the recipes for organization and government are accordingly simple. "I was just realizing how much better it is to reason with these poor wayward fellows," Plastic Man observes as he drives a left to the jaw. His philosophy is popular.

Occasionally, the feelings that make for a strong-arm government within the government (the "party" of the super state) are catered to by means of private "justice societies," which young readers are encouraged to join. A modest cash outlay provides them with badges and assurance that they are a part of the management. In achieving its success, the Superman strip has patterned itself not only on the blind hero-worship motif developed by Hitler and Mussolini, but also on the pagan Hellenistic values so useful to a super state. Superman's permanent orgy of muscularity is a correlative of the glorification of youth that is part of the pagan economy in its original habitat as well as in Nietzsche, Wagner, and in Hitler's reconditioned Valhalla. (This resurgence of official paganism in Germany was foreseen as a part of the new Germany by the prophet Nietzsche in his vision of the "rebirth in Germany of the Hellenic world.") Moreover, as Nietzsche and the official civilizations of the Nazi and Russian super states like to do, Superman dreams in accurately adolescent dreams of tomorrow's world. Indeed, his creators label him openly the "Man of Tomorrow." This tomorrow is the team world of the maladjusted child, and it is ruled by the steady application of brute force.

The same Hellenistic apotheosis of youth is carried on with great enthusiasm by Wonder Woman, too. This streamlined American Amazon gives evidence of the cult, for instance, in a morbid retrogressive fancy, reminiscent again of proto-Nazi melody out of Nietzsche or Stefan George. This fancy settles upon a return to the child's world as the most desirable goal in life. Here is the defeatism of the individual overwhelmed by the threat of herd existence at its worst. In Wonder Woman's dreams, which are staple items in her adventures, the frustrated adult returns to the world of impulse in order to discover a life pattern free of the intellectual activity proscribed by existence in the herd. In this world where adult problems are evaporated as the twitching of the mind subsides, Wonder Woman on one occasion finds herself arraigned before a judge who is an infant still unable to talk. "Da-de, da-dah," (I quote) is his studied verdict. Here is the new recipe for the good life.

Such adventures are not symptomatic of a condition among children, who are incapable of making youth the object of retrogressive fancy and who, in their desire to be grown up, are probably left quite cold by this adulation of childhood. These adventures are canards flown in from an adult world.

The idealization of youth manifests itself in other ways, too, in Wonder Woman. In one issue she qualifies as the heroine of a really redoubtable womanhood by turning over ten times in a somersault without touching the ground. As one adventure begins she prescribes for the whole American scene in a flip analysis, which substitutes faked assurance for insight: "The Amazon maiden believes that America's greatest need today is more fun, recreation, and health giving amusement."

This total athleticism finds its outlet everywhere in the comic world, where one runs across a "blue beetle," a batman, a star-man, and other mighty cosmic wayfarers, as well as the plastic man we encountered earlier, who can stretch himself indefinitely in any direction. It flowers in the breakfast cereal advertisements that the comics display. It puts the emphasis where the new order likes to have it.

As an originator of one of the comics himself explains these picture stories feed their readers' desires for "feeling big, smart, important, and winning the admiration of their fellows." The same approach and emphasis are reflected when we are advised by the comics' backers that, "the wish to be super-strong is a healthy wish, a vital, compelling, power-producing desire."

The publishers of these strips, acutely aware of the charges to which comics lie open, have of course been stumping for what patriotism they can. Syphoned off a volatile world of wish fulfillment, this patriotism is necessarily of a highly vaporous type. The characters in the strips are occasionally signed up as F.B.I. men or as other government agents so that the flag can be waved at objections. But the headiest patriotism of all is that bottled with the bromide "In the comics, crime never pays." At the level of reading response at which the comics are propelled, it is plainly questionable whether such a fact is operative or even noticed, and it would be interesting to know whether to the juvenile comic book addict crime means anything more than opposition to the character with the highest emotional appeal.

Indeed, the constant traffic with the world of crime provides a suitable culture for the paranoiac patriotism which Dr. Richard M. Brickner, writing recently in the *Atlantic Monthly*, found festering at the roots of recent Germany. It is Dr. Brickner's considered opinion that the fact that Germany provided environments friendly to paranoia largely explains that country's present plight. "Clark Kent," Superman is told, "you're a pessimist! To listen to you, anyone would think this town was full of crooks!" The guardian of American ideals glances casually over his shoulder. Crooks everywhere. It is not far to go from this world of total crime to the persecution complex of the neurotic.

Added to all this, the frank exploitation of sex which has become a primary circulation builder in the comic field parallels the neo-paganism with which the super state manipulates the herd. We don't ordinarily think of it this way, but it might be noted here that the sexy and synthetic pastoralism of *Li'l Abner*, even in its comic phase, is akin to what has been regarded as a mark of a decadent society in ancient Greece, ancient Rome, the eighteenth-century French court. I prescind from the manifest cleverness of this comic, which is another thing.

Sex exploitation has often taken such sharp turns in the direction of sadism and masochism that groups of interested persons have felt it necessary to protest. Thus a Child Study Association report on the comics calls attention to the objectionable character of the "pictures of chained women, of captive women being driven by men, and other sadistic themes."

These are the tendencies. They are not by any means apparent in all the comics, for there remain such features as *Gasoline Alley* or *Blondie* that are quite free of the play of these weird forces. But it is disconcerting and sobering to see how these forces have moved irresistibly into the comic field.

Recent developments have caused no little consternation in quarters where the comics have been considered as one of the outposts, one of the citadels, of the American way of life.

"Sidney Smith gets a laugh out of the millions because he shows us folks as they are . . . we *are* the Gumps," a magazine writer in 1923 was preaching to Andy Gump's apparently numerous understudies. This is reassuring. But it won't work for Dick Tracy or Tarzan or Blue Beetle or Mandrake the Magician, who have shouldered Andy aside but who are *not* the kind of people you expect to find moving in next door.

You still hear a gouty protest here and there that the older comics were best. That is not what the comic readers as a whole think. As newspaper publishers have gained experience, they have found it more profitable when the same public which used to be satisfied with the likes of Happy Hooligan is supplied with more and more comics turned out according to more advanced formulas.

For the audience as a whole is not very discriminating: it likes comics. Just comics. Sinclair Lewis portrays Babbitt in his Main Street home plodding "nightly through every picture" of the comic section "with the solemn face of a devotee, breathing heavily." Babbitt read them all. His picture is still being multiplied everywhere and the abiding accuracy of Lewis's reporting can be checked on every streetcar. A great section of comic readers read them all. There seems to be nothing in the good comics that keeps readers from liking the others. Both kinds slide comfortably along the same neural ruts. It is not unusual for a comic book to feature, as one current book does, *Blondie* and *The Katzenjammer Kids*, both humorous, plus *Tim Tyler*, a typical thriller, and *The Phantom*, a sex and horror piece—all under a cover displaying only a Katzenjammer Kid honorably engaged in his round of perpetual badgering. *The Captain and the Kids*, *Ella Cinders*, and the resolute burlesque of *Nancy* share another book with *Tarzan* and a *Spark Man* piece that ends with a wanton-looking female hung up by the hands. Another book featuring a generous number of humorous pieces displays quite frankly on its cover only a crude sex-lure. In the last winter issue of *Wonder Woman*, the reader, finished with his heroine's adventures among the mermaids, turns the page for more satisfaction. There he finds—*Mutt and Jeff*.

Historically, the "healthy" comics seem not to have retained an isolated group of followers but to have fed their readers into the indiscriminating audience where the tendencies we have examined earlier are welcomed and given free play.

If we are at a loss to explain why this change has taken place in so "healthy" a type of reading as the comics were, it is perhaps because we have developed some mental squints toward them. We have a hard time seeing them as they really are. Responsible for this are several beliefs that have acted as blinds behind which the ideology of the new orders could safely enter the comic field.

The first is the normalcy superstition. This belief holds that a taste for the comics is an indication of a healthy emotional life because it is "normal," that is, because everyone indulges it. This superstition plainly makes an objective evaluation of the comics impossible. It deflects our attention from the comics to ourselves; instead of making us sharp-sighted, it makes us self-conscious and worried about our own reactions.

The operation of this superstition can be seen in a current writer who settles the value of the comics by a deft blow which clubs his readers into line: if you are "inclined to deplore" the influence of the comic strips, you are a "snob," he says. That settles it. The conclusion is completed before examination of the comics has begun. You will never notice very much about the comics that way.

Another and a related belief which has developed in us a mental squint toward the comics is the folklore superstition. A recent plea for the comics, for instance, tracks witches, cruel stepmothers, and wholesale poisoning from the comic strips back to their lairs in the older folk literature, such as Grimm's fairy tales. That makes everything all right.

This path has been worn smooth by defenders of the comics. The comic strips are supposed to have "created some of the towering figures of our American mythology," and "they are definitely a part of our native folklore," newspaper articles assure us.

There is, of course, an intelligent interest in the folk: an intelligent love of one's own people and culture we are best capable of loving, since we know them best. This interest in one's people thrives on study and mature emotion.

Itself a product of a genuine cultural tradition, it is capable of discerning the valuable products of that tradition from its byproducts. Being intelligent, it can evaluate its own performance, and expects to do so.

This is not the folklore superstition.

The folklore superstition is pretty sloppy about artistic or social values. You can recognize it by its thoroughgoing indiscrimination, its persistent refusal to bother seriously about forming really critical estimates. If it can father a literary or any other work on the *Volk*, the *Volk* will be the work's entire justification. Mass approval has a magic value, and one must ask no questions.

One current writer observes that a recent report on the comics by a group of sociological, educational, and psychiatrical experts was rather awesome "until we realized that they were merely saying that the reason for the success of comic strips (and books) is that they fill in our generation the place of the old folk tale."

Here *is* the superstition.

Only say that the comics are like folk tales, and all misgivings vanish. The taut muscles of the mind relax. The mind bows before its fetish and is reassured. Why? The reason seems traceable, historically as well as logically, to an attitude toward *das Volk* on which the new orders build.

In the nineteenth century many scholars were so blinded by notions that the masses of men were endowed with magical powers that they constructed a spurious pedigree for the so-called "popular ballads." These pieces of folklore were supposed, according to this pedigree, to be the result of some magic, resident in the herd: things that "grow," that "fall out of the air," creations that "spring from the very heart of the people and flit from age to age, from lip to lip of shepherds, peasants, nurses, of all that continue nearest to the natural state of man." Miss Louise Pound pointed out the inaccuracy of this pedigree some years ago in her *Poetic Origins and the Ballad* (the quotations just given, from Andrew Lang and Theodor Sturm, are to be found in this book). When you realize that, as she points out, in every case where we can trace their origins, the ballads are not of such lineage at all but are confused or even quite incoherent versions of "art poetry"—that is, poetry composed like everything else, including the comics, by someone who sets himself down to a definite task—and that the "art poetry," before it got transmogrified into a popular ballad by being passed around with no great care from mouth to mouth, was almost always better work than afterward; when you realize, in other words, that contact of an imaginative work with large groups of people who pay only passing attention to it does not make the work inevitably worthwhile—when you realize all this, you are not so scrupulous about regarding *all* folk literature as an automatic artistic and sociological success.

But the new order is scrupulous about this. Men such as Wagner, whose work has got itself sufficiently entangled with folk superstition, were all snapped up as props for the official civilization of the Third Reich. The defense of the comics, which adopts as the ultimate criterion of worth an indiscriminating enthusiasm for mass likes and dislikes, is in the same tradition. To the proto-Nazi herdists, the ballads were beyond cavil because they were seen "flitting from age to age, from lip to lip of shepherds, peasants, nurses . . . " The present-day defender of the comics, aware of his audience's prejudices, falls back on the same dodge, almost word for word. Here is no *people* critical of itself, but only a turgid and luckless mass made to bear the weight of a bogus infallibility.

As one reflection of the folklore superstition, there is abroad this belief: that readers will find their native shrewdness whetted when they apply themselves to the better comics. But even rid of the normalcy and folklore superstitions, it is hard indeed to find instances where the comics give reason for this belief. Close scrutiny of even the best comics does not reveal anything that would lead to the conclusion that their readers are inoculated against infection with any of the notions blowing about in the most miasmic geopolitical wind.

However wholesomely some comics may bring out the good points in our civilization, they are powerless to evaluate any factors in the civilization on any other terms than those of its own prejudices. Since the reader must never be unseated from his easy chair, the standards he takes for granted are beyond question. *Mr. and Mrs.* and other family comics poke fun a lot in the American home, but their creators are acutely aware that they must do so only in unposted territory where the audience feels its position so secure that it can afford to indulge a self-complacent laugh. Such questions as divorce, for instance, or the aberrations of our educational efforts, or our national pride which makes us often odious as a nation to other groups of people—things which a serious satirist of our way of life could never keep clear of—are studiously hushed.

Al Capp's satirization of the gruesome mores of his synthetic hillbillies in *Li'l Abner* is irrelevant enough to be amusing: when he poked fun at Margaret Mitchell, he had to apologize in full Sunday color and shut up. What would happen if he began to show his whole audience what he really could do with *their* mores and folkways makes an engaging subject for macabre speculation.

The most wholesome comics have to follow the marked trails, and the satirical strips have to direct their fire at specified targets. Yet the comics do create the illusion of giving an overview of life. To many persons, they seem critical. Orphan Annie does not philosophize into thin air but into readers' opened ears. All the while, there can be no keenness without depth, and depth is too much to require of the comic strip audience. The result is that an unedged satire and unconditional surrender to the least common denominator of readers' ideals, far from developing really canny readers, encourages instead habits of self-complacency and cultural narcissism.

The plain fact is that the comics, although for a time they exhibited no very objectionable phenomena, impose on their audience reading habits that are dangerous. Our attitude toward the comics may often make little difference in itself, but it is important as an index of our attitude toward the great mass of reading which operates at the same level of awareness—reading made for effortless absorption, reading on the level at which propaganda moves. We are inclined to forget that when a man gives himself to reading, he has to keep his wits about him or at least to collect them from time to time. Otherwise he is not safe. Neither is the man next to him.

This is not a condemnation of everything in the comics nor a plea to abolish them. Neither is it an attempt to picture the publishers of the comics as diabolic schemers designedly attempting to foist herdist ideals upon America. Even the worst of the comic publishers are essentially businessmen intent only on making money. This is simply a plea to recognize the comics for *all* that they are, to face the facts, but all of them.

The comic publishers' wares are in great part not devices for warming man's five wits but drugs that tend to induce intellectual anesthesia. Like other drugs, they can often build in the addict a false confidence while they are crystalizing the very habits that blunt his powers of perception. The rocketing popularity of the comics among servicemen under the abnormal strains of war is itself evidence of the qualifications of the comics as a soporific.

We cannot wipe out literature prepared for this level of response. But a lot depends on our outspoken awareness of what it is. As matters stand, instead of scrutinizing the comics, we too often make over them. We make over them so much that workbooks built around sensational comic characters have been in use in schools. It may be unlikely that the comics will overpower all other educational devices; but the ease with which they can be presented as an educational nostrum shows how far gone is the uncritical attitude toward them. In our educational processes there will be more encouragement than ever to combine technological accomplishment with a sprawling literary helplessness. Military victory or no, this is preparation for the age of the new order.

The important point is not that so many forces at work in the comics today fall into a herdist pattern. The herdist pattern serves here only as a general area of reference to show how an uncontrolled type of reading will reproduce and magnify the forces lurking in the hidden corners and back alleys of civilization. The important point is that the comics are a sounding box where the infra-rational waves of human behavior irresponsibly amplify themselves, and we must be aware of this fact.

A vague uneasiness about the comics is common enough today. Most discussions handle this uneasiness in either of two ways. Some proffer a set of ready-made windmills for the uneasiness to spend itself on: comics pervert grammar, they stunt vocabulary growth, they are "unartistic." Such windmills induce fits of harmless and irrelevant activity that wears off the uneasiness and supplants it with a sense of achievement. Other discussions of the comics simply asphyxiate the mind in the vapors of truisms and prejudices. Thus one magazine writer can conclude his study of the comics with the motto "*Know folks* if you want to sell something to them."

Fogged by smug observations such as this, the mind drops off into a reassured slumber.

The Superman Conceit

FREDRIC WERTHAM

Reprinted from *Seduction of the Innocent* (Main Road Books, 2004 [1954]), 94–102 by permission of the President and Fellows of Harvard College.

THE ATMOSPHERE OF CRIME COMIC BOOKS IS UNPARALLELED IN THE HISTORY OF children's literature of any time or any nation. It is a distillation of viciousness. The world of the comic book is the world of the strong, the ruthless, the bluffer, the shrewd deceiver, the torturer, and the thief. All the emphasis is on exploits where somebody takes advantage of somebody else, violently, sexually, or threateningly. It is no more the world of braves and squaws, but one of punks and molls. Force and violence in any conceivable form are romanticized. Constructive and creative forces in children are channeled by comic books into destructive avenues. Trust, loyalty, confidence, solidarity, sympathy, charity, compassion are ridiculed. Hostility and hate set the pace of almost every story. A natural scientist who had looked over comic books expressed this to me tersely, "in comic books life is worth nothing; there is no dignity of a human being."

Children seek a figure to emulate and follow. Crime comic books undermine this necessary ingredient of ethical development. They play up the good times had by those who do the wrong thing. Those who at the tail end of stories mete out punishment use the same violence and the same lingo as those whom they punish. Since everybody is selfish and force and violence are depicted as the most successful methods, the child is given a feeling of justification. They not only suggest the satisfaction of primitive impulses but supply the rationalization. In this soil children indulge in the stock fantasies supplied by the industry: murder, torture, burglary, threats, arson, and rape. Into that area of the child's mind where right and wrong is evaluated, children incorporate such false standards that an ethical confusion results for which they are not to blame. They become emotionally handicapped and culturally underprivileged. And this affects their social balance.

Whatever may give a child some ethical orientation is dragged down to the crime-violence level. Inculcation of a distorted morality by endless repetition is not such an intangible factor if one studies its source in comic books and its effect in the lives of children. It is of course a question not of pious slogans like "Crime never pays" but of the emotional accents within the stories themselves.

In one comic an old man is killed during the hold-up of his jewelry store. He had not obeyed the order to back up against the wall quickly enough. After other crimes and murders the captured criminal says: "It was not right to kill him. . . . That man couldn't have obeyed me? . . . That old man was STONE DEAF!"

The moral principle is clear. If you hold up a man and he does not obey quickly enough because he is deaf, you are not supposed to shoot him. But if he is *not* deaf, shooting him is all right.

In one comic story called "Mother Knows Best," the mother advises her children: "I brought you kids up right—rub out those coppers like I taught you!"

One son answers: "Don't worry, ma! We'll give those flatfeet a bellyful of lead!"

Several boys have shown me this story. They themselves condemned and at the same time were fascinated by this anti-maternal story.

In the same comic book, a man attacks a high school girl ("All I want is a little kiss? C'mon!"), and chokes her to death.

What in a few words is the essential ethical teaching of crime comics for children? I find it well and accurately summarized in this brief quotation:

> It is not a question of right, but of winning. Close your heart against compassion. Brutality does it. The stronger is in the right. Greatest hardness. Follow your opponent till he is crushed.

These words were the instructions given on August 22, 1939, by a superman in his home in Berchtesgaden to his generals, to serve as guiding lines for the treatment of the population in the impending war on Poland.

In modification of the Fernald method of letting children judge the severity of offenses, I have often asked them about punishment. Why do people get punished, what is just punishment, how does it come about that people get punished? Frequently the reply is that it serves the criminal right, whatever the punishment may be: "He got caught, didn't he?" My clinical findings leave no room for doubt that children learn from crime comics that the real guilt is getting caught. They have little faith in any ordinary public processes of having an offense evaluated and justly and humanely dealt with. The law enforcers are criminals in reverse. They use the same methods. If they are also stronger and there are more of them, they win; if not, they lose. In many subtle and not so subtle forms the lynch spirit is taught as a moral lesson. Many children have told me that lynching is all right and have shown me examples from their comic books. In one such story the townspeople get together, hunt the criminal and he is finally shot and killed. The lesson is in the last sentence: "The story of Lee Gillon proves that fearless people banded together will always see that justice triumphs."

In the same book, a man slaps a girl's face and says: "Give me trouble and you'll have a board full of spikes smashed into your kisser!"

The form in which this distrust for democratic law and the morality of taking punishment—or rather vengeance—into one's own hands has done most harm to the ethical development of young people is the superman conceit. Analyzing children's fantasies and daydreams, I have often found in them a wish for overwhelming physical strength, domination, power, ruthlessness, emancipation from the morals of the community. It may show in various half-repressed ways or openly as admiration for these traits. Spontaneously children connect this with crime comic books of the Superman, Batman, Superboy, Wonder Woman type. In the individual case this superman ideology is psychologically most unhygienic. The would-be supermen compensate for some kind of inferiority, real or imagined, by the fantasy of the superior being who is a law unto himself. I have had cases where children would have had a good chance to overcome feelings of inferiority in constructive ways at their disposal if they had not been sidetracked by the fancied shortcuts of superman prowess.

The superman conceit gives boys and girls the feeling that ruthless go-getting based on physical strength or the power of weapons or machines is the desirable way to behave. When I have had to examine young adults at the Clinic off and on for driving recklessly, I was interested to find the same attitude. Particularly dangerous is the superman-speed-fancy in girls who in turn influence boys. One young girl told me that she would only go out with boys who would not let other cars pass them on the road. That was the idea of the proper male behavior that she had got from comics.

In these children there is an exact parallel to the blunting of sensibilities in the direction of cruelty that has characterized a whole generation of central European youth fed on the Nietzsche-Nazi myth of the exceptional man who is beyond good and evil. It is an ethical confusion. If such persons are analyzed psychiatrically, it is found that the trouble lies not so much with the impulse to do the wrong thing as with the false rationalization which permits the impulse to grow and to express itself in deeds. The very children for whose unruly behavior I would want to prescribe psychotherapy in an anti-superman direction have been nourished (or rather poisoned) by the endless repetition of Superman stories. How can they respect the hard-working mother, father, or teacher who is so pedestrian, trying to teach common rules of conduct, wanting you to keep your feet on the ground, and unable even figuratively speaking to fly through the air? Psychologically, Superman undermines the authority and the dignity of the ordinary man and woman in the minds of children.

When I described how children suffer in their ethical development through the reading of comic books, the industry countered by pointing with pride to the "moral" lesson imprinted on many crime comics, that "crime does not pay." In the first place, this is not true. In comic books crime usually does pay, and pay very well, until the last picture or two. The crimes are glamorous; the end is dull. Frequently the ratio of "crime" to "does not pay" is as high as fifty to one. More important, the slogan "Crime does not pay" is *not* moral, but highly immoral. It is strange how responsible adults have accepted this slogan and refer to it on platforms, over the radio, and in articles as admirable. Great harm has been done by teaching children that they should not play hookey, that they should not steal or lie, that they should not hit girls (as comic-book figures so often do)—*because it "doesn't pay"*! I have seen many children who were confused by this vicious crime-comic-book morality. The reason why one does not hit girls, even if comics have made it so attractive, is that it is cowardly and that it hurts them; the reason why one does not steal or break into stores is that that is not how one lives in a civilized community; that whether crime pays or does not pay, it is not what a decent person wants to do. *That* should be the lesson for children.

When I pointed out the hypocrisy of the "Crime does not pay" slogan and its bad effect on children, the industry accused me of "unfairness" in attacking their highest endeavors and introduced some more slogan morality. In one comic book are two pages by a police captain attacking me: "Don't let reformers kid you!" He is "shocked by what I read today about the people who condemn crime comics. These people are the menace." He goes on: "Children don't like to be kicked around by reformers who want to decide what's good for them to read." And he extols "the strong moral force" that comics exert on children.

Frequently I have been in the position of having to defend children who have received harsh judgments in courts and on psychiatric wards and equally harsh treatment in places of detention and reformatories. There is no better illustration of the state of affairs where we first victimize children and then put all the responsibility on them, the victims, than this same comic book. It has a story where two policemen are killed—and a real police captain pointing out what a "strong moral force" such a book is!

In the midst of bloody scenes in another book are two full-page announcements, one advocating "better schools" and the other with an oversized headline in capitals: WITH GOD ALL THINGS ARE POSSIBLE!" advocating "a new way of prayer." If one tried to set out deliberately to create ethical confusion in children, better ways could hardly be devised. No wonder that a minister heard his young son exclaim: "Hands up, in the name of the Lord!"

The detrimental effect on character is if anything worse on girls than on boys. Their ego-ideal formation is interfered with by the fascination of the sadistic female comic-book heroines. Comic books do not permit these children even in their imagination to view a non-violent life. A girl of eleven examined because of stealing showed in her Thematic Apperception Test a profusion of stories with murder and hostility. Her drawing of a woman showed a masculine type with violent aggressivity. Of average intelligence, she had a reading retardation undoubtedly caused by constant reading of comics. She had incorporated the comic-book morale into her character.

"I read about ten a day," she stated. "I like the stories when you get in trouble and everything. You learn like it does not pay if you kill a person for nothing that isn't right[!]. They have to go to prison for a certain length of time, then they come out and do it all over again. Then they go up the river again."

Without rationalization and without an ideal image of oneself one cannot learn to exert self-discipline. That is why good reading is such a character-building influence. Comic books work in the opposite direction. A thirteen-year-old girl examined because of "truancy and disobedience" said about her reading, "I used to buy a love comic every day. I like to read *Sheena* because I like the way she fights. She fights like a man, swings on the vines, and kicks people in the face."

Ethical development of children, so intimately bound up with their mental development, has to do not only with relations with an individual but also with integration in groups. The development of the superego, of conscience or, more simply, the sense of decency, takes place not only on the basis of identification with parents but also with successive parent-substitutes who are at the same time representatives and symbols of group demands and group responsibilities. In this sphere, comic books are most pernicious. They expose children's minds to an endless stream of prejudice-producing images. This influence, subtle and pervasive but easily demonstrable by clinical psychological methods, has not only directly affected the individual child, but also constitutes an important factor for the whole nation. It is currently fashionable to speak of "inter-group tensions," "group adjustments," and so on. The old term *race hatred* (or *race prejudice*) is more honest and more to the point. What we call "minorities" constitute the *majority* of mankind. The United States is spending at present millions of dollars to persuade the world on the air and by other propaganda means that race hatred is not an integral part of American life. At the same time, millions of American comic books are exported all over the world which give the impression that the United States is instilling race hatred in young children.

If I were to make the briefest summary of what children have told us about how different peoples are represented to them in the lore of crime comics, it would be that there are two kinds of people: on the one hand is the tall, blond, regular-featured man sometimes disguised as a superman (or superman disguised as a man) and the pretty young blonde girl with the super-breast. On the other hand are the inferior people: natives, primitives, savages, "ape men," Negroes, Jews, Indians, Italians, Slavs, Chinese, and Japanese, immigrants of every description, people with irregular features, swarthy skins, physical deformities, Oriental features. In some crime comics the first class sometimes wears some kind of superman uniform, while the second class is in mufti. The brunt of this imputed inferiority in whole groups of people is directed against colored people and "foreign born."

When the seeds of prejudice against others first appear in a child, or when he first becomes aware of belonging to a group against which there is prejudice, depends on many diverse factors: family, education, community, social stratum. From my studies, the second apparently appears later. But in general both feelings appear much earlier than is commonly supposed. A four-year-old can imbibe prejudice from comic books, and six- or seven-year-olds are quite articulate about it. Sometimes their feeling of dislike for a group ("They are bad." "They are vicious." "They are criminals." "They are dirty." "You can't trust them.") is derived from crime comic books. In other cases, distorted stereotypes acquired at home, on the street, in school, are given new nourishment and perpetuation by comic-book reading. These conclusions are based entirely on *what the children themselves say*.

The pictures of these "inferior" types as criminals, gangsters, rapists, suitable victims for slaughter by either the lawless or the law, have made an indelible impression on children's minds. There can be no doubt about the correctness of this conclusion.

For example, when a child is shown a comic book that he has not read and is asked to pick out the bad man, he will unhesitatingly pick out types according to the stereotyped conceptions of race prejudice, and tell you the reason for his choice. "Is he an American?" "No!"

Attacks by older children on younger ones, inspired or fortified by the race prejudice shown in comic books, are getting more frequent. I have seen such cases (which do not always come to the attention of the authorities) with victims belonging to various minorities. For the victims, this is frequently a serious traumatic emotional episode. Some juvenile gangs make it a practice to beat dark-skinned children, and they do it with comic-book brutality. So comic books provide both the methods and the vilification of the victims.

Comic books read with glee by many children, including very young ones, teach the props of anti-Semitism. There is the book with the story of the "itch-ray projector," with illustrations that might be taken directly from Nazi magazines like Streicher's *Stuermer*. One particularly popular comic book features the story of "Mother Mandelbaum, A True Story." Depicted as an unmistakable and repellent stereotype, she "aspires to be the biggest fence in New York." She finances bank robberies, starts a school for pickpockets, and also has a class for safecrackers and another to teach assorted kinds of violence. She personally orders and supervises the beating up of "slow payers."

When you see groups of children reading this and hear them chuckle and fill in the derogatory epithets and appellations, the result of the indoctrination is clear. It partially explains some recent episodes of vandalism and attacks on children.

The Great Women Superheroes

TRINA ROBBINS

Reprinted by permission of the author from *The Great Women Superheroes* (Kitchen Sink Press, 1996), 2–14.

IN 1938 TWO TEENAGE BOYS, JERRY SIEGEL AND JOE SHUSTER, INTRODUCED their creation, Superman, in *Action Comics* #1, and superheroes entered the world's consciousness. Their story of a superpowered foundling from another planet had been rejected by every comic strip syndicate and comic book editor to whom it had been submitted before being accepted by Harry Donenfeld for publication in his new *Action Comics*. Inspired by the energetic leadership of President Franklin Delano Roosevelt and the attempts of the government to alleviate the Depression through the programs of the New Deal, the Superman stories struck a chord in the minds and hearts of Americans. Within a year, Superman had his own comic book; within two years, Siegel and Shuster's oft-rejected creation was also a syndicated comic strip appearing in over 250 newspapers, and the comic book was selling a million copies per month.

The success of the Superman character naturally led to imitation, and new superheroes popped up almost faster than a speeding bullet. In 1939, Batman emerged from his batcave to avenge his murdered parents in *Detective Comics* #27, and within a year he had his own book. By 1940, National Periodical Publications had concluded that superheroes were here to stay, and introduced the Flash, the fastest man alive, in his own title, while DC featured superheroes like Hawkman, who dressed like a hawk and spoke to birds, in features in anthology books like *Detective Comics*.

1940 saw other comic book companies create their own superheroes. The Fawcett Company was the home of Captain Marvel, really a twelve-year-old boy who said the magic word "Shazam" to become invincible. Timely Comics followed suit with the Human Torch, who possessed the unique ability to burst into flame, and Sub-Mariner, who swam up from the depths of the ocean to fight humans, but later switched his enmity to the Axis.

Accompanied by colorful sound effects like *Bam*, *Crash*, and *Pow!*, scores of other costumed heroes flew, swam, raced, and punched their way through the pages of comic books. Aside from their brightly colored longjohns, the one thing these heroes had in common was their gender. But the first costumed superheroine also appeared in 1940. In the pages of *Thrilling Comics*, undercover policewoman Peggy Allen decided she could do a better job solving crimes if she donned a disguise—a long red hooded robe and matching mask. Evildoers and the police she assisted had no idea that The Woman in Red was actually a policewoman, and thus she was also the first superheroine with a secret identity. The Woman in Red appeared sporadically in the pages of *Thrilling Comics* throughout the next five years, but unlike most of the superheroes who appeared in the initial burst of creativity that followed the appearance of Superman in *Action Comics*, the character was never given her own book and is almost completely forgotten today.

This was the plight of most comic book action heroines. None had ever appeared in her own book, and they were invariably short-lived, rarely lasting for more than three appearances before fading into permanent obscurity. Often they were merely sidekicks of the more important male hero. For the most part, when women appeared in comics they were relegated to the role of girlfriend, and their purpose was to be rescued by the hero. Girl readers could find little in the way of heroic role models in the pages of comic books.

In December 1941, a psychologist named William Moulton Marston remedied this sorry state of affairs forever. As early as 1937, Marston and comic book entrepreneur Max Gaines had discussed the creation of a comic book superheroine. Marston is certainly one of the more unusual figures in the history of comic art. The inventor of the lie detector, Marston was a member of the Massachusetts Bar, holder of a doctorate in psychology from Harvard University, a successful advertising man, and the author of popular and scholarly books and articles on psychology.

Marston and Gaines came up with several concepts that they hoped would attract women readers, including a female version of Tarzan named Diana (after the classical goddess of the hunt), but none was immediately translated into comic book form. However, in 1941, Marston's heroine at last debuted, first in *All Star Comics* #8, and one month later in *Sensation Comics* #1. This character was the Amazon Princess Diana, who became Wonder Woman when she left the land of the Amazons to become a costumed superheroine.

It had taken both Superman and Batman a year after their first appearances to get their own books, but less than six months after her appearance in *Sensation*, the Summer 1942 issue of *Wonder Woman* #1 arrived on the newsstands, and the amazing Amazon had her own title. At its peak, the monthly *Wonder Woman* comic book sold around two and a half million copies, and by 1944 she even had her own newspaper comic strip.

Marston knew exactly how to go about creating a superheroine for girls. In 1943, he wrote an article for *The American Scholar* in which he described the reasoning that went into Wonder Woman's creation:

> It seemed to me, from a psychological angle, that the comics worst offense was their blood-curdling masculinity. . . . It's smart to be strong. It's big to be generous, but it's sissified, according to exclusively male rules, to be tender, loving, affectionate, and alluring. "Aw, that's girl stuff," snorts our young comics reader. "Who wants to be a girl?" And that's the point: not even girls want to be girls so long as our feminine archetype lacks force, strength . . . Women's strong qualities have become despised because of their weak ones.

Marston went on to describe the reactions of publishers to his suggestion that girls might want to read about and identify with a strong heroine:

> My suggestion was met by a storm of mingled protests and guffaws. Didn't I know that heroines had been tried in pulps and comics and, without exception, found failure? Yes, I pointed out, but they weren't superwomen.

Although Marston's article in *The American Scholar* was published under his own name for an audience of his professional peers, indicating that he was proud to have been the creator and scriptwriter for *Wonder Woman*, all his comic book work appeared under the pseudonym Charles Moulton. The writing of his early *Wonder Woman* scripts was a family affair. Marston's wife, Elizabeth Holloway Marston, was also a psychologist, and she had a hand in the Amazon princess's creation. His son, Pete, sent in story ideas from college and was paid twenty-five dollars for each one that was used.

Writing his scripts in longhand, Marston combined his knowledge of psychology with elements from mythology and fairy tales to create the mystical Paradise Island, the homeland of the Amazons where men are forbidden to tread. Princess Diana's origin springs directly from classical mythology. The mythic hero is usually born from the union of a virgin and a god, and when the virginal Amazon queen Hippolyta desires a child, the goddess Aphrodite instructs her to mold one out of clay, then breathes life into the statue. Thus, Wonder Woman's divine parent is, in this case, a female deity, and little Diana has two mommies.

When Steve Trevor, an intelligence officer from the United States, crashes his plane on Paradise Island, he is rescued and nursed back to health by

Princess Diana. She saves his life with the "purple ray," falls in love with him, and eventually takes him back to America. Disguised as an Army nurse, and later as Lieutenant Diana Prince, she stays in "the man's world" to fight injustice as Wonder Woman. With her she brings some accouterments of science fiction and fantasy: a magic golden lasso which compels anyone caught in its links to obey the lasso's holder, an invisible plane which Wonder Woman can contact telepathically, and a "mental radio," which resembles a small TV set in the shape of a Greek temple.

Just as one can't envision Lewis Carroll's *Alice in Wonderland* without the illustrations of Sir John Tenniel, nor imagine the world of A. A. Milne's *Winnie the Pooh* in any other way than that created by the Ernest H. Shepard illustrations, so Wonder Woman was defined for all time by her original illustrator Harry G. Peter. H. G. Peter's art appeared as early as the teens, when he did cartoons for the humor magazines *Judge* and *Leslie's*. He also contributed some minor stories to other comic books, but nothing else approached the level of his *Wonder Woman* art. Working in a style utterly unlike that seen anywhere else in comics, perhaps because he was older than most comic artists, Peter lent an almost *art nouveau* air to the fairy tale-like stories. With bold brushstrokes he fleshed out Marston's Amazon maiden, giving her thick, curly Mediterranean hair, a strong, well-defined chin, and the slim, muscular body of an Olympic swimming champion.

Marston and Peter were a perfect creative team—a rare occurrence in comics—and it is impossible to imagine one without the other. In 1943, for a reason we will probably never know (perhaps illness kept Peter from meeting his deadlines), the Wonder Woman stories in two issues of *Sensation* were drawn by cartoonist and illustrator Frank Godwin. Godwin was an excellent artist, better than Peter, and he had many book illustrations to his credit as well as two successful comic strips, *Connie* and *Rusty Riley*, yet the comic looks wrong. It's beautifully drawn, but it just isn't *Wonder Woman*.

On Harry G. Peter's elegant pages, there are often entire sequences in which not one male can be found. *Wonder Woman* as written by Marston is, like Paradise Island, a women's world. Women are always the strongest characters in the stories. The handsome but befuddled Steve Trevor exists because of an unwritten law of superhero comics: the hero must have a love interest so there will always be someone to rescue. He is the Lois Lane to Wonder Woman's Superman.

Even the majority of the villains are women. They are always very beautiful, and eventually wind up seeing the error of their ways, thanks to the message of love and humanitarianism that Wonder Woman carries to the world as she rights wrongs. In a 1947 *Wonder Woman*, Queen Atomia, the exotic, dagger-nailed ruler of an atom world, tries to destroy Wonder Woman. The Amazon princess subdues her and takes her to Reform Island, the Amazons' reform school. On the way her invisible plane flies over Starr Sanitarium for crippled children, and they see children on crutches. The flame-haired villainess asks, "Why are those children leaning on wooden sticks?" In response to Wonder Woman's explanation, she sneers, "Bah! Why bother with weak people?" But on Reform Island, the Amazon Mala puts a girdle of Venus metal on the Atom Queen, explaining that "While she wears it she will have new understanding!" And indeed, "No sooner is the magic girdle around her than Queen Atomia falls repentantly on her knees." She says, "This girdle makes me feel so different. It makes me hate all the evil things I've done!" Eventually the goddess Aphrodite herself welds the girdle permanently on Atomia, telling her, "I weld thy Venus girdle on thee with the powers of eternal love! . . . Forever thy heart shall overflow with kindness. Thou shalt ever be devoted to the worship of love, beauty and humanity!" Returning to her atom world, she informs her subjects, "We must love, not hate!" Finally, she cures the crippled children of Starr Sanitarium. In a last panel that demonstrates America's postwar faith in atomic power as a miracle cure, the children have thrown aside their crutches and are playing ball and leapfrog, while Wonder Woman says, "The atomic universe shall ever shine to help humanity—its radio rays healing children's diseases."

The most powerful humanistic message in Wonder Woman, and the one most constantly repeated, is that super powers are not necessary for a girl to become a superheroine; the Amazon princess herself does not really possess super powers. Her incredible strength, speed, and agility are the results of superior Amazon training, and with comparable training any woman or girl could become a wonder woman. This was demonstrated not just in the stories about Wonder Woman herself, but also in a feature that appeared in every issue of the comic book, "Wonder Women of History." Credited to associate editor and tennis champion Alice Marble, these short comic stories told about real-life heroines like Florence Nightingale and Amelia Earhart who made and changed history.

To prove this point, Wonder Woman sometimes brought her message to real girls. In a story that ran in *Sensation Comics* in 1946, she meets little Olive Norton, who wants to play baseball with her brothers, but is a failure. "Girls can't play ball! Olive's no good," says one brother. Wonder Woman consoles the crying girl, who has just struck out: "Let's face the facts. You're not as good as the boys. Why? Because you haven't practiced and developed your muscles the way they have." She continues, "You can be as strong as any boy if you'll work hard and train yourself in athletics, the way boys do." Olive returns to Paradise Island with Wonder Woman and undergoes a crash course in Amazon training. She succeeds admirably—Wonder Woman exclaims, "I knew Olive could be a real athlete. All she needed was our Amazon training"—and leaps from the invisible plane right onto the diamond where her brothers are playing ball. The new, improved Olive proceeds to hit a home run, rescue her brother Jimmy from quicksand, and even help Wonder Woman capture a band of spies.

The Amazon's sidekicks are women, too, mostly students hailing from Holliday College. In contrast, most male villains, like Dr. Psycho or the Duke of Deception, are grotesque and stunted creatures who are beyond redemption. Wonder Woman has to battle them over and over again.

This emphasis on the female has led a great many writers (all male) to comment on what they have seen as lesbianism in the early Wonder Woman comic books. As early as 1954, Dr. Fredric Wertham, in his critical book about the harmful effect of comics on children, *Seduction of the Innocent*, referred to Wonder Woman "as the Lesbian counterpart of Batman." This set the theme for future writers, like Jim Harmon, writing in the anthology *All in Color for a Dime*, who called the comic "a very sick scene." He wrote that Wonder Woman would "exchange hugs and kisses of delight with the readily available Holliday Girls."

Actually, in twenty-five Wonder Woman comic stories from the forties, I counted five portrayals of Wonder Woman embracing another woman. Twice she hugged a little girl, once a dying woman. Princess Diana also often embraces her mother. Presumably this is permissible. Of course, what Harmon and other male writers are not taking into account is that women do show their emotions, and do hug. On the other hand, American men are notoriously afraid of being considered homosexual, and never touch each other except when playing sports. These writers also conveniently ignore their favorite superhero comics, where the action takes place in an almost entirely male world. Marston understood that just as young boys tend to avoid anything female, girls of the same age are not interested in boys or men, and identify most strongly with other girls and women.

Marston has also been accused of filling his comic book stories with bondage and with male bashing. In his 1970 book, *The Steranko History of Comics*, James Steranko stated, "Wonder Woman delighted in beating up men." Similarly, Richard Reynolds went so far as to write in *Super Heroes: A Modern Mythology*, that Wonder Woman was "developed as a frank appeal to male fantasies of sexual domination"! In fact, the stories rarely depicted the Amazon princess using physical force on her protagonists, except in defense of someone weaker. In her own defense, she usually resorted to the Amazon game of "bullets and bracelets"—deflecting the bullets with her heavy steel bracelets. And, rather than punching them out, she used her magic lasso to capture the bad guys and compel them to obey her. Compared to most male-oriented action comics, *Wonder Woman* was pretty nonviolent. In a 1948 *Wonder Woman*, Queen Hippolyta expresses once again the constant humanitarian theme of the comic: "Wonder Woman never relaxes her vigilance against those who seek to rule people by brute force! She teaches that love is the greatest force . . . "

As far the accusations of bondage, the fact is that in comics from the 1940s, if the heroes weren't getting tied up so that they could escape from their bonds, their girlfriends were getting tied up so that they could be rescued by the heroes. Some heroes got tied up more than others. Aside from the word "Shazam," the most frequently used expression in Captain Marvel comics was "Shaz-ugh," as little Billy Batson got knocked unconscious before he could utter the magic word that turned him into a superhero. This was the story's conflict. The poor kid would always awaken bound and gagged, thus unable to say the word, until he somehow managed to loosen his gag, shout "Shazam!," become Captain Marvel, and bring the villains to justice. Still, I have never read anything about the bondage in *Captain Marvel*. Wonder Woman's situation was somewhat similar to that of Billy Batson. Symbolically, Wonder Woman could not break her chains if she had been chained by a man. So, in story after story, she had to find some other way of escaping her bonds and emerging victorious.

Most men who have written about comic book history are not particularly kind to superheroines, but they seem to reserve their most unkind observations for Wonder Woman, the longest-lasting and most popular superheroine of all. Les Daniels demonstrated his awareness of this when he wrote in his 1970 book, *Comix: a History of Comic Books in America*: "Masculine critics have viewed her [Wonder Woman] with a mixture of contempt and alarm." But then he betrayed his own masculine attitudes when he added: "In the hands of artist Harry Peter she was perhaps the least visually attractive of comic book heroines . . . " He neglected to inform the reader by what standard he made this judgment, and one wonders if it was not the same standard Jules Feiffer used in his 1965 book, *The Great Comic Book Heroes*. Among his comments on Wonder Woman, Feiffer refers to his younger self as wondering, "Why was she so flat-chested?" Alone of all male critics, Feiffer had the self-awareness to declare, "I never knew they [girls] read her [*Wonder Woman*]—or any comic book. That girls had a preference for my brand of literature would have been more of a frightening image to me than any number of men being beaten up by Wonder Woman." Perhaps Fredric Wertham was correct when he wrote, "For boys, Wonder Woman is a frightening image."

Marston himself foresaw these reactions when, in his 1943 article, he described the negative reactions to his proposed superheroine. "Well, asserted my masculine authorities, if a woman hero were stronger than a man, she would be even less appealing. Boys wouldn't stand for that; they'd resent the strong gal's superiority."

But for generations of girls, the inspiration received from stories of the amazing Amazon is best expressed by pioneer feminist Gloria Steinem who, in her introduction to a 1972 collection of Wonder Woman stories, described "the relief, the sweet vengeance, the toe-wriggling pleasure of reading about a woman who was strong, beautiful, courageous, and a fighter for social justice."

Fandom and Authorship

WILL BROOKER

Reprinted by permission from *Batman Unmasked* (Continuum, 2000), 250–79.

THE DISCOURSES OF COMIC FANDOM AND COMIC AUTHORSHIP WERE BORN AS twins and have grown up together over the last few decades, siblings locked into a relationship of debate and mutual dependence. Both originated in the early 1960s [in fact the history of letters pages and fandom in comics predates the 1960s, but Brooker is focusing here on their role in superhero comics specifically—*eds.*]. While artists like Bob Kane were lucky enough to enjoy a rare cult of authorship during the 1940s, taking working vacations in Hollywood and posing for publicity snaps with glamour girls on Miami Beach,[1] and the first DC Comics fanzines appeared in the early 1950s, just before the crackdown,[2] these were exceptions rather than early signs of a trend.

According to Gerard Jones in *The Comic Book Heroes*, it was DC that first opened its pages to reader response through the letter columns of *Superman* and *Justice Society of America*, edited respectively by Mort Weisinger and Julius Schwartz.[3] The year was 1960. That September, "at a Pittsburgh science fiction convention . . . two young couples simultaneously conceived fanzines that devoted regular attention to comics." The editors of *Xero* and *Comic Art* "were far removed from Weisinger's young letter-writers":

> the new fanzine publishers were adults looking back, with little emotional investment in the present, while Weisinger's kids were the opposite, all waiting for the next issue of Superman with no sense of comics history. Before fandom could have any real effect on the field, the gap between them would have to be bridged. And who else could engineer that bridge but Mort's old partner in fandom, Julius Schwartz?

Jones has the journalistic tendency of turning comics history into a comfortable yarn, eliding ambiguity for the sake of a good story teleologically told. It is hard to know, as was the case with his account of William Dozier's epiphany over the *Batman* title, whether the scheme of events was really this simple: but as he relates it, the two fields of fanzine culture and comic book "letterhacks" were brought together as Julius Schwartz and Gardner Fox invited one of their *JSA* fans, Jerry Bails, into the National Periodicals office in New York. Over lunch, "Schwartz explained the ins and outs of 'fanzines' and fan networking." The date was now February 1961. That month, a new edition of *Hawkman* comic hit the stands, its letter column bearing—for the first time—the street addresses of every correspondent. Jerry Bails, fired up from his lunch meeting wrote to every fan whose letter appeared in that issue, explaining his vision of "comics fandom . . . I know now (for sure) . . . that I want to bring out a 'fanzine' dedicated to the Great Revival of the costumed heroes." Within a few months, Bails was publishing *Alter-Ego* with Roy Thomas, a fellow letter-writer.

> Other fanzines popped up like mushrooms all across the country: *Komix Illustrated*, *The Rocket's Blast*, *The Comic Reader*, *Batmania*, and scores more. Most were done by adults, but some came from precocious kids just discovering comics. . . . Bails even added two more fanzines to his little home publishing business: *Capa-Alpha*, a sort of communal fanzine called an "amateur press alliance" or "apa" and *The Comicollector*, "the companion to *Alter Ego*," featuring ads for people selling, buying, and swapping old comics.[4]

The network expanded rapidly, mapping out links between publishing and self-publishing, readers and writers, buyers and sellers; and the relationship between editors and fans was for this time a happy, mutually beneficial one. Bails paid for that lunch in kind by forming an Academy of Comic Arts and Sciences whose fan panel awarded every prize to Julius Schwartz and his crew; Schwartz promoted *Alter-Ego* in the pages of his own comics. Prominent fans, writes Jones, "drove cross-country to visit each other, tally votes, and plan conventions."[5] A community had been established. "For years, fans had nurtured their obsessions alone in silence. Now, suddenly, they'd found their lost race."[6]

The lettercols had made this fan-network possible; and while Jones neglects to mention it, the slippery concept of the comic book "author" clearly evolved through the same columns and the same process. Julius Schwartz, Jones notes, "encouraged . . . the controversy over whether Joe Kubert was the right artist for *Hawkman*, criticism over *Mystery in Space* . . . and the fight about whether superheroes were better suited for science fiction or human interest stories in *Green Lantern*."[7] Through the discourse between fan and editor, then, comics "authorship" was created and debated. The inverted commas are needed here because, as I will suggest, the "creator" of a comic book—that construction of words, pencils, plots, inks, colors, letters, and editing—is especially hard to pin down, and comics fandom, unlike film scholarship, rarely takes the easier option of singling out a single individual from the creative team for sole praise or blame. Even at this early stage, we can see that the responsibility is being jointly attributed to artists as well as writers; and we might also note that Schwartz, as editor, is also responsible in a very real way for the "creation"—the commission or cancelling, at least—of the stories under discussion. Schwartz's crucial role in the cultivation of the "authorship" discourse is comparable to the part he played in fandom; for instance, when artist Carmine Infantino made the unprecedented demand in 1964 that the signature "Bob Kane" be left off his work, it was Schwartz who came through for him.[8]

The culture of the comic fan and accompanying discourse around the comic author went from strength to strength during the 1960s. Fans organized the first New York Comicon in 1964—a whole convention devoted to comics, rather than just a corner of a sci-fi meet. As Jones reports, most of the professionals invited declined to attend, but Spider-Man artist Steve Ditko's arrival highlighted an important function of the comic book convention: not only did it unite fans from across the country, it brought fans together with producers. Ditko had set a precedent; the second New York Con guest-starred, among others, Mort Weisinger, Gardner Fox, and Bill Finger, and the massive annual gatherings of the San Diego Con or Britain's UKCAC today are still built around author signings, sketch sessions from visiting artists, and discussion panels where professionals sit alongside fanzine editors and field questions from an active audience.

Comic book authors had remained, for the most part, unknown and unheralded until the 1960s. Julius Schwartz first allowed Gardner Fox and the artists of *The Atom* credit in 1961:[9] readers and writers alike were therefore seeing their names in print for the first time, at the same time. It is perhaps for this reason that comic book fandom has always had a particularly close relationship with the text's creators. The boundaries between comic author and fan, writer and reader, have always been thin and often dissolve entirely.[10]

Even by publishing a mimeographed fanzine for ten people, of course, a fan like Jerry Bails or Roy Thomas, was becoming a comic book "writer"; and often a comic book artist too, as the pages of comic zines were and continue to be filled out with amateur art. The crossovers occasionally became even more dramatic, though, as "elite" fans actually began to work for the major companies. Roy Thomas was hired to work for Mort Weisinger. F. Nelson Bridwell had already been taken on by Weisinger as an editorial assistant. Both had come to the editor's attention through their letters to *Superman*.[11] "The signal had been sent," Jones notes. "Fans could become pros. They could actually *shape* the comics."

• • •

In this brief case study I want to step aside from the historical overview for a moment and examine the actual nature of fan discourse within the letter columns of *Detective Comics* during 1965. This was a significant cultural moment in terms of fandom's evolution; readers had only recently been given the chance of a public voice, of having their discourse on Batman validated by publication, and of joining in debate not just with editors, but with fellow aficionados. One enthuses that "I seem to be becoming a 'regular' in the *Detective* and *Batman* letters pages, and I like it!,"[12] and others report that their published comments have led to pen-pal relationships with other fans. It was also a moment of transition in terms of comic book authorship, for Bob Kane's signature was still appearing on some stories with which he had no connection, while at the same time the names of other artists and writers were beginning to be credited for the first time. This inconsistency led fans into a pleasurable to-and-fro with the editors as they attempted to deduce the identity of unnamed writers and artists, and so effectively shaped the concept of the comic book "author"—an individual who, whatever his role in the creative process, contributes a recognizable, personal style—at the same time as they were building their own fan-networks.

Readers had already been invited to play guessing-games with the editors on issues of plot and long-term narrative, as in the "Outsider" story where letterhacks attempted to identify the mysterious villain—"is he the American Hydra-Head, as per *Batman* #167, out for revenge?"[13]—until he was revealed as Alfred the Butler. This puzzling over deliberately created narrative enigmas was just part of an extended discourse which dominated the lettercols of the mid-to-late Batman titles; it is tempting to wonder whether this relationship between reader and editor was in any way an unconscious reflection and enactment of the Batman's own role as "darknight detective," musing over the riddles posed by his trickster enemies. It doesn't seem entirely farfetched to suppose that part of the readers' pleasure in pitting their skills of observation against the comic text came from an identification with Batman and his co-stars, the "ductile detective" Ralph Dibney, and detective J'onn J'onn, the Martian Manhunter. In this sense, the title *Detective Comics* referred not just to its featured characters, but to the role of the reader; and it was largely the readers who created this role for themselves.

There was, it seems, no initial editorial invitation to identify the writer or artist on each uncredited story: but this is the task *Detective*'s fans set themselves, performing it with diligence, shrewdness, and a substantial background knowledge of the creators' distinctive styles.

> The artwork was noteworthy in that you've put another inker to work on Carmine Infantino's pencils. I'm not exactly sure, but my guess is that Sid Greene handled the job.[14]

> I am somewhat mystified about the inker. I think it's Infantino himself, with a slightly modified style, Yet certain parts looks like the work of Murphy Anderson, or even John Giunta.[15]
>
> Infantino's art-job? Great! It could have been super-great if the great Carmine had inked his own pencils, which leads to an interesting suggestion. How about teaming up Bob Kane and Carmine Infantino as a pencil-ink combo on a Batman story? It should be superb![16]

Note that, in these early days of fan discourse, the concept of "author," or at least "creator," is already taken to include the artist as a vital contributor to the construction of the Batman story, and that this role is recognized as comprising the two distinct tasks of pencils and inks. Writers receive an approximately equal attention, again with a sometimes astonishing attention to detail.

> The inside story was written with a touch of genius by . . . John Broome?[17]
>
> I think the author of this story was John Broome, because of the way the Gotham Gladiator stopped in the middle of his sentence in panel one of page five.[18]

Guy H. Lillian, singled out by editor Julie Schwartz as "our favorite Guy correspondent," receives a lengthy answer to his venture that a particular story "was written by Gardner Fox, I'll wager." The reply emphasizes the spirit of competition that had emerged in *Detective*, suggests the role of editors in keeping their fans guessing, and indicates the relative complexity that the lettercol discourse of authorship had attained by 1965.

> It wasn't hard for you to tag Gardner Fox as the writer of the Elongated Man yarn . . . especially as he's written all the Elongated Man stories that have appeared so far in *Detective Comics*. Strangely enough, the Elongated Man stories that appeared in *The Flash* were written by John Broome. One of these issues, we're going to give Broome a crack at his original character . . . and then let's see who can tell the difference between a "Fox" and a "Broome."[19]

Note, though, that it was the fans who created the cult of authorship around recognizable styles and creative traits, and the editors who seem to follow, taking up the game and providing new challenges. Clearly, there would be no puzzle if writer, inker, and penciller were given full, explicit credit in the pages of *Detective*; and in this regard DC seems markedly different from its rivals, Marvel, who gave enthusiastic billing to everyone from star artist "Jolly Jack"

Kirby down to the secretary "Fabulous Flo" Steinberg.[20] Although Gerard Jones claims that Schwartz had credited Gardner Fox and his team in *The Atom* from 1960 onwards, my own research suggests that Bob Kane's signature continued to dominate *Batman* up until the mid-1960s, and inconsistencies remain even once his monopoly seems to be broken. Credits for Gardner Fox, Sid Greene, and Carmine Infantino begin to appear in *Detective* #357 of November 1966, but the next issue, while correctly attributing the Elongated Man story to Fox and Greene, has Kane's signature returning to Batman artwork which is clearly by another hand. It was presumably this ambiguity, which led to comments like the following, as the variable art style of "Bob Kane" defied the guessing game:

> I'm writing this because of Bob Kane's magnificent artwork. I can really say I didn't think Bob Kane was much of an artist, with his square-jawed, stiff-looking characters, but in the October *Detective* he really did a good job.[21]

> I must congratulate Bob Kane on his ever-improving artwork. However, in some panels, too much of Batman's nose shows below his mask.[22]

Ultimately, though, the discourse around authorship in these columns goes no further than a sophisticated parlor game of identifying writers, pencillers, and inkers. While it constructs each for the first time as a creative individual, vital to the completed work, and associates them with an "individual stamp"—Broome's unfinished sentences, Kane's square chins—the identification is enough; there is no real discussion of what these distinct creative traits contribute to mood, theme, or characterization. The lack of printed credits in *Detective* of the early to mid-1960s creates a mystery, and the fans take pleasure in solving it. It is as though *Cahiers du Cinema* in the 1960s had been made up of letters guessing that "Gregg Toland is the cinematographer on *Citizen Kane*, I'll wager—his deep focus on the snowstorm scene is unmistakable," or that "the music in *Psycho* sounds like Bernard Herrmann. I never enjoyed his repetitive string motifs before, but this theme is more to my taste." The analysis is in many ways informed and intelligent, but it clearly has its limits; and it was only once the guessing-game was made redundant that lettercolumn fans were able to ask more searching questions of the comic text.

In the Batman comics, then—which, probably because of Kane's sustained monopoly over "authorship," differ from DC's other titles in that they lack accurate credits until the mid-to-late 1960s—the cult around writers and artists as joint authors was born from the combination of fan curiosity and editorial teasing. When full credits began to appear around 1966, fans had the opportunity to direct their discussion around authorship further, beyond mere identification for the sake of it. The guessing game was over, on one level; but with the identities of writer and artist provided, readers could begin to theorize and conject about the ways in which these authors interpreted the Batman formula, and the differences between them in a wider sense. Consider, just as a brief indication of what followed, these extracts from a *Detective* lettercol of 1980, typical of the contemporary discourse in their discussion of character, narrative, the relation between writing and art, and the relative merits of different individual contributions.

> Don [Newton] and Dan [Adkins] are hanging in there, creating page after page of truly beautiful, moody, exciting storytelling artwork. Denny O'Neil's story this time was a little SILLY—a group of assassins killing a nobody on the slim chance that he MIGHT know something about them . . .[23]

> Now the writing. Jack C. Harris is steadily improving, although he still has a way to go to match Bob Rozakis's work. But Jack is doing great things with the Barbara Gordon character, fleshing her out and giving her substance. I am especially delighted with the warm and believable relationship Jack has established between Babs and her father. He also has attained a perfect ratio of action to characterization in his stories. But it is in the plotting that Mr. Harris falls down.[24]

> Don Newton and Dan Adkins' artistic rendition of the tale by Denny O'Neil shows just how important the artist is in comics. The splash page conveyed the entire feeling of the story in one glance. Throughout the 17 pages the art never faltered even once to convey the storyline and enhance the plot and dialogue. I must also compliment Adrienne Roy for her outstanding coloring, especially the movie theater scene with the shadows playing off of the main figures.[25]

It should be obvious that these letters represent a progression from the spot-the-artist games of the mid-1960s, and show fan discourse engaging with some of the complex issues arising from the nature of comic book storytelling. We can see that the readers are no longer concerned with the identity of the creators, but with what the distinctive talents that those creators bring to the story under discussion, and with the struggle to express the dynamic between several different contributors in terms of the final result.

Leaping forward again, just to show that debate around authorship was still a going concern in the lettercolumns of the late 1990s despite the instant accessibility of Internet boards, here is a comment on Grant Morrison's writing of Batman, published in the *Justice League of America* comic dated July 1998,

> Morrison writes the Dark Knight as a double paradox: a sullen misanthrope devoted to protecting others and a resolutely human figure who nevertheless can perform the impossible. Crucially, Morrison understands that Batman is never a single character, but rather a host of Batmen: a wealth of possibilities existing behind that costume, cowl, and symbol.[26]

I'm still quite proud of that letter.

* * *

As Alan Moore wrote, in his introduction to Frank Miller's The Dark Knight Returns, *"Everything is exactly the same, except for the fact that it's all totally different."*

I wrote this essay in 1998, some fourteen years ago, before I had a PhD—indeed, it was my PhD thesis, published in 2000. In 1960, as I discuss above, DC Comics introduced letters columns for fan response and correspondence. In 2002, it phased them out, clearly feeling that the immediacy and near-infinite space of Internet discussion had made a monthly mailbag redundant. In 2011, DC announced that it was reinstating letters pages, though with a shift of focus to digital comics sales through tablet and phone formats—and with the fan correspondence centered around a website, www.dcletterspage.com, rather than a printed forum, things were never going to be quite the same.

That the online letters site is a dead link, less than a year later, is characteristic of DC's current tendency to dodge, switch, and frantically second-guess, chasing the market rather than leading it. Dennis O'Neil, former Group Editor of the Batman titles—whom I interviewed in his New York office, in 1998—conceded in the early years of the new century that comics had become the "R&D division of the entertainment industry," a "hidden asset" of Warner Bros., rather than an autonomous narrative medium in its own right. In September 2011, attempting to grab back some of the market share from Marvel's successful cross-platform Avengers franchise, DC cancelled all its current titles and launched fifty-two of them ("the New 52") from issue #1. Less than six months later, it withdrew half a dozen of those titles, which were already suffering poor sales, and launched a "second wave" of replacements. Batman's official history and continuity is constantly being written and rewritten in a series of editorial earthquakes, and as reboot after reboot is forced through, secondary female characters like Stephanie Brown and Barbara Gordon often have their backstories crudely retconned or simply wiped off the record.

I wrote this chapter years before Twitter, Facebook, and Tumblr were founded, but the rise of an increasingly widespread and sophisticated online culture—where legions of fans now protest the loss of Stephanie Brown's role as Batgirl or the unconvincing fix of Barbara Gordon's spine, after twenty-five years of disability—has made little difference to DC's corporate project. Editors Jim Lee and Dan DiDio post on Twitter now, using the same platform as the comic book readers and, theoretically, entering into a vast, democratic discussion, but their word—or their 140 characters, in this case—is still final.

"if Bruce is Batman only 5 yrs how can he have 10 yr old son (Damian)?" asks one fan, @kingmob29.

"Batman around b4then as urban legend only public last 5," @jimlee replies firmly.

If anything, the shift to online media has made it easier for DC's editorial to erase swathes of character history and backstory and cover up the traces. The aesthetic of the reboot and the retcon, the decision that continuity has changed and certain aspects of the remembered past never took place, is ideally suited to electronic records that can be instantly changed and covered up. Shifting and dodging, like copying and pasting, are easier in the age of Wikipedia; digital archives of comics can be swiftly rearranged, official histories can be re-edited, and if the fans' shelves of printed comics and collected editions contradict the current status quo, they can be reclassified as old-school, quaint, and out of date.

Specific details of the history I propose in this chapter have also been rewritten. As Marc Singer points out in his recent book, Grant Morrison: Combining the Worlds of Contemporary Comics *(2011)*, Grant Morrison originally imagined Arkham Asylum *as drawn by Brian Bolland, "and my vision was of it being ultra-real to the point of being painful." As Singer notes, "even if we set aside Morrison's stated preference for Bolland's style, the disjunctions between the art and script of* Arkham Asylum *suggest that Morrison's symbolically overburdened story would have benefited had it been grounded in Bolland's solidity and verisimilitude." The 2004 "Anniversary Edition" offers a glimpse not of Bolland's version, but Morrison's, through his thumbnail sketches; everything is the same as the final, original* Arkham Asylum, *except for the fact that it's all totally different.*

And of course, everything is totally different now, in 2012, just prior to the release of Christopher Nolan's third Batman film. Everything changed in Summer 2005, when Nolan wrote firmly in black ink over the cultural memory of Joel Schumacher's Day-Glo Batman & Robin *(1997)*, the last entry in the franchise; everything changed again in 2008 when Nolan's The Dark Knight *was seen by many reviewers to transcend not just the character but the superhero genre, earning comparison with classic gangster cinema like* The Godfather, *and even reaching the heights of Greek tragedy and Shakespearean drama.*

Everything changed, and yet in some ways everything is still exactly the same. In this essay, I was working toward a sense of the comic book author as—in Roland Barthes's term—the "scriptor," an editor of existing material, producing novelty from the familiar; and Nolan's Batman was enthusiastically received by comics fans in much the same way that they had previously embraced Miller's Batman, Morrison's Batman, and Moore's Batman, as a new spin on the old myth. We wait to see what the marriage of seventy-year-old icon and hotshot auteur will bring next: it's this alchemy, this chemistry, which fuels the Dark Knight. Fans won't be picking up the phones when Nolan's Dark Knight Rises *is released, as they did when* Dark Knight Returns *was first published—or if they do, it will be to text, rather than call. But the buzz is the same.*

The central truth about Batman is that he remains essentially unchanged, even though, in each incarnation from each author, in each new version for each new decade, we seek something different and find him, in turn, reflecting back our culture and concerns from a fresh angle.

Batman survives, and rises again after each fall, because of this dynamic.

NOTES

1. See Bob Kane with Tom Andrae, *Batman and Me* (Forestville, CA: Eclipse Books, 1989), 120–121, 130.
2. Gerard Jones and Will Jacobs, *The Comic Book Heroes* (Roseville, CA: Prima Publishing, 1997), 63.
3. Ibid.
4. Ibid, 64.
5. Ibid, 65.
6. Ibid, 64.
7. Ibid.
8. Ibid, 97.
9. Ibid, 65.
10. Not to suggest that this phenomenon is unique to comics. Tulloch and Jenkins note that "many important science fiction authors came from fandom, while many writers within the genre regularly attend fan conventions." John Tulloch and Henry Jenkins, *Science Fiction Audiences* (London: Routledge, 1995), 187–188.
11. Jones and Jacobs, 67.
12. Letter from Mike Friedrich, *Detective Comics* #335 (New York: DC Comics, January 1965).
13. *Detective Comics* #338 (New York: DC Comics, April 1965).
14. Letter from Mike Friedrich, *Detective Comics* #335 (New York: DC Comics, January 1965).
15. Letter from Kenneth S. Gallagher, *Detective Comics* #336 (New York: DC Comics, February 1965).
16. Letter from Leon J. Tirado, *Detective Comics* #335 (New York: DC Comics, January 1965).
17. Letter from Doug Potter, *Detective Comics* #337 (New York: DC Comics, March 1965).
18. Letter from Guy H. Lillian III, *Detective Comics* #335 (New York: DC Comics, October 1966).

19. Editorial reply, ibid.
20. Jones and Jacobs, 65.
21. Letter from John Wilson, *Detective Comics* #336 (New York: DC Comics, February 1965).
22. Letter from Walt Smith, *Detective Comics* #340 (New York: DC Comics, June 1965).
23. Letter from Henry R. Kujawa, *Detective Comics* #492 (New York: DC Comics, July 1980).
24. Letter from Scott Gibson, ibid.
25. Letter from Mark Ryan, ibid.
26. Letter from Will Brooker, *JLA* #20 (New York: DC Comics, July 1998).

Section Two

THEORY AND GENRE

A GENRE IS AN EMPIRICAL SOCIAL REALITY: NOT ONLY A CRITICAL CATEGORY FOR organizing works, but also a tradition and pastime upheld by an audience attuned to such works. Indeed a genre is something on the order of a loose social compact, a set of concepts and practices that groups of people use to help them sort through and make sense of things. It therefore has a lived-in quality. If today we can study the superhero as genre in quite specific terms, that is because it plays important roles—communal, aesthetic, intellectual, and psychological—in the lives of many people. By now the genre is entrenched, having achieved a high degree of specificity and self-awareness. It constitutes a little conceptual universe. Criticism now assumes the superhero narrative's distinctive nature (and of course this *Reader* presupposes as much).

Yet academic analysis of the superhero has not always been able to assume this. Historically, academic studies, which lagged behind fandom's highly specific understanding of the genre, first sought to place the superhero within other, larger generic contexts. Early analyses tended to treat superhero narratives as a vague subset of other, more inclusive categories. John G. Cawelti, a pioneer in the academic study of what he called formula fiction (1977), subsumes the superhero in the mega-genre of the adventure story. All such stories, he notes, express the basic fantasy of the hero "overcoming obstacles and dangers and accomplishing some important and moral mission." To Cawelti, the superhero constitutes simply a particularly childish type of the adventure hero, one subject to unabashed adulation as a beloved parent is by a child. These are stories, he suggests, "constructed for children and young people."

Roger B. Rollin, in an article for *College English* in 1970, "Beowulf to Batman: The Epic Hero and Pop Culture," had also categorized the superhero within the adventure tale. Rollin's article uses the specific term *pop romance* to denote "television programs, films, and comic strips in the adventure category" (note that he does not distinguish between newspaper strips and comic books, another sign of his generalizing approach). The pop romance, Rollin argues, offers not mere escapism, in the pejorative sense, but rather a way of reflecting and coping with "tensions and problems [. . .] not usually very far removed from present reality." Furthermore, he proposes that pop romance and epic poetry—*Beowulf*, Spenser, Milton—have "significant esthetic and intellectual parallels," which may be exploited to introduce students to the classics by analogy. Underlying his argument is, first, a concern for relevance to his (Vietnam War–era) students, whom Rollin sees as resistant readers staring back at teachers across a yawning generation gap; and, second, the model of archetypal criticism constructed by Northrop Frye in his seminal *Anatomy of Criticism* (1957), a model that enables critics to highlight commonalities between classics and pop.

The team of Robert Jewett and John Shelton Lawrence also writes from an outside or nonexclusive perspective, albeit one at least vaguely aware of comics' history. Their study *The Myth of the American Superhero* (2002), though much later than Rollin and Cawelti, builds conceptually on their earlier *The American Monomyth* (1977) as well as Jewett's *The Captain America Complex* (1973). In some ways their concerns and methods hark to an earlier era. Like Rollin and Cawelti, they view the comic book superhero as part of a larger cultural pattern, indeed what they call, drawing on Joseph Campbell, a monomyth. This pattern, they argue, manifests in and is reinforced by heroic tales that encourage an "attitude of credulity" and a pseudo-religious "yearning for fantasy redemption." For Jewett and Lawrence, the specificity of the superhero genre matters little (the cover of their book juxtaposes Superman and Batman with Clint Eastwood in gunslinger guise). What matters is a political argument about the hazards of hero worship: the monomyth they descry is fundamentally antidemocratic, and, via its dissemination across popular culture, controlling; it "manag[es]" consciousness and dictates behavior. In essence, Jewett and Lawrence express concerns about media effects and ideology similar to those of Wertham and Ong—though nearer cousins to their work are Cawelti on formula and Richard Slotkin's study of American frontier myth, *Regeneration through Violence* (1973).

Unlike Cawelti or Rollin, Jewett and Lawrence do comment on the historical emergence of the comic book. They christen the 1930s, the decade of the superhero genre's arrival, "the axial decade." However, their interest rests not on the particular history of the comic book superhero but rather on a greater cultural trend; they argue that the 1930s laid the template for "monomythic entertainments" across media and genres. In the superheroes of the axial decade, including Superman and Batman, they locate the blueprint for subsequent pop culture heroes such as "Kirk and Spock, Dirty Harry, Rambo, and the Steven Seagal characters" (their argument operates on a level at which all these heroes appear alike rather than different). Perhaps as a result of this larger focus, they are less precise in their dates and facts than a comic book fan or historian might wish them to be. However, their comments on the superhero's "segmented" identity and sexual renunciation give real insight into the genre.

The arrival of Richard Reynolds's *Super Heroes: A Modern Mythology* (UK 1992; U.S. 1994), seemingly the first academic monograph devoted to the comic book superhero, signaled a change in scholarly approaches to the genre. Reynolds derives his understanding of the superhero from reading widely among superhero comics and consulting the lore of fans and creators. He sees superhero fandom as a "very cohesive subculture," one that "tightly define[s] and defend[s]" the genre and "has built up its own lively and heuristic critical discourse." He charts the history of the comic book, albeit briefly and from a superhero fan's point of view (the Golden Age gives way to the Silver Age, and so on). Further, he notes the range and diversity of superheroes, stressing their differences rather than their generic identity alone. Also, he explores changes within the genre by reading the comics against each other, rather than simply gesturing outward toward broad social changes. In essence, his analysis of contemporary superhero texts stresses the ways they respond to and reinterpret the tradition of which they are part.

Reynolds's was the first monograph to acknowledge something fans already knew: the intertextual richness of the superhero tale as a *comic book genre*, that is, the extent to which superhero comics were in dialogue with each other. He takes superhero comics as critical sources in their own right. For example, he begins inductively by reading that *ur*-text of the genre, Superman's first adventure in *Action Comics* #1 (1938). He identifies the essential elements in that comic that would later become generic markers: the orphan hero, the hero as demigod, the devotion to a personal rather than legal sense of justice, the contrast between the human and the superhuman, the secret identity (cf. Jewett and Lawrence on *segmentation*), the hero's doubtful relationship to political order, and the indiscriminate blending of science and magic. Aspects of Reynolds have dated: for example, his comments on superhero films clearly predate the digital blockbusters of today. However, his comments on the comics' visual rhetoric, the genre's essential setting in the modern metropolis (New York), and its conservative function as an upholder of the "social order" all remain provocative.

Reynolds signaled a new, more specific superhero criticism based on expertise in the comics themselves, a trend borne out by the rest of this section. Geoff Klock's *How to Read Superhero Comics and Why* (2002) carries Reynolds's method to a logical extreme by way of Harold Bloom's model of the anxiety of influence, wherein an artist-poet's "strong misreading" or "misprision" of her/his precursors results in new works and in the renewal of the genre. By this model, all "poetry" becomes "criticism"—or, in this case, extending the logic of Reynolds, new superhero comics become self-reflexive critical texts on the genre. What interests Klock is the "comic book whose 'meaning' is found in its relationship with another comic book," and the possibility of "approach[ing] superhero comic books on their own terms." Genre self-awareness is Klock's starting point, as he posits the 1980s' so-called revisionary superhero movement—in particular its taproots texts *The Dark Night Returns* (1986), by Frank Miller, and *Watchmen* (1986–87), by Alan Moore and Dave Gibbons—as the moment when the superhero genre crossed over from infantile "fantasy" to "literature."

According to Klock, these texts are the first to gather in, organize, and comment on the entire history of the genre: essentially, texts that reflexively pose allegorical arguments about the genre itself. Klock's argument favors a type of Bloomian "strong" reader (Miller, Moore) whose willful reinterpretation of the tradition can subsume "weak" readings, making generic elements his own and striving after a simultaneous "negation" and yet strengthening of the genre. Miller, says Klock, uses realism to intensify the genre, while Moore uses it to "empty out" and defeat the genre, thus to "take [his] place at [its] head."

There is always a risk that this direction in criticism will prove insular, that such criticism may come down to a self-regarding fascination that replays the excesses of fan discourse at its most parochial. However, both Reynolds and Klock continue to pay attention to the larger social, ideological, and political issues in play around the superhero. Reynolds sees the superhero as enacting a tense relationship between political order (the state) and individual conscience (vigilantism), a topic also of concern to Jewett and Lawrence. Klock moves in this direction too, analyzing Miller's Batman (*Dark Knight*) as both a revolutionary and the source of a new, potentially hegemonic order. The divisive political meanings of the genre, in particular its association with fascist ideology (again, cf. Ong and Wertham), at once motivates and complicates Klock's readings.

One aspect of superhero fandom's specialization if not insularity is its fascination with *continuity*, that is, the way serial superhero comics seek to maintain the semblance of a single overarching world shared by many heroes. The eruption of a superhero "universe" into a "multiverse" of divergent timelines multiplies the potential for baroque continuity-based stories. While this issue might seem to be of only narrow fannish interest, in fact it intersects with larger issues including the pleasures of serial narrative and narratological theories about the making of "storyworlds," i.e., the mental models readers develop for understanding stories. According to cognitive narratologist Karin Kukkonen, the complexity of superhero multiverses challenges these models, and challenges narrative theory as well, calling on scholars to develop a more complex theory of how readers understand such tales. The teeming cosmologies and intricate narrative clockworks of today's superheroes have made the genre something of a test case for the possibilities of vast narratives assembled in piecemeal, serial form. How do readers learn to construct storyworlds that will enable them to navigate these byzantine multiverses? How do readers learn to juggle multiple Earths, when the narratives do not insist on elevating one Earth over other and reducing the others to phantasmal "subworlds," or dreams? Kukkonen shows how two devices help readers navigate these multiversal narratives: one, the use of a stable visual iconography that distinguishes each hero (and each version of a hero); two, the prevalence of characters who must be guided through the multiverses and therefore serve as reader surrogates. Thus readers are enabled to distinguish among the various alternate worlds given in the narratives.

The superhero genre's emphasis on branching and multiplying "continuities" may appear highly specialized and inward-turning. The proliferation of alternate worlds speaks to the extreme self-awareness of the genre and its fans, and is thus another aspect of the almost overbearing sense of tradition also charted by Klock. At this point the genre may seem well nigh hermetic. Scott Bukatman, however, in "A Song of the Urban Superhero," reminds us how powerfully the genre reflects the dreams and realities of twentieth-century urban life. According to Bukatman—and here he extends Reynolds—superheroes belong to the modern City, indeed are "vehicles of urban representation," acting out the City's utopian and dystopian possibilities. In their flamboyance and mobility across the cityscape, in their panoptic vision (from above) and defiance of urban order and rationalization, and yet too in the anonymity of their "secret identities"—an anonymity that confers a type of freedom—superheroes mythologize what the City is, and what it makes possible. Bukatman's free-ranging, very personal argument, a lattice of unexpected references and connections, unites the social and political perspectives of earlier critics with fandom's deep knowledge of the genre, finding a new relevance by simultaneously digging in and looking outward, to phenomena beyond the boundaries of the genre narrowly conceived. Everything from ideology, commerce, fashion, architecture, and the history of communications media (newspapers, comics) becomes part of Bukatman's web. The challenge of theorizing the superhero as genre is met precisely here, as Bukatman reveals a fan's passion for and minute knowledge of the tradition, yet places all this within a much larger cultural matrix, where ideology and aesthetics are indissolubly linked and where pleasure and skepticism collide.

Literary Formulas

JOHN G. CAWELTI

Reprinted by permission from John G. Cawelti, *Adventure, Mystery, Romance: Formula Stories as Art and Popular Culture* (University of Chicago Press, 1977), 39–41.

THE CENTRAL FANTASY OF THE ADVENTURE STORY IS THAT OF THE HERO—INDIvidual or group—overcoming obstacles and dangers and accomplishing some important and moral mission. Often, though not always, the hero's trials are the result of the machinations of a villain, and, in addition, the hero frequently receives, as a kind of side benefit, the favors of one or more attractive young ladies. The interplay with the villain and the erotic interests served by attendant damsels are more in the nature of frosting on the cake. The true focus of interest in the adventure story is the character of the hero and the nature of the obstacles he has to overcome. This is the simplest and perhaps the oldest and widest in appeal of all story types. It can clearly be traced back to the myths and epics of earliest times and has been cultivated in some form or other by almost every human society.

At least on the surface, the appeal of this form is obvious. It presents a character, with whom the audience identifies, passing through the most frightening perils to achieve some triumph. Perhaps the basic moral fantasy implicit in this type of story is that of victory over death, though there are also all kinds of subsidiary triumphs available depending on the particular cultural materials employed: the triumph over injustice and the threat of lawlessness in the western; the saving of the nation in the spy story; the overcoming of fear and the defeat of the enemy in the combat story. While the specific characterization of the hero depends on the cultural motifs and themes that are embodied in any specific adventure formula, there are in general two primary ways in which the hero can be characterized: as a superhero with exceptional strength or ability or as "one of us," a figure marked, at least at the beginning of the story, by flawed abilities and attitudes presumably shared by the audience.

Both of these methods of characterization foster strong, but slightly different, ties of identification between hero and audience. In the case of the superhero, the principle of identification is like that between child and parent and involves the complex feelings of envious submission and ambiguous love characteristic of that relationship. This kind of treatment of the hero is most characteristic of the adventure stories constructed for children and young people. The superhero also frequently embodies the most blatant kind of sexual symbolism. More sophisticated adults generally prefer the "ordinary" hero figure who is dominant in the fictions of those who are usually considered the best writers of "grown-up" adventure stories such as H. Rider Haggard, Robert Louis Stevenson, or, to take a more recent example, Alistair MacLean. Some of the most popular writers of this type have managed to combine the superhero with a certain degree of sophistication as in the James Bond adventures of Ian Fleming.

Beyond the two general adventure patterns of the superhero and the ordinary hero, specific adventure formulas can be categorized in terms of the location and nature of the hero's adventures. This seems to vary considerably from culture to culture, presumably in relation to those activities that different periods and cultures see as embodying a combination of danger, significance, and interest. New periods seem to generate new adventure formulas while to some extent still holding on to earlier modes. Adventure situations that seem too distant either in time or in space tend to drop out of the current catalog of adventure formulas or to pass into another area of the culture. Thus, tales of knightly adventure, still widely popular in the nineteenth century, no longer play much of a role in adult adventure literature. More recent cultural situations—crime and its pursuit, war, the West, international espionage, sports—have largely usurped the battle with dragons and the quest for the grail.

Crowds of Superheroes

ROBERT JEWETT AND JOHN SHELTON LAWRENCE

Reprinted by permission from Robert Jewett and John Shelton Lawrence, *The Myth of the American Superhero* (Wm. B. Eerdmans Publishing, 2002), 43–47.

FOLLOWING THE PHENOMENAL SUCCESS OF SUPERMAN COMICS IN 1938, THE axial decade closed with a proliferation of superheroes. The masks, uniforms, miraculous powers, and secret alter egos combine with sexual renunciation and segmentation to complete the formation of the monomythic hero. Batman, Sandman, Hawkman, and The Spirit all sprang to life in 1939; Flash, The Green Lantern, The Shield, Captain Marvel, and White Streak followed in 1940; and Sub-Mariner, Wonder Woman, Plastic Man, and Captain America were born the following year. [Jewett and Lawrence are not quite accurate here: The Spirit (star of a weekly newspaper insert) launched in June 1940; both Hawkman and the Flash began in *Flash Comics* No. 1, cover-dated Jan. 1940; and the Sub-Mariner first appeared in *Marvel Comics* No. 1, cover-dated Oct. 1939 (or, for sticklers, in the undistributed *Motion Picture Funnies Weekly* No. 1, 1939). The obscure White Streak is perhaps an odd example, having appeared only in *Target Comics* (Novelty Press) in issues cover-dated from Feb. 1940 to Dec. 1941.—*eds.*] The opening captions of these comic superhero tales reveal the degree to which the monomythic definition of mission, character, and powers was permanently crystallized by the axial decade.

The first episode of Batman in May 1939 introduces the disguised isolate as "a mysterious and adventurous figure fighting for righteousness and apprehending the wrongdoers, in his lone battle against the evil forces of society . . . his identity remains unknown."[1] The initial issue of *Captain Marvel* comics announces itself in these monomythic terms: "Whiz Comics proudly presents THE WORLD'S MIGHTIEST MAN—POWERFUL CHAMPION OF JUSTICE—RELENTLESS ENEMY OF EVIL." In the story, Billy Batson is confronted by a divine personage looking suspiciously like the "Ancient of Days" in old Sunday school material. "All my life," the figure says, "I have fought injustice and cruelty. But I am old now—my time is almost up. You shall be my successor merely by speaking my name. You can become the mightiest man in the world—Captain Marvel. Shazam! Blam! Captain Marvel, I salute you. Henceforth it shall be your sacred duty to defend the poor and helpless, right wrongs and crush evil everywhere."[2] Thus a new superhero takes up the redemptive task from a senile religious symbol, offering for the fantasy life of every schoolboy an opportunity to be transformed by a magic word into the all-powerful redeemer.

The connection of these superhero materials with the American religious heritage illustrates the displacement of the story of redemption. Only in a culture preoccupied for centuries with the question of salvation is the appearance of redemption through superheroes comprehensible. The secularization process in this instance did not eliminate the need for redemption, as the Enlightenment had attempted to do, but rather displaces it with superhuman agencies. Powers that the culture had earlier reserved for God and his angelic beings are transferred to an Everyman, conveniently shielded by an alter ego. Even the most explicit references to the mythology of the ancient world are conditioned by this new superhero paradigm. This can be documented in materials created long after the axial decade. The television version of the goddess Isis began in 1975 with these mysterious-sounding lines:

> "O mighty queen," said the royal sorceress, "with this amulet you and your descendants are endowed by the goddess Isis with the powers of the animals and the elements. You will soar as the falcon soars, run with the speed of gazelles, and command the elements of sky and earth."

But as the narrator extends the context, it is clearly the familiar redemption scheme with a segmented superheroine in disguise.

> Three thousand years later a young science teacher dug up this lost treasure and found she was heir to the secrets of Isis. And so, unknown to even her closest friends . . . became a dual person—Andrea Thomas—teacher—and Isis—dedicated foe of evil, defender of the weak, champion of truth and justice.[3]

The references to ancient gods and amulets may sound archaic to some, but the format was shaped during the axial decade of the twentieth century.

As the superhero genre was elaborated in the years following the axial decade, the displacement of traditional religious symbols was frequently articulated. An issue of *Flash* from August 1971 seems archetypical: a gang of urban thugs has taken over a church to store and divide their loot; when the faithful nuns pray for relief, one of their oppressors pours scorn on the thought of divine intervention.

"Haw! Whatcha doin'? Askin' your own top man to help you? No way! Nothin's gonna stop us from keepin' this loot!"

The gang then accuses the nun's brother of being an informer. Flash arrives just in time to save him from death as they throw him off the roof of a tall building. The boy decides to go straight, but the chief has hidden the loot. The boy confides his problem to Sister Anne, who says that she will pray for help. Flash overhears the conversation and comments: "There's only one way of quickly finding that hidden loot . . . and that's *scientifically*!" The superhero becomes a rapidly moving radar unit, systematically projecting grids over the city and searching until he finds the cave where the loot is hidden. He saves the young informer and his girlfriend from retaliation by secretly warding off hostile bullets and making clubs disintegrate while increasing the strength of the good guy's fists. After triumphing over the crooks, the young man tells his girlfriend, "Might makes right!" The nuns get control of their church again, the juvenile delinquents are reformed, and, as Vic recounts the events, "It all seems like a miracle!" Barry Allen, alias Flash, mutters to himself, "Made possible by the miracle of superspeed!"

In the final scene, Sister Anne expresses her thanks to God for deliverance. As Barry acknowledges that it has been "a *kind* of miracle," the caption reads: "Perhaps, Barry—but to those who believe, 'the moment of a miracle is like unending lightning.'" The miraculous intervention of the modern superhero has confirmed the faith of the naïve sister. She thinks God still works in mysterious ways, and if this story is right, he does—through the jet-age counterpart of the Lone Ranger's speedy horse.[4] The superheroes thus provide a secular fulfillment of the religious promise articulated in the endings of *The Birth of a Nation* and *The Virginian*. They cut Gordian knots, lift the siege of evil, and restore the Edenic state of perfect faith and perfect peace. It is a millennial, religious expectation—at least in origin—yet it is fulfilled by secular agents. The premise of democratic equality is visible in that superhuman powers have to be projected onto ordinary citizens, yet their transformation into superheroes renders them incapable of democratic citizenship. Moreover, total power must be pictured as totally benign, transmuting lawless vigilantism into a perfect embodiment of law enforcement. That such fantasies suddenly became credible in the popular culture is the abiding legacy of the axial decade. Although they had not yet appeared in the minds of their creators, the parameters for Kirk and Spock, Dirty Harry, Rambo, and the Steven Seagal characters were already defined. They were ready to play out their roles of redeeming the American Dream, along with their nonviolent cohorts from Heidi and Mary Poppins to Lassie and Flipper. All that remained was for the subplots to vary and the scenes to change. Henceforth, materials for mass audiences would have to undergo a kind of mythic alchemy to fit the new monomythic consciousness. A story paradigm as potent as Hercules or Odysseus had been born, spawning its offspring in a popular culture that would soon encircle the world. It would not be long before the American monomyth became a subculture of Planet Earth, managing especially the consciousness of youth and adults, evoking a wide array of imitative behaviors.

By the end of the axial decade, a new mystical consciousness shaped by the American monomyth was already emerging. E. E. Smith's vivid description of the mindset at the end of the axial decade is equally applicable today. Asked to define the meaning of the First International Science Fiction Convention for its participants in 1940, he did so in terms that are disarmingly religious:

> What brings us together and underlies this convention is a fundamental unity of mind. We are imaginative, with a tempered, analytical imagination which fairy tales will not satisfy. . . . Science fiction fans form a group unparalleled in history, in our close-knit . . . organization, in our strong likes and dislikes, in our partisanship and loyalties . . . there is a depth of satisfaction, a height of fellowship which no one who has never experienced it can even partially understand.[5]

Although Smith felt that science fiction fans would never comprise more than a fraction of the population, and that outsiders would have trouble grasping the basis of their fervor, the attitude of credulity and the yearning for fantasy redemption were already visible within the widespread audience for monomythic entertainments. A revolution in spiritual consciousness was underway, allowing for the emergence of formal and informal pop religions in which the various superheroic rites could be conducted. Fandom began to emerge as a new form of religious community, and in the alter ego feature of the superhero fantasies every worshiper could become a god.

NOTES

1. Jules Feiffer, *The Great Comic Book Heroes* (New York: Bonanza Books, 1965), 26; italics omitted.
2. Ibid, 68; some caps omitted.
3. "Shazam-Isis," CBS (November 1975).
4. *Flash Comics* #208, August 1971.
5. E. E. Smith, "What Does This Convention Mean?" in *All Our Yesterdays: An Informal History of Science Fiction Fandom in the Forties*, ed. H. Warner, Jr. (Chicago: Advent, 1969), 96.

The Epic Hero and Pop Culture

ROGER B. ROLLIN

Sections I–III and V of Rollin's essay are reprinted by permission of the National Council of Teachers of English from *College English*, Vol. 31, no. 5 (February 1970), 431–449.

> The student's unmediated responses are to his comic books and television programs, while his response to *Macbeth* has every conceivable kind of inhibition attached to it.
> **NORTHROP FRYE**

MANY A TEACHER OF ENGLISH VIEWS WITH TREPIDATION THE PROSPECT OF INtroducing members of the present student generation to the study of *Beowulf*, *The Faerie Queene*, or *Paradise Lost*. The poems themselves have always posed enough scholarly and critical problems to make teaching them a problem, but nowadays the students themselves seem to make that pedagogy still more difficult. Many of them, more than is sometimes realized, are deeply concerned about the race problem in America or are involved in it, have fought in Vietnam or fought going there, have demonstrated against the brutality of police or of college administrators, have been actively engaged in politics or social work, have complained about their education's lack of relevance, or have tried to do something about it. For such students the great old poems of the Anglo-Saxon *scop*, of Spenser, and of Milton may well seem not merely remote, but irrelevant. Even the best among them, those who despite their other real concerns can still be responsive to esthetic or scholarly appeals, may feel that reading the great English epics is reading only for art's or history's sake. Encountering Spenser's proud claim in his letter to Raleigh that "The generall end thereof of [*The Faerie Queene*] is to fashion a gentleman or noble person in vertuous and gentle discipline . . . ," they may at worst scorn or at best savor what seems to be the poet's quaintly Elizabethan squareness.

Yet these same serious students, when they temporarily put aside their socio-political and academic cares, will watch television programs like *Mission Impossible* or *Star Trek*, will follow installments of *Steve Canyon* or *Batman* in the comics, or will read Ian Fleming or attend "James Bond" films, all of which have a "generall end" similar to Spenser's: "to fashion a gentleman or noble person" for the age. The students themselves, however (and not a few of their teachers), think of such extra-curricular, extra-political activities as "escape."

But what is "escape"? If it means a temporary psychological and intellectual disengagement from the tensions and problems of "real" life, the type of entertainment referred to above will not serve. For "pop romance" (a term that will be used throughout this paper to designate television programs, films, and comic strips in the adventure category) is typically replete with tensions and problems, and those not usually very far removed from present reality. A few years ago it might have been argued that the frequent threats and acts of violence to be found in pop romance made the genre escapist by virtue of sheer hyperbole, but our growing awareness of how violent our reality actually is weakens that case.

It might better be argued that the "escapism" of pop romance resides paradoxically in the security it generates: we know, deep down in our hearts, that Batman will not be turned into a human shish kabob by "The Joker," that Steve Canyon will in the end foil the attempt of the Chinese Reds to defoliate Central Park. If this argument has some validity, it follows that the "escapism" provided by pop romance involves not only emotional catharsis, the purgation of pity and fear, but also what might be called "value satisfaction," that confirmation or reaffirmation of our value system which results from our seeing this value system threatened, but ultimately triumphant. For at least one of the things that happens when a hero like Batman or Steve Canyon wins out in the end—and not the least important thing—is that we experience *at some level* the defeat of Evil (as we imagine it) by the Good (as we have learned it). Even though we consciously are aware that such victories do not always occur in reality, there is a part of us which very much wants them to occur. We are of course unwilling to have such victories take place too easily, as the epic poets well realized, for an easy victory not only lacks dramatic force but paradoxically cheapens the value system the victory is to affirm by making it almost irrelevant.

"Escapism" then, connoting a retreat to a state of mindlessness or euphoria, may well be the wrong term to use to justify or to attack anyone's involvement in pop romance. Though adventure films, television programs, and comic strips (*Cahiers du Cinema* and Roy Lichtenstein notwithstanding) may be only pseudo- or semi-art, they need not be more "escapist" than "true" art. Or, as W. R. Robinson claims in his defense of films, "escape" (into the higher reality of moral truth) can be seen as a function of all forms of art:

> The most persistent and unjust criticism leveled at the movies has been that they are *sui generis* "escapist." But this critical term, the nastiest epithet conceivable within a very narrow-minded aesthetic of truth which sprung up alongside realism, absurdly distorts our sense of what art is or should be. It implies that only an art as grim and dour as the realist thought life to be under the aegis of materialism can qualify as serious aesthetic achievement.... Yet even in the dourest realistic view truth is a human triumph; through it man transcends suffering and determinism. Nikolai Berdyaev saw this clearly when he argued that all art is a victory over heaviness. It is always escape.[1]

Even popular art forms, Robinson continues, "are a part of man's intellectual armament in this war to liberate himself from heaviness...," for "by incarnating the Good, a spiritual entity, in a concrete form, art frees it to be."

That even pop romance is concerned with moral truth—by "incarnating the Good" in its hero figures—is easily shown. The more primitive films, television programs, and comics—those produced mainly for children—explicitly purport to be morality tales: The Lone Ranger is identified as a "champion of justice,"[2] for example, and Batman is plainly if infelicitously described as "fighting for righteousness and apprehending the wrong-doer."[3]

In more sophisticated pop romance the same process is handled more subtly and may even result in the establishment of fairly complex levels of meaning. Steve Canyon, for example, is clearly an incarnation of moral Good, but he is also the means by which Milton Caniff, his creator, idealizes and glorifies the military, devalues civilians and civilian life, advances a Dullesian posture on international affairs, and in general espouses a conservative sociopolitical philosophy. Though Caniff is hardly less didactic than Spenser or Milton, and the thrust of his didacticism is such that he too invariably alienates some readers, he, like these poets, makes complete rejection of his "art" almost impossible by incorporating his specific socio-political views within the general framework of the Judeo-Christian value system. Left with a choice between desiring a victory for militantly militarist Steve Canyon (and Western Civilization) and a victory for The Other Side, only the most resolute radical has a real alternative.

There is still another level at which pop romance, both primitive and sophisticated, incarnates the Good. This is the level where personal ethics and ego meet to define individual spiritual and material aspirations. We tend to admire and identify with Batman, for example, not only because he is clean, upright, reverent, etc., an adult Boy Scout, square but undeniably *good*—all the things we should be—but also because he is handsome, athletic, intelligent, and rich—all the things we would like to be. He is the fulfillment of our fantasies as well as of our moral sense. And though Freudian psychology may lead us to expect that the former function is more crucial, this does not seem to be the case: a hero figure may be ugly or poor (and some are) but he can still be acceptable; if he should fail to honor his father and mother or if he should covet his neighbor's wife he will not be. Whatever different values may be stressed in various heroes of pop romance (and there is some variation), they tend to have the basic values of our culture in common. Thus their repeated triumphs, whether we are fully conscious of it or not, can help to reinforce our confidence in our value system and to encourage our conformity to it.

Clearly, his readers' conformity to the values he anatomized in *The Faerie Queene* was one of the main effects Spenser hoped to achieve through his art. But if the Instruction that effects moral conformity was his main purpose, Spenser, like all makers of fiction, also recognized that "the most part of men delight to read, rather for variety of matter, then for the profit of the ensample"; therefore, as he explained to Raleigh, instead of having "good discipline delivered plainly in way of precepts, or sermoned at large," he wrote an epic poem, in which the Instruction was "most plausible and pleasing, being coloured with an historicall fiction. . . ." It is of course far more likely that Delight rather than Instruction is the main conscious intent of most of the creators of pop romance. It is Delight that brings in the dollars. But to succeed in delighting a whole culture or even a sizeable portion of it is neither automatic nor easy. The chances for such success for example are diminished considerably if the Delight comes at the expense of the culture's value system. Thus neither epic poets nor the creators of pop culture are true cultural revolutionaries. (Even devout Royalists could accept *Paradise Lost*.) Whether Delight or Instruction then is uppermost in the mind of the creator of the fiction, if the fiction is successful the results will likely be the same: the culture will find reiterated in that fiction most of the values it passed on to the creator in the first place. It is almost inevitable therefore that pop romance, for example, instruct in spite of itself.

Milton Caniff has said: "The American hero lives in all of us . . . and if we are not all heroes, we are all hero ridden. Descendants of a legend, we persist in identifying with it."[4] To summarize the argument of this paper, if today's students can be made conscious of this truth about themselves by having their attention called to their involvement in pop romance, and if, by analyzing the nature and functions of the hero in pop romance and epic poems, they can begin to perceive significant esthetic and intellectual parallels between the popular and the classic, then their heightened awareness of the unity and the relevance of all art will help to make their study of literature easier, more enjoyable, and more pointed. To some extent Marshall McLuhan has made even the ordinary student more receptive to such an approach than he might have been a few years ago, and Northrop Frye of course has done even more for the well-read student. And Frye, in addition, is helpful in providing some guidelines by which such an approach can to an extent be systematized.

ONE

In *Anatomy of Criticism*, Frye classifies five types of fictive hero, each type being determined "by the hero's power of action, which may be greater than ours, less, or roughly the same." (Frye's fourth type, the hero "superior neither to other men nor to his environment" and his fifth type, the hero who is "inferior in power or intelligence to ourselves," do not concern us here, though they would if the limits of this essay extended beyond the literary epic and the pop romance.)

Type I. "If superior in *kind* both to other men and to the environment of other men, the hero is a divine being, and the story about him will be a *myth* in the common sense of a story about a god." Frye adds that "Such stories have an important place in literature, but are as a rule found outside the normal literary categories," but as we shall see, *Paradise Lost* is a noteworthy exception to this rule, as is, less obviously, *The Faerie Queene*. The pop hero who best illustrates Type I is Superman, who to all intent and purposes is absolute in his power, his glory, and his goodness. Superman, like other such mythic figures, is not only perfect, but is capable of donning imperfection—of voluntarily assuming a human role, in the playing of which he suffers what Jules Feiffer has called his "discreet martyrdom."[5]

Type II. "If superior in *degree* to other men and to his environment, the hero is the typical hero of *romance*, whose actions are marvelous but who is himself identified as a human being. The hero of romance moves in a world in which the ordinary laws of nature are slightly suspended. . . ." The fact that these laws frequently seem to be suspended by the hero himself gives the Type II figure a semi-divine aura even though he is of earthly mold. Though limited, he is still overwhelmingly powerful and overwhelmingly virtuous. He is, however, capable of error (though seldom of crime or serious sin) and ultimately he is vulnerable. In pop romance Batman is a familiar example of this type.

Type III. "If superior in degree to other men but not to his natural environment, the hero is a leader. He has authority, passions, and powers of expression far greater than ours but . . . is subject both to social criticism and to the order of nature." Although a number of pop heroes are of this type, Steve Canyon is fairly representative. He is a leader, an Air Force lieutenant colonel, passionate about the U.S. Air Force, the U.S., and—occasionally—a female (in that order), but what he does is sometimes criticized (most often by ignorant or malicious civilians) and the jet planes he flies are subject to the laws of physics. He is vulnerable, not only physically but also intellectually and psychologically, and he is capable of, though not prone to, error.

The Type I hero is what we would all like to be ("faster than a speeding bullet," having "X-ray vision," capable of flying), but outside of our dreams of wish fulfillment, we recognize that we could not possibly be him. The Type II hero, being more human than superhuman, is a more attainable ideal, but again our conscious selves will acknowledge that we can never have all the powers and virtues he possesses nor have them to the degree that he does. The Type III hero is also greater in the sum total of his powers and virtues than we could be, but because he shares with the rest of humanity certain limitations upon his embodiment and exercise of these powers and virtues, some of them are at least theoretically within our reach and in a few we could even exceed him: we could conceivably fly airplanes as well as Lt. Col. Canyon; we might even become generals.

All of these heroes are larger than life; some are merely larger than others. But what the hero is and does in terms of objective reality are less important than what he represents to our inner reality. The local man who saves a child from drowning is of less enduring interest to us than our fictive or historical heroes: the former wants symbolism, and unless local mythopoeia provides him with it, we tend to displace him in our consciousness with the more value-charged heroes we seem to need. The heroes of the great English epics represent attempts by poets of genius to fulfill that need for their own times. In our time, supposedly the age of the "anti-hero," the writers of pop romance knowingly or unknowingly fulfill the same need. Thus, what Northrop Frye claims about popular literature in general is particularly true of pop romance: it is "literature which affords an almost unobstructed view of archetypes."

Specific illustrations of how the analogies between epic and pop heroes can be used to provide one kind of approach to *Beowulf*, *The Faerie Queene*, and *Paradise Lost* comprise the next three sections of this paper. The focus will be on the hero figures and the value systems in which they are involved rather than upon structure or imagery or the like. Nor will any attempt be made to justify on esthetic grounds the examples of pop romance considered. Whether primitive or slick, they seldom even approach the threshold of what is generally regarded as "art"—although they do qualify if we accept Norman Holland's definition of art as that which exists for our pleasure, requires us to suspend disbelief in order to experience that pleasure, and gives us that pleasure by "managing" or "controlling" our fantasies and feelings.[6] But whether they are regarded as "art" or not, pop romances can shed light on art and on our responses to it, as both Holland and Frye have suggested.[7] The same conclusion is arrived at by a student of the comic strip phenomenon, Kenneth E. Eble, even though he rejects the comics as an art form:

> The comics fail badly as art despite their pretension to seriousness—or perhaps because of it. They have about the same relation to serious art that a tract like *Pierce Pennilesse* has to *Paradise Lost*. . . . As objects of serious study, they rank considerably higher. They will offer much information to future historians as to how we lived, how we acted, and, in a large sense, how we (the thickening mass) responded. . . . As factors in shaping a nation's emotional and intellectual responses, they deserve much more study than they have yet received.[8]

TWO

In his consideration of "The Primitive Heroic Ideal," E. Talbot Donaldson says: "put most simply, the heroic ideal was excellence. The hero-kings strove to do better than anyone else the things that an essentially migratory life demanded . . . "[9] Fighting was of course the primary activity, as it is so often in pop romance, and it is on those few violent hours in Beowulf's life when he wins his three great victories that the Anglo-Saxon *scop* concentrates rather than upon his youth or years of kingship. Violence, it might be added, is also a preoccupation of Spenser in *The Faerie Queene*, and it gets its due in *Paradise Lost* as well, in spite of Milton's intention to frame a "higher Argument." Pop romance is frequently attacked for its own preoccupation with violence, but its critics do not always recognize that violence is seldom gratuitous; as in epic poems it is usually if not always effectively moralized: the resounding "Pow!" as Batman's fist connects with the Joker's jaw signals not only retribution but the reestablishment of moral order.

The plot of the first section of *Beowulf*—the bringing of order to the chaos that is Heorot through the deeds of the stranger-hero, and thus bringing stability and security to a community near collapse—has been utilized so often as to seem formula by now. The Western, of course, employs it over and over again.

In a popular television series of a few years back, *Have Gun, Will Travel*, this formula shaped almost every episode. The hero, a gun-fighter-knight-errant (appropriately named Paladin), continually rode out to rid a variety of communities of a variety of Grendels. A typical episode begins in San Francisco, where Paladin lives like royalty, surrounded by retainers male and female. When the call comes, however, he abandons his sybaritic life without hesitation and exchanges his foppish apparel for a basic black Western outfit symbolic of his deadly role. Although he usually rides alone, he is often joined by a decent citizen or two who serve as his temporary retainers. Upon these retainers and the community he succors Paladin bestows something of the courtesy that Beowulf shows to Hrothgar and the Geats. The rewards Paladin receives for his victories are, like Beowulf's, commensurate with the grave risks he takes, but he too is capable of exercising his talents for violence on the strength of a friendship or a principle, receiving for his victories only renewed fame.

The series which fixed the stranger-savior most firmly in the imagination of mid-twentieth century America was of course *The Lone Ranger*. Conceived for juveniles, this series was so well received that it has appeared in all of the popular media. It is possible that the messianic overtones of the formula which *The Lone Ranger* so obviously played upon were partly responsible for its wide appeal: in times of crisis we look for a deliverer, a Beowulf or a Lone Ranger. The vague origins and the sudden departures of such heroes also serve to enhance their legends. These legends in time take on almost religious status, becoming myths that provide the communities not only with models for conduct but with the kind of heightened shared experiences which inspire and unify their members.

The final sequence of *Beowulf*, the hero's fight with the dragon, embodies still another formulaic plot, that of the resident-hero who champions the community in its struggle for self-preservation. This hero may or may not be the titular leader of the community, but he is always the present exemplification of the primitive kingly ideal (Hrothgar's heroism was in the past). "Dodge City," the archetypal community of the television Western *Gunsmoke* has a mayor, but it is the city's marshal, Matt Dillon, who guarantees its stability and security. "Gotham" not only has a mayor, but a police commissioner, a police chief, and squads of officers, but it is Batman who defeats the city's dragons. The ineffectuality of the forces of law and order and of the law itself seems almost a basic assumption both of epics and of pop romance.

The law frequently appears to be too complex or too cumbersome to deal with crises, so the hero, whether he is a real or titular king, becomes a law unto himself. Ian Fleming's "James Bond," a true primitive hero updated to espionage agent, is "licensed to kill." He is above the law not only of his own community but of the international community as well. So too are the agents featured in the television series, *Mission Impossible*. Unlike the individualistic Bond they operate in concert (the committee-as-hero?) and their numbers include the mandatory black man (a modern Tonto?) and the mandatory beautiful woman (a modern Britomart?). In their adventures these organization-man-heroes so frequently and blithely violate not only laws but human rights that they are warned before every mission that, if captured, they will be disavowed by the very national community which sends them forth. The legal and moral assumptions behind their activities are seldom questioned because these heroes, like Beowulf, are understood to be "on God's side," i.e., the community's. (It is only in the "low mimetic" and "ironic" modes that the question of whether God is on our side or on that of the big battalions can be entertained.)

The hero's antagonists, on the other hand, are depicted as being unresponsive to the community and the community's values, even if they happen to be residents. The antagonist may represent an alien community or only the community of the self, but the fact that he acts as a law unto himself is *not* glossed over. The *Beowulf*-poet stresses this: Grendel is of the exiled race of Cain, he inhabits that no-man's land where the influence of the community ends and what is in effect the jungle begins, and from that dark region he peers at the community and envies its happiness. Though he comes within the pale of the community by gaining control of Heorot, if only during the night, his natural element, his means of doing so puts him beyond the pale. The rules therefore need not apply to him: the only good renegade is a dead renegade.

Primitive heroes do not, however, have *carte blanche*. Although the community may be quite willing to waive *all* of its laws to ensure the defeat of its enemy, the hero cannot, for otherwise he loses face and his force as the repository of the community's values (which supposedly he is struggling to preserve). For heroes there seems to be a law of diminishing legal returns. He can violate some laws—against illegal search and seizure, for example—but he cannot violate others, particularly the unwritten laws of the community: killing the villain can eliminate the expense and delay in the community's vengeance entailed by the observation of due process, but the execution must take the form of a sword point or a bullet in the villain's chest, not in his back. It is to such a "code of the West" that Beowulf conforms when he undertakes to battle Grendel with his bare hands and Grendel's dam with a sword (a compensation for the disadvantage of fighting under water). This form of chivalry only allows for "equalizers"—in the "shootdown" it must be .38 against .38. Of course this code is binding upon heroes only; it is one of the crosses they bear but without which they might be difficult to distinguish from their codeless antagonists, the merely instinctual Grendels and cattle-rustlers.

In spite of the fact that the community itself is usually inferior in the quality of its collective life to the life of the hero, it is still in some sense above him. Its survival is the *summum bonum*, and the issue of community survival is one which can conveniently be invoked in any crisis in order to justify its actions, even the sacrifice of its best, the hero himself. For the community in both epic and pop romance is not only a social unit but a quasi-religious one. It is that which nurtures, controls, and protects the non-heroes who comprise it: the community giveth and the community taketh away. Its wars are holy wars and its champions, as noted above, become quasi-religious figures. Thus the Unferths or the cowardly shopkeepers whose action or inaction undermines the hero (and thus the community) come close to being not only traitors but apostates.

Invariably this community religion becomes cosmic: in Hrothgar's view Beowulf has been divinely sent to deliver his people from a monster who is "at war with God" (although he appears to give real trouble only to the Geats). And Beowulf himself feels that he is under God's protection. His status as a messiah-figure receives the heaviest stress in the poem's climactic sequence, the fight with the dragon. This "worm" that flies by night, that is associated with fire, that lives somewhere below, shares at least in the archetype of Satan, whom Milton (in the "Nativity Ode") called "the old dragon underground." Beowulf's determination to save his people singlehandedly, his going-forth with a band of twelve, one of whom initiated the chain of events which will lead to his death, and the *scop*'s final description of him—"of world-kings the mildest of men and the gentlest"—all suggest an imitation of Christ. The image of the hero as gentle man which seems almost an afterthought in *Beowulf* is close to the formula in pop romance. "Clark Kent" is always "the mild-mannered reporter," and Steve Canyon's pipe-smoking is an obvious clue to his character. The image thrives too in the Western, the classic example being the mild hero (played by Gary Cooper) of the film *High Noon*.

Heroes cannot, however, remain lambs: crises call for lions. And whether they take place in epics or in pop romance, crises usually require violent solutions. Violence indeed seems to be the reality of their worlds, and it is in violent situations that the heroes are defined. Superman is somehow more "real" than the mousey "Clark Kent," Batman more "real" than the do-gooder "Bruce Wayne." Indeed, in this "civilian" alter ego, each of these heroes is suspected of being, like the youthful Beowulf, "slack, a young man unbold."

Beowulf must, in spite of his divine aura, be classified as a Type II hero. He is "of mankind . . . the strongest of might," a prestigious swimmer, a supreme fighter, yet if you cut him, he bleeds. He belongs to the company of Batman and Paladin. One significant difference, however, between *Beowulf* and romance, pop or otherwise (and to some extent between *Beowulf* and *The Faerie Queene*), is the distinction between mortality and vulnerability. Spenser's heroes, like Batman and Paladin, are always being threatened with death but never die (or even age), whereas Beowulf not only ages but dies. And, unlike these other heroes he is intensely aware of fate and almost preoccupied with death. Transiency is his reality and this gives his story an additional dimension. The world of *The Faerie Queene* and, frequently, of the American Western is largely static, a version of pastoral. "The Wild West," which existed for only a heartbeat in history, in fiction seems to exist out of time. Marshall Dillon's Dodge City resembles the town on Keats's Grecian urn, fixed forever. (This is very much the case with Spenser's "Faerie Land" and Batman's "Gotham" as well.) Though populated, these places do not change nor does their populace. Only their heroes seem quite alive—and their villains also, who come and go and occasionally die. This tendency moves a romance-epic like *The Faerie Queene* and pop romance toward comedy while *Beowulf* approaches tragedy. And even though *Paradise Lost* involves tragic action in its story of Satan, the to-be-continued story of Adam and Eve takes the shape of elevated tragicomedy, and the poem as a whole, with its promise of good coming out of evil, takes on the form of a history-play which is also a divine comedy.

THREE

In spite of the New Morality, the New Theology, and all of the other forces which are said to be radically altering American society, it is possible to question whether real changes have taken place on all of the levels at which that society responds to art. If, for example, a social scientist were to perform a study to determine which are the twelve moral virtues of most importance to Americans, is it necessarily the case that he would come up with a list that would differ significantly from that of Edmund Spenser? The answer would seem to be "No," if one can trust the impressions one receives from editorials and letters-to-the-editor, from high-circulation magazines ranging from *Life* and the *Reader's Digest* to *Playboy*, from pulpits and from the soap boxes of television news and documentaries. Additional evidence to validate this hypothesis can be extracted from an examination of the heroes of pop romance, in whom the virtues treated by Spenser in *The Faerie Queene*, for example, live still.

While the main task of these heroes is to insure that justice is done (American justice, community justice), in the process of doing so they, like Sir Calidore, exhibit Courtesy (in the narrow sense of chivalric manners and in the broad sense of integrity); they exemplify Friendship's highest ideal, *agape*, by being willing to lay down their lives for their friends; and finally, although some might deviate slightly from Temperance conceived of in terms of wine and women (though even this is not usual), the life of moderation is generally their way of life. Even the virtues of Chastity and Holiness, whose very naming can elicit smiles from the God-Is-Dead, Sexual Freedom generation, seem deeply rooted in the consciousness of even the young. Holiness may perhaps be redefined in terms of Zen or drug-expanded awareness or Peace Corps-type service, and Chastity in terms of "I-Thou" relationships for sexual partners, but the spirit of the ideal still moves among us.

In pop romance, it is true, Holiness is something of a negative virtue. Men of the cloth and other pious folk are treated deferentially by a Superman, a Batman, or a Steve Canyon, but these heroes do not themselves espouse patently ecclesiastical causes. Churches remain sacred places and church-goers are often depicted as that segment of the populace which requires and merits secular as well as divine protection. Villains in pop romance, on the other hand, not infrequently appear as false religious figures (heirs of Archimago and Duessa), whether they be the phony parsons of Westerns, the leaders of obscure and evil cults in modern adventures, or atheistic Communists of the type that Steve Canyon battles. Thus, although the heroes of pop romance appear to be essentially secular figures—and their creators take pains to avoid obvious religious controversy—they are in fact modern exemplars of Holiness, in the broad sense of having respect for religion, of being virtuous, and of being "on God's side." While they are not Christian militants, for the Word they spread is not the Gospel but "Justice" or "America," many pop heroes are not very far removed from the Puritan heroes of the seventeenth century. They are by implication and by default Protestants—there are rarely any Catholics, Jews, Muslims, or atheists in the foxholes of the fictive war against evil. And in his dogged and irresistible militancy on behalf of his cause, each pop hero resembles a one-man New Model Army.

Although their Chastity, like their Holiness, is more often implicit than explicit, the majority of the heroes of pop romance are still in the Spenserian tradition. Some viewers of *Gunsmoke* have long suspected that Miss Kitty, proprietress of the Dodge City saloon that Matt Dillon frequents, is no better than she should be, but the sexual overtones of their relationship remain muted. It is a standing joke among cinema buffs that the "Code of the West" permits the cowboy to kiss only his horse, but even today, in an era of attempts at making "realistic" Westerns, the hero is seldom permitted to be a rake. A really strong interest in sex is, in Westerns as in *The Faerie Queene*, usually reserved for villains.

Spenser's heroes are attractive to women, good and bad, and are sometimes attracted to women as other than objects of chivalric fulfillment. They are not professional virgins, even Britomart, but sex without full ecclesiastical and social sanctions is denied them. This is likewise the case with many of the heroes of pop romance; here as in most pastorals, sex is often portrayed as an intrusive force, leading the hero to unaccustomed excess and interfering with his performance of his duties. The male hero's dilemma is perfectly symbolized in the plight of Superman, who is forever having to rescue Lois Lane and forever rejecting her advances, but who, as "Clark Kent," degrades himself by making advances which she always spurns. Spenser's creation of the magnificent Bower of Bliss and his ruthless destruction of it show hardly more rigor than the tendency of the creators of pop romance to condemn their heroes to a largely sexless and even loveless existence. An exception to this tendency is to be found in recent "swinging" versions of the espionage-romance genre. Spy-heroes like James Bond and "Napoleon Solo," title-figure of the television series, *The Man from U.N.C.L.E.*, who, as noted above, are already to a great extent outside both the law and the culture, apparently have licenses to fornicate as well as to kill. They are hedonist-heroes of the New Morality. Yet their popularity, enormous for a year or two, already seems on the wane, which may indicate that Spenser's ideal of Chastity is still operative beneath the surface of our supposedly liberated culture.

Spenser's very idealism makes the classification of his hero-types difficult. The deliberately non-realistic world he creates complicates the establishment of correspondences with our own world by which the hero is partially defined. The world of *The Faerie Queene*, being itself supernatural, is sometimes superior to the heroes and sometimes not. Since this world does not operate according to natural law in the first place, it seemingly cannot accommodate the Type III hero at all. Furthermore, Spenser's heroes themselves, informed as they are by so many levels of allegorical meaning but so little characterization, cannot readily be distinguished from each other. "Ordinary" human characters (like Colin Cloute perhaps), who might establish some kind of norm by which the heroes might be measured, are relatively few and far between; "Faerye Land" seems to be populated mainly by heroes and villains. The majority of the former are clearly Type II heroes; in a few cases, however, there is another possibility.

As Spenser's letter to Raleigh explains, Prince Arthur is "perfected in the twelve private morall vertues, as Aristotle hath devised." Such perfection, summarized in the supreme virtue of Magnanimity, makes him "superior in kind" to even the other great heroes in the poem, and he is also superior to them in that he possesses a shield whose powers go beyond even the supernatural. This being the case, he is also superior to his "environment," the supernatural land of Faerie. Spenser does not call him a god, for this would compromise the Christian level of his allegory, but he gives the impression of being one. He is the deliverer, one who comes in glory, and will come again. Thus, along with his beloved, "That greatest glorious queene," Gloriana, the descendent of "either spright/Or angell," Arthur can be considered a Type I hero.

Two other possibilities for this classification present themselves. Although Talus, the "yron man" of Book V, is Artegall's squire, like God he is "Immoveable, resistlesse, without end" and like Christ he "thresht out falshood, and did truth unfould." In his inhumanity—or more precisely, his a-humanity—he foreshadows Superman, whose human traits really emerge only when he is "Clark Kent." In Talus and in Superman the *deus ex machina* has become "the machine god," but in the case of the latter a poetic fantasy has been replaced by a technical fantasy; Superman, the man of tomorrow, "is the promise that each and every world problem will be solved by the technical trick."[10]

The mechanical savagery of Talus in some respects has its counterpart in the "natural" savagery of Calepine's rescuer [the Salvage Man in Book Six of *The Faerie Queene*]. Although he is, like Talus, a minor character, the "salvage man" is very close at least to being a Type I hero for he is quintessentially good, invincible, and rendered invulnerable through "magicke leare." A Superman *sans* cape and leotards, he is also a "Clark Kent," capable of being "enmoved" to feel compassion. Without losing his god-like powers or his identity he can exhibit "milde humanity and perfect gentle mynd." His case is an example of how in its smallest as well as its largest developments Spenser's poem moves toward unity and identity whereas Superman's story illustrate what seems to be the schizoid tendency of twentieth-century imaginings.

Although a Redcrosse or a Britomart is so far above us that we may be lulled into thinking of them as gods, if we remain responsive to Spenser's descriptions and his narrative, it is evident that they are Type II heroes. Like Batman they are vulnerable and capable of error, though Batman's errors tend to be tactical, theirs human or moral; they can be overpowered by human, natural, or supernatural forces (technological forces in the case of Batman). Their human weaknesses get them into difficulties from which neither their physical nor their moral strength can extricate them. Unlike Adam they are not "sufficient": all Type II and Type III heroes are in fact fallen men. Being fallen and thus incomplete they frequently need assistance. Indeed, assistants are a fixture of Type II heroes: as Redcrosse has his Una, Britomart her Glaucé, and Artegall his Talus, so Batman has his Robin. Assistants come in handy for purposes of plot: they can be separated from the hero and become involved in sub-plots of their own, from which they may need to be rescued by the hero, or the separation, which weakens the hero, can create a crisis in his own plot from which the assistant can extricate him. An assistant can serve as confidant or as foil to the hero. As foils they are both like the hero and unlike him—Una's Revealed Truth complements the Holiness of Redcrosse as Robin's boyish exuberance complements Batman's mature energy. In general assistants are inferior both physically and mentally to the Type II hero, but together, as a "dynamic duo," they approach the perfection of the Type I hero. Nonetheless, they still lack his invulnerability. [. . .]

FIVE

There can be little doubt, among scholars at least, that Milton, Spenser, and the *scop* of *Beowulf* believed that their epics were relevant to their times, and in the case of Milton certainly, Spenser probably, and the Anglo-Saxon poet possibly, relevant for all time. While the intentions and assumptions of the creators of pop romance may be less evident, there can be little doubt that a part of the vast popularity their efforts enjoy must be due to the special kinds of relevancy that they have for their audiences. If the present generation of students is to be introduced to *Beowulf*, *The Faerie Queene*, and *Paradise Lost* mainly because of their esthetic and historical importance, that introduction may be facilitated and perhaps even enriched if these students can be brought to recognize that our western values have persisted remarkably down through the ages to even the present time through a variety of literary forms and through diverse media; that on this level alone the great English epics can speak to them and to their condition; and that they can speak in language and in modes to which the popular forms so familiar to them sometimes aspire, but seldom achieve.

NOTES

1. W. R. Robinson, "The Movies, Too, Will Make You Free," *Man and the Movies*, ed. W. R. Robinson (Baton Rouge, LA, 1967), 117–18.
2. Quoted in Jim Harmon, *The Great Radio Heroes* (Garden City, NY, 1967), 203.
3. Quoted in Jules Feiffer, *The Great Comic Book Heroes* (New York, 1965), 26.
4. Quoted in David Manning White and Robert Abel, "Comic Strips and American Culture," *The Funnies: An American Idiom*, eds. David Manning White and Robert Abel (New York, 1963), 33.
5. Feiffer, 19.
6. Norman N. Holland, *The Dynamics of Literary Response* (New York, 1968), 74–75.
7. Holland, xiii–xiv; Frye, *Anatomy of Criticism*, 103, 116–17.
8. "Our Serious Comics," *The Funnies*, 109.
9. In *The Norton Anthology of English Literature*, gen. ed. M.H. Abrams, rev. ed. (New York, 1968), 1, 3.
10. Heinz Politzer, "From Little Nemo to Li'l Abner," *The Funnies*, 51.

Masked Heroes

RICHARD REYNOLDS

Reprinted by permission from *Superheroes: A Modern Mythology* (University Press of Mississippi, 1994), 7–25.

BATMAN, SUPERMAN, SPIDER-MAN, AND WONDER WOMAN ARE AMONG THE most widely known fictional characters ever conceived. Created as comic-book heroes, they remain more widely known through television, the movies and (in the case of Batman and Superman) through a vigorous presence in American and European popular culture that ensures their recognition by millions who have never read a Batman comic or seen a Superman film. Superman, Batman, and Wonder Woman[1] have remained continuously in print and involved in an unbroken sequence of new adventures for over fifty years [now seventy—*eds.*]. Yet the medium from which they spring—the 6" x 9" four-color comic book—continues to be (at least in North American and British culture) a marginalized channel of communication held by many to be an irredeemably corrupt and corrupting form of discourse, or else suitable only for children and the semi-literate.

In consequence, the adult superhero readership (a sub-section of the adult comic readership as a whole) has come to identify itself as a small and very cohesive subculture. Specialist comic-book retailers, "marts," and full-scale conventions are the outward signs of this cohesion, as is the highly organized marketplace for buying, selling, and collecting old comics. If connoisseurship and value to the collector alone gave access to the privileged world of high culture, superhero comics would have been there long ago.

For the cultural student, superhero comics present a number of immediate paradoxes: a popular art form traditionally known for its apparently hegemonic and sometimes overtly authoritarian texts; a publishing genre which began to gain a degree of cultural respectability by ducking "underground" at least partially for its distribution; an art-form which has been handled (if at all) with disdain by the literary establishment, and yet has built up its own lively and heuristic critical discourse through what is still rather misleadingly known as the "fan press";[2] and, finally, a body of contemporary mythology from which television and Hollywood have plundered material as diverse as the campy 1960s Batman TV show, the apparent artlessness of the Christopher Reeve Superman cycle, and the overwrought gothic bravura of the 1989 Batman movie.

The superhero genre is tightly defined and defended by its committed readership—often to the exasperation of writers and artists, many of whom have proclaimed it to be a worn-out formula from as long ago as the 1970s. But the dinosaur refuses to keel over and die, and dominates the economics of the American comics industry. The chief superhero characters remain its most widely understood and recognized creations—to the annoyance of writers and artists who would like to bring the wider possibilities of the comic book (or graphic novel)[3] to the attention of the general public.

An attempt to define the limits of the genre can best be made as part of a broader exploration of the heroes themselves—differing as they do from each other sometimes as much as Gandhi and the Lone Ranger. The costumed superhero burst into seemingly fully fledged existence in June 1938, with the appearance on American newsstands of *Action Comics* #1, featuring Superman's first ever appearance in print. The new arrival proved enormously popular, and quickly led to a host of imitations and new ideas along similar lines—from Batman, Wonder Woman, and the Sub-Mariner—all with us to this day—to such obscure creations as The Arrow, Shock Gibson, and the Masked Marvel.[4]

America's entry into World War Two gave the superheroes a whole new set of enemies, and supplied a complete working rationale and worldview for a super-patriotic superhero such as Captain America.[5] This so-called Golden Age[6] of comics and superhero comics in particular lasted up to the late 1940s, when the bulk of the costumed superhero titles folded as a result of falling readerships. Only Superman, Batman, and Wonder Woman came through the lean years of the early 1950s without a break in publication. The spotlight had shifted elsewhere—to crime comics, western comics, horror comics.

As is well known, it was the excesses of the horror comics that led indirectly to the renaissance of the superhero genre. The bloody guts and gore of Entertaining Comics'[7] *Tales from the Crypt*, *Vault of Horror*,[8] and other titles both from EC and rival publishers led to the censorious publication *Seduction of the Innocent*[9] by Dr. Fredric Wertham and the 1954 Congressional hearings on juvenile delinquency and comics.[10] [While Reynolds understandably stresses the notoriety of EC and other horror comics, it should be noted that objections to comic books predated the horror boom of the early fifties, and indeed predated Wertham.—*eds.*] The comic publishers responded to the adverse publicity of the report and the hearings with the self-censoring Comics

Code. The Code involved a voluntary ban by the publishers themselves on violence, explicit sex, gratuitous gore, and the triumph of evil or antisocial behavior. In a move against the "true crime" comics that had peaked in popularity in the late 1940s, the Code stipulated that law enforcement officers should never be shown in a disrespectful or unsympathetic light.

Clearly, the climate had changed. Detective Comics (DC) decided to expand their small list of superhero comics that had, in the early 1950s, shrunk to no more than Superman, Batman, and Wonder Woman. A re-born and re-costumed Flash (1956)[11] paved the way for the return of the Green Lantern (1959),[12] a new heroine, Supergirl (1959),[13] and then a whole superhero team in the shape of the Justice League of America (1960).[14] Under the editorship of Stan Lee, Marvel Comics re-entered the superhero market with new titles such as *The Fantastic Four* (1961),[15] *Spider-Man* (1963),[16] and the *X-Men* (1964).[17] Norse Gods were added to the genre with *The Mighty Thor*,[18] and horror wedded to the superhero format in *The Incredible Hulk*.[19] Golden Age characters such as Captain America and the Sub-Mariner were brought back out of retirement.[20]

This is the period usually referred to as the Silver Age, dating from the revival of The Flash in 1956. Marvel dominated the scene in the 1960s and early 1970s, its writers and artists creating a wealth of exciting new titles that mixed protagonists more in tune with the mores of the period, and kept an eye for the visual and verbal ironies inherent in situating superpowered characters against a background that purported to represent the "real" world. It was the Marvel line of this period which first began the expansion of comics into a teenage and college readership. DC, however, remained the leading publisher of superhero comics in terms of sales, benefiting from the enormous appeal of the 1960s Batman TV series. Batman and Superman titles made up nine of the ten best-selling comics in the U.S.A. by 1969. DC also developed innovative titles of its own, such as the Green Lantern/Green Arrow team-up of the early 1970s, which featured artwork by exciting new talent Neal Adams.[21] [Adams was not quite new to comic books, having begun working for DC in 1967—and he made his debut as a comic strip artist with *Ben Casey* in 1962.—*eds.*]

But by the 1980s, the Marvel phenomenon had gone stale. DC reasserted itself as the leading comic book publisher, by means of a shrewd and imaginative revamping of its classic titles, and the promoting of exciting and innovative work both in the superhero genre (such as *Watchmen*) and in the linked genres of fantasy and horror, with titles such as *Hellblazer*. By the mid-1980s the Comics Code, once a force powerful enough to bring even EC's William Gaines to heel, had become a spent force, with both Marvel and DC insouciantly advertising many of their comics as "Suggested for Mature

Readers." Such confidence in the labeling bespoke the strength of their adult readership. There is currently a feeling amongst some comic publishers that the "adult" trend may have gone too far, and that comics may be running the risk of provoking another Wertham-like backlash against explicit violence and sexuality.[22]

Superman, the first superhero, was conceived by the teenage Jerry Siegel as early as 1934, lying sleepless one night in bed:

> I am lying in bed counting the sheep when all of the sudden it hits me. I conceive a character like Samson, Hercules, and all the strong men I have ever heard tell of rolled into one. Only more so. I hop right out of bed and write this down, and then I go back and think some more for about two hours and get up again and write that down. This goes on all night at two-hour intervals, until in the morning I have a complete script.[23]

But the concept of a character with superhuman strength and invulnerability was simply too unfamiliar for the comic book publishers of the early 1930s. Siegel and artist Joe Shuster established themselves in the comics business with the private-eye strip "Slam Bradley" (1934). Superman finally made his debut in *Action Comics* #1 (1938),[24] using material hastily adapted by Siegel and Shuster from a story which had originally been intended to form part of a newspaper strip.

Superman's arrival created a wholly new genre out of a very diverse set of materials. Today, many aspects of the first Superman story and its narrative approach have the appearance of cliché: it is necessary to keep in mind that the origin of what later became clichés lies right here.

Page one introduces the reader to the dying planet Krypton (unnamed) and explains that "a scientist" has placed his infant son in a spaceship, launching it towards earth. The "sleeping babe" is discovered and grows up in an orphanage (Clark Kent's parents in Smallville are a later addition to the mythology). On reaching maturity, the young man discovers that he can "leap ⅛th of a mile, hurdle a twenty story building . . . raise tremendous weights . . . run faster than an express train. . . ."[25]

Moreover "nothing less than a bursting shell" can penetrate his skin. Considerable powers, though modest when compared with the godlike abilities Superman would acquire later in his career. Clark decides to dedicate his strength to the benefit of mankind and elects to assume the identity of Superman—all this in the first page of the story, which concludes with a "scientific" explanation of Clark's superhuman abilities, comparing his strength with the proportionate strength of ants and grasshoppers. Pure hokum, but anticipating by twenty-five years Stan Lee's Spider-Man and that character's "proportionate strength of a spider."

Pages two to four relate how Superman prevents an innocent woman going to the electric chair. On page five Clark gets an assignment from the (unnamed) editor of the paper that employs him, the *Daily Star* (later to be renamed the *Daily Planet*):

> "Did you ever hear of Superman?"
> "What?"
> "Reports have been streaming in that a fellow with gigantic strength named Superman actually exists. I'm making it your steady assignment to cover these reports. Think you can handle it, Kent?"
> "Listen Chief, if I can't find out anything about that Superman, no one can!"[26]

Pages five and six see Superman intervene in a wife beating ("You're not fighting a woman now!"). Next, Clark encounters his smart and stylish colleague Lois Lane ("What do you say to a ... er ... date tonight, Lois?" "I suppose I'll give you a break ... for a change"). At the roadhouse, however, Clark is hustled away from his date by brawling Butch Matson, who has nothing but contempt for Clark's pacifist attitudes ("Fight ... you weak livered polecat!" "Really, I have no desire to do so!").

Lois leaves the club in disgust, but finds herself bundled into Matson's car. But even as they hustle their captive away, Matson and his cronies find the road blocked by the imposing figure of Superman, who tips both Lois and the roughnecks out of the car and then trashes the automobile, in a panel which also provides the subject matter for the comic's famous car-throwing cover. Superman carries Lois to safety, and on page ten we find her telling the *Daily Star*'s editor of her meeting with the Man of Steel. Clark in the meantime has been given an assignment to visit the South American republic of San Monte to stir up news for the *Star*'s front page. Instead, he travels to Washington DC to investigate a case of corruption in the U.S. Senate ("The bill will be passed before its full implications are realized. Before any remedial steps can be taken, our country will be embroiled with Europe"). A cliffhanger has Superman and the captured foreign agent failing to complete a leap between two adjacent skyscrapers.

Much that would become central to the superhero genre is established in these thirteen pages. As a first step towards a definition of the superhero, some of the features of the story could be listed as follows:

1. *Lost parents*

A key preoccupation. Superman is separated from his natural parents, and so his extraordinary powers are not represented in a straightforward parent-to-child relationship. Few superheroes enjoy uncomplicated relationships with parents who are regularly present in the narrative.

2. *The man-god*

The language of the story's first page mimics the King James Bible. A "passing motorist, discovering the sleeping babe within" echoes the Magi on the road to Bethlehem, or Moses among the Bulrushes—both clearly appropriate notes to strike. The sky-spanning spaceship crashes into the Earth, leaving—in later versions of the myth, at least—a deep gash in the soil. So Superman is born from a marriage of Uranus (Heaven) and Gaia (Earth). In due course, Superman will acquire his Father on Earth (Kent senior) to go with Jor-El of Krypton, his Father in Heaven.

3. *Justice*

Superman's devotion to those in need involves coming to the help of those victimized by a blind though well-intentioned state. Superman's first ever exploit involves breaking into the State Governor's bedroom in order to save an innocent woman from the electric chair. Superman does, however, leave the real murderer bound and gagged on the Governor's lawn.[27]

4. *The normal and the superpowered*

The momentary (illusory) power of the individual who threatens the superhero with a gun, knife, or speeding car leads with deliberate inevitability to the astonished realization of the superhero's invulnerability. This is a note that most superhero stories strike from time to time, lest the contrast between superpowered hero and the average individual becomes lost—and the sense of wonder blunted by showing nothing but superpowered characters slugging it out with each other.

Page three of *Action Comics* #1 includes a fine use of this contrast linked to the structure of the panels and the necessity of turning the page to follow the story. The final panel of page three shows the Governor's butler firing a revolver at Superman from point blank range. Page four, panel one, shows an unharmed Superman reaching out to grab the revolver.

5. *The secret identity*

Why doesn't Clark let Lois know that he's Superman? The discourse of the story, the soap-opera continuity that investigates the Clark/Lois/Superman triangle, would be shattered if Lois were to realize Clark and Superman's unity. The Clark/Superman duality needs a constant supply of new dramatic situations to reveal new facets of the hero's split personality. The explicit reasons given within the story—such as "they could use my friends to get at me," reasons which have become common throughout the genre and do not need to be spelt out when establishing a new character—are only secondary to the structural need for characters to have secret identities.

This first-ever Superman story establishes the convention by using it as if it already existed. The reader is called upon to adduce adequate reasons for the disguise. And Lois's extreme scorn for the "morning-after" Clark establishes the width of the Clark/Superman gulf by way of a one-sided conversation:

I'm sorry about last night—
please don't be angry with me.[28]

But Lois coldly stares in the opposite direction. She has become a different person from the warm and yielding individual Superman held in his arms just two panels before: panels which occupy opposite ends of a three-panel sequence in the center of the page. The visual distance between Superman and Lois in the left-hand panel is similar to the distance that separates them on the right, but the emotional relationships implied by the figures are wholly different.

What has been established is in the nature of a taboo. Refraining from a certain act (in this case, revealing oneself to be Superman) wards off a potential disaster. Illogical perhaps, but the situation strengthens the appeal of our hero by establishing certain specific restraints which are peculiar to him and him alone. He pays for his great powers by the observance of this taboo of secrecy—in a manner which is analogous to the process in which warriors in many traditional societies "pay" for their strength in battle by abstaining from sex, eating special foods, and other taboos designed to isolate and protect the "masculine" in their characters.[29] Such concern with what amount to the rites of passage from adolescence to manhood is clearly of interest and concern to a teenage audience.

6. *Superpowers and politics*

The theme of restraint and limitation leads rather nicely to the question of the superheroes and the politicians. In fact, this theme is only lightly touched on in *Action Comics* #1. All that is established is Superman's ability (and willingness) to act clandestinely and even illegally if he believes that national interests may be at stake. His loyalty and patriotism are above even his devotion to the law. This entails some important consequences for a superhero such as Superman, who is beyond the power of the armed forces, should he choose to oppose state power. Endless story possibilities can be designed around the theme of the superhero wrestling with his conscience over which order should be followed—moral or political, temporal or divine.

7. Science as magic

This feature is fundamental to the nature of the universe that the superhero comic portrays. Science is treated as a special form of magic, capable of both good and evil. Scientific concepts and terms are introduced freely into plots and used to create atmosphere and add background detail to artwork—but the science itself is at most only superficially plausible, often less so, and the prevailing mood is mystical rather than rational. Explicitly "magic" powers are able to coexist quite comfortably with apparently scientific ones. A good example of this is the partnership between Iron Man (science) and Thor (magic) developed over the years in Marvel's *Avengers* title.

Although further removed from the character of the heroes themselves than the other points raised above, the depiction of science as magic is crucial to the way in which the superhero comic mythologizes certain aspects of the society it addresses.

These seven headings can be pulled together to construct a first-stage working definition of the superhero genre; a definition that at least has the authenticity of being constructed from the motifs of the first ever superhero comic.

1. The hero is marked out from society. He often reaches maturity without having a relationship with his parents.
2. At least some of the superheroes will be like earthbound gods in their level of powers. Other superheroes of lesser powers will consort easily with these earthbound deities.
3. The hero's devotion to justice overrides even his devotion to the law.
4. The extraordinary nature of the superhero will be contrasted with the ordinariness of his surroundings.
5. Likewise, the extraordinary nature of the hero will be contrasted with the mundane nature of his alter-ego. Certain taboos will govern the actions of these alter-egos.

6. Although ultimately above the law, superheroes can be capable of considerable patriotism and moral loyalty to the state, though not necessarily to the letter of its laws.
7. The stories are mythical and use science and myth indiscriminately to create a sense of wonder.

Turning some of these laws on their heads, such as three and six, would give us a good working definition of the superhero's opponent, the supervillain. Such characters are implicit in the set of governing codes supplied to Superman in his first ever appearance, although they did not become a regular feature of superhero comics until around 1940.[30]

The early Superman stories were a resounding success. Readers asked for more of "that magazine with Superman in it." Publisher Harry Donenfeld—initially skeptical—realized that he had a phenomenal success on his hands. The superhero market boomed. By 1942, several dozen superhero titles were on the American market, forming the largest share of the 150-odd individual comic book titles on sale. Some were blatant copies of Superman: a lawsuit killed Fox Features' Wonderman, and another case was soon outstanding against Fawcett's Captain Marvel.[31] Other characters only derived from the Superman model in the most generic way: famous heroes already well-established included Batman, the Human Torch, the Sub-Mariner, Captain America, Hawkman, Wonder Woman, and the Green Lantern.[32] The new medium had created a new genre all its own, and one perfectly suited to the comic-book's ability to create unfettered fantasy at a price that even children could afford. Moreover, the idealistic but law-abiding superheroes fitted the mood of a United States about to go to war against the fascist powers.

Budgetary considerations make the superhero particularly suitable for the comics medium. Parallels can be drawn between the comic book and the cinema, but in one respect the two media are totally unalike. Film is an expensive art form. Budgets for feature films today rarely go lower than $4 million—they may go as high as $50 million or more. Comics are cheaper, and they are cheaper just where the cinema is most expensive. It costs DC comics no more to have John Byrne draw Superman replacing a space-station in orbit or bathing on the surface of a star, than to show Clark Kent crossing the street on his way to the office. Clearly, any film producer has a much tougher and tightly constrained set of choices to make about a project which may be perfectly sound when viewed simply from the angle of character and plot development.

The comic artist develops a familiarity, indeed almost a casual ease, in handling extraordinary and exotic locations. Such scenes can be casually introduced, for a few panels only, or a bewildering variety of settings can be made use of in one story, if required. The film producer, having decided to let his director build one or two expensive sets, is more or less obliged to "shoot the money"—i.e. to make all this costly set-building pay off as part of the climactic action of the movie. Often this presents no insoluble problems, but it remains an additional pressure on story structure from which the comic-book artist-writer team remains refreshingly free.

Superman and the superhero emerged at the end of the Great Depression and during the run-up to the outbreak of the European war. Millions of Americans had experienced poverty and unemployment; millions more had had their faith in the notion of uninterrupted economic progress seriously undermined. Avenging Lone Wolf heroes abounded in popular narrative of the 1930s and 1940s on both sides of the Atlantic: from Doc Savage to Philip Marlowe, from Hannay in Hitchcock's *39 Steps* to the Green Hornet, from Rick Blain in *Casablanca* to Captain Midnight of the radio serials.[33] A new kind of popular hero had emerged: the self-reliant individualist who stands aloof from many of the humdrum concerns of society, yet is able to operate according to his own code of honor, to take on the world on his own terms, and win. For Americans, the historical path from Munich to Pearl Harbor coincides with the emergence of Superman and Captain America—solitary but socialized heroes, who engage in battle from time to time as proxies of U.S. foreign policy. A darker side of the Lone Wolf hero is embodied by the Batman, a hero whose motivations and emotions are turned inward against the evils within society, and even the social and psychological roots of crime itself. The tension between these two veins in the superhero tradition remains to the present day.

The locus of superhero comics was then, as it largely remains, New York. Writers and artists living in the city depict it in their work—so successfully that superhero stories set in any other city may require a certain degree of justification for their choice of locale. The New York of the early 1940s was a place seemingly chosen for the preservation of the values of European civilization, and a destination for large numbers of artists and intellectuals seeking refuge from the Nazi conquest of Europe: Auden, Isherwood, Ernst, Tanguy, Mondrian. The anthropologist Claude Lévi-Strauss described his reactions on arriving in the city in the essay "New York in 1941":

> The French surrealists and their friends settled in Greenwich Village, where, just a few subway stops from Times Square, one could still lodge—just as in Balzac's time—in a small two- or three-story house with a tiny garden in back. A few days after my arrival, when visiting Yves Tanguy, I discovered and immediately rented, on the street where he lived, a studio whose windows faced a neglected garden. You reached

it by way of a long basement corridor leading to a private stairway in the rear of a red-brick house. . . . Just two or three years ago, I learned that Claude Shannon had also lived there, but on an upper story and facing the street. Only a few yards apart, he was creating cybernetics and I was writing *Elementary Structures of Kinship*. Actually, we had a mutual friend in the house, a young woman, and I recall that, without mentioning his name, she once spoke to me about one of our neighbors, who, she explained, was busy "inventing an artificial brain."

If I did not have it now before my eyes, it would be hard to believe that I bought one day a sixteenth-century Tuscan sideboard for a few dollars. However, New York (and this is the source of its charm and its peculiar fascination) was then a city where anything seemed possible. Like the urban fabric, the social and cultural fabric was riddled with holes. All you had to do was pick one and slip through if, like Alice, you wanted to get to the other side of the looking glass and find worlds so enchanting that they seemed unreal.[34]

This is the New York (or Gotham City, or Metropolis) that dominates the superhero story and has become its almost inevitable milieu. New York draws together an impressive wealth of signs, all of which the comic-reader (of the 1940s or the 1990s) is adept at deciphering. It is a city that signifies all cities, and, more specifically, all modern cities, since the city itself is one of the signs of modernity. It is the place where—since the comedies of Terence—the author takes the reader in order that something may be made to happen. And New York has always been the great point of disembarkation in the history and mythology of the New World (although today, Ellis Island has been opened as a museum and migration now occurs through El Paso, Los Angeles, or Miami). New York is a sign in fictional discourse for the imminence of such possibilities—simultaneously a forest of urban signs and an endlessly wiped slate on which unlimited designs can be inscribed—cop shows, thrillers, comedies, "ethnic" movies such as *Mean Streets*, *Moonstruck*, or *Do The Right Thing*, and cyclical adventures of costumed heroes as diverse as Bob Kane's *Batman* and Alan Moore's *Watchmen*.

Artists and characters might even rub shoulders with each other on Madison Avenue. Marvel under Stan Lee and Jim Shooter has often blurred the distinction between New York as fictional milieu and New York as publishing center—as in Doctor Doom's appearance in the Marvel offices in *Fantastic Four* #10, explaining his escape from a runaway meteor.[35]

Sometimes a thin disguise is the easiest way of summoning up an all-too-familiar subject. Batman writer Bill Finger describes the origin of a famous by-name in the following way:

Originally, I was going to call Gotham City "Civic City." Then I tried Capital City, then Coast City. Then I flipped through the phone book and spotted the name Gotham Jewelers and said, "That's it, Gotham City." We didn't call it New York because we wanted anybody in any city to identify with it. Of course, Gotham is another name for New York.[36]

New York, however, couldn't be done away with so easily. The 1940 story "Batman and Robin visit the 1940 New York World's Fair"[37] is one of the earliest stories involving Robin, the Boy Wonder. The story commences with Bruce Wayne and his young ward Dick Grayson striding towards the Fair, taking in and being impressed by everything they see.

> Dick: Wow I heard it was big, but I didn't think it was this big!
> Bruce: Big is a mild word. It's stupendous . . . Look over there!—the trylon and the perisphere!
> Dick: Say, let's go inside the perisphere! . . . And see the city of tomorrow![38]

Clearly, it's appropriate that Bruce and Dick should spend their time keeping themselves abreast of the latest developments in technology, the better to prosecute their joint war against crime. Where better to do this than at New York's World's Fair? But the off-duty Caped Crusaders have barely begun their day of enjoyment when they are faced with an unwelcome interruption: a radio exhibit broadcasting the news that the great Westriver Bridge has just melted away "as if someone had played an acetylene torch upon it." Bruce and Dick leave the World's Fair to investigate—but without changing into their costumes.

Wayne visits Commissioner Gordon and quizzes him about the bridge. While he's in the Commissioner's office, a Mr. Travers of Travers Engineering arrives carrying a blackmail note that threatens destruction of a second bridge unless a ransom of $300,000 is paid. Commissioner Gordon advises Travers to ignore the threat—"Probably a crackpot trying to cash in on easy money." Meanwhile, Dick inspects the site of the disaster. Two men attack a woman. Dick intervenes, only to be informed that both men are detectives—"Sure, we was takin' her to stir!" After the detectives have gone, Dick begins to have doubts. "Those men didn't act or talk like detectives! I wonder?"

Two days later, the Travers Bridge collapses as threatened. $500,000 is demanded—or a third bridge will be destroyed in the same way. This time, Batman and Robin sweep into action and surprise the hoods, who are positioning a box-like contraption on the bridge. As the duo examine the box, the young woman who Dick saved from the "detectives" reappears. She explains that the box is the work of her father, Doctor Vreekill, a scientist who has discovered a short-wave ray that can "decompose the elements that make up steel." He intends to use his invention to blackmail construction firms into paying protection money. His daughter tells Batman of her father's plans to "free some dangerous prisoners tonight at the state prison so that they may join his organization! Then he's going to destroy the half-finished Monarch building!" Batman and Robin foil the prisoners' escape, then race to the Monarch building site, where they battle more hoods, before flying the Batplane to Doctor Vreekill's laboratory.

Who?

The Batman . . . about to take you to jail!

Jail? You'll never take me to jail! Never![39]

Vreekill electrocutes himself on some bare wires. "Well, he saved the state the job" is Batman's verdict. The story concludes with another Batman and Robin endorsement of New York's World Fair.

It's got as many thrills as one of our adventures!

And he's not kidding! If you want to see something that will not only educate you, but thrill you, by all means see the New York World's Fair.[40]

In its construction and organization, this text is typical of a certain kind of superhero narrative of the 1940s—historically, the period in which the genre was formulating rules and approaches which later artists and writers could obey or flout—but not ignore. The structure and preoccupations of this text are typical of the so-called Golden Age.

Batman and Robin expend considerable effort and risk themselves in unarmed combat against men with guns in defense of—what? One answer might be "law and order," but clearly a man and boy who have no official connection with the police force and operate in disguise and through the use of secret identities are not agents of the law in the same way as the heroes of (say) an Edgar Wallace novel. The splash page at the beginning of the story comments:

Wealth, lust for power, these are the roots of evil that tend to plant themselves in man's heart and mind . . . crime, havoc and destruction, these are the fruits. Once again it remains for the Batman and Robin, the boy wonder, to pit their amazing skill against one who would become a king of crime . . . a king of evil. . . .[41]

These words are positioned over the image of an enthusiastic Bruce and Dick arriving at the World's Fair, symbolic of rational and utopian values. Crime erupts into this ordered environment, and—significantly—crime against the fabric of the city, undertaken through the misappliance of science: Vreekill's machine that can "decompose the elements that make up steel." Though not quite a supervillain, Vreekill's bald head and functional costume signify him clearly as a "mad scientist." There is no exploration of the psychology that leads Vreekill to use his discovery for the pursuit of crime:

> With my machine I can become the most powerful man in the world! I can hold it as a club over those who deal in steel constructions.[42]

This is clearly not a sociological view of the roots of crime. The mythology underlying the text is that of the Old Testament, and, most specifically, the Temptation and the Fall. Vreekill is a prototype for many "Fallen" characters which Batman and other superheroes have encountered through the years—the Joker, Two-Face, Lex Luthor, Doctor Doom, Magneto, Ozymandias. All are corrupted by power, and power in the particular form of knowledge. "Ye shall be as gods, knowing good and evil," promises the serpent in Genesis. Barthes, in the essay "Myth Today"[43] and elsewhere, has highlighted many of the ways in which mythology can be used to represent culture as nature and thus "explain" as natural and inevitable many of the social and political structures of our society. "Batman and Robin visit the 1940 New York World's Fair" mythologizes the idea of crime, dramatizing the individual's criminal potential through the decisions taken from a position of power (i.e., knowledge). If history is to be understood as a progress toward Utopia, a significant tension can be adduced between superheroes (assisting this process) and villains (thwarting the Utopia builders, or "those who deal in steel constructions").

This mythologizing of the dangers of scientific knowledge is one of the mainstream currents of science fiction, from *Frankenstein* through to the famous Spock/McCoy reason/conscience conflict in *Star Trek* (a conflict which is spuriously resolved by the *deus ex machina* of Kirk's overarching "humanity," which embraces such contradictions and thereby resolves them). However, the more traditional split of knowledge and conscience that is signified by comic book supervillains cannot be so easily reconciled within the confines of the genre. A villain such as the Joker continues year after year, story after story, sabotaging the social order in an endless treadmill of destruction, which Batman struggles to control and contain.

Such would be the "preferred" reading of a text such as "The World's Fair." Clearly, a number of contradictory readings can be advanced. For example, certain oppositional readings identify with the personal exploitation of knowledge and power espoused by Dr. Vreekill. In an early superhero text such as this, however, the difference between the preferred and oppositional readings remains clear-cut. The weight of moral decisions and their preferred interpretation are clearly inscribed in the construction of the narrative. Kane's art signals moments of moral decision very precisely, often by the use of a circular panel framing the character or the character's head. This is a narrative device akin to a film director's "holding" on a close-up, but the tight circular story panel serves the additional function of breaking up the visual flow of the narrative, acting as a giant-sized full-stop.

Such visual punctuation abstracts the contents of the panel from their context, a process which is helped on its way by the absence of any detailed backgrounds—although the panel in which Bruce and Dick agree to investigate the first bridge collapse shows both figures against a schematized New York skyline, the city they have pledged themselves to defend. The central conflict of the story is resolved in two circular panels on the last page. They are placed one above the other, although separated in narrative space by the two intervening panels that form the left-hand side of the bottom row. The upper circular panel shows Vreekill in the act of grabbing at the bare electric wire, destroyed by the forces he intended to exploit. The lower panel shows the triumphant Bruce and Dick, delivering their final homily on the virtues of the World's Fair. The reader is invited to participate, along with the story's heroes, in the alliance of knowledge and social order that the narrative has made visible.

NOTES

1. Superman has been in continuous publication since 1938, Batman since 1939. Wonder Woman has been in continuous publication since 1941, barring a short hiatus in 1986–87.
2. *The Comics Journal*, edited since 1976 by Gary Groth, is the premier fan publication—its intellectual range and acuity of critical discourse are very impressive. *The New Comics* (Berkley Books, 1989) is a collection of interviews with notable artists and writers from the pages of the *Journal*.
3. When does a comic become a graphic novel? "The most useful distinction in comics is to be drawn between periodical and book-style publication. A periodical is comprised of issues, one of which always replaces the previous one. The title is continuous, but one issue always differs from another. A book is a publication in which the title and issue are the same. A new printing does not require abandoning the contents in favor of a new set. A graphic novel is a unified comic art form that exploits the relationship between the two: book and periodical" (Steve Edgell, private communication to the author, 1992).
4. Batman first appeared in *Detective Comics* #27, 1939; Wonder Woman in *All Star Comics* #8, 1941; the Sub-Mariner in *Marvel Comics* #1, 1939. The Arrow first appeared in *Funny Pages* #21 (1938), Shock Gibson in *Speed Comics* (October 1939), and the Masked Marvel in *Keen Detective Funnies* #11 (1940).

5. Captain America first appeared in *Captain America Comics* #1 (1941). The story is reproduced in Jules Feiffer's *The Great Comic Book Heroes*.
6. The Golden Age lasted from 1938 to 1949 [Reynolds's precise end-date here is not universally agreed upon—*eds*.]. The Silver Age is agreed as having begun in 1956; there is no agreed terminal date, but most would accept that it lasted until around 1967–70.
7. Plastic Man also survived the slump of the early fifties, but never cashed in on the new impetus of the Silver Age: publication ceased in 1956.
8. EC's major horror titles were *Vault of Horror*, *Haunt of Fear*, and *Crypt of Terror* (later *Tales from the Crypt*), all launched in 1950.
9. Although *Seduction of the Innocent* was published in 1954, Wertham had been campaigning against violence in comic books since the late forties. In 1948 he presided over a New York Department of Hospitals' symposium called "The Psychopathology of Comic Books."
10. The hearings took place as part of the Senate Subcommittee to Investigate Juvenile Delinquency in the United States.
11. Flash reappeared in *Showcase* #4, October 1956. This date is usually regarded as the beginning of the Silver Age.
12. The Green Lantern returned in *Showcase* #22, October 1959.
13. Supergirl premiered in *Action Comics* #252, May 1959.
14. The Justice League of America first appeared in *The Brave and the Bold* #28, March 1960. The super-team acquired its own title in October 1960.
15. The Fantastic Four made their debut in *Fantastic Four* #1, November 1961.
16. Spider-Man made his first appearance in *Amazing Fantasy* #15, August 1962—the very last scheduled issue before this title was axed. *Amazing Spider-Man* #1 followed in March 1963.
17. The X-Men made their debut in *X-Men* #1, September 1963.
18. The Mighty Thor first appeared in *Journey into Mystery* #83, August 1962. In March 1966 the comic was retitled *The Mighty Thor*, though keeping the numbered sequence from the earlier title.
19. The Incredible Hulk burst on the scene in *The Incredible Hulk* #1, May 1962.
20. Captain America returned to action in *Avengers* #4, May 1964. The Sub-Mariner had resurfaced earlier, in *Fantastic Four* #4, May 1962.
21. The Neal Adams Green Lantern/Green Arrow sequence runs from *Green Lantern* #76 to #89.
22. See, for example, "Drawing the Line" by Buddy Saunders, *The Comics Journal* #138, 109–122.
23. Quoted in "The Man of Tomorrow and the Boys of Yesterday," by Dennis Dooley, from *Superman at Fifty! The Persistence of a Legend!*, ed. Dennis Dooley and Gary Engle (Octavia Press, 1987), 26.
24. *Action Comics* #1 was cover-dated June 1938. This comic is reprinted in *The Smithsonian Book of Comic Book Comics*, ed. Michael Barrier and Martin Williams (Smithsonian Institution Press and Harry N. Abrams, 1981), 19–31. A very similar story appears in *Superman* #1, Summer 1939. This story is reproduced in Feiffer's *The Great Comic Book Heroes*.
25. *Action Comics* #1, page 1.
26. *Action Comics* #1, page 5.
27. *Action Comics* #1, page 4.
28. *Action Comics* #1, page 10.
29. See for example *The Golden Bough*, by Sir James Frazer (abridged ed., Macmillan, 1957), 277–279.
30. The first appearance of the Joker is in *Batman* #1, Spring 1940.
31. This long-running dispute eventually led to the cancellation of *Captain Marvel* and the

whole Marvel Family line of comics in 1953. There have been several unsuccessful attempts to revive the original Captain Marvel since. Marvel Comics' Captain Marvel is a completely different character, who (paradoxically) was much closer in conception to Superman than Fawcett's character ever was.

32. By 1942, there were 143 different comic book titles being published in the United States, with an annual industry revenue of some fifteen million dollars.
33. Several of these characters have appeared in comic book form. Pulp hero Doc Savage appeared in his own comic in May 1940, when longtime Doc Savage publisher Street and Smith decided to enter the comic book market. The Green Hornet and Captain Midnight—both heroes of the radio serials—entered the comic medium in 1940 and 1942 respectively.
34. Claude Lévi-Strauss, *The View from Afar* (Peregrine, 1987), 259–260.
35. *Fantastic Four* #10, page 5.
36. Quoted in Bob Kane, *Batman & Me* (Eclipse Books, 1989), 44.
37. This was a special Batman edition by Kane and Finger, published in the 1940 issue of *New York World's Fair Comics*. The story is reprinted in Kane's *Batman & Me*, 58–70.
38. "New York World's Fair," p. 1.
39. "New York World's Fair," p. 13.
40. "New York World's Fair," p. 13.
41. "New York World's Fair," p. 1.
42. "New York World's Fair," p. 8.
43. Ronald Barthes, *Mythologies* (Hill and Wang, 1972), 109–159.

The Revisionary Superhero Narrative

GEOFF KLOCK

Reprinted with permission from *How to Read Superhero Comics and Why*, 25–52, by the Continuum International Publishing Company. Geoff Klock © 2006.

IN HIS INTRODUCTION TO *BATMAN: THE DARK KNIGHT RETURNS*, ALAN MOORE gives the reader the first hint toward understanding the relation that this work has with the complex tradition in which it participates. He writes:

> [Miller] has taken a character whose every trivial and incidental detail is graven in stone on the hearts and minds of comic fans that make up his audience and managed to dramatically redefine the character without contradicting one jot of the character's mythology. Yes, Batman is still Bruce Wayne, Alfred is still his butler and Commissioner Gordon is still the chief of police, albeit just barely. There is still a young sidekick named Robin, along with a batmobile, a batcave and a utility belt. The Joker, Two-Face and the Catwoman are still in evidence amongst the roster of villains. Everything is exactly the same, except for the fact that it's all totally different.[1]

Batman: The Dark Knight Returns is the first work in the history of superhero comics that attempts a synthesis of forty-five years of preceding Batman history in one place. Prose summaries giving a sense of how the Dark Knight has been portrayed over the decades have already been written.[2] To avoid redundancy, let me cite one example of Batman's contradictory portrayal as emblematic. The adventures of a superhero are published serially, and thus continuity is established from episode to episode, as in television. Unlike television, however, the serial adventures of individual superheroes have been running for decades, and as fictional characters these heroes do not age. Batman, for example, has remained a perennially young twenty-nine-year-old since his appearance in 1939, even though the environment in which he fights has changed month by month to remain contemporary.

While certain writers and artists have had long runs with a single character, each superhero has had a number of different writers and artists over its run, crossing decades in American history. Since no single creator is essential to the continuation of any given character across the run of a series, many successful superhero titles are still in publication. Comic books are open-ended and can never be definitively completed, as even canceled titles might be revived and augmented by creators. This creates a number of interesting paradoxes that the revisionary superhero narrative will deal with uniquely, as we will see. The reader is given to understand, for example, that the Batman fighting crime in 1939 saying, "Well, Robin, he was a pilot during the war"; the cherry, goofy, campy 1960s Batman reciting the proverbial "Good job, old chum" (the basis for the Adam West *Batman* television show); and the solitary, grim, nearly psychotic, nocturnal 1980s Batman who watches Ronald Reagan on television are one and the same continuous character. Frank Miller's *Dark Knight Returns* is a radical move in the history of the superhero narrative because it is the first work that tries to compose a story that makes sense of its history, rather than mechanically adding another story to the Batman folklore. It must participate in the tradition in order to be recognized as a Batman story, but it consciously organizes that tradition in such a way as to comment on forty-five years of Batman comic books. This serves to complicate the assumptions and structure of that tradition. This is why, as Alan Moore notes, every aspect of the Batman that every reader knows so well finds expression here. This reworking organizes the Batman canon's contradictory parts into a coherent whole.

The Dark Night Returns is one of the most important works in the tradition of superhero narratives because it is the first strong misreading of comic book history, specifically the history of Batman. Miller's work, and some of the work of those around him, can be located near Harold Bloom's concept of revisionary literature, which Bloom describes as "a re-aiming or a looking-over-again, leading to a re-esteeming or a re-estimating. The revisionist strives to *see* again, so as to *esteem* and *estimate* differently, so as to *aim* 'correctively.'"[3] Bloom's theory of revisionism is useful in understanding the way recent superhero narratives function, but the important moments will be where superhero comic books differ, rather than line up, with theories of poetry and other literature. An analysis of *The Dark Knight Returns* will serve as a good introduction to, and paradigm for, the way in which recent superhero narratives function, as it was one of the first, and still one of the strongest, superhero misprisions.

One difference from Bloom's understanding of poetry may already be asserted. Miller is not writing a poem within the determination of strong poetic influence, but writing a character whose aspects are literally formed by his predecessors' works: he cannot come to the character fresh, because everything his predecessors on *Batman* wrote, on some level, did happen to the character he is writing. Batman, like many superheroes, wears his tradition on his sleeve. The writer of an established superhero finds not only anxiety in past reading (which determines present writing), but in the very *bricolage* of the character's previous narrative. Poetic influence, which Bloom primarily identifies in stylistic terms, often emerges in superhero comic books as elements of the ostensible diegetic narrative. Miller's task differs from, say, strong poetry in America, because his misreading of Batman is an organization of a host of contradictory weak readings of a single, overdetermined character rather than an overcoming of previous strong effort within a poetic tradition; his effort in organizing them is to converge those weak readings into his own strong vision.

The first aspect of Miller's reorganization is an intense level of realism, the hallmark of his gritty, hard-boiled work on Marvel's *Daredevil* in the early 1980s (more influenced by the novels of Raymond Chandler and Dashiell Hammett than by fantasy/science fiction).[4] This trend reaches its culmination in *The Dark Knight Returns*, in which the Bat-mobile is sensibly reconceived as a Bat-Tank, and Arkham Asylum, usually portrayed as some kind of medieval dungeon, becomes an actual hospital for the mentally disturbed, complete with doctors and nurses. Miller forces the world of Batman to make sense. On a broad scale, this means introducing realistic time into comic books in a way never done before. First, Batman has aged, a move unheard of in a genre where characters persist for decades untouched by the passage of time. *The Dark Knight Returns* is set in Batman's "future," where he has been in retirement for ten years and is now in his mid-fifties. Gotham City, which in the history of comics has been a kind of abstract fictional stand-in for any urban setting, is given a temporal and spatial specificity very much in line with the New York City of the mid-1980s: the Twin Towers are a clear part of the city's skyline, and Ronald Reagan is president of the United States. So, while the reader is intended to understand *The Dark Knight Returns* as taking place in Batman's "future," it is a future relative to his age. The setting is in fact the contemporaneous 1980s. Miller accomplishes this level of realism—taking time seriously—without breaking from the superhero tradition of always setting the story in contemporary urban America. Aging Batman is the only way to accomplish this and still make narrative sense.

Miller also finds ways to synthesize Batman's confused and contradictory history on a smaller scale. Batman appears throughout *The Dark Knight Returns* in a number of different uniforms, with various Bat-Shield chest emblems reflecting forty-five years of costume design. In one amusing example, readers are finally given an explanation for one of the confusing aspects of the garb, the eye-catching yellow Bat-Shield on a uniform meant to blend in with shadows. When Batman takes a rifle shot to the chest, which any reader assumes would kill him instantly, it reveals metal shielding. Batman says. "Why do you think I wear a target on my chest—can't armor my head,"[5] and with that one line a thirty-year mystery dissolves as every reader runs mentally through previous stories, understanding that plate as having always been there. This example of Miller's realism is paradigmatic of his revisionary strategy and is more clearly illustrated by the way he incorporates violence into his narrative.

Miller has often stated that the only thing contemporary comics have learned from *The Dark Knight Returns* is the extreme level of violence it presents.[6] His own work is not so much violent as it is more graphic and more realistic about the violence that has always inhabited superhero narratives. With *The Dark Knight Returns*, the reader is forced to confront what has been going on for years between the panels. Miller's realism operates as a kind commentary on a genre that has treated its inherent violence with kid gloves. Take, for example, the fact that Batman has in the course of his history gotten into many fights in which he is outnumbered and his opponents are armed with guns. Using only a Batarang and his fists, Batman manages to defeat them all without breaking a sweat. Miller never treats his hero so gently—his Batman is almost always wounded, sometimes badly, and the Batarang is reconceived as a kind of bat-shaped throwing star that disarms by slicing into the forearm, rather than its former, sillier portrayal as a boomerang that disarms criminals by knocking weapons out of their hands. The strength of Miller's portrayal leaves readers with the impression that all of Batman's fights must have been of this kind, but that they have been reading a watered-down version of the way things "really happened." It is important to note that powerful reading in superhero narratives often functions in this way, making all other readings appear to have "fallen away" from the strongest version that is retroactively constituted as always already true.

In [Umberto] Eco's oneiric climate [as described in his essay "The Myth of Superman"], strong work comes to define truth, as narrative continuity is fuzzy at best. Miller's revisionary realism is only another version of what comic books often accomplish in the narrative, a literal revising of the facts of a comic book character's history on the basis of recent interpretation. Take, for example, the design of Superman's home planet, Krypton. The rendering of a "futuristic" world looks very different today than the rendering done in 1938. Today, however, Krypton is portrayed anew and is expected to be understood by readers as the true rendition of how Krypton *has always* looked. Miller's writing is very conscious of this process and actively strives to participate in comic book tradition, invoking various recognizable aspects in such a way as to recast readers' understanding of what they have seen before. Harold Bloom's remarks on Milton are amusingly relevant. Substituting Miller for Milton, the reader may conceive that—within its field of signifiers—*The Dark Knight*

Returns has "the true priority of *interpretation*, the powerful reading that insists on its own uniqueness and its own accuracy. Troping on his forerunners' tropes, [Miller] compels us to read as he reads, and to accept his stance and vision as our origin, his time as true time."[7]

Miller's work internalizes not only fictional determination but also intertextual/historical influence. Early in *The Dark Knight Returns*, Bruce Wayne finds the film *The Mark of Zorro* on television,[8] and the reader is given to understand that this was the movie from which Bruce Wayne and his parents were returning when his parents were killed. Batman creator Bob Kane has admitted that *The Mark of Zorro* (1920) was an influence in the creation of his superhero.[9] Miller makes the trail of influence in Bruce Wayne's creation of the Batman persona within the fictional history parallel the influence on Kane's portrayal of the character. This is only the first example of how *The Dark Knight Returns* engages and synthesizes not only the fictional tradition of its main character but also the very real history that has surrounded the comic book as a medium.

One key historical intertext for Miller's work is Dr. Fredric Wertham's notorious book, *Seduction of the Innocent*. Published in 1954, the 397-page opus condemned the comic book industry for degrading American values, and for spreading social and moral perversion. His words on superhero comic books still echo in the genre today:

> What is the social meaning of these supermen, superwomen, superlovers, superboys, supergirls, super-ducks, super-mice, super-magicians, super-safe crackers? How did Nietzsche get into the nursery? . . . Superheroes undermine respect for the law and hardworking decent citizens.[10]

He had this illuminating passage specifically devoted to Batman:

> Only someone ignorant of the fundamentals of psychology and the psychopathology of sex can fail to realize a subtle atmosphere of homoeroticism which pervades the adventures of the mature "Batman" and his young friend "Robin" . . . Robin is a handsome ephebic boy, usually shown in his uniform with bare legs . . . he often stands with his legs spread, the genital region discreetly evident.[11]

Bruce Wayne and Dick Grayson's life in Wayne Manor is described as "the wish dream of two homosexuals living together." The shine on this observation was only made to sparkle more brightly in light of the Adam West *Batman* show that graced the airwaves in the 1960s. Since that time, these terms have colored the impression of Batman for the non-comic book reading public and have forced on the defensive those fans reading the more "serious" Denny O'Neil/Neal Adams Batman of the 1970s, readers who viewed this perspective as insulting, but had no terms in which to reply.[12]

Miller responds to the instincts of mainstream fandom and "refutes" these passé charges without denying Wertham his observation that homoeroticism plays a role in the superhero story. He synthesizes both perspectives, both aspects of the comic book tradition, while remaining inside the framework of the Batman folklore. His conciliatory (and revisionary) move is to cast a girl in the role of the new Robin. The original Robin, Dick Grayson, makes no appearance in *The Dark Knight Returns*; Bruce cryptically informs Commissioner Gordon that they have not spoken for seven years. The second Robin, Jason Todd (whose uniform is seen in a glass case at the center of the Batcave), died, and because Batman feels responsible for Todd's death, he retired ten years ago. Carrie Kelly, the new Robin, is picked up in the course of *The Dark Knight Returns*, and through her gender provides interesting commentary on the role of her young male predecessors.

Several scenes are particularly germane to this discussion. The first occurs after Carrie Kelly is initially brought to the Batcave with an almost mortally wounded Batman. She has saved his life (albeit barely) and tagged along in the Batmobile with conscious plans of becoming the next Robin (she has already crafted a uniform by hand). A young girl waiting with anxiety to discover if her hero will live, she is placed in the role of a concerned wife or lover. Two small panels at the bottom right of the right-hand page show a large hand being placed on her shoulder as she turns her head: the page turn reveals a full-page spread (the comic book equivalent of "music swells"), which is not a reunion kiss, suggested by the lead-in drama, but a completely non-sexual embrace, almost a parody of the lover's embrace.[13] In another scene, Robin nearly falls to her doom but is rescued by Batman. Safe from death but still hovering over the water, she straddles Batman's crotch and clutches to him tightly. Here, the female Robin is cast in the role of the damsel in distress (cf. Superman's characteristic swoop downward to catch the recurrently falling Lois Lane), but again the result, which, like the earlier embrace, could be read as sexual (and in the damsel in distress role would be), simply defies the reader to interpret it in this manner.[14] It is difficult to find sexual tension in Batman's "Good soldier. Good soldier."[15]

In both these scenes, the setup hints at the possibility of a sexual reading, then frustrates the fulfillment of this desire. Rather than provide more sexual tension (as a similar situation might in early Hollywood films, which often coded sexual moments in such a way as to be suggestive while avoiding the censors), the dissonance between the erotic frame with which the reader is provided and the ostensible content short circuits the sexual reading altogether.

Those who are familiar with Wertham's book or its echoes—ubiquitous in popular culture parodies of Batman—will be on the lookout for these kinds of homoerotic signifiers and discover Miller toying with them. Casting Robin as a girl places the sexual relation of Batman and Robin in a more socially acceptable light, as if the sexuality can and thus will be brought out into the open, then still denies that the sexuality is there. The reader is invited to conclude that it never was, that age is the obvious barrier to this reading of the Batman-Robin relationship, not homosexuality. The one moment that does suggest sexuality in Robin comes when she sees the corpses left behind by the Joker. Batman narrates, "A tiny hand tightens its grip on my arm . . . A girl of thirteen breathes in sharply, suddenly, her innocence lost,"[16] but this must be read in the context of Batman's relationship to the Joker, and the Joker's relation to sexuality within the narrative.

Having evaded Wertham's claims for Batman and Robin, Miller is not so naive as to insist that homoeroticism is entirely absent from the Batman narrative, and in fact provides for it a consequential role in *The Dark Knight Returns*. The final joke on Wertham is Miller's ability to avoid homoeroticism in the Batman-Robin relationship while at the same time raising the question, transferring it to the antagonistic relationship between Batman and the Joker. Miller caters to instincts that Batman and Robin's relationship is not a thinly disguised homoerotic fantasy, but also gives Wertham his due by not invoking a reactionary position (as C. S. Lewis did in regard to Shakespeare's sonnets), that the homoerotic has no place at all.

The Joker's role in *The Dark Knight Returns* brings homoeroticism out into the open for one of the first times in mainstream superhero comic books. Like Batman, the Joker has been the subject of various disparate portrayals in the Batman titles and has gone through an equal amount of instability regarding his history and character. A disturbed murderer in the 1940s and early 1950s, he becomes silly rather than evil after the crackdown on violence in comics in 1954 (led by Wertham's book), then slowly returns to his earlier viciousness as comics begin to recover. Miller's Joker has the personality of an aging, degenerate rock star, as murderous as he is effete. *The Dark Knight Returns* portrays the Joker in a role that synthesizes these dual and opposing personae. The dialogue between hero and villain unearths Wertham's general charges of homoeroticism in Batman, and the shift from Batman/Robin to Batman/Joker makes the claim significantly more interesting and complex. The effect is not, as some have claimed, simply a homophobic attempt to align homosexuality with evil, but rather provides a subterranean connection between two characters who seem, on the surface, to be diametrically opposed.

Sketching out a specific level of connection between antagonists in this work, however, cannot be appreciated without at least mentioning the more general part Batman's villains play in the series. Every major member of the villain's gallery operates as a kind of reflection of some aspect of Batman's personality or role so that an understanding of one of the villains always sheds light on Batman himself. Some examples, expanding Reynolds's observations on the Penguin and Two-Face,[17] will make this clear. Two-Face is always given at least some part in every major Batman story because of his parallel relation to Batman: a successful upper-class socialite, the district attorney of Gotham City had half his face scarred by acid thrown when he was prosecuting the mob. This trauma resulted in a split personality and an obsession with duality and the number two. Bruce Wayne, upon seeing his parents murdered, suffered a similar personality split: the creation of the Batman alter ego. The Penguin reflects the dark side of Bruce Wayne's millionaire capitalist playboy routine. Mr. Freeze points out the dark side of Bruce Wayne's utter lack of emotion as Batman. The shape-shifter, Clayface, suggests the anti-essential nature of the Batman/Bruce Wayne relationship, both of which are seen as personae (Batman to scare criminals, Wayne to cover up Batman under the role of a disaffected rich fop). Poison Ivy uses criminal activity (and Batman's vigilante status is, of course, illegal) for a good cause, ecology. The Scarecrow, whose entire existence is devoted to fear, recalls that the intention of the Batman persona is the edge provided by terror. The Mad Hatter's mind control reflects the extremities of Batman's methods of coercion. The Riddler parodies Batman's role as the great detective. Man-Bat provides another example of a Jekyll-and-Hyde transformation that, like Batman, only emerges at night. The Ventriloquist questions, in terms of split personality, who is the puppet and who is the puppeteer. Even a ludicrously silly villain like the Calendar Man, who commits theme crimes once a month, reflects Batman's monthly publishing schedule. Miller actually conceives of Ronald Reagan, who wants Batman brought down, in terms of his reflective relation to the Dark Knight: a spokesman for the president informs the news that "it's noisy, all right. That big cape and pointy ears—it's great show biz. And you know the president knows his show biz."[18] The political similarity between the two is a major theme of *The Dark Knight Returns*. Miller is very aware of this function of Batman's villains and draws the reader's attention to it early. Confronting Batman face-to-face (as it were), Two-Face asks him what he sees: "I see a reflection, Harvey. A reflection."[19] Under this schema, any understanding of the Joker—violent, insane, or sexually deviant—will reflect an aspect of Batman.

The Joker is clearly in some kind of dormant state at Arkham Asylum, watching television in a common room without his trademark smile—until he hears news reports of Batman's return to the streets. As the smile slowly grows, his only reaction is to say, "Darling"[20] (by which the Joker will refer to Batman throughout *The Dark Knight Returns*). Claiming rehabilitation, he appears on a kind of David Letterman show (along with Dr. Ruth Westheimer). Dr. Wolper, the Joker's psychotherapist, claims, "My patient is a victim of Batman's psychosis," and that the nature of this psychosis is "sexual repression, of course."[21] "We must not restrain ourselves," says the Joker, as he begins his killing spree by kissing the sex therapist, poisoning her.[22]

In a later apostrophe to Batman, remarking to himself that he no longer keeps track of how many people he has killed, the Joker coyly notes, "But you do. And I love you for it."[23] Were this sexuality only found in the Joker it would suggest a simple connection between sex ("deviant" sexuality) and evil, but Batman's dealings reveal a complex dynamic at work. Earlier in the narrative, Batman and Two-Face crash through a window together: Batman narrates: "We tumble like lovers,"[24] and the Joker's intriguing combination of feminine and masculine signifiers—the delicate application of makeup, a "tough guy" build, speech affectations, aggressive physical violence—must be seen in light of the fact that the issue devoted to him opens with Batman dressed as a woman.[25] As Batman descends on his most hated villain, the reader is privy to this piece of Batman's interior monologue, ostensibly about finally killing the Joker but suggestive of something else:

> Can you see it, Joker? Feels to me ... like it's written all over my face. I've lain awake nights ... planning it ... picturing it ... endless nights ... considering every possible method ... treasuring each imaginary moment ... from the beginning, I knew ... that there's nothing wrong with you ... that I can't fix ... with my hands. ...[26]

The final battle between the two occurs in the Joker's most often-used site, the carnival. A skirmish in the House of Mirrors suggests that the two are dark reflections of each other, and the Joker's death, the consummation of the Batman-Joker relationship referred to in the passage above, occurs, appropriately, in the Tunnel of Love. All this serves to address Wertham's earlier claims about the subtext of superhero literature; in addressing nearly fifty years of comic book history, in trying to make sense of a chaotic tradition, Miller cannot avoid it. He is able to write a Batman without the camp and silliness of the Adam West series (the Dick Sprang years of the comic book) but while still understanding the character as operating over a background informed by a homoerotic subtext. By moving the focus from Robin to the Joker, he swerves from understanding this subtext as specifically linked to superhero narratives (through the sidekick, an archetypal role in superhero stories), suggesting, rather, that it operates in all antagonistic narratives: a relatively pedestrian illustration of the widely accepted Freudian thesis on the link between sexuality and violence (regardless of sexual preference). Miller brings together hero and villain, and hints at the collapse between them. This thesis is reinforced by the observation that, moments before his death, the Joker's word bubbles take on the color and shape used to distinguish Batman's speech. [. . .]

The collapse between antagonists, however, only points to a larger, more dangerous, pattern of collapse between Batman and his more shadowy reflective antagonist: the political. *The Dark Knight Returns* is also known for overtly engaging political issues, but this observation misses the point that Miller makes in bringing political realities to Batman: comic books have always had a political dimension, usually supporting whatever hegemonic discourse (most often conservative) the decade at hand had to offer. (It is interesting to note in this context that the father of all superhero stories—*Action Comics* #1 (1938), the first appearance of Superman—involved Superman stopping fifth columnists trying to get America "embroiled" in the war in Europe.)[27] Like the issues of homoeroticism and violence, Miller wants to foreground a submerged aspect of comic book tradition. He chooses, along with cold war Reagan-era politics, a more structural aspect of superhero politics: its fascistic tendencies.

Three aspects of superhero comic books are at work here. First, superheroes, and Batman especially, always rely on physical violence and intimidation to fight crime. Batman himself is not unwilling to be physically brutal to acquire information, for example, and often relies on the threat or implied threat of violence to keep criminals in line. Second, it is often the case that the superhero is a kind of criminal—a vigilante. In these two respects, many masked crime fighters differ from the Ku Klux Klan only in that they are usually afforded socially acceptable status on a large scale.[28] As masked men who take the law into their own hands, superheroes come dangerously close to some of the great evils in American history. Third, superheroes most often occupy a reactionary role, traditionally emerging only to meet a threat to the status quo. Large-scale social changes are a supervillain signature, manifesting when one wishes to take over the world or, alternatively, to destroy all human life, allowing nature to grow without humanity's ecological poisoning, for example. However well intentioned, these kinds of moves almost always mark someone whom the superhero must stop, even in the case of a fellow superhero. Miller takes into account each of these aspects of the comic book tradition, especially the first two (Alan Moore's *Watchman* focuses on the third). Where in most superhero stories these issues are usually accepted as assumptions, *The Dark Knight Returns* foregrounds their role as determiners of the text, and complicates them.

Violence in Miller's work has already been discussed in the context of his revisionary realism, but it should be kept in mind when understanding Batman's status as a vigilante, also highlighted in *The Dark Knight Returns*. The work is interspersed with debates about the level of danger this kind of activity entails, and the degree to which Batman himself is a hero or villain. In the context of Batman's overdetermination by his multivectored history, and Miller's organization of that history, the question of Batman's signification is raised in a television debate. An anti-Batman spokesperson debates publicly with Lana Lang, once a love interest for Clark Kent, and thus debating the more idealistic view of superheroes:

> Lana: One almost expects to see the Bat-Signal striking the side of one of Gotham's Twin Towers. Yes, he gave us quite a night.
> Morrie: Sure kept the hospitals busy.
> Lana: Yes, Morrie, but I think it is a mistake to think of this in purely political terms. Rather, I regard it as a symbolic resurgence of the common man's will to resist. A rebirth of the American fighting spirit.
> Morrie: Ease up, Lana. The only thing he signifies is an aberrant psychotic force, morally bankrupt, politically hazardous, reactionary, paranoid. . . .[29]

The difficulty is, of course, that Batman has at times signified all of these things. Here, Miller allows Batman's interpretations to engage in dialectic rather than choosing a single perspective. Once again, Miller complicates a key assumption of the Batman tradition: his vigilante, and thus illegal, status. Unlike readers of the comic books that came before, Miller's reader cannot wholeheartedly agree with Batman's methods, but is instead invited to question his extremity.

Batman's disregard for civil rights arises only three pages after the debate quoted above. As Batman questions a suspect whom he has already left in a neck brace and crutches, the following Clint Eastwoodesque exchange takes place:

> Batman: You're going to tell me everything you know, sooner or later. If it's later—I won't mind.
> Man: No!—Stay back—I got rights. [Batman throws him through a closed window onto a fire escape]
> Batman: You've got rights. Lots of rights. Sometimes I count them just to make myself feel crazy. But right now you've got a piece of glass shoved into a major artery in your arm. Right now you're bleeding to death. Right now I'm the only one in the world who can get you to a hospital in time.[30]

Batman's obsession with control and order, his disregard for civil rights, and his use of violence to force others, though often criminals, into submission to his will point to comic books' (sometimes alluring) flirtation with fascism. Illegal, physically violent coercion plays a role in all superhero stories; it is practically a genre convention. Miller questions its role, highlighting an aspect of those narratives in which every reader has, perhaps unwillingly, participated.

The implied threat of large-scale fascistic control must necessarily underlie superhero stories because of a fundamental power differential. In *Leviathan*, Thomas Hobbes writes that the reason men can bond together in equality to create a civilization is that all men are basically equal: where one excels in physical strength, another may excel in mental ability. The power differences among men are never so great that a few might not band together to stop one.[31] In the world of superhero comics, this is simply not the case. It is conceivable that the seven core members of DC's flagship superhero team, the Justice League of America (which includes Batman, Superman, Wonder Woman, and the Green Lantern), could reduce the world to rubble in a matter of days. So even in regard to "do-gooders," the threat of paternalism cum fascism is always present. Other superhero works, like *Squadron Supreme* and *Kingdom Come*, deal with this aspect of superhero tradition more specifically. In *The Dark Knight Returns*, it remains more of an implied threat, but clearly factors into the notable absence of other superheroes in such a global narrative.

Miller's adumbrated explanation of where all the superheroes have gone suggests the reactionary politics of McCarthy-era America, when those who refused to come before the committee investigating communism were blacklisted. More specifically, it recalls Wertham's report, which called the entire comic book industry into question and caused the cancellation of more than a few titles. Superman's fragmentary internal monologue gives only the briefest hints of what happened in Miller's fictional world, but clearly Batman's role must be understood in this context:

> The rest of us learned to cope. The rest of us recognized the danger—of the endless envy of those not blessed. Diana [Wonder Woman] went back to her people. Hal [Jordan: The Green Lantern] went to the stars.[32]

> They'll kill us if they can, Bruce. Every year they grow smaller. Every year they hate us more. We must not remind them that giants walk the earth.[33]

> You were the one they used against us, Bruce. The one who played it rough. When the noise started from the parents' groups and the subcommittee called us in for questioning—you were the one who laughed . . . that scary laugh of yours. . . . "[S]ure we're criminals," you said. "[W]e've always been criminals. We have to be criminals."[34]

I gave them my obedience and my invisibility. They gave me a license and let us live. No. I don't like it. But I get to save lives—and the media stays quiet. But now the storm is growing again. They'll hunt us down again—because of you.[35]

After *Seduction of the Innocent*, the criminal and subversive aspects of comic books were played down but not eradicated. Batman, perhaps the most rebellious of the superheroes, is calling attention to himself again and ignoring the rules, just as Miller's work ignores the Wertham report and the "Comics Code Authority" (the comic book industry's reaction to Wertham, similar to the Production Code Administration which was designed to protect "values and decency" in Hollywood in the 1930s and 1940s).[36] Miller's work consistently flouts the principles of the code, and is thus the point at which comic books become more interesting for adult readers. Miller puts himself in the position of Batman: Batman's indictment of Superman and the subservience he now stands for is Miller's indictment of the comic book industry for crumbling under the weight of the charges in *Seduction of the Innocent*. [It should be noted that Wertham's work did not automatically result in the founding of the Comics Code Authority, and in fact Wertham disapproved of the Code. Also, though Wertham certainly attacked the idea of the superhero, the genre no longer dominated the comic book market at the time of *Seduction of the Innocent* in 1954. Klock's reading of Miller's intention, however, strikes us as spot-on.—*eds.*]

Miller places this difficult structural observation in the context of Reagan-era politics, and once again raises dual aspects of the Batman folklore: Batman's position is that of both a rebel and a dispenser of a new hegemonic discourse. The one must necessarily imply the other because superheroes are in a position of fighting for a world in which they will no longer have a place, in which they will no longer be needed. A successful rebel is a new hegemony, and the sheer power many superheroes wield threatens that success. Because comic book superheroes are produced serially and always take place in contemporary America, it is possible (if not necessary) for characters to be rebels forever. They can continue to fight threats in each issue but still never approach the total eradication of crime. Miller raises the fact that, at least theoretically, each superhero is fighting for an overall change in society, even if in each individual issue the hero is usually reactionary in maintaining the status quo. The rebel/hegemony split once again nods to Wertham's observation that "superheroes undermine respect for the law and hardworking decent citizens" and the historical observation that comic book politics have consistently aligned themselves with dominant social trends. Superman, father of all superheroes—and thus in metonymy for all standard superhero narratives—enters into this discussion as the spokesperson for the latter. Batman speaks to him in apostrophe: "You've always known just what to say. 'Yes'. . . to anyone with a badge—or a flag."[37] In Miller's conception, Superman is a stooge and soldier for an enfeebled Ronald Reagan who wants to see Batman stopped because his empowerment—and empowerment of others by example—threatens the social control Reagan has in place. Reagan says:

> I like to think I learned everything I know about running this country on my ranch. I know it's corny but I like to think it. And well, it's all well and good, on a ranch I mean, for the horses to be all different colors and sizes, long as they stay inside the fence. It's even okay to have a crazy bronco now and then, does the hands good to break him in. But if that bronco up and kicks the fence out and gets the other horses crazy, well it's bad for business.[38]

The climax of *The Dark Knight Returns* is the final face-off between Batman and Superman. The rebel threatening a new hegemony against the keepers of the old hegemony and the status quo represents the facing-off of the dialectical aspects of comic book tradition. Both of these aspects have been inherent in the superhero comic tradition, of which Miller has been trying to make sense, attempting a synthesis. Here, the two positions literally battle for control, and the implications of the ending are clear in this context. Batman is clearly the winner before collapsing of a heart attack; but his death is only a ruse, and he lives underground. No longer the visible threat he once was, he allows Superman to ignore him as he prepares students to go above and continue the fight. "The American fighting spirit" (as Lana Lang puts it) appears to have been crushed under the heel of reactionary politics, but it is not dead, only dreaming.[39] The rebellious incarnation of the superhero can never be entirely vanquished, but it will always lurk beneath and haunt the genre, no matter how it may try to conform to external standards.

In this respect, *The Dark Knight Returns* can be read as a kind of fable for comic book tradition, warning against the fascistic impulses inherent in superheroics, in which both the reader and Batman come to a realization of the role that this must play in the superhero narrative. *The Dark Knight Returns* once again responds to contradictory aspects of Batman's fictional history or tradition: at times, Batman has been written with the understanding that he is low profile, that at least part of his power comes from his status in Gotham City as a kind of urban legend that the criminal underworld fears is real. Batman comes out only at night and might be some inhuman demon or vampire. At other times, particularly in the sunny 1950s and 1960s, but also randomly throughout his career, this has been forgotten, and the reader has seen

Batman walking the streets in the daytime, shaking hands with the mayor and Commissioner Gordon, marching in parades, even touring college campuses with Robin. Miller acknowledges both mutually exclusive portrayals, presenting Batman's return as Batman-out-in-the-open-with-a-vengeance—a kind of "return of the repressed" 1960s Batman—then reestablishing his urban legend status at the end of the narrative.

When Miller's Batman emerges from retirement, the immediate issue in question is his visibility. The Bat-Tank in particular lacks a certain level of subtlety. Oliver Queen, known to those with knowledge of the DC universe as the Green Arrow, makes the key statement for understanding the Batman's role in the political in this work:

> You've always had it wrong, Bruce . . . giving them such a big target. Sure, you play it mysterious—but it's a loud kind of mysterious, man. Especially lately. You've got to learn how to make those sons of bitches work for you. Look—it's been five years since I blew out of prison—and you know I've kept busy—
>
> [. . .] And they've been covering for me, just like they covered up my escape. Sure, they'd love to frost me . . . long as they can do it without admitting I exist. But you, Bruce—man, they *have* to kill you.[40]

Batman's use of conspicuous force parallels the Reagan-era cold war politics: both Batman and Reagan are "fighting crime" in a conspicuous display of power (the Bat-Tank, Reagan's missile,[41] and "real-life" Reagan's Star Wars missile defense shield) to impress the population they want to control. In Miller's realism, where the subtlety of Batman-as-urban-legend is much more believable, any conspicuous display of power will be used for, or by, the government (e.g., Superman's involvement as a tool of the White House) to drum up fear or to gain support for the government (to fight the Russians in Miller's fictional Corto Maltese subplot; or, on the local level, the anti-Batman stance, used to get support for a new and unpopular police chief). In the course of *The Dark Knight Returns*, Batman becomes the worst sort of reactionary fascist terrorizing people into his control with cheap theatrics.

Batman's former status as an urban legend kept him outside of this kind of political struggle (outside being co-opted by the White House or being used in a "Big Brother will save you from the Batman" campaign). In the urban legend position, a warrant for Batman's arrest would have been laughable to a disbelieving public, as if the police department were trying to rid Gotham City of the bogeyman. In the end, Bruce Wayne realizes that the Batman persona is being manipulated and publicly destroys it. An early, proposed ending for *The Dark Knight Returns*[42] placed Batman on a throne, in a cave surrounded by disciples waiting to return, but the finished version makes better sense in the story's context. Bruce Wayne becomes a teacher, on the floor of the cave, kneeling in plain clothes and speaking to students—some of whom are actually standing above him. The narration tells us he has learned that the world is "plagued by worse than thieves and murderers,"[43] presumably the methods used in fighting them. Miller's text reinstalls Batman as a rebel, as subversive, but with a greater understanding of the power structures involved. As with Shakespeare's, Miller's innovation within his tradition is to allow reflection to result in character development.

Batman's understanding of himself must also be seen in terms of Miller's understanding of tradition. The final page of *The Dark Knight Returns* is a vision of Batman overcoming his previous interpretations. On the narrative level, this occurs as the destruction of the Batman persona because of the "interpretations" of the media and the government. On the level of trope, it means the placement of Miller's Batman for the Batman of other creators (e.g., Bob Kane and Dick Sprang). As Bloom says of Childe Roland, "There is only Roland himself to serve both as hero and villain. . . . The Childe stands in judgment against his own antithetical quest and, however lovingly, against his antithetical precursors as well. . . . He is an interpretation of his precursors' quest."[44] Batman's metatextual act of knowledge is of himself and his tradition, of his razing of preceding visions of the Batman: "Here, in the endless cave, *far past the burnt remains of a crimefighter whose time has passed* . . . it begins here—an army—to bring sense to a world plagued by worse than thieves and murderers."[45] Miller's is the Batman who, in his strength, burns his predecessors "whose time has past" (the Batman of 1939; the Batman of 1968; his own Batman persona within *The Dark Knight Returns*, literally burned in the destruction of Wayne Manor), but who also understands that the Batcave, and the Batman comic book, is "endless," that is, serially published. However strong a reading Miller might perform, "it begins here" rather than ends. Batman will continue to be published in the hands of other writers.

The feeling of finality in the last moment of *The Dark Knight Returns* is juxtaposed with a statement of beginning. Just after calling for a lamp to illuminate the darkness of the cave—a new fire, a new Batman past the burnt remains of the old—he informs his students that "we haven't got all night," but thinks to himself, "That's not true . . . we have years—as many as we need."[46] The last we hear of Batman's pedagogy is Miller's imparting of the fecundity of the Batman mythos to future writers, "First we get a steady supply of water. There's a spring right beneath."[47] Miller's powerful misprision of comic book history ends with a troping of superhero narratives as an "endless cave" with a "spring" of contradictory but rich tradition to be drawn upon "right beneath." *The Dark Knight Returns* becomes the *fons es origo* (the fountainhead and the origin) of the revisionary superhero narrative. Miller himself has gone into Batman's fictional history and selected elements for use in his work, taking many elements a lesser writer would have simply ignored, and made them his own. The reader can understand that in his last act of knowledge on the final page, Miller's Batman, to quote Bloom again on Childe Roland:

> negates the larger part of the poem, a negation that strengthens rather than weakens the poem, because there [he] suffers a unique act of knowledge, an act that clarifies both his personal past and tradition, though at the expense of both presence and present. By "presence" I mean both [his] self-presence [the willing destruction of both the Bruce Wayne and Batman personas past and present], and also the virtual existence of any opposing force in the poem other than [his] internalization of the precursors.[48]

This is what Miller's work is about. Batman (and Miller's) struggle is not to control any villain but to master preceding visions of himself and his tradition. When the new chief of police confronts Commissioner Gordon as to why he supported a vigilante during his tenure, Gordon's words express an understanding of the interpretive process:

> I'm sure you've heard old fossils like me talk about Pearl Harbor, Yindel. Fact is we mostly lie about it. We make it sound like we all leaped to our feet and went after the Axis on the spot. Hell, we were scared. Rumors were flying, we thought the Japanese had taken California. We didn't even have an army. So there we were, lying in bed pulling the sheets over our heads—and there was Roosevelt on the radio, strong and sure, taking fear [read: anxiety] and turning it into a fighting spirit [cf. Lana Lang's description of Batman as the return of the American fighting spirit]. Almost overnight we had our army. We won the war. . . . A few years back a lot of people with a lot of evidence said that Roosevelt knew Pearl Harbor was going to be attacked—and that he let it happen. . . . I couldn't stop thinking how horrible that would be, and how Pearl was what got us off our duffs in time to stop the Axis. But a lot of innocent men died. But we won the war. It bounced back and forth in my head until I realized I couldn't judge it. It was too big. *He* was too big . . .[49]

"I don't see what this has to do with a vigilante," Yindel says. "Maybe you will," is the reply. The relation to Batman is obvious, but in terms of Miller's text, it serves as a statement on the power of the single interpretive (revisionary) stance. There is no stable point from which to pass judgment, no standard other than the strength of the vision—the strength of the personality, be it Batman or Miller. This passage is quoted at length, because it is paradigmatic of a move many revisionist superhero narratives will make, from *Watchmen* to *The Authority*.

The role of fascism, the role of forced control in *The Dark Knight Returns*, is clearly reflexive. Batman's imposition of control over the chaotic streets of Gotham City cannot be seen as distinct from Miller's imposition of control over Batman's chaotic narrative tradition and intertexts.[50] In his battle with Superman, Batman narrates:

> You sold us out, Clark. You gave them the power that should have been ours. Just like your parents taught you to. My parents taught me a different lesson, lying on the street, shaking in deep shock—dying for no reason at all—they showed me that the world only makes sense when you force it to.[51]

Miller's take on the history of the Dark Knight, and on the contradictory tradition of superhero narratives, is that it will only make sense when you force it to. In a psychomachia, the retired "Batman" taunts the aging Wayne, "You are nothing, a hollow shell, a rusty trap that cannot hold me—smoldering, I burn you."[52] Miller holds the chaos of signifiers that is Batman and ultimately shows his character in the cave "far past the burnt remains of a crimefighter whose time has passed." Miller organizes the contradictory signifying field that surrounds the subject of Batman—which includes figures like Wertham and issues as far apart in the American political sphere as fascism and homosexuality—and forms them into a coherent story that is itself a commentary on the history that has come before, as well as on the tradition of the genre. To (mis)quote Bloom on Milton again: "[Miller's] design is wholly definite, and its effect is to reverse literary tradition. . . . The precursors return in [Miller], but only at his will, and they return to be corrected."[53] Every convention that allows superhero narratives to function, and every intertext, is exposed to the reader with a clarity that at once cleans up comic book history and also complicates it. The superhero narratives of any worth that follow *The Dark Knight Returns* can no longer ignore these determiners on the genre, but must confront both comic book tradition and Miller's influential handling of it: the superhero narrative will forever be under the shadow of the bat.

NOTES

1. Alan Moore, "Introduction," *The Dark Knight Returns* (New York: DC Comics, 1986).
2. See Les Daniels, *Batman: The Complete History* (San Francisco: Chronicle Books, 1999).

3. Harold Bloom, *A Map of Misreading* (Oxford: Oxford University Press, 1975), 4 (Bloom's emphasis).
4. Frank Miller, interview with *Writers on Comics Scriptwriting*, ed. Mark Salisbury (London: Titan Books, 1999), 187. I find it useful to separate the superhero narrative from fantasy and science fiction. The former [fantasy] is most often set in a mythical past with a distinct cosmology, whereas the latter [science fiction] is set in the future and often uses science in a completely different manner. The lines are, of course, blurred but some useful distinctions can be made.
5. Frank Miller, Klaus Janson, and Lynn Varley, *Batman: The Dark Knight Returns* (New York: DC Comics, 1986), 51.
6. Miller, "Batman and the Twilight of the Idols: An Interview with Frank Miller," in *The Many Lives of the Batman*, ed. Roberta E. Pearson and William Uricchio (New York: Routledge, 1991), 45.
7. Bloom, *A Map of Misreading*, 132 (Bloom's emphasis).
8. Miller et al., *Batman: The Dark Knight Returns*, 22.
9. Greg S. McCue with Clive Bloom, *Dark Knights: The New Comics in Context* (London: Pluto, 1993), 22.
10. Fredric Wertham, *Seduction of the Innocent* (New York: Rinehart and Company, 1954), 15.
11. Ibid, 191. McCue cites these same passages in *Dark Knights*.
12. See Will Brooker, *Batman Unmasked* (New York: Continuum, 2000), 101–170, for an extremely sensitive and cogent discussion of homophobia, Wertham, and *Batman*.
13. See Miller et al., *The Dark Knight Returns*, 91–92.
14. Ibid., 138.
15. Ibid.
16. Ibid, 140 (Miller's ellipsis).
17. Richard Reynolds, *Superheroes: A Modern Mythology* (Jackson, MS: University Press of Mississippi, 1994), 68.
18. Miller et al., *Batman: The Dark Knight Returns*, 66.
19. Ibid., 55.
20. Ibid., 41.
21. Ibid., 126.
22. Ibid., 127.
23. Ibid., 140.
24. Ibid., 54.
25. Ibid., 106.
26. Ibid., 142 (Miller's ellipses).
27. *Action Comics* #1 (New York: DC Comics, 1938).
28. This description is perhaps more accurate for DC than the Marvel universe: Captain America and the Avengers are not vigilantes, whereas Spider-Man and the X-Men do not enjoy social acceptance.
29. Miller et al., *Batman: The Dark Knight Returns*, 41.
30. Ibid., 44–45.
31. Thomas Hobbes, "Leviathan," in *From Plato to Nietzsche*, ed. Forrest E. Baird and Walter Kaufmann (Upper Saddle River: Prentice Hall, 1997), 471–512.
32. Ibid., 120.
33. Ibid., 129–130.
34. Ibid., 135 (Miller's ellipses).

35. Ibid., 139.
36. See Amy Kiste Nyberg, "Seal of Approval: The Origins and History of the Comics Code" (Ph.D. diss, University of Wisconsin-Madison, 1994).
37. Miller et al., *Batman: The Dark Knight Returns*, 190 (my ellipsis).
38. Ibid., 84.
39. Cf. the end of Chuck Palahniuk's *Fight Club*, a work that also engages the problem of the rebel's institution of a new hegemony.
40. Miller et al., *Batman: The Dark Knight Returns*, 185–186 (Miller's ellipses).
41. Ibid., 164.
42. Ibid., appendix.
43. Ibid., 199.
44. Bloom, *A Map of Misreading*, 117.
45. Miller et al., *Batman: The Dark Knight Returns*, 199 (my emphasis, Miller's ellipsis).
46. Ibid. (Miller's ellipsis).
47. Ibid.
48. Bloom, *A Map of Misreading*, 116.
49. Miller et al., *Batman: The Dark Knight Returns*, 96 (my ellipses).
50. This having been said, it would be simply ignorant to deny that *Batman: The Dark Knight Returns* is a conservative text in the Reagan-era style. It assumes that psychiatric care and civil liberties allow more crime than they prevent, and portrays those trying to curb fascism as Nazis themselves, effectively avoiding debate. Such an inversion of political realities allows comics, and Miller especially, to claim to be attacking what, in practice, they support. Though I believe I offer a persuasive argument for the metaphorical weight of Commissioner Gordon's Pearl Harbor anecdote and Batman's imposition of order on the streets of Gotham City, this should supplement, rather than replace, the knowledge that President Franklin Roosevelt's actions and Batman's formation of an underground "army" (Miller's term) represent the obverse of any democratic process. To quote Whit Stillman's film *Barcelona*, one probably shouldn't forget

   -the message or meaning that's right there on the surface completely open and obvious.
   They never talk about that. What do you call what's above the subtext?
   -The text?
   -OK, that's right, but they never talk about that.

   (*Barcelona*, dir. Whit Stillman, perf. Taylor Nichols and Christopher Eigeman. Castle Rock Entertainment, 1994). Edgar Allan Poe's short story *The Black Cat* should also be remembered in this context. Like the anti-abolitionist's short story about the hanging of a black cat from a tree limb, stories exceed intentions.
51. Miller et al., *Batman: The Dark Knight Returns*, 192.
52. Ibid., 25.
53. Bloom, *A Map of Misreading*, 142.

Jack Kirby and the Marvel Aesthetic

CHARLES HATFIELD

Reprinted by permission from *Hand of Fire: The Comics Art of Jack Kirby* (University Press of Mississippi, 2011), 124–142, with minor edits by the author.

THE MARVEL MYTHOS

IT HAS OFTEN BEEN SAID, THOUGH NOT SO OFTEN CONVINCINGLY, THAT SUPER-heroes constitute "a modern mythology," and that the Marvel Universe in particular called forth or made more obvious this mythic quality. Such arguments are inexact. If Marvel constitutes a *mythos*, then it is one that does not carry all the meanings that attach, or once attached, to the word: it does not consist of traditional stories built around putatively historical events; it does not constitute, at least not in any sacred or authoritative way, a body of widely shared beliefs about the world; it does not bear the cosmogony or eschatology of a people (though it has its own privileged stories of genesis and Armageddon, making and unmaking). In short, the Marvel mythos does not seem to perform much of the cultural work performed, or once performed, by the traditional mythoi so often invoked for the sake of the comparison. Notwithstanding Richard Reynolds's useful *Super Heroes: A Modern Mythology* (1994) and other, lesser books, no thorough study has yet been done to substantiate the notion of superhero comics as a mythology, at least in terms other than metaphorical.

Yet, if the comparison is too often loosely made, Marvel did draw inspiration from mythology, particularly artist Jack Kirby's appetite for mythic tales, a hankering seen even very early in his work. From such tales Kirby inherited a sense of scope, a habit of representing moral and philosophical conflicts by using godlike and symbolically counterpoised characters, and a penchant for creating families of such characters that both reinforce and yet also blur the differences between "good" and evil." Explicit borrowings from ancient myth, including internecine feuds and symbolically opposed figures, structured Kirby's

Thor and "Tales of Asgard," in which Kirby tended to design characters by the handful rather than singly (ditto for his later Fourth World and *Eternals*). These myth-making gestures weren't just tokens of archaism: they were very much at home in Cold War America, testimony to the beliefs and fears of the time. Implicitly, Kirby's personal mythologies testify to and make sense within the Cold War's totalizing ideological conflict. This is why Marvel's vintage superhero comics have a time capsule-like quality. They also attain, not least because of Kirby's graphic mythopoesis, some of the timeless, deeply resonant qualities of mythology and legend.

Under Kirby, Marvel's approach to superheroes became more complex, less settled, and, if I may hazard the word, pantheonic. By this I mean that, over time, Marvel's heroes and villains came to counterbalance each other, in a sort of rough-hewn grand design defined by symbolic symmetry. All of them, heroes and villains, belonged to a great, sprawling, superhuman family whose interweaving, often violent relationships were tangled and confusing, but also compelling. Good and evil forces were paired in a Manichean struggle in which the victory of the good, though expected and hoped for at the end of each tale, turned out to be temporary, provisory, and fragile. Conflict reigned. The heroes' omnipotence was not guaranteed (though the coddling moralism of the Comics Code did ensure that heroes almost always won the battle if not the war).

To some extent this pattern of unceasing conflict had always been the case for superheroes; Superman's career, after all, was famously described as a "never-ending battle." But the Marvel characters were not blessed with that forgetfulness which, in earlier superhero comics, almost always ushered the antagonists back, in ritualistic fashion, to an atemporal stasis, or what Neil Gaiman has called a "state of grace," between episodes, so that the beginning of each new story could be a fresh starting point (see "Change or Die!" 195–196). Instead, the Marvel characters remembered—and so did their readers.

Gaiman's concept of the "state of grace" echoes Umberto Eco's famed analysis of narrative time in his essay "The Myth of Superman" ("Il mito di Superman e la dissoluzione del tempo," 1962, re. and trans. 1972), which was one of the earliest and is still one of the smartest academic analyses of superhero comics (and of "time" in popular series fiction more generally). Eco, writing in the early sixties prior to Marvel's big changes, argues that Superman comics, indeed superhero comics on the whole, embody a "paradoxical" approach to narrative temporality, so as to reconcile the demands of the mythic—that is, the archetypal, the "emblematic," the fixed and predictable functions of the superhero—with the different demands of the popular romance, that is, the novel. Per Eco, the novel depends on the invocation (yet also violation) of the everyday and "typical," and thrives on unpredictability, "the ingenious invention of unexpected events," and, above all, the possibility of development (148–149). The demands of novelistic development call for the hero to *accomplish* something, that is, "to ma[k]e a gesture which is inscribed in his past and which weighs on his future." Such accomplishments, such meaningful happenings, constitute, Eco says, "a step toward death"—for to act is to "consume" oneself, to use up or foreclose some of one's future possibilities and to add to the archive of events that will shape (and hem in) one's future actions (150). To act is to surrender to time's passage. Superman comics therefore depend on a temporal paradox, not because the "time" depicted within a given story is odd (though time travel stories were common in Superman comics then) but because the inferred time "which ties one episode to another" is canceled or ignored or continually rewound to a notional status quo, denying change (153). In short, Superman comics—and by extension all superhero comic series of that era, according to Eco—neglected time between episodes or treated it only very selectively. They followed a logic of repetition rather than development: what Eco calls an *iterative* structure, in which "each event takes up again from a sort of virtual beginning, ignoring where the preceding event left off" (157).

This had already begun to change before Marvel, Tom De Haven argues, in the Weisinger-edited Superman titles circa 1958 and after. During that era, Superman developed a supporting cast of other survivors from his native planet of Krypton, his alien status was increasingly stressed, and the stories tilted hard in the direction of science fiction, focusing on Kryptonian lore. Weisinger, De Haven notes, "devised a preposterous yet consistent series history and culture," so that, gradually, "the permanent cast members were endowed with charged and significant memories" (115). Indeed memories and revisitations of Krypton proved a reliable story engine for years. Superman and his fictive world were thus greatly enriched: "In depicting, for the first time, Superman *as* an alien, *as* an immigrant, *as* a survivor, and in presenting these attributes as consequential and defining, the comic books [. . .] developed a coherence and an inviting, elevated *meaningfulness* [. . .]" (117) This, De Haven notes, presaged the development of tighter continuity at Marvel, and had the unintended consequence of hooking a new, more dedicated kind of reader (137).

By this light, Eco's analysis of Superman had already become outdated by 1962. Yet Eco does note that Superman stories take place in an "oneiric climate" that selectively admits time and enables a kind of ritualistic return to and elaboration of the character's origins and history (153–54). His analysis acknowledges the embroidering of the Superman universe under Weisinger, including Weisinger's frequent recourse to "imaginary" (what-if) stories and "untold" or retold tales (154–55). What does *not* happen in these comics, Eco argues, is anything that would draw Superman into developments likely to dictate his future actions. Yes, the Weisinger-era Superman had backstory, that is, a history, but not one that necessarily imposed on each successive installment. Despite the many recurrent motifs and the burgeoning cast of characters in Superman comics during this period, almost every tale was self-contained. New readers could jump on with any issue. Between-issue temporality was still vague or deniable.

In contrast, Marvel became addicted, soap opera–like, to continuing stories and unresolved problems. Marvel's heroes and villains had baggage. They shared memories and carted them around, seldom forgetting. As Kirby, Stan Lee, and company chased the notion of continuity, those memories often (though not always consistently) impinged on present struggles. For example, the Fantastic Four were haunted by villains-at-large such as the Sub-Mariner and the Frightful Four, whose escapes left the team with troubling loose ends between issues. References to preceding issues became common. Even as intertitle continuity became Marvel's main selling tool, individual titles such as *Fantastic Four* and *Amazing Spider-Man* began to experiment with cliffhanger stories of two or more issues each. By late 1964, *Amazing* was a nonstop soap opera, and the same was true of the *FF* by mid-1965. If these series lacked the cohesiveness of the ideal novel, if over the long term they were still indefinitely repeating *series* rather than whole stories published by part, still they boasted, individually and collectively, an additive and even genealogical quality that turned them into an unending "saga." A saga, as Eco has said elsewhere, entails the passage of time; it is able to let characters grow, change, and perhaps even die; it is prone to a treelike branching into various narrative lines. Admittedly, an open-ended, commercial saga is still, as Eco observes, essentially "a series in disguise," repeating, albeit in a pseudo-historical framework, the same old story, the same ideas; there is a contradiction between the saga's effort toward novelistic development and the series' effort to avoid consumption, so as to maintain the infinite exploitability of the characters (*Limits* 87). Yet a saga at least allows the potential to develop an immense, ongoing fictive network, what scholars Pat Harrigan and Noah Wardrip-Fruin have called a *vast narrative* (2–3). Marvel, building on hints in Superman and other comics, activated the idea of vast narrative for comics.

This vast narrative—the Marvel Universe—started tentatively, and only later was consolidated and elaborated on by diverse hands. It represents a case of multiple authorship on a massive scale, carried out over the decades following Marvel's first success. However, some of the elements that made this mass effort possible were present early on in Kirby's work. Indeed they arose from his drawing board. For example, one of the keystones of the Marvel saga was (and is) *family resemblance*: the fact that heroes and villains often come from common roots and boast similar or complementary powers. Kirby introduced this idea to Marvel, specifically the topos of symbolic pairings or matches between hero and villain. This fretful dualism spoke to the cultural moment: to the Cold War, to its global diffusion of conflict, its comprehensiveness, and its insistence on ideological opposition and mirroring (clash of civilizations, ahem!). What this meant, practically, is that good villains never stayed dead and never stayed away for long. They became regular supporting characters.

Superheroes had always required super-antagonists, of course. From the forties on, many heroes had faced recurrent signature villains who seemed, always, to escape captivity and renew the old feuds. Batman's rogues' gallery is probably the best-known example (Joker, Penguin, et al.). But at Marvel the villains often evaded capture and simply withdrew at the end of an episode, leaving plot points dangling. Earlier superhero comics, by contrast, typically jailed or even killed off the villains at story's end, only to bring them back later. For instance, the Brain Wave is one of the signature villains for the Justice Society of America (the team featured in DC's *All Star Comics* between 1941 and 1951), yet he faced the JSA only four times during the Golden Age, each time ending in "death" or capture. Super-villains who appeared much more frequently, so frequently as to become part of a hero's supporting cast, were unusual: the best example would be Captain Marvel's archenemy Dr. Sivana, who appeared continually in Fawcett Comics' various Captain Marvel series (1940–1953) and who often evaded capture. Sivana's absurdly comic presence became a staple ingredient of Captain Marvel's world (this Captain Marvel, note, was no relation to Marvel Comics the publisher). More typical were villains who recurred often but whose presence was not considered essential to a series' premise: Batman's Joker, Superman's Lex Luthor, Captain America's Red Skull.

By contrast, Marvel in the sixties not only let the villains get away but also made the unresolved threats they posed a continual and defining aspect of the heroes' world. By the mid-sixties Marvel had developed powerful pairings of hero and villain whose continual conflicts could sustain stories indefinitely: the Fantastic Four and Dr. Doom, Thor and Loki, Spider-Man and Dr. Octopus, Spider-Man and the Green Goblin, the X-Men and Magneto. What's more, Marvel's villains were often tied to the heroes by shared origins—connected symbiotically, almost like family. There were few precedents for this in earlier superhero comics. One example could be Black Adam, a villain introduced in Fawcett's *Marvel Family* series in 1945 who shared the same magic origins and basic costume design as the heroes (again, this *Marvel Family* was unrelated to Marvel Comics). Black Adam, however, was originally a one-shot character, and would not be reused for some thirty-two years. Marvel took this idea of the villain as hero's counterpart and, over the years, ran with it: for example, the Fantastic Four's resident scientist, Mr. Fantastic, nearly met his match in Dr. Doom, a mad genius whom he had met and tried to befriend years before when both were in college. Doom often seemed to be motivated as much by fraternal rivalry with Mr. Fantastic as by innate evil: a popular villain, he became a near-constant presence in the lives of the Fantastic Four and a pillar of the Marvel Universe (he has starred in several series of his own). In the *X-Men* series, the hate-filled Magneto fulfilled a similar but even more central role, growing in stature so much that, long after Kirby's tenure, the character would hover uncertainly between villain and misguided antihero.

Nemeses were everything. Numerous Marvel comics in Kirby's wake pursued the idea of the villain as inverted hero, as rival and opposite. The Hulk clashed with other radiation-induced monstrosities, the Abomination and the Leader; Iron Man battled a rival armored character, the Titanium Man; and Dr. Strange faced off against rival sorcerer Baron Mordo, who shared his origins. Meanwhile, Ditko's Spider-Man faced foes such as Dr. Octopus and the Sandman, who, like Spider-Man, gained their powers through nuclear accidents and who, equally like Spider-Man, were freakish in power and appearance (indulging Ditko's penchant for elastic, ever-morphing body types and curving, serpentine shapes). Much, much later, well past Ditko, Spider-Man would face evil doppelgangers whose looks were closely patterned after his own costume (Venom, Carnage). The villains often seemed to be distorted shadows of the heroes.

Surely Kirby cannot be credited or blamed for most of this? Of course not. These trends did not pop out suddenly in 1961–62, but over time as the Marvel Universe grew, fitfully, erratically, at first more the result of cross-promotional improvising than some considered, long-range plan. Many creators beyond Kirby and Lee were involved in its growth. It was under Kirby, though, that Marvel decisively latched onto the idea of unresolved, never-ending conflict between superpowered opposites, and, revealingly, Kirby's subsequent work often explores this kind of dualistic premise in distilled or exaggerated form. This sort of mirroring obviously appealed to him, as both a storyteller and a designer of characters.

The *X-Men* series, launched in 1963, is the keystone example. It introduced the germ of an idea that was to emerge full-blown in many of Kirby's later creations: that of superhuman heroes and villains springing from a common origin, vying with each other like rival gods in some epically dysfunctional family. Humankind, of course, was caught in the middle. *X-Men* approached this concept through the then-novel idea of mutants, that is, superbeings who were simply born that way. *X-Men* #1 (September 1963) establishes the blueprint straight off: a perpetual conflict between "evil" mutants, represented by

Magneto, and "good" (that is, pro-human) mutants, represented by Professor Charles Xavier and his young students, the titular X-Men. Linked by a common name and nature (*mutant*), yet starkly divided by philosophies and means, Xavier and Magneto define opposite poles in a struggle that was to become a foundational element in the Marvel Universe: Magneto seeks to rule over humankind as "homo superior," while Professor X seeks peaceful coexistence with humans and strives to defend the world from Magneto's ambitions. This fundamental conflict is at work even in the first story.

Originally, neither Magneto's specific origin nor Xavier's was important. Their common mutanthood was a given. What mattered was the struggle between X-Men and evil mutants to define the relationship between mutantkind and humankind. In this struggle, humanity became the fulcrum and victim, just as, so often in ancient mythology and epic, humans are proxies in or victims of conflicts among gods and goddesses. In the *X-Men*'s premise, then, there was a promise, a seed, of mythological scope. There had never quite been anything like this in comic books before: never had super-villains played such a fundamental role in a series, and never had comic books focused on a "race" of superbeings simply born with their unique powers. The X-Men needed no magic words, no mystic thunderbolts, no cosmic rays or attacks by radioactive bugs to explain their abilities. Neither did their most potent and enduring antagonist, Magneto. From this simple idea came, gradually and without fanfare, a new approach to the superhero.

Granted, Kirby and Lee did not fully exploit this potential in the early *X-Men*. The Lee and Kirby *X-Men* of 1963–66 was an underachieving series that, after a promising launch, came to seem cramped and uninventive alongside Kirby's best work. Kirby departed the series on the cusp of 1966 to focus on other work; by then he had fully penciled *X-Men* issues 1–11 and provided layouts for other artists, mainly Werner Roth, in issues 12–17 (dated July 1965 to February 1966). He would provide covers or cover layouts for most issues through late 1966. But this was not his sharpest work; frankly, *X-Men* was a second-stringer. Lee handed over the scripting to protégé Roy Thomas as of #20, and what followed was largely undistinguished until the arrival of artist Neal Adams in 1969. Shortly after the fondly remembered Adams/Thomas run, the series died, only to be revived as a reprint book, in which status it continued quietly for almost five years before its widely touted revival in 1975, years after Lee and Kirby. Even the earliest issues of *X-Men*, those penciled fully by Kirby, had been comparatively weak: the only essential villains introduced in the early run were Magneto and the robotic Sentinels, and, as had *The Fantastic Four* before it, the series cast about uncertainly for subplots, hooks, and distinctive characterizations. Kirby and Lee returned to Magneto monotonously throughout their two-plus years on the title, without deepening the conflict among mutants or expanding the scope of the action in such a way as to capitalize on the series' premise. Though said premise held extraordinary promise, when handled in an ordinary way it confined and hobbled the series, making it dully repetitive. Truthfully, the X-Men languished in the shadow of the Fantastic Four; the series demanded a bigger treatment than it got. The early issues remained trapped in month-to-month superheroics, often against colorless villains, the only novelty coming from Professor X as teacher and the hovering presence of Magneto as antagonist. Years would go by before other creators (Chris Claremont et al.) would begin to extrapolate from the original and exploit the series' potential.

Though *X-Men* had the glimmer of an idea, it was Kirby's peak period on Marvel's *Thor* that most successfully explored a pantheonic approach to superheroes. The mythological Thor had held a special fascination for Kirby for decades: witness "Villain from Valhalla," a 1942 *Sandman* story by Kirby and Joe Simon, or "The Magic Hammer," another Thor-related story for DC's *Tales of the Unexpected* in 1957. However, the early Thor stories in Marvel's *Journey into Mystery* failed to capitalize on the character's mythic origins. Like many of the early-sixties Marvel series, *Thor* began with one foot in the Kirby/Lee monster comics; then, after Kirby's brief initial run, it had little offer besides standard crime-fighting stories in mythological drag. However, once Kirby returned to the series and hit his stride—especially in 1966 and after—his *Thor* became a launch pad for epics of unprecedented scope and mythic resonance. Building on, though also offhandedly distorting, the patterns laid out in Norse myth, Kirby and Lee made Thor's unpredictable half-brother Loki into a pure villain and central figure, while also spotlighting other mythic characters, both heroic (e.g., Sif, Balder, Heimdall) and villainous (e.g., Hela, goddess of death; various giants and trolls). Thor's pitiable human alter-ego, the lame but well-intentioned doctor Don Blake—in superhero parlance, his *civilian identity*—disappeared for issues at a time, as Kirby's interest in conventional superheroics waned and he instead explored the possibilities of a godly pantheon.

Prior to this, *Thor* had been dominated by romance-styled plotting about Thor/Don Blake's stymied relationship with love interest Jane Foster, his nurse. This was *Superman* with a vengeance: Blake, kindly, lame, and a bit dull if not outright "mild-mannered," desired Jane, but his true self, Thor, could not cleave to her because his godly father, Odin, forbade him to love a "mortal." Jane was often in need of being rescued; Thor/Blake was torn by his divided nature. In essence, Don Blake was a mashup of Clark Kent and the then-popular Dr. Kildare. In the *Thor* of the mid-to-late sixties, though, things were cosmic: often, nothing less than the end of everything was at stake. Jane Foster was eventually shunted to the side and the series went Blake-less for long periods. Plots occasionally wobbled back to earthbound crime-fighting and soap opera, but most often slipped the traces, giving free rein to Kirby's off-the-cuff mythopoeic barnstorming. Kirby's design and drawing went wild, the elastic plots giving affordance to spectacular graphic invention.

Equally grand in scope from the mid-sixties onward was Kirby's *Fantastic Four*, which used the team's science-fiction roots to explore a range of hidden worlds, alternate realities, inhuman species, and space-spanning superbeings. In fact it was the *FF* that first and most clearly heralded Kirby's new outsized approach to the superhero genre. The much-praised "Galactus trilogy" in *FF* #48–50 (March–May 1966), which first introduced the seminal characters Galactus and the Silver Surfer, is similar in outline to many of the conflicts acted out in the peak-period *Thor*: the Godlike Galactus, not so much a villain as an amoral, impersonal force, struggles with his once-servant, the Silver Surfer, to decide the fate of the world. Again, humanity is the fulcrum: the Silver Surfer's sympathetic regard for humans resembles Thor's own, and, eventually, the Surfer would be cast as an almost Christlike sufferer for humanity's sins (a symbolic burden most weightily depicted in the Stan Lee-scripted, post-Kirby *Silver Surfer* series of 1968–1970). In the Galactus trilogy, even the most powerful of humans, the Fantastic Four, are forced into the role of bystanders—until the intervention of another Godlike extraterrestrial, the Watcher, helps humanity save itself. Humankind thus tips the scales, though in an almost childlike, unknowing way, in a mythic struggle to decide its own destiny.

The "Galactus trilogy," a prime example of Kirby's technological sublime, was to prove supremely influential, indeed epochal, for Marvel and its fans. Tellingly, it isn't so much a cohesive trilogy as three months' worth of issues placed within a larger continuity. *Fantastic Four* #48 actually begins with the resolution of the Inhumans storyline launched several issues earlier, while #50, though titled "The Startling Saga of the Silver Surfer," resolves the threat of Galactus halfway through, quickly ushers off the Surfer, and then concentrates on domestic happenings in the lives of the FF: tension between newly-weds Reed and Sue, the tortured wanderings of Ben, who is convinced that his girlfriend Alicia has rejected him for the Surfer, and—this was evidently a selling point—Johnny's first day at "Metro College," where he meets new supporting character Wyatt Wingfoot. The "trilogy," then, has none of the formal separateness or claims to historic importance that we might expect in the marketing of "event" series in today's comic books. Rather, the operative mode is that of a soap opera. Yet what these three issues are remembered for is their unprecedented scale: Galactus intends to devour the earth's energy not because he is malicious or evil (the usual super-villain stuff) but because he is a force "above good and evil," to whom the Earth's inhabitants are simply beneath notice. The story's resolution hinges on forcing Galactus, through the Silver Surfer, to *take* notice. The central character, it turns out, is the one who mediates between the human and the godlike, the Surfer, who unpredictably blossoms from a mere functionary of the plot—a cold, unemotional harbinger of doom—into an articulate and tormented hero.

Much of the story's drama stems from the Surfer, as he transitions from plot device (his arrival heralds the coming of Galactus) to character. Introducing the Surfer, as eccentric a gimmick as any Kirby had come up with, was an ingenious narrative stroke, brought to the boards by Kirby without Lee's input in order to foreshadow the threat of Galactus on a more human scale. The device of the Surfer allows us to approach Galactus obliquely, to imagine what kind of being would need a "herald" this imposing to prepare the way for his arrival. The first chapter's climactic splash, a full-page panel dominated by the big "reveal" of Galactus, derives its power from the way it fulfills the suspense generated by the dozen or so pages preceding it. The chapter's title, "The Coming of Galactus," anticipates its end, for which we are prepared in two ways: first, by seeing the Surfer's progress through space, toward Earth; second, through apocalyptic signs—a sky filled with flames, then with floating rocks or "debris"—that strike terror into the people of New York City. These unexplained phenomena inspire panic in the streets, provoking confrontations between Johnny and Ben and a fearful crowd. (Ben knocks out one man with a tap of his finger, a bit of comic drollery that offsets the story's lowering sense of threat.) Afterwards, the omniscient Watcher, a frequent supporting character in *Fantastic Four*, appears at the group's headquarters and reveals that the "fire-shield" and orbiting debris were his own unsuccessful attempts to hide the Earth from the Surfer, Galactus's "advance scout" (oddly enough, the orbiting debris does nothing to dim the light of the sun!). Even as the Watcher speaks, the Surfer slips through the barrier of debris and lands—as luck or narrative economy would have it—right on the roof of the FF's headquarters. Ben dispatches the Surfer with one punch, but to no avail: the signal having been given, Galactus arrives suddenly, announced by a full-page photomontage splash that shows the opening of his spherical starship. Galactus disembarks, in a costume of baroque complexity festooned, funnily enough, with a "G" on the chest (like Superman's "S" chevron or the FF's own "4" logo). Arm outstretched, dwarfing even the giant Watcher, Galactus makes a singular impression: "My journey is *ended!* This planet shall *sustain* me until it has been drained of all elemental life! *So speaks Galactus!*" (20). Part of what makes this work so well, in spite of its unselfconscious absurdity, is the cumulative effect of the narrative teasing that leads up to this moment. This cliffhanger must have been quite a stunner to Marvel readers in 1966.

The Silver Surfer, a clear example of the kind of improvisation that characterizes mid-sixties Marvel, is the device that makes this first chapter tick. He is introduced as a cosmic traveler "zooming along the starways like a living comet—with the freedom and wild abandon of the wind itself," but also as an object of terror for the villainous Skrulls "of the Andromeda Galaxy," past enemies of the Fantastic Four, whose fearful determination to hide their entire social system already tells us about the scope of the threat the Surfer represents (7–8). The Surfer is later shown surfing the cosmic explosion of a "supernova" and then detecting our own solar system, all the while shooting through Kirby's overstuffed, decorative idea of outer space, which is alive with closely packed stars, planets, and fizzing energy (apparently it didn't occur to Kirby that space is mostly emptiness, or dark matter). When the Surfer arrives, he is a portent, a promise, of impending apocalypse. What's interesting about the construction of this drawn-out narrative tease is that it apparently came from Kirby alone.

Stan Lee, in his book *Son of Origins of Marvel Comics* (1975), credits Kirby with creating the Surfer. According to Lee, Kirby penciled the first chapter of the story after an informal conference with Lee, in which the two agreed on the broad concept of a huge, godlike being "who could destroy entire planets at will" (205)—a pretty generic idea, it must be admitted, and of course Lee's account is so short on specifics as to be unconfirmable. What is most specific about Lee's account is that, when Kirby eventually delivered the pages for the trilogy's first installment, Lee was, he said, startled to see an unfamiliar figure on a flying surfboard, upon which Kirby explained that a being as powerful as Galactus ought to have a herald, "an advance guard" to come before him and pave the way—a good call, but, one is tempted to say, a storyteller's call, not one justified by any logic other than that of the narrative. Lee recalls being intrigued by, even "wild" about, the Surfer, whom Kirby had created on his own, out of whole cloth (206). What this tells us is not only that Lee did not have a hand in the initial design of the character, but also that he was not in control of the pacing of the narrative, since the Surfer is critical to the dramatic structure of the story's first chapter. He is the story's pacemaker. Lee's account thus inadvertently reveals much about the nature of the Kirby/Lee collaboration at this stage and about the central role Kirby played as a conceptualist and storyteller. By inventing/inserting the Surfer, Kirby in effect plotted the story. He paced the telling. He even provided the character that, in the end, would steal the show, in "The Startling Saga of the Silver Surfer."

In other words, the Silver Surfer is a character that grew out of Kirby's process of narrative drawing rather than a prior intention or any literary considerations. The bulk of the "writing" (in the sense of story-plotting and storytelling) was in the art. Character design and movement, facial expressions, the compositions of panels, the leap from panel to panel, the gridding of the page: all of these crucial cartooning/storytelling elements were the province of Kirby, the artist. Regarding this particular story, Mike Gartland unpacks the process of its creation in *The Jack Kirby Collector* issues 22 and 23, which provide facsimiles of penciled pages from *Fantastic Four* #49 that include Kirby's original plot notes. Gartland concludes: "Despite whatever input Stan might or might not've had at the conceptual phase, these margin notes show the action and dramatic impact of this pivotal episode . . . begin with Kirby" ("Failure," Part Two 38). In his role as dialoguer, Lee responded to what Kirby gave, at times seriously, at times playfully, always adding a new layer to the total work. In the case of the Surfer, a character for whom Lee has great affection and over whom he reportedly tried to exert a proprietary claim for a while (McLaughlin 98), the meeting between Kirby's pencils and Lee's scripts resulted in a new layer of characterization. As the story builds (#49–50), the treatment of the Surfer deepens, infusing Kirby's initially cold, enigmatic conception—a being of energy, wholly alien and unfeeling—with a "nobility" and an awaking "conscience" that will shape the story's outcome and in fact provide the crucial stalling action: the Surfer will turn on his master, Galactus, and battle him, buying time for Johnny Storm to fetch the cosmic super-weapon with which Galactus can be overcome. In short, the Surfer, at first improvised by Kirby simply for the sake of storytelling, ended up becoming the story's thematic linchpin and thereby a major Marvel character.

It would seem that, during the production of *FF* #48, both Kirby and Lee saw something they wanted to use in the Surfer, and so Kirby elaborated. As Lee recounts in *Son of Origins*: "Later, as I started to write the dialogue for the strip, I realized that The Surfer had the potential to be far more than just a high-flying, colorful supporting character. Studying the illustrations, seeing the way Jack had drawn him, I found a certain nobility in his demeanor, an almost spiritual quality in his aspect and his bearing. [. . .] I was tempted to imbue him with a spirit of almost religious purity" (206). Accordingly, issues 49 and 50, as they emerged from Kirby's drawing board, pushed the Silver Surfer to the fore. Out of Kirby's improvisation, then, came a signature character, one in which both Kirby and Lee developed a keen interest. They would return to the character repeatedly, first, in *Fantastic Four* #55, then in the epic *FF* #57–61 and subsequent issues, often casting the Surfer as a victim and emphasizing his innocence and suffering, qualities that Lee, finally, underscored in the *Silver Surfer* series of 1968, with its pathetic, blatantly Christlike hero. By the late sixties Lee had been so charmed by the character that he came to regard it as specially his, and, insisting on an anguished, Romantic, and sacrificial treatment of the character, took it far from what had emerged on Kirby's drawing board (McLaughlin 97; Raphael and Spurgeon 123). Ironically, Kirby's impromptu narrative problem-solving resulted in one of Lee's most self-consciously ambitious literary efforts—a testimony to the odd results often achieved through the Marvel production method.

The Silver Surfer, then, is Kirby's fingerprint on the Galactus trilogy. Most relevant to my interest, though, is the way the character's expanded role affected the shape of the story. The Surfer's rebellion against Galactus constitutes a key example of Marvel's signature dualism: master versus herald, with humanity in the middle. *The Fantastic Four* thus experimented with the same sort of conflict hinted at in the early issues of the *X-Men*. It opened the door to the grand-scale, cosmic adventures that would appear in *Thor*. Other ideas introduced in the *FF* likewise recalled the *X-Men*'s premise: most notably, that of the Inhumans, a race of beings superhuman by nature yet forced to live in a Hidden Land, shielded from human eyes. In the first Inhumans story, immediately prior to the Galactus trilogy (November 1965–January 1966), Kirby and Lee again discarded the conventions of accidental origins and secret identities in favor of a more mythic approach, creating a pantheon of good and evil characters (the Inhumans' royal family) with a shared origin and destiny. One senses Kirby—the evidence shows that it *was* mainly Kirby plotting the series at this point—straining at the limits of formula here, cramming whole series' worth of concepts into *The Fantastic Four*. The existence of other worlds or dimensions allowed for similar explorations; new settings, such as the Negative Zone and Wakanda, became breeding grounds for new characters and ideas. In Kirby's run on *The Fantastic Four*, then, and especially between late 1965 and late 1967, the Marvel Universe began to sprout.

This sudden afflatus may in part have been due to Martin Goodman's plans to expand the Marvel line: biographer Ronin Ro claims that Kirby had been apprised of such plans and even promised a share of the profits from expanded merchandising, and thus was incentivized. By Ro's account, Kirby, when he realized that Goodman in fact could not expand the line so quickly, ended up grafting his ideas onto *The Fantastic Four*. In any case, as the Marvel Universe went through this growth spurt it began to diverge drastically from the ordinary life-world of its readers, blooming into a strange world all its own. The month-to-month *Fantastic Four* serial—the cornerstone of Marvel—gestured toward a saga, a vast, rambling narrative. To the low-fantastic appeal of the costumed urban hero was added an emphasis on invented landscape and infinite powers akin to high fantasy. The frontier ethos of the vigilante hero—and the questions of justice, vengeance, and law that go with it—were sidelined in favor of pure, marvelous invention.

THE EPIC APPROACH AND ITS CONSEQUENCES

Kirby's transformation of the superhero dates back to the basic, then-unfulfilled premise of *The X-Men*. Through the ongoing conflict between good and evil mutants, Kirby felt his way tentatively toward what would become, for him, an irresistible new idea. Instead of defending the status quo, that is, the everyday life-world assumed by their readers, the X-Men redefined the world by their very presence. Instead of defending against random "crime," the X-Men battled other mutants, for humanity's sake. Unlike the superhero comics that came before it, then, *The X-Men* started from a premise that was not conservative but potentially transformative. Harking back to the genre's science fiction roots (recall Philip Wylie's *Gladiator*, for example), it had the potential to make the whole world look different. This possibility would be more fully exploited as Marvel's continuity developed into an ever-tighter generative (and restrictive) mechanism. *X-Men*, in short, opened the door to a speculative approach to superheroes, an approach much influenced by Kirby's reading of SF. Kirby then gladly walked through that door in *Fantastic Four* and *Thor*, taking those series to new heights.

In sum, Marvel under Kirby introduced an epic approach to the superhero genre that was "mythic" both in its scale and in its pantheonic complications. At Marvel, heroes and villains shared common origins and each side was defined by its constant struggle against the other. This idea has had a great impact on the structure and iconography of the genre in the years since. By establishing pantheons of rival superbeings, Kirby infused a once tapped-out genre with the potential for more complex character relationships, sustained and meaningful conflict, and spectacular narrative drawing. Drawing of course was at the heart of it all: Kirby the designer was questing for new things to do. But the narrative consequences were far-reaching. Kirby's outsized take on the genre at last gave superheroes threats worthy of them, villains and dangers that could fill the historical gap left by the defeat of "the Axis" at the end of WWII, the genre's first boom period. Thus superhero comics could implicitly rehearse the ideological struggles of the Cold War without sinking to naked jingoism (though early on there was plenty of that too), and could speak to the era's looming sense of apocalypse. This mythic approach of Kirby's paved the way for series in which heroes not only saved the world but redefined it. It also gave the contemporary superhero a reason for being. With *X-Men* and *Thor*, Kirby began to weave into comics the kind of complex narrative designs found in classical myth or the Old Norse Eddas, while yet upholding a stark, sharply drawn, Comics Code-sanctioned moral dualism, a Manichean tug-of-war between Good and Evil.

Admittedly, said dualism fails to capture, in fact refuses, the frequent moral ambiguity of so many myths and Eddas, with their capricious, often self-serving, sometimes self-destructive gods and heroes. For the most part, the Marvel Comics of the sixties skirt tragedy and uphold a staunchly prescriptive morality. As Code-approved superhero comics of their era, they remain locked into a pinched, earnestly moralistic idea of children's fiction; as partial heirs to the bathos of muted, post-Code romance comics, they work on emotional registers that call to mind formula adolescent fiction. These are stories conceived with young readers—or, rather, a frankly conservative, moralizing approach to young readers—in mind. Their explorations are often blunted by that assumption. And yet Marvel's fallible heroes, the moments of genuine pathos scattered through their stories, and the expanded fictional world in which they adventured, all these took the superhero comic book in vital new directions. Monster-heroes like the Thing and the Hulk, as well as misfits like Spider-Man, sharpened the superhero's internal agon, his driving self-conflict, resetting the genre's basic tensions. At the same time, Marvel's supergroups—its families of heroes and villains—introduced complex interpersonal dynamics, far from either solo hero tales or the blandly collegial, clubhouse-like atmosphere of DC's then-Justice League (which gave no hint of personality conflicts, nor indeed of distinct personalities, among its members). The ever-expanding storyscape around them, meanwhile, was stuffed with things to respond to, recurrent menaces to fight, dreamlike locales to visit, and the possibility of relationships to rekindle.

Marvel thus made formula superhero comics both more welcoming of emotional complexity and much wider in scope. In the latter quality, their epic scope, Kirby's handprint shows through especially clearly; Marvel's new sense of scale afforded him a grand canvas. It liberated him. As a result, the Marvel of the sixties boasted some of the most inventive graphic design and cracklingly vital narrative drawing ever seen in comic books. But this accomplishment did not end in the sixties, for Kirby would go on, after his classic period at Marvel, to explore still more shaded and conflicted characters and more expansive worlds.

If, fortified by Kirby, Marvel rebuilt and revitalized the superhero, then this success prodded Kirby further, stoking his ambition. He began to see that he could treat superheroes as vehicles for personal expression and for the conflict of ideas, at a time when ideas seemed to animate conflict on a global scale. As the rhetoric of the Cold War pitted rival ideologies against each other in a bid for world dominance, so Kirby worked out the conflict of ideas with a rugged graphic immediacy. More and more, he assayed themes that haunted and provoked him. More and more, he made abstract concepts leap off the page, personified. In his hands, some of the genre's axial conflicts—between justice and authority, for example—became less important, while others—such as the superhero's status as both insider and outsider—were boldly redefined. A peculiar *otherness* crept into his superheroes: they became gods, and pulled humans into the orbit of their conflicts. They worked the cosmos, not just the city, but brought the cosmos *to* the city too, imbuing the city with layers and mysteries. Asgard and New York, Supertown and Metropolis—Kirby made the mundane settings of the earthbound hero and the grand settings of mythology part of one vast narrative design. By this point he was less interested in the kinds of conflictedness that first gave life to the superhero—masculine self-doubt, urban paranoia, the allure and wickedness of crime—but very interested in doing new things with what was there, the established and understood language of the genre. He turned this language toward mythic fantasy. His best work gave ideas an embodied urgency and an archetypal obviousness but at the same time a quirky and surprising visual richness.

Kirby's work, in short, pursued the possibility of superheroics as allegory, a possibility he broached at Marvel, then went on to plumb in his visionary and bizarrely eccentric Fourth World for DC. Through the Fourth World he introduced multiple innovations that have influenced superhero comics ever since. One such innovation, the idea of simultaneously launching several new series within a single larger storyline, has since become common industry practice. Other innovative features of the Fourth World were its deliberate symbolic parallelism; its ideological subtext, if indeed we may call it *sub*text (it's pretty obvious); and the way it used an overarching conflict and shared cast to revive and exploit various subgenres. Like *The X-Men*—and indeed it underscores in hindsight Kirby's distinct contribution to *The X-Men*—the Fourth World establishes a conflict among demigods, of which humans become the focal point and deciding the fate of humanity the main objective. The saga's titanic villain, Darkseid, attacks Earth in hopes of plucking a fateful secret from human minds, while Darkseid's opposites, the gods and heroes of "New Genesis," spring to humanity's defense. This is where *The Fourth World* begins: with human life, ever the disputed stake in Kirby's epics. Here Kirby's mythic approach to the genre emerges in its pure form; here archetypal figures are locked in world-defining struggle. Having established this struggle, Kirby developed symbolically fraught characters and cast them in variations of traditional comics genres.

It may be that, in 1971, all this was too much for the comic book's tottering newsstand market to handle. After all, the original incarnation of the Fourth World proved short-lived. However, the concept has been revived repeatedly, insistently, over the decades since, usually in diminished or more readily containable form. Even though the series posed trouble for the putative continuity of the DC Universe, subsequent writers have found its concepts irresistible and sought to reintroduce them, or versions of them, into the company's expansive menu of characters. In fact Kirby's pantheonic treatment of superheroes, of which the Fourth World is the very distillation, has since transformed the narrative strategies of the whole superhero genre. Four decades after the Fourth World began, creators intuitively recognize that superheroes demand not only worthy antagonists but also coherent worlds and shared origins. So this is how Kirby reshaped the superhero genre: the notion of "continuity" prevalent in superhero comics today rests not only on the phenomenal success of the Marvel Universe that Kirby did so much to create, but specifically on the mythic approach to the genre that emerged, tentatively, in *The X-Men* and then blossomed into the Fourth World. More than any other creator, Kirby opened up this rich and habitable space.

I make this claim not to exult in an easy triumph, nor to make the case for Kirby as the only important contributor to Marvel. We know that Kirby was not the sole architect of Marvel; the company's achievement was collective and contingent on a set of circumstances impossible to be repeated, including the facts of Kirby's availability and financial desperation. Moreover, despite his contributions to the Marvel aesthetic, thus to superhero comics in general, Kirby did not vault directly from Marvel to due recognition, compensation, or a general sense of ownership—editorial, financial, or professional—over his own work. Though gush about Kirby as "King" was common enough, his co-authorship of Marvel remained veiled behind company rhetoric. He had to wait until retirement for a measure of vindication, critical reappraisal, and partisan fan support. Finally, Kirby was not interested in the workmanlike upkeep of continuity, nor did he have much of a share, in later years, in the Marvel continuity he helped to create. Rather, he was interested in high concepts and the overflowing of ideas, designs, and visions. By the mid-seventies, continuity was his nemesis. He professed disinterest in subsequent revisions of his characters by other creators, did not return to old series with the intention of recreating the terms of their earlier success, and was sometimes held to task for either wrenching old properties in new directions or failing to notice that new directions had already come. That Marvel continuity post-1970 fostered a sense of comparative realism only proved to be a thorn in Kirby's side, and, in later years, the freewheeling, childlike qualities of many of his comics frankly alienated many of the fans that had lapped up his work (under Lee's imprimatur) back in the sixties. The Marvel Universe, more generally the settled and hyper-rationalized version of the Marvel aesthetic that overtook the comic book field, turned out to be inhospitable to Kirby's talents.

Kirby's position vis-à-vis the superhero genre is therefore a curious one. At Marvel he co-created a vast narrative that, on the one hand, fired his ambitions and pushed him further along artistically, and yet, on the other, bred a fan culture whose expectations for consistency and systemization would only have straightjacketed him, had he been able to meet them at all. If it is possible for one person to be both a father figure and an outcast, Kirby has been both of those. While the repertory of contemporary superhero comics, specifically the vast narratives of Marvel and DC, is based largely on his work, today's comics are so thoroughly enmeshed in the custodial upkeep of continuity that the actual history and rude specificity of Kirby have been effaced, and the daffier, more outré elements of his comics have been kept at arm's length. Perhaps this is why writer Chris Roberson has referred to the late Mark Gruenwald (1953–1996), onetime Marvel editor and continuity expert, as the real "father of modern superhero comics": "The current state of superhero comics, with its obsessive attention to continuity and rationalization, line-wide crossovers, multiple realities, and increasing divergence from the real world, resembles nothing so much as a Mark Gruenwald comic writ large" ("Mark Gruenwald" no page).

This "current state" is as much the achievement of fandom as of publishers. It is designed for sharing. We know, after all, that genres are not simply formulas or lists of conventions or clichés, but social compacts, ways of acting and relating in the world. We know that the superhero genre isn't simply a textual but also a social network, that knowledge of continuity grants cultural capital within said network, that continuity generates both fan fiction and professional comics, and that by now the difference between the two is practically no difference at all. The superhero genre and its collective, its fandom, are now online, "cross-platform," and invested in the shared universe model; the genre has become a big playground. Why not?

Recent genre theory has reminded us that a genre's social purposes are at least as if not more important than its formal and aesthetic components; indeed, Amy Devitt has shown that genres are defined "less by their formal conventions than by their purposes, participants, and subjects." The "purposes" of fandom include participation—on a social level as close by as one's local comic book shop—in the vast narratives of superhero comics, and fans have collectively embroidered on those narratives in ways quite alien to the original comics of Jack Kirby. Indeed, vast narratives may function best for fans when their points of historical origin are elided, when launch points are multiple and slightly blurry, and when there is no single, unquestionable, canonical source text to follow (or when claims to canonicity are bracketed off). In any case, Kirby provided the raw material for shared universes that have gone on and will continue to go on without him.

WORKS CITED

De Haven, Tom. *Our Hero: Superman on Earth*. New Haven: Yale University Press, 2010.
Devitt, Amy J. "Integrating Rhetorical and Literary Theories of Genre." *College English* 62.6 (July 2000): 696–718.
Eco, Umberto. "The Myth of Superman" [Il mito di Superman e la dissoluzione del tempo]. 1962. Rev. version trans. Natalie Chilton, *Diacritics* 2.1 (1972): 14–22.
Gaiman, Neil, et al. "Change or Die!" Afterword. *The One*. By Rick Veitch. West Townshend, VT: King Hell, 1989. 188–209.

Gartland, Mike. "A Failure to Communicate: Part Two," *The Jack Kirby Collector* 22 (Dec. 1998): 36–43.

Harrigan, Pat, and Noah Wardrip-Fruin, eds. *Third Person: Authoring and Exploring Vast Narratives.* Cambridge, MA: MIT, 2009.

Lee, Stan. *Son of Origins of Marvel Comics.* New York: Simon and Schuster, 1975.

McLaughlin, Jeff, ed. *Stan Lee: Conversations.* Jackson: University Press of Mississippi, 2007.

Raphael, Jordan, and Tom Spurgeon. *Stan Lee and the Rise and Fall of the American Comic Book.* Chicago: Chicago Review Press, 2003.

Reynolds, Richard. *Super Heroes: A Modern Mythology.* 1992. Jackson, MS: University Press of Mississippi, 1994.

Ro, Ronin. *Tales to Astonish: Jack Kirby, Stan Lee, and the American Comic Book Revolution.* New York: Bloomsbury, 2004.

Roberson, Chris. "Mark Gruenwald, the father of modern superhero comics." *The Myriad Worlds of Chris Roberson.* Blog. 2 July 2007. Web. 29 July 2010.

Navigating Infinite Earths

KARIN KUKKONEN

"Navigating Infinite Earths: Readers, Mental Models, and the Multiverse of Superhero Comics," by Karin Kukkonen, is reproduced from *Storyworlds* 2, with permission from the University of Nebraska Press. ©2010 by the University of Nebraska Press.

IN A RECENT STUDY OF MULTIPLE WORLDS IN PHYSICS, PHILOSOPHY, AND NARRAtive, Marie-Laure Ryan argues that our "private encyclopedia" is deeply rooted in the classical notion that there is one world in which we live and through which we think—rather than many such worlds. As Ryan puts it, "[f]or most of us, the idea of parallel realities is not yet solidly established in our private encyclopedias and the text must give strong cues for us to suspect momentarily our intuitive belief in classical cosmology" (Ryan 2006: 671). Cognitive-psychological research on mental models, that is, scenarios we mentally develop in order to reason, also stresses that situations triggering the creation of multiple mental models are difficult to process (see Jarvella, Lundquist, and Hyönä 1995), and that we construct mental models in order to eliminate alternatives and create coherence (Johnson-Laird 1983; Garnham and Oakhill 1994). Thus, when reading fiction, interpreters construct "a three-dimensional model akin to an actual model of the scene" (Johnson-Lair 2006: 37) in order to locate the characters in a story, monitor the events and project the narrative's progress (see Harman 2002). In such contexts readers' mental model is called a "storyworld," and it relies on the same one-world ontology that Ryan associates with "our intuitive belief in classical cosmology."

Readers of contemporary superhero comics, however, seem to be less fully invested than others in this classical cosmology—a cosmology that favors singular over multiple realities, in narrative texts as well as everyday life. The stories of heroes like Superman, Batman, and Wonder Woman have been published for decades on a weekly or biweekly basis, written by ever-changing authors. As a result, inconsistencies emerged in the different storyworlds and encounters involving these characters, and continuity, or the coherent and consistent development of the characters and their storyworlds, became a problem. In response, superhero comics made a virtue out of necessity and presented their storyworlds as part of a larger "multiverse," in which a variety of mutually incompatible narrative worlds existed as parallel realities. Villains aim to turn the entire multiverse into their dominion, and superheroes unite to maintain the status quo across storyworlds.

Insofar as it involves a set of incompatible storyworlds, the multiverse of superhero comics differs from other narratives that cluster storyworlds. Ryan outlines several strategies through which multiple worlds are accommodated in narratives, in a way that can be reconciled with classical cosmology: they can be explained as the product of a character's imagination (mentalism), as a computer-generated world (virtualization), as a symbolic world (allegory), through reference to the author (metatextualism), through magic, or through an explicit invitation to the reader to choose his or her own story (2006: 669–71). Superhero comics, however, take a multiworld model of reality—the multiverse—largely as an ontological given. The storyworlds of the superhero multiverse involve not just plural private worlds or "subworlds," that is, the imaginings, hopes, and beliefs of characters (see Ryan 1991: 116–23; Ryan 1992; Werth 1999: 210–58), but rather fully parallel, equally actualized realities. And even though these comics feature metareferences outside the storyworld to authors and readers (see Kukkonen 2009), these are not always used to reduce the multiplicity of comics storyworlds. At issue in the superhero multiverse, rather, are mutually incompatible realities—unrelated (or at least highly distinctive) narrative worlds featuring different sets of superheroes as well as counterfactual scenarios involving alternative developments in the story of a known superhero. These cannot be reconciled as subworlds within the larger storyworld, and a baseline "textual actual world" (Ryan 1991: 113) is not always established. In superhero comics, multiple scenarios are the case, and it can be a challenge to determine when and how storyworlds of the multiverse form a set of counterfactuals, that is, "what if" alternatives departing from what is the case.

This essay explores the sometimes labyrinthine complexity of the superhero multiverse, as well as the means by which readers navigate that ontological labyrinth, via three tutor texts: Marv Wolfman's *Crisis on Infinite Earths* (1985–86), Warren Ellis's *Planetary* (1999–2009), and Alan Moore's *Tom Strong* (1996–2006). In *Crisis on Infinite Earths* the superheroes of the multiverse of the publishing house DC unite to face the threat of expanding antimatter. Superman and Kal-El (a version of Superman who ages and marries Lois Lane), different versions of The Flash, and other superheroes from across the multiverse team up in a final stand against the onslaught of antimatter. *Crisis on Infinite Earths* is a classic instance of the narratives of the multiverse, setting a precedent for later superhero comics like *Planetary* and *Tom Strong*, which likewise feature threats from alternative worlds and several character versions that meet each other. In *Planetary* a team of superheroes investigates the popular culture of the twentieth century. They travel through numerous fictional worlds and encounter alternative versions of other superheroes. Meanwhile, in the stories of the *Tom Strong* series, Strong is incarnated as a hero in the various popular-culture styles of the twentieth century, including those associated with its pulp fiction and superhero comics. Chronicling the history of these various styles and the heroes who figure in them, Moore portrays Tom as repeatedly encountering other versions of himself.

My argument is that although the storyworlds of the superhero multiverse are not easily reconcilable into storyworld and subworld, or into one baseline storyworld and its alternative versions, you do not need to be a super-reader, mentally juggling the innumerable storyworlds of the multiverse, in order to read superhero comics. Rather, the creators of superhero comics deploy a range of strategies to help readers navigate this multiverse of mutually incompatible realities, including iconographic elements in the portrayal of different character versions and the strategic use of reader surrogates, i.e. characters whom readers follow and identify with as the story unfolds. In fact, the *Crisis on Infinite Earths* mini-series was conceived as an attempt to unify the DC multiverse, to clear up the problems with narrative continuity that had been created through decades of storytelling in weekly installments (see the Introduction to Wolfman 2000). But ever since superhero comics featured the multiverse, they also cued readers to establish a mental model of multiple parallel realities, enabling them to navigate the multiverse and cope with its violations of classical cosmology.

The first part of this article begins by exploring how readers move from the comics text to a mental model of the events as they read the story. In an effort to extend previous research based on verbal propositions and narratives, I argue that images provide visual clues from which readers construct the mental model of the storyworld, rather than a direct, analogue representation of the storyworld. The next section then turns to continuity and counterfactuals and examines the challenges that the multiverse in the superhero narratives of *Crisis on Infinite Earths*, *Planetary*, and *Tom Strong* poses to human cognition. Cognitive-psychological research on counterfactual thinking and mental models shows that generally only a very limited set of counterfactual options is kept in mind. Superhero narratives, however, present their readers with uncounted numbers of storyworlds and character versions who travel between them. The remainder of the article explores strategies superhero comics use to mitigate these challenges to human cognition. For one thing, superhero comics have developed a very detailed encyclopedia of costumes and visual attributes, an iconography that provides shortcuts into readers' knowledge structures, enabling readers to keep different character versions distinct and connect them to their original storyworlds. Further, reader surrogates—characters whom readers follow as the story unfolds—move on a path through the multiverse that connects only a limited number of worlds at a given time and thus reduces the cognitive load for readers. And when reader surrogates are given explanations of the structure of the multiverse in the story proper, readers acquire by proxy the mental model that the surrogates construct at the diegetic level.

FROM COMICS TO MENTAL MODELS

Comics are a medium employing three modes of expression: words, images, and sequence. On the level of meaning-making in the reading process, that is, for understanding what the story is about, these three modes of expression work together. Because a cognitive approach to narrative is not tied to one mode of expression, it promises to be a particularly useful paradigm for comics studies. However, research on storyworlds in narrative, and mental models more generally, has been developed largely on the basis of verbal narratives or propositions. Thus, in order to move from the comics text to the level of storyworlds, we need to explore in some detail how the components of comics narratives prompt the construction of mental models.

Time and space are the basic categories in terms of which we conceptualize our world as human beings. In his *Critique of Pure Reason* Immanuel Kant describes time and space as "pure forms of intuition" (1986: 44) that precede and structure our experience, and Kant's contemporary Gotthold Ephraim Lessing details in his essay *Laokoon* how the various arts engage with time and space. Lessing holds that there are "arts of time," such as prose and poetry, and "arts of space," such as painting and sculpture. Arts of time unfold through the reading process of a written text; arts of space attempt to capture a "pregnant moment" and provide us with a holistic but punctual impression that does not itself unfold through time (Lessing 2003: 23)—even though it may evoke or connote a temporal sequence. Thus, suggesting that the arts of time and arts of space differently engage with our "pure forms of intuition," Lessing provides in *Laocoon* an early account of what media studies today calls "media affordances" (see Kress 2003): that is, how different means of expression, different semiotic channels such as words and images, enable us to communicate different things or, for that matter, the same thing in different ways.

Images seem to provide an analogue mode of representation, depicting the world and its spatial extension "directly." Does this mean that what we see in an image in comics translates directly into the mental models we construct when engaging with the narrative? Most likely it does not. For one thing, even in the case of photographs in newspapers and films, images do not depict the world through pure analogy or iconicity but are deliberate means of communication, anchored in particular discourse contents and imbued with rhetorical purposes (see Aumont 1997). Further, even though Johnson-Laird describes his mental models as "icons," he distinguishes them clearly from visual images as such (2006: 37). Johnson-Laird's qualification is part of a larger debate about whether we use "mental imagery" when thinking and the extent to which this "imagery" corresponds to actual visual images (see Block 1982 for a collection of basic positions in this debate and Ganis et al. 2004 for a more current overview).

Thus, whereas the images of graphic narratives such as comics provide cues for constructing both the spatial and temporal dimensions of the storyworld, they are more like blueprints than photo-ready copies of the mental models that inform the design of the storyworld. Significantly, it is not obligatory for storyworlds to follow the principles of Euclidean space; for example, the distances between characters and objects in a room that figures in a narrative do not always correspond to our construction of the room in the mental model (see Langston, Kramer, and Glenberg 1998). Storyworlds, in this sense, are not representations of the content of the text, but representations of content that we take to be important or especially worthy of notice. Driven by the requirements of text comprehension, our primary goal is not to process spatial information accurately, as we might if the spatial details were presented on the flat, two-dimensional plane of Euclidean geometry, but rather to process the information thematically and according to the forms of embodiment such information enables.

Let's consider an example from *Promethea*, written by Alan Moore and penciled by J. H. Williams III, in order to flesh out this claim more concretely.

As Sophie Bangs travels through the storyworlds of the previous incarnations of the heroine Promethea, she is pursued by reptile warriors in Hy-Brasil. Hy-Brasil is the storyworld of the 1930s Promethea, which harks back to the adventure comics of the time. In the upper half of the page, we see Grace, the Promethea of Hy-Brasil, kill the two reptile warriors in a single somersault. We also see Sophie from the front as she observes the event in shock. In the lower half of the page, Grace has landed from her somersault and calms the animals. She is still in full swing from the movement, her sword drawn and bloody. Sophie, however, has changed her position completely: we see her back and no longer her face as she looks at the events. We can make sense of the relation between these two images by supplying the events that can be assumed to lie between them.[1] In other words, as readers process the visual clues of this page, they do not focus on the discrepancy between the panel images as such, but instead understand them as being tied to separate "events" (Walsh

2006). In this example from *Promethea* we first see Sophie shocked and overwhelmed by the events. Her facial expression and gestures communicate this information directly to us. In the second image we take a distanced position alongside her as she tries to make sense of what has just happened. This is the important narrative information in relation to Sophie here, not how much ground she really covered or the exact coordinates of her trajectory through space.

More generally, visual clues are integrated into a broader model of the world of the narrative, rather than being treated as iconic reproductions of features of that world. That is why the depiction of events on a page of comics does not need to be continuous in order for us to develop a coherent mental model of those events. In fact, panel images in comics are usually to some degree disjunctive or discontinuous, to stress the event-like character of the "pregnant moment" they depict—that is, the way that moment is caught up in a larger flow of happenings or occurrences. Readers scan both images and words for salient information as they imagine the storyworld. Even though images have different media affordances from words, their differences are not crucial for the construction of mental models; both provide clues about how to build a storyworld.

THE MULTIVERSE: CONTINUITY AND COUNTERFACTUALS

The previous section identified how readers use the text of comics to construct mental models or storyworlds; this section explores some of the challenges the alternative realities of the multiverse pose for the construction of mental models.

As we have seen, the continuity of the story a comic tells is not necessarily provided by the coherence of its clues, but by the (more or less coherent) mental model readers construct on the basis of those textual clues. The storyworld is not a reproduction of the visual information the story represents, but a model of what the interpreter takes to be relevant for understanding the story. Johnson-Laird develops the notion of a mental model on the premise that reasoning is a semantic process (Johnson-Laird 1983; see also Johnson-Laird, Byrne, and Schaeken 1992: 418). Human beings do not compute abstract logical formulae but construct a mental model for reasoning and develop a causal scenario to make sense of facts (2005: 203). Such mental models are also at the basis of meaning-making when we read fiction. We develop mental models in which we locate the events, characters, and settings about which we read. We use the mental model to draw inferences about what has happened in the story and to project what is going to happen. Out of this process of reasoning within a model—of answering pertinent questions of the narrative from a stock of knowledge that is organized in a mental model—continuity and coherence in storytelling emerge. Different paradigms of reader-oriented research have developed their own accounts of mental models: van Jijk and Kintsch (1983) call them "situation models"; Werth (1999), Stockwell (2002), and Gavins (2007) call them "textworlds"; and Herman (2002) calls them "storyworlds."

Mental models are akin to modal logics in philosophy and its possible worlds in that they build models of possibilities. In turn, counterfactuals are alternative sets of such possibilities. Ruth Byrne shows how our reasoning is based not only on mental models but also on our negotiation of different counterfactual possibilities. In what Byrne calls the "rational imagination," there are a number of "fault lines" along which the counterfactuals of the superhero multiverse unfold are different from those of reality, which Byrne discusses, readers can imagine them as alternative sets of possibilities afforded by a mental model.[2] In Wolfman's *Crisis on Infinite Earths*, for example, there is Earth-1 on which Superman as we know him lives. On Earth-2 Superman ages and marries Lois Lane. On Earth-3 Superman is the villain Ultraman, and his nemesis Lex Luthor is a science hero who defends Metropolis. For each of these storyworlds, one element of its basic premises has been changed. They work as counterfactuals, "what if" versions, relative to one another.

As Johnson-Laird and Byrne show, alternative mental models are used in everyday reasoning to determine the relative significance and truth-value of different propositions. However, the more possibilities we construct, the more counterfactual scenarios there are to negotiate, the more difficult it becomes to process them in our working memory (see Johnson-Laird 2006: 46–47, 112–13). In written narratives, as Danenberg (2008) has demonstrated, counterfactuals have been present in the novel throughout its history. The novel generally provides a baseline reality relative to its counterfactuals, either in the storyworld (for characters' and narrators' speculations and imaginations) or in the actual world (for historical counterfactuals). By contrast, though readers can consider Earth-1 and the young, unmarried Superman as a baseline reality from which an infinite number of earths diverts counterfactually, superhero comics like *Crisis on Infinite Earths* generally do not posit any single storyworld as the baseline reality or textual actual world. Rather, these comics develop mutually incompatible counterfactual versions of their storyworld—and more of these than anyone's working memory can hold. In one of its most recent treatments, the series *52* (2006–7), the DC multiverse comprises no less than fifty-two distinct storyworlds.

Constructing counterfactuals is, to be sure, part and parcel of our imagination and reasoning, and this accounts for the readiness with which readers accept the multiple storyworlds of superhero multiverses. Yet the cognitive load imposed by dozens of counterfactuals is immense, and without an established baseline reality it is very difficult to maintain a clear sense of all the different states of affairs that are the case in the multiverse. In order to cope with these challenges of the multiverse, superhero comics need to provide readers with means to identify character versions and the storyworld(s) to which they belong, and they need to present some basis, in lieu of a single, core reality, to which readers can relate the counterfactuals of the multiverse. In the following sections, I turn to *Crisis on Infinite Earths*, *Tom Strong*, and *Planetary* and show how these superhero comics guide their readers through the multiverse with the help of iconography and reader surrogates.

ICONOGRAPHY AS A SHORTCUT TO KNOWLEDGE STRUCTURES

In his essay, "The Myth of Superman," Umberto Eco describes superhero comics as cyclical, because their serial nature prevents the heroes from developing, growing, and dying. The novel, in contrast, is linear, and its author can make irrevocable changes, such as having the hero marry, die, or grow old. Even when his essay was first published in English (in a revised version, 1972), Eco's argument was not quite up-to-date with then-current superhero comics. For the Golden Age superheroes of the 1940s and 1950s, his characterization of comics as cyclical and devoid of development is apt. Yet as early as 1961, DC Comics had already introduced the concept of the "multiverse" with the story of *Flash of Two Worlds*. In this story, the current Flash, Barry Allen, moves so fast that he enters another storyworld, that of the original Flash, Jay Garrick.[3] As DC Comics continued to set its stories in numerous, noncongruent storyworlds, individual development of the superheroes and irrevocable events became possible, because in this way series would not have to end. Superheroes like Kal-El on Earth-2, the DC storyworld based on the Golden Age, could marry and grow old, while Superman on Earth-1, the current DC storyworld, is still young and courting. Different from other serial forms like the TV series or the novel in installments, superhero comics do not need to resolve "the possible" (see O'Sullivan 2009 on "the possible" and serial form); instead, they can keep it unresolved by representing several alternative realities simultaneously in their multiverse.

Although migration across narrative worlds is possible, each of these superhero versions is anchored in his or her own storyworld. Therefore superhero comics need to provide a way for readers to keep the character versions distinct and to relate each version to its own storyworld. The image from

Promethea discussed earlier suggests how readers identify characters and their storyworlds: Grace wears Egyptian-style headgear and antiquish body armor that fit well into the storyworld of 1930s adventure comics; Sophia's white shirt and jeans, on the other hand, put her at odds with the expectations tied to 1930s adventure comics and show that she is probably an interloper from another storyworld. Here the costumes, or in more general terms the iconography, of the characters allows readers to identify the storyworlds in which they are anchored.

Iconography refers to the visual attributes with which one can identify characters and allegories. Pallas Athene, for example, can be identified through her helmet, shield, and spear. The apostle Peter carries a key, and the cardinal sin Wrath is accompanied by a lion in visual depictions. Iconography has been defined by the art historian Erwin Panofsky (1955) as one of the levels on which we understand images. It is closely tied to the cultural knowledge that forms part of the readers' general world knowledge. For readers with little knowledge of ancient mythology or Christianity's folklore, it might be difficult to identify Pallas Athene, the apostle Peter, or the cardinal sin Wrath. Readers well versed in these conventions often recognize the figures instantly and tie them in with their general knowledge structures. For example, Pallas Athene can be identified as the daughter of Zeus and goddess of wisdom and rationality, and as belonging to the pantheon of antiquity. The iconography of the image works as a shortcut to the readers' knowledge of the character and narrative world she inhabits.

The creators of superhero comics have developed their own iconography of costumes and visual attributes, which can be used to identify character versions and their storyworlds. In Wolfman's *Crisis on Infinite Earths*, different versions of The Flash are distinguishable by their costumes: the Golden Age Flash wears a helmet with wings, while the Silver Age Flash wears a red suit, and the current Flash wears a yellow-red suit (later to be swapped out for the suit of the earlier, Silver Age Flash). Readers of superhero comics know which Flash is supposed to wear which costume and can thus distinguish among the different character versions with the help of these iconographic elements. Needless to say, after more than seven decades of superhero comics, the superhero iconography has become at least as complex as the iconography connected to ancient mythology, and at times its interpretation requires a similar degree of expert knowledge on the part of readers.

In Warren Ellis's *Planetary*, the Planetary team are called to Gotham City to investigate a series of gruesome murders (2003: 3). As it turns out, a "partial multiversal collapse" fused different storyworlds together, as well as the bodies of whoever happened to be at the same place (*multatis mutandis*) at the same time (2003: 3.7).[4] The Planetary team hunt down through the streets of

Gotham City the culprit who caused this collapse, following him through the different versions of the Batman storyworld created throughout the series' history. They encounter Batman from 1939 (2003: 3.38), from the 1960s TV series (2003: 3.25), from Frank Miller's *Dark Knight Returns* (2003: 3.27), and from Jeph Loeb's *Hush* (2003: 3.40). Readers know that they move through historically different versions of the Batman storyworld, because Batman looks, talks, and behaves like the different versions of the character in the Golden Age comics, the TV series, and Miller's and Loeb's more recent versions. With the help of superhero iconography, Warren Ellis takes readers on a guided tour through the history of the multiverse.

In Alan Moore's *Tom Strong*, iconographic elements provided a similar navigational function but without actually referring to existing series. *Tom Strong* is itself a commentary on superhero conventions and traditions. The series also tackles the concept of the superhero multiverse repeatedly. In one instance, Tom Strong's daughter Tesla wants to take a joyride into the multiverse through the hero's "search board" (2003: 3). She opens a portal through which multiple alternative versions of her character also step.

The Telsa of the *Tom Strong* storyworld we know from earlier stories encounters a cowgirl version, a Golden Age superhero version, a cartoon version, an adventure comics version, and a version inspired by the series *Judge Dredd*.[5] The appearance of these alternative versions of the character allows them to be anchored in different generic contexts, such as the Western, the adventure comic in the tradition of the *Tarzan* series, or science fiction. With the help of their contrasting superhero costumes and related iconographic features, readers can connect the different versions of characters to the alternative storyworlds from which they come and thus keep them distinct.

READER SURROGATES, THE PATHS, AND EXPLANATORY MODELS

In addition to the problem of keeping track of which character version belongs to which storyworld, the multiverse poses a second challenge for readers: the absence of a baseline reality against which various storyworld scenarios might be compared in order to identify the counterfactual versions. The most common version of a superhero character, like Superman working as a newspaper reporter and eternally courting Lois Lane, can be posited as the baseline reality for that character; but superhero comics more often make use of a specific textual strategy to provide a sure footing for their readers: characters who function as reader surrogates.

As the narratives of the superhero multiverse unfold in *Crisis on Infinite Earths*, *Planetary*, and *Tom Strong*, readers do not navigate these storyworlds by formally constructing a set of premises, as in the examples of logical reasoning that Johnson-Laird presents. Instead, readers usually mentally accompany a character as he or she explores the storyworld or, in this case, the superhero multiverse. I call these characters "reader surrogates." Surrogates venture on a path through the multiverse. Along this path they are faced with a manageable number of alternative realities, and the path itself connects this constellation of worlds into a larger, more or less coherent whole. Characters cross from one storyworld to another using several means, such as Tom's "search board," which rides the "quantum foam" between worlds in *Tom Strong* (2001: 3; 2003: 3.8), or the "travelstones" of the ship that sails the "bleed" between storyworlds in *Planetary* (2000: 4.15). Thanks to these devices, characters like Tom Strong and the Planetary team can physically migrate from one storyworld to another. Other means by which worlds in the multiverse are connected include the superpowers of heroes like The Harbinger, who can move back and forth between the alternative worlds of the multiverse in *Crisis on Infinite Earths*, and the portals that facilitate the change of storyworlds in *Tom Strong*.

All these narrative devices provide physical paths that connect storyworlds. As readers follow reader surrogates on their paths through the storyworlds of the multiverse and experience events with or rather through them, they understand together with these characters that they have moved from one storyworld of the multiverse to another. But readers do not merely follow their surrogate characters experientially on their physical paths through the multiverse; they are also privy to the explanatory models of the multiverse that these characters either develop on their own or have conveyed to them by others. In *Crisis on Infinite Earths*, the superheroes aboard The Monitor's satellite are told how the multiverse emerged and how anti-matter and the villain, appropriately named The Anti-Monitor, threaten to annul the many worlds of the multiverse one by one. Only merging the multiverse together into one storyworld again, and uniting all the superheroes to take up the fight against The Anti-Monitor, will save the day. Hence The Monitor and his helpers, The Harbinger and The Pariah, explain to the superheroes, and by proxy to readers, how the multiverse was formed, what threatens it, and how they can work against it (see Wolfman et al. 2000: 114–15, 182–90).

Tom Strong and *Planetary* feature more abstract explanatory models. When Tom Strange, Tom Strong's alternative version from a storyworld called Terra Obscura, is introduced in Alan Moore's *Tom Strong*, readers learn that Terra Obscura relates to Tom Strong's world in the same way that a particle relates to a "ghost particle" (2003: 4). As Tom Strange arrives in Tom Strong's world,

Strong explains to his family that Strange is like a mirror image of him and that Terra Obscura developed similarly to their own storyworld. Later on Tom Strong gives the physical explanation of the ghost particle to Tom Strange. The mirroring of storyworlds in particle and ghost particle provides an explanatory model that is based on a continuous spatial expansion partitioned by a limitation, that of the mirror, into different realities or worlds.

In *Planetary*, meanwhile, the explanatory model is the "snowflake." The main storyworld of *Planetary* is embedded in a multiverse structured in the shape of a "snowflake," as the ship explains to one of the characters (2000: 4.15). At this point in the narrative the comic portrays such a snowflake, reflecting light in many different colors. These reflections represent each storyworld within the snowflake. As readers learned earlier on, a group of 1930s pulp heroes reproduced this snowflake of reality in order to end the Second World War. A projection shows the snowflake as one of the pulp heroes explains the plan to his fellows and by proxy to us readers (2000: 1.19). Like *Tom Strong*, then, *Planetary* draws on an explanatory model of the multiverse that is rooted in physics and geometry and suggests a continuous space within which the multiverse unfolds, be it in the mirror reflection of the ghost particle or in the monster group symmetry of the "snowflake."[6] As in *Tom Strong*, in *Planetary* this physical model is explained to characters who function as reader surrogates.

Reader surrogates can form a replacement for the lost baseline reality of the multiverse. Even though no storyworld works as a textual actual world in the multiverse against which all the other storyworlds might be contrasted as counterfactual, reader surrogates can provide a basic point of departure for the process of constructing a mental model of the multiverse. The surrogates' path through the multiverse limits the number of alternative storyworlds with which readers need to be concerned, even as the explanatory models encountered along those paths provide keys to navigating the multiverse.

CONCLUSION

Superhero comics feature surprisingly complex storyworlds. Because their adventures have been narrated serially over the last seven decades, these characters' initially continuous narrative worlds have diversified into a vast multiverse. This multiverse holds different versions of different characters from different epochs and different series, in comics written by different authors. Indeed, like the characters' double identities and superpowers, the multiverse has become a convention of the superhero genre.

The multiverse is a set of mutually incompatible storyworlds. In principle these storyworlds can be viewed as counterfactuals: changing particular elements of the characters' situations, they relate to one other as "what if" versions. But because a baseline reality is often difficult to discern within this constellation of worlds, the multiverse poses considerable processing challenges. On the one hand, the iconography of superhero costumes provides readers with something of a shortcut, helping them identify and distinguish between different character versions. On the other hand, reader surrogates take paths through storyworlds that, in conjunction with explanatory models they (and thus readers) acquire along the way, enable interpreters to connect these worlds into the larger whole of the multiverse. As the narrative unfolds, readers can with the help of surrogates construct a more or less continuous mental model of the multiverse, incrementally moving through its different parts and sets of possibilities.

Drawing on our capacity for imagining and reasoning via mental models, the creators of superhero comics have developed strategies to facilitate storytelling—and story understanding—in the multiverse. These strategies provide new ways of characterizing, or contextualizing, the "intuitive belief in classical cosmology" that Ryan (2006) describes. The one-world commitments of classical cosmology stem from the coherence and parsimony of the mental models grounded in that world picture. But as superhero comics show, those same mental models can be adapted and extended to accommodate the imaginative wealth of the multiverse, which invites us to inhabit a different, postclassical cosmology.

NOTES

1. Note that the two animals no longer bear their riders and that Grace's sword is in her left hand in the top panels, but in her right hand in the lower panel.
2. Byrne distinguishes between several fault lines of counterfactuals in everyday reasoning, such as taking an action or not taking an action, socially acceptable or prohibited actions, and strongly causal or merely enabling relations. It would be an interesting extension of this article to investigate which of these fault lines also underlie the counterfactuals of the superhero multiverse. Note that superhero counterfactuals emerge not only from basic actions like Superman marrying Lois Lane, but also from rather outlandish propositions like alien invasions and purely narrative changes such as a switch of the dominant generic model organizing the text. DC's Elseworlds series features, besides the multiverse, several counterfactual narratives, such as Superman assuming leadership in the Soviet Union (in Mark Millar's *Superman: Red Son*) or superheroes getting caught up in the Apocalypse (in Mark Waid's *Kingdom Come*).
3. Most superhero personae are tied to a particular costume and mask, and sometimes they also have magical items that afford superpowers. In comics history, these superhero personae are assumed by different human characters. The costume and superpowers of The Flash

were donned first by Jay Garrick (from 1940) in the Golden Age and then by Barry Allen (1956–1985) in the Silver Age. Currently, Wally West (1986–) is The Flash [actually, Barry Allen became The Flash once again in 2011, after the writing of this essay—eds.].
4. Since the comics in question are nonpaginated, I quote from the texts according to the following convention: (year: issue, page number).
5. The Golden Age superhero version reproduces Mary Marvel's costume. Alan Moore himself wrote some of the *Judge Dredd* stories first published in the British science fiction comics magazine *2000 AD*.
6. The "monster group" is a mathematical symmetry group of 196,882 dimensions, which supposedly reflects the structure of the universe (see Roman 2007). "Ghost particle" is a term used by Isaac Asimov in his novel *The Neutrino* (1966).

WORKS CITED

Aumont, Jacques (1997). *The Image*. Trans. Claire Pajackowska. London: BFL.
Block, Ned, ed. (1982). *Imagery*. Cambridge, MIT Press.
Byrne, Ruth M. J. (2005). *The Rational Imagination: How People Create Alternatives to Reality*. Cambridge, MIT Press.
Dannenberg, Hilary (2008). *Coincidence and Counterfactuality: Plotting Time and Space in Narrative Fiction*. Lincoln: University of Nebraska Press.
Eco, Umberto (1972/1986). "The Myth of Superman." *Contemporary Literary Criticism: Modernism through Poststructuralism*. Ed. Robert Con Davis. London: Longman, 330–44.
Ellis, Warren, et al. (2000). *Planetary 1: All Over the World and Other Stories*. New York: Wildstorm-DC.
——— (2004). *Planetary: Crossing Worlds*. New York: Wildstorm-DC.
Ganis, Giorgio, William L. Thompson, Fred Mast, and Stephen M. Kosslyn (2004). "The Brain's Images: The Cognitive Neuroscience of Mental Imagery." *The Cognitive Neurosciences*. Ed. Michael S. Gazzaniga. Cambridge: MIT Press.
Garnham, Alan, and Jane Oakhill (1994). *Thinking and Reasoning*. Oxford: Blackwell.
Gavins, Joanna (2007). *Text World Theory: An Introduction*. Edinburgh: Edinburgh University Press.
Herman, David (2002). *Story Logic: Problems and Possibilities of Narrative*. Lincoln: University of Nebraska Press.
Jarvella, Robert J., Lita Lundquist, and Jukka Hyönä (1995). "Text, Topos and Mental Models." *Discourse Processes* 20.1: 1–28.
Johnson-Laird, Philip (1983). *Mental Models*. Cambridge: Harvard University Press.
——— (2005). "Mental Models and Thought." *The Cambridge Handbook of Thinking and Reasoning*. Ed. Keith J. Holyoak and Robert G. Morrison. Cambridge: Cambridge University Press: 185–208.
——— (2006). *How We Reason*. Oxford: Oxford University Press.
Johnson-Laird, Philip, Ruth Byrne, and Walter Schaeken (1992). "Propositional Reasoning by Model." *Psychological Review* 99.3: 418–38.
Kant, Immanuel (1781/1986). *Critique of Pure Reason*. Trans. J. M. D. Meiklejohn. London: Dent.
Kress, Gunther (2003). *Literacy in the New Media Age*. London: Routledge.
Kukkonen, Karin (2009). "Textworlds and Metareference in Comics." *Metareference across Media: Theory and Case Studies*. Ed. Werner Wolf. Amsterdam: Rodopi. 499–514.

Langston, William, Douglas C. Kramer, and Arthur M. Glenberg (1998). "The Representation of Space in Mental Models Derived from Text." *Memory and Cognition* 16.2: 147–62.
Lessing, Gotthold Ephraim (1776/2003). *Laokoon, oder: Über die Grenzen der Malerei und Poesie.* Stuttgart: Reclam, 2003.
Moore, Alan, et al. (2000). *Promethea 1.* La Jolla: America's Best Comics.
——— (2001). *Tom Strong: Book 1.* La Jolla: America's Best Comics.
——— (2005). *Tom Strong: Book 2.* La Jolla: America's Best Comics.
O'Sullivan, Sean (2009). "Reconstructing the Rim: Thoughts on Deadwood and Third Seasons." *Third Person: Authoring and Exploring Vast Narratives.* Ed. Pat Harrigan and Noah Wardrip-Fruin. Cambridge: MIT Press: 323–32.
Panofsky, Erwin (1955). *Meaning in the Visual Arts: Papers in and on Art History.* New York: Doubleday.
Roman, Mark (2007). *Symmetry and the Monster: One of the Greatest Quests in Mathematics.* Oxford: Oxford University Press.
Ryan, Marie-Laure (1991). *Possible Worlds, Artificial Intelligence, and Narrative Theory.* Bloomington: Indiana University Press.
——— (1992). "Possible Worlds in Recent Literary Theory." *Style* 26.4: 528–53.
——— (2006). "From Parallel Universes to Possible Worlds: Ontological Pluralism in Physics, Narratology, and Narrative." *Poetics Today* 17.4: 633–74.
Stockwell, Peter (2002). *Cognitive Poetics: An Introduction.* London: Routledge.
Van Dijk, Teun, and Walter Kintsch (1983). *Strategies of Discourse Comprehension.* New York: Academic Press.
Walsh, Richard (2006). "Narrative Imagination across Media." *Modern Fiction Studies* 52.4: 855–68.
Werth, Paul (1999). *Text Worlds: Representing Conceptual Space in Discourse.* Harlow, Longman.
Wolfman, Marv, et al. (2000). *Crisis on Infinite Earths.* New York: DC Comics.

A Song of the Urban Superhero

SCOTT BUKATMAN

Chapter originally titled "The Boys in the Hoods: A Song of the Urban Superhero," reprinted by permission from *Matters of Gravity: Special Effects and Supermen in the 20th Century*, 184–223. © 2003 Duke University Press. All rights reserved. Reprinted by permission of the publisher. www.dukeupress.edu.

> There is a city, a glorious and singular place. Old and yet pristine, ornate and yet streamlined. A metropolis of now and then and never was.
> **STARMAN #1**

IN THE STORIES THEY COME STRAIGHT AT YOU, IN BOLD, BLURRED STREAKS OF color against the ground of the great metropolis. At first glance they are terribly crude—especially in their first decades of existence—but familiarity and developing history endow them with copious nuance. Cloaking themselves in vibrant tones, they come straight at you in a blur and streak across the panel, the page, the city, the mind, and then they stop: wondrous polychrome monuments, somehow intimate and solid and untouchable in the sky.

I find it fascinating, or at least noteworthy, that superheroes, many of whom could, let's face it, live anywhere they want, invariably reside in American cities.[1] Other comics bring us to the 'burbs (*Archie*) or beyond known space (*Star Wars*), but superheroes are homebodies as much as homeboys: Superman is generally content to operate in and around Metropolis, Batman's name is synonymous with Gotham City, Opal City is Starman's official place of residence, and for a strange while, all the Marvel superheroes jostled for room (and, presumably, apartments) in—where else?—New York. Crime remains at the level of heists and elaborate capers, the crowd exists only to gawk, and an anticorporatist populism marks the sole intrusion of a realpolitik. In the mid-1980s, creators began to explore the relation between heroic figure and urban ground, and the city became something more than a generic background for superheroic derring-do.[2] The superhero-city link has become increasingly explicit in such recent comics as Kurt Busiek's *Astro City* and Alan Moore's *Top 10*.

Let me propose that American superheroes encapsulated and embodied the same utopian aspirations of modernity as the cities themselves. Superhero narratives thus comprise a genre that joins World's Fairs, urban musicals, and slapstick comedies in presenting urban modernity as a utopia of sublime grace. These comics dream impossible figures in ideal cities. Even if those cities themselves were hardly individuated in the first decades of superhero comics—Coast City and Central City served as backdrops more than fully felt environments—still, they were cities, and while superhero comics don't produce an urban analysis that city planners can use, they nevertheless provide a compelling iconography of a rich urban imaginary, unfettered and uncanny.

Because the audience for superhero comics largely consisted of adolescent and postadolescent males (as any visitor to a comics shop can attest), explanations of comics' appeal have stuck to well-worn paths mostly trodden by Oedipus. Superheroes have been regarded as power fantasies for boys who have not yet acclimated socially (as with kids' fascination with less-than-human/more-than-human dinosaurs). Superheroes are also said to embody the displacement of sexual energy into aggression (which is why comics are profligate with property damage and evenly matched opponents locked in nonlethal slugfests). And of course superheroes are authority and order incarnate, innately fascist at their core (especially Superman, our homegrown *übermensch*). Still further, superheroes negotiate dichotomous roles: the child (the orphaned Bruce Wayne) and the father (Batman), the servant of the law (crime fighter) and the autonomous outsider (vigilante) are condensed into a single, titanic figure. Displacement and condensation are the real superpowers. Thus have superheroes been reduced to a standard set of psychoanalytic and sociological maneuvers. No wonder they were neurotic by the 1960s.

The stories themselves generally tell it this way (and creators and fans alike generally concur): the superhero is a figure of great independence who chooses to serve the laws and moral values of our society. He is an urban dweller because that's where the criminals are; he operates beyond the strict parameters of the law the better to enforce its values; he supports the status quo but remains uncorrupted by the constant corruption he encounters. As comics creator Howard Chaykin observed, not inaccurately, "The comic book reader has very proscribed ideas about how comic book heroes behave. It comes back to Raymond Chandler's line about Alan Ladd: 'A small boy's idea of a tough guy.'"[3] The superhero is Philip Marlowe in tights.

I would say that as avatars of law and order and justice and authority go, superheroes are a trivial and unconvincing lot. For the most part, nothing really changes through their actions. Their enemies are only marginally freakier than they. The battles leave the "real" problems of society sporadically acknowledged and hardly addressed. Further, if ideas of preserving order are present at all, it is only at the level of narrative: the sequence of images, with their candy-colored costumes, dynamic and irregular layouts, movement beyond the boundary of the frame, fragmented temporalities, sound effects, and further abstractions, insist on a pervasive and appealing chaos, more Midway than White City. The hyperbolic spectacle of the color comics page easily undermines and, yes, subverts, thin fantasies of social order.

Superhero comics present something other than, or apart from, aggressive fantasies of authority and control; something more closely aligned with fantasy and color but at the same time specific to the urban settings that pervade the genre.[4]

Grids and Grace

To ensure a more rational system of urban growth in New York, in 1811 a gridded projection dividing the entire territory of the island into a system of 155 streets and 12 avenues (a total of 2,028 blocks) was superimposed on the topography of Manhattan: "a blueprint for the island's manifest destiny," the architect Rem Koolhaas wrote in *Delirious New York*. The system was at once totalitarian (only Broadway, cutting a broad diagonal swath across the grid, was allowed to deviate from the system) and democratic (a leveling of irregularities, an erasure of difference), an order that would permit expansion and prosperity. With the advent of the grid, rationalist order ruled the city, or at least that's how the story goes. Koolhaas, on the other hand, views the two-dimensional array as little more than a blind for the irrational fantasies that lay at the heart of Manhattan, "the neutralizing agent" that structured the "subutopian fragments" of the city upon which urban planning never completely foreclosed. Horizontality was balanced, perhaps even contradicted, by the upward thrust of the city into vast skyscrapers, each disconnected block and each building, every separate floor and room defined by its own unique and grandiose designs and imaginings. "Through the establishment of enclaves such as the Roman Gardens—emotional shelters for the metropolitan masses that represent ideal worlds removed in time and space, insulated against the corrosion of reality—the fantastic supplants the utilitarian in Manhattan."[5] The irrational dreams of the city only *seemed* constrained by the even tempos of the urban grid.

The urban newspaper was also characterized by the regularity of its columns and the compaction of vast amounts of information within a limited space. In Pulitzer's and Hearst's wooing of New York's vast immigrant and laboring population, the newspaper, once a source of dry information central to the mercantile economy of the nation, became a conduit for fantasies of urban existence. With the introduction of illustrations and multicolumned headlines, the organization of the page owed more to the grid, but this was a grid characterized by new, more open spaces that broke from the strict constraints of even columns. Illustrations and headlines were the signs, lights, and marquees of Broadway and perhaps, too, the invigorating expanse of Olmstead and Vaux's Central Park or sometimes even the playground of Coney.

Newspaper comics, whether in their initial single-panel incarnation or later horizontal sequences, also offered entertainment and respite for eyes regulated by columnar precision, although their legibility also depended on the grid's regularity. In his *New York Journal*, William Randolph Hearst pushed sensational stories, multicolumned headlines, and plenty of multicolumned illustrations. The papers increasingly reflected the kaleidoscopic experience of life in the city, and the Sunday color supplements gave readers a fantasia of familiar urban types in sumptuous settings. While newspapers established their centrality as a set of information discourses through reportage, advertising, and editorials, comics remained distinct: aesthetically through their color and varied organization; and in their content, which generally stressed fantasy, if not outright metamorphosis. Comics were the most conspicuous noninformational feature, or at least the only one that had no pretensions about uplifting the masses. In their deployment of color and fantasy, they were a deliberate departure from the rest of the paper.

The most visually striking strips luxuriated in the space of a full page, and artists frequently played with (and, in the case of one memorable Winsor McCay strip from 1905, exploded) the grids and boxes that dominated the rest of the paper.[6] The fluid metamorphoses that mark nearly all of McCay's *Little Nemo* pages introduce the reader to built environments of surprising yet inevitable complexity. *Nemo* summons thoughts of visionary architecture, but the pages are also reminiscent of the ornate and singular facades on the apartment buildings of the *belle époque*. In contrast, the compressed and formulaic pages of early comic books suggest the overcrowded tenements—democratic, graceless, and durable—that defined immigrant neighborhoods.[7]

The superhero city is founded on the relationship between grids and grace. The city becomes a place of grace by licensing the multitude of fantasies that thrived against the "constraining" ground of the grid. Grace is a function of elegant precision but also implies a virtuosic transcendence of the purely functional, and the city thus possesses a grace of its own. Superheroes are physically graceful, but they are also graced through their freedom, their power, and their mobility. Superhero comics embody the grace of the city; superheroes are graced by the city. Through the superhero, we gain a freedom of movement not constrained by the ground-level order imposed by the urban grid. The city becomes legible through signage and captions and the hero's panoramic and panoptic gaze. It is at once the site of anonymity and flamboyance. Above all, soaring above all, the superhero city is a place of weightlessness, a site that exists, at least in part, of playful defiance of the spirit of gravity.

PART ONE
THE PHENOMENOLOGY OF SUPERHERO CITIES

The twentieth-century city put new concentrations of information into increasingly rapid circulation, coincident with new modes of perception and social definition. The now familiar litany of modernist tropes usually includes the problem of mapping an urban space that had become so big, complex, and dynamic as to evade easy comprehension by both its residents and its ostensible controllers. There were anxieties about urban concentration and the concurrent impact of new technologies on mundane life. The city was a contradictory field: the humans within it were reduced to economic units of undifferentiated labor value, and yet, as Georg Simmel famously argued, liberation might lie within this anonymity. The city was its faceless masses, but it was also the new opportunities to make (or remake) a self (or selves). Cities were hardly panoptic spaces of total control: the perfect gaze of the authorities worked most efficiently in fiction that still seemed to posit an amateur sleuth as the last, best, hope.

In fiction, journalism, and cinema, the uncentered city appeared as a dark maze or labyrinth, a site of disappearance and murky invisibilities, a giant trap for the unwary, but it was also a stage for spectacular, kaleidoscopic experience. The city was described in a set of clichéd but not inappropriate dichotomies: the familiar and the strange, the sunlit and the shadowed, the planned and the chaotic, the sublime and the uncanny. This was the poem of the city, so compelling that one could almost see the crosswalks filled with bedazzled, entranced citizens, all struggling to retain their balance on the mesmerizing streets of modernity. Flying over the horizon relatively late in this history, superheroes nevertheless inherit and embody many of these paradoxical tropes. Some define perceptual paradigms and tactics of negotiation appropriate to city life.

Flying in the City

The experience of the city (and the comic book) is less one of static order than dynamic negotiation. "Within the network of its rectilinearity, movement becomes ideological navigation between the conflicting claims and promises of each block," writes Koolhaas.[8] The city, in his seductive view, is not the logical place of business that it pretends to be; it is instead a multitude of fantasies projected in three dimensions. The superhero, in his costumed extravagance, muscular absurdity, and hyperkineticism, superimposes the fantastic on the face of the utilitarian, bringing the city back to the fact of its fantasy. First of all, superheroes negate the negation of the grid—they move through space in three dimensions, designing their own vehicles, choosing their own trajectories. To be a superhero, you've got to be able to move. Superhero narratives are sagas of propulsion, thrust, and movement through the city.

New York City is a city of intense circulation. Vivian Gornick finds comfort in its incessant turbulence: "The street keeps moving, and you've got to love the movement. You've got to find the composition of the rhythm, lift the story from the motion, understand and not regret that all is dependent on the swiftness with which we come into view and pass out again. The pleasure and the reassurance lie precisely in the speed with which connection is established and then let go of. No need to clutch. The connection is generic not specific. There's another piece of it coming right along behind this one."[9] But while it might be a city of intense circulation, it also quickly became a place of blocked circulation. The grids of Manhattan imposed regularity on the traffic but channeled it into narrow streets that worked against the flow as well as the logic of the island's narrow, hilly topography.[10] And so, not surprisingly, nearly every superhero worthy of the name has enhanced powers of motion. Superman, Green Lantern, Mighty Mouse, and Captain Marvel can fly, Wonder Woman has an invisible airplane, The Flash has superspeed, and Batman swings on a rope, drives the Batmobile, flies the Batgyro, and so on.[11] The Spectre can walk through walls, Iceman can ride an ice slide, the Fantastic Four have a hovercar, Hawkman and the Angel have wings, and Daredevil and Spider-Man leap and swing. Some of them can teleport, but I can't remember who.

Plastic Man is perhaps the most urban of them all—maybe because he doesn't seem to own a car. When Plastic Man needs to be somewhere, he runs, and Jack Cole's art deploys an enormous array of such forms of urban clutter as lampposts, subway entrances, cobblestoned streets, peeling posters, and moldering brick walls. We are often placed so low to the ground that even the curbs loom menacingly. Cole continually varied perspectives on a single page as Plastic Man's body snaked from panel to panel, his stretched body itself linking the spaces of the panels, the city.[12]

The best of them move with more than swift efficiency, their poise and elegance also speaking a kind of poetic appropriation of space. Batman's eloquent cape, Green Lantern's slightly arched back, Daredevil's acrobatic virtuosity, and Superman's vibrant coloration all speak to more than the business at hand.[13] Alan Moore's "imaginary" last Superman story finds Lois Lane describing one of her innumerable rescues: "What happened next had all the familiarity of a recurring dream. I was falling, and a violet comet was falling alongside me. The reds and blues ran together, you see, so that's how he looked when he flew . . . a violet comet."[14] In the consciously mythic *Superman for All Seasons*, Tim Sale represents Superman's blurred superspeed with a thick patina of crayon.[15] There is an appealing childlike wonder in these kinetic views. Superheroes preserve the order of the city but need not submit to it. What they must do, however, is partake of its movement.

The Legible City

Cities were also "word cities," as Peter Fritzsche calls them, spaces to be literally and continually read. Newspapers, magazines, and comics helped to constitute the word cities of the United States, as did a wealth of private and municipal signage.[16] Comics superimpose text on the space of the city.[17] In signs, labels, captions, word balloons, and sound effects, words become a fundamental aspect of urban space. Captains are placed in colored boxes, sound effects are depicted in BRIGHT! BOLD! FORMS! These texts compete for the eye's attention, but the overall effect is usually to guide the eye through the complex space. The reader simultaneously juggles words that are part of the landscape (signs), words that are constitutive of narrative (captions, word balloons), and words that produce sensational impact (sound effects). In the later 1970s, such artists as Walt Simonson and Howard Chaykin refined the interplay of image and text: in *American Flagg!*, *Time²*, and *Manhunter*, reading and looking overlapped as they hadn't before.

The city's many layers are also made legible in the superhero city. Superman tunnels through the city, and the reader is given a cross section of buildings, streets, substructures, and even the rocky substrate. The Hulk shoves The Thing down a manhole, and Jack Kirby divides the panel to show both the street above and the embarrassin' space below. Otomo Katsuhiro's *Akira* is set in a postapocalyptic Neo-Tokyo rendered in meticulous detail. Broken slabs of steel-reinforced concrete, jumbled slabs of asphalt, and the dense underpinnings of the city are all newly exposed to harsh light.

Further, superhero comics are filled with schematic diagrams, like the one of the Fantastic Four's high-rise headquarters. Everything is carefully labeled, from the Giant Map Room and the Hidden Elevator to the Fantasticar Hangar, Trophy Room, and Weapon Collection and the Long Range Passenger Missile (able to reach any point on Earth in minutes). These schematics provide a way of reading the city and are great instances of skyscrapers as both rational and fantastic spaces. The Baxter Building is the Fantastic Four's place of business. The labels are signs that this is a working environment (they're also a further set of signs in the legible city), and they also provide some tantalizing clues as to how the environment works. But, while my childhood mind could well imagine that skyscrapers contained Conference Rooms and Computers, did they also have Missile Monitoring Rooms? The Hidden Elevator ran up and down the length of the building, which the Fantastic Four shared with other, presumably less fantastic, tenants, and another label explained how "Rocket exhaust travels down these pipes to expend its heat in fire pits beneath the city surface." Fire pits beneath the city surface? Wow! So labeling gave me a rational city that was anything but, while cutaway views showed me high-tech hiding places nested within the modern spaces of adulthood.

The superhero city is experienced in a rush but opened to contemplation: it is distinguished by this dialectic of exuberant motion and a legible stasis. By exposing and labeling the multiple layers of the city, superhero comics enact something equivalent to the superhero's panoramic and panoptic gaze, just as the dynamic organization of figures and panels enact something of the city's constant hustle.

The City in Our Grasp

Before there was a Giant Man, an Ant Man, or an Atom, McCay's Little Nemo grew to the size of Manhattan's rising skyline, as he and Flip stepped over the buildings like toy blocks. Decades later, Bill Watterson's Calvin underwent a similar metamorphosis.[18] In the comic strips, fantasy and dreams explicitly licensed the transformation: superhero comics relied on radioactivity or Red Kryptonite to do the same job. Whatever the cause, scale is constantly refigured in the superhero's city.

Bill Finger, a Batman cocreator, was fond of battles at trade exhibitions, where the Caped Crusader and Boy Wonder would hop along the keys of giant typewriters. The expanding list of Kryptonian survivors included the entire city of Kandor, which had been shrunk, bottled, and stolen by Brainiac before the planet exploded. The citizens of Kandor live their normal, albeit tiny, lives on a shelf in Superman's Fortress of Solitude, apparently undismayed by the giant faces of Superman or Lois Lane peering down at them. The most uncanny aspect of Kandor was not simply its portability, although that was pretty interesting, but the notion that a city could be detached, isolated, and removed from its surroundings. The city was a clearly bounded, self-enclosed, self-sustaining environment, something like Manhattan Island without the outlying suburbs. Who feeds the people of Kandor, and how do they dispose of waste? Do these people have jobs? What do they *do* in there? While these are the kinds of questions that earthbound urban planners might well ponder, Kandor's secrets remain its own. Susan Stewart reminds us that the miniature erases labor and cause and effect; it also arrests time.[19]

Humans loom above Kandor, a display city, Krypton's Futurama. In a recent Batman animated film, the Joker and Batman do battle at the abandoned site of the Gotham City World's Fair in a Futurama-style exhibition space.[20] The antagonists are the size of buildings. The Joker even wears the spire of the Chrysler Building, just as its architect, William Van Allen, did at a 1931 masquerade ball. The city, then, becomes a toy, a pocket city, a dream house. The body of the child, as with Nemo and Calvin or the ostensible adults of the superhero comics, becomes adequate to the size of the city. The city moves from sublime unknown to marvelous object, its blocks now children's blocks to be rearranged at will. These shifts of scale put the body into a fundamentally different, more tactile relation to the city. "The hand is the measure of the miniature," Susan Stewart writes.[21] Enlarging the body or diminishing the city permits one to "grasp" the city as whole. "To toy with something is to manipulate it, to try it out within sets of contexts, none of which is determinative."[22]

The city is shrunken and distilled in the superhero comic in ways that recall the distilled urbanism of world's fairs. The World of Tomorrow, in the guise of the 1939 New York World's Fair, had opened to the public only one year after the appearance of Superman, the Man of Tomorrow. Fairs organized the city into a set of panoramic views, with ample opportunities to see it all from the air. Towers and Ferris wheels and parachute jumps swept the visitors aloft to experience a "fiction of knowledge" and to satisfy "this lust to be a viewpoint." And the fair was the city reduced in scale, open to view, an educational, sensational, but nonlinear immersion in an ideal urban experience. They were progressive and nostalgic in exactly the ways that superheroes were. They humanized the future in terms of the past. Two issues of *World's Fair Comics* appeared, with Superman and Batman sharing the covers, and the fair marked the first public appearance of a "live" Superman (played by Ray Middleton) as part of 1940's "Superman Day." And then there was a short-lived superhero called The Fantom of the Fair, who lurked in utopia's basement (ok, its substructure), fighting crime at, well, world's fairs. In the last decade, a striking number of superheroes have managed to visit the 1939 fair: The Squadron Supreme, Superman, the citizens of Terminal City, and Batman all return to this locus of American urban utopian aspiration as if they recognized their ideological complicity in producing a distilled, controllable urbanism.[23]

PART TWO: SUPERHERO CITY TOURS

Superman's Metropolis

Superman was inevitable. Jerry Siegel and Joe Shuster had already tried the name out on a mad villain, which made some kind of sense against the background of an incompletely grasped Nietzschean philosophy and the growing sense of impending war in Europe. Even two Midwestern lads could sense a change in the air. America needed a Superman of its own, an American Superman—a boy's Superman. Actually, they gave us a pretty good one.

Superman entered a substantial tradition of hero AS America. With his ability to fly and his inhuman endurance, he became a worthy successor to Lindbergh, while he was also, like Babe Ruth, a power slugger. He was a fine and willing celebrity, frequently sighted by ordinary citizens ("Look! Up in the sky!"). For consumers he incarnated the dreams of personal flying machines, and he was always comfortingly collectible. In a country dedicated to propositions of progress and the "new," Superman appeared with his invulnerable body: the body that retains no marks, on which history cannot be inscribed.

Superman's city, Metropolis, was named for the darkly modern urban center in Fritz Lang's 1926 film, but our Metropolis is more democratic and far less decadent. Its vertical lines cut cleanly to the sky. Our Metropolis is soaring lines and vivid colors. Superman belongs here. Kryptonian skyscrapers tumbled like dominoes in the first panel of Superman's first daily strip. Jor-El bundled his only begotten son into a prototype rocket and aimed it toward Earth. The little rocket, streamlined and slightly bulbous, resembles Siegel's skyscrapers, and the little baby, of course, becomes something of a skyscraper himself. The icon of Superman and the icon of the modern American skyscraper are closely associated. (Superman is raised in the Midwest by Jonathan and Martha Kent before setting out for Metropolis. Immigrant Kryptonian orphan *and* rural American: Superman comes to the city from both directions.) Shortly after his arrival in Metropolis (which went unnamed until 1939 and *Action Comics* #16), Clark Kent took a job at the *Daily Planet*, whose building probably wasn't designed by Raymond Hood but might have been.

Superman *is* a skyscraper, "able to leap tall buildings in a single bound," as I just mentioned: a monument of the modern city, to be gawked at as part of the landscape. He is blessed with panoramic perception, a magisterial gaze upon a known and controlled urban landscape. His body is clothed in a skintight uniform, ornamented only by a functional *S* and a red cape cum banner. There are no hidden secrets to his power—he just hovers there, a Super-Every-Man. Light informs him, from his brightly colored togs to the yellow sunlight that endows him with strength and the beams of heat vision that he can direct at will. No mask hides his face with false ornament: his features are clear, his focus direct. The magisterial gaze becomes democratic, and the "inhuman" skyscraper is mastered by a visibly human body.

There were some precedents. In 1931, the world watched the construction of the Empire State Building, and the photographs taken by Lewis Hine celebrated the young American men who lived and worked in the sky. One figure straddles a guy wire, his right arm stretched above him, his left curved against his body. The city is visible in the distance far below his strikingly casual body. Seven years later, on the cover of *Superman* #1, a smiling Superman rises above the city in a similar pose, the buildings again arrayed below. And people could climb the Statue of Liberty, or be lifted to the top of the Empire State itself, attempting "to find the machinery hidden in the god and approach a transcendent view of the city himself or herself."[24]

If there is a tectonic honesty to this so-called Man of Steel, let's note that he represented, in 1938, a kind of Corbusierian ideal. Superman has X-ray vision: walls become permeable, transparent. Through his benign, controlled authority, Superman renders the city open, modernist, and democratic: he furthers a sense that Le Corbusier described in 1925, namely, that "Everything is known to us." Knowledge depended, for Corbusier, on the mass media, but for Superman "knowledge coincides with sight"—natural sight, I'd add.[25] His X-ray vision imposes transparency, and it manages to reinvent and undermine the city as a private space. There are still secrets behind the old stone walls, but Superman punctures the walls with his gaze and fists and brings the secrets to life.

The aerial perspective provides a powerful liberation. De Certeau wrote of riding to the top of a New York skyscraper that it is "to be lifted out of the city's grasp. One's body is no longer clasped by the streets that turn and return it according to an anonymous law: nor is it possessed, whether as player or played, by the rumble of so many differences."[26] Superman is, as much as anything else, a magisterial view of Metropolis, a way of seeing and negotiating the space of seeing. "The exaltation of a Gnostic and scopic drive: the fiction of knowledge is related to this lust to be a viewpoint and nothing more."[27]

Superman seems to be an incarnation of Corbusier's panoramic authority based on perfect transparency, control, and knowledge. He is democratic, open, and idealistic, carving a space for the little guy. A walking, flying figure of utopian progress, Superman prefigures in his mode of perception and spatial negotiation the development of the city of tomorrow. But fantasies of urban planning were rarely so nobly realized, especially in America, and by the later part of the century Corbusier's vision seemed myopic, overly centralized, and terrifyingly corrupted. Highway systems had displaced the centrality of the metropolis, and the emergent configurations were as distant from the Radiant City of Corbusier as from the Broadacre City of Frank Lloyd Wright. The Metropolis of To-Morrow had become the Suburbia of To-Day. Urban "renewal" tended toward the obliteration of both history and nature, demolishing neighborhoods, air quality, and ethnic pluralism in shortsighted obeisance to the engorged networks of automobile circulation.

Eight years before Superman appeared above the streets of Metropolis, Corbusier polemicized against modernity's assault on the human sensorium.

Using language that first recalls Benjamin, Kracauer, and other nascent critical theorists of the early twentieth century, his shock polemic abruptly turns toward severe social realignment: "man lives in a perpetual state of instability, insecurity, fatigue, and accumulating delusions. Our physical and nervous organization is brutalized and battered by this torrent; it makes its protest, of course, but it will soon give way unless some energetic decision, far-sighted and not too long delayed, brings order once more to a situation that is rapidly getting out of hand."[28] Superman was the New Man, the Man of Steel, the Man of Tomorrow, a "far-sighted" fellow, "not too long delayed" (faster than a locomotive) who could suffer the brutalizing shocks of modernity with neither broken bones nor neurasthenic breakdowns. Superior senses and a body so strong that "nothing less than a bursting shell could penetrate his skin" made him the first perfect citizen of the modern Metropolis. But if Superman was the perfect citizen, Lex Luthor is its perfect manager. Lex was retooled in the 1980s and 1990s as the flip side of Superman's democratic radiance. He emerged as the Master of Metropolis—a corporate city planner discontented with this unpredictable individualist sailing through his skies. Luthor, not Superman, best personifies Corbusier's call to order and energetic decision. "Metropolis was nothing until I rebuilt it according to my vision," he ruminates. "All in all, it's a perfect picture of order." But Superman, "an alien with freakish powers," threatens the control of "me, the true Master of Metropolis." Luthor combined the instrumental reason of Corbusier, the independent bureaucratic clout and self-aggrandizement of Robert Moses, and the ruthless baldness of Edward Arnold in *Meet John Doe*. And so Metropolis, whether operating under the gaze of Superman or Luthor, remains primarily on Corbusier's turf.

Batman's Gotham

Gotham City, it hardly needs to be said, has no master. It is a city askew, defined by angular perspectives, impenetrable shadows, and the grotesque inhabitants of the night. The screenplay for Tim Burton's 1989 film sums up what Gotham City had become through the 1970s and 1980s: "stark angles, creeping shadows, dense, crowded, airless, a random tangle of steel and concrete, as if Hell had erupted through the sidewalk and kept on growing."[29] Batman's nemesis is the id figure of the Joker rather than Luthor's cool capitalist. Gotham is a city of massed solidities: heavy stone and thick fog cloak its goings-on. The physiognomies here are as warped as the perspectives (Chester Gould's *Dick Tracy* was a precursor) but as solid as the buildings. The city became a "backdrop which was sometimes a mood-setting frieze, sometimes an enveloping or even choking atmosphere that mirrored the twisted preoccupations of villains."[30]

Here, as in the detective fiction of the Victorian era and the American pulps and early narrative cinema, crime links the spaces of the city—high and low, penthouses and sewers. All of the city's sunshine and shadow dichotomies are knitted together, and every place is equally susceptible to criminal infection and infestation. Frank Miller's *Dark Knight Returns* was central to bringing this version of Gotham City to the fore, with doses of *Blade Runner* and *Road Warrior* compounding the sense of nihilistic gloom. Gotham became an even more grotesque, gothic, claustrophobic environment. The bird's-eye view—Superman's magisterial, panoramic perception—is insufficiently panoptic. Gotham is a city defined more by its underworld. It's a concatenation of hidden spaces, corners, and traps. This city needs to be read, deciphered, made legible, and the one to do it lives among the bats in his own subterranean hideout.

Tom Gunning has shown how around the turn of the century surveillance and counter-surveillance structured the urban detective story. Disguise became a major weapon, and acts of deception and unmasking increasingly structured the narratives.[31] Superman's X-ray vision is too natural, its worldview too rooted in transparency, to get to the bottom of things. Superman's naturalism yields to the dark ratiocinations and high technologies of Batman. Batman inherits from the urban pulp tradition of The Shadow and The Spider, and there is more than a little Holmes and Dupin in his ratiocentrism. His effects are carefully considered, and his endless training has made him a self-made fighting machine—perhaps more steely than his Metropolis counterpart. He is rational, if monomaniacal, but throws fear around him. Superman, appearing in *Action Comics*, inspired wonder, curling across the sky like a rainbow. Batman summoned a more sublime terror. But both figures, all of these figures, are lingeringly uncanny—childhood anxieties and desires granted crudely concrete form.

Terry Castle has argued that the rise of the Enlightenment was inevitably accompanied "like a toxic side effect" by its uncanny underside, and it is indeed striking how quickly the nocturnal figure of the Batman followed the vivid blur of Superman onto the world stage.[32] Metropolis and Gotham City were variations on New York, but Gotham was the dark side while the sun tended to shine a whole lot more brightly on Superman's city. Recent Superman/Batman teamings, beginning with Frank Miller's *The Dark Knight Returns*, have emphasized the dichotomous nature of these two heroes and their two cities. While Luthor and the Joker have their admirers, many revisionist writers have become increasingly intent on exploring the evident (and all too often mechanistic) dualism of these two.[33]

The Joker serves as another double, a psychotic funhouse mirror image of the somber and obsessed hero.[34] He first appeared in *Batman* #1, only a year after the Caped Crusader's own debut: a grotesque figure with a permanent maniacal grin ripped from the posters for Coney Island's Steeplechase Park, chalk-white features and a green shock of slicked-back hair, all dressed up in a purple flat-brimmed hat and zoot suit. The eerie whiteness of the Joker's face signals its opposite: it's the "dark" version of Batman's removable disguise, even more unnatural against the prevailing gloom. Tim Burton's film updated him as a jive pimp, but the Joker was always racial ambiguity incarnate—the original "white Negro."

Spider-Man in New York

In an early issue of *Spider-Man*, Peter Parker decides he needs a study break and sets off, as his arachnid alter ego, to swing around the city for a while. It's hard to imagine Batman or The Hulk making the rounds for the sheer joy of moving, but Spider-Man is after all a healthy teenager with a need to grandstand.[35]

Spider-Man is something of an all-around pariah. Parker began as a nerd's nerd, overly fascinated with chemistry class and oblivious to embodied subjectivities. A bite from a radioactive spider gave him proportionally great strength, the ability to climb walls, and enhanced "spider-senses." But the police suspect him, the press is waging a vendetta against him, and the public perceives him as a menace. While Batman courts his vigilante status, Spider-Man has it thrust on him. His first impulse was not to fight crime but to become a TV star, and his self-centeredness led to the death of his beloved uncle. Guilt, rather than righteous vengeance, provides his primal motivation. Not surprisingly, given the level of self-torture involved here, Spider-Man's main foes have turned out to be his own doppelgangers. As the theme song for the Spider-Man cartoon show once jauntily summed it up: "To him, life is a great big hang-up!"

All this high-flying neurosis would have been impossible to take without the exuberant depictions of Spider-Man swinging through New York City. New York: not Metropolis, not Gotham City, not Coast City. Real neuroses demand a real city (or vice versa, I'm not sure which). And New York is a complex organism that, especially by the 1960s when Spider-Man and other Marvel Comics heroes appeared, defied easy apprehension. Superman's magisterial gaze and Batman's profound urban knowledge were revised by Spider-Man's more improvisational, sensational style. When his spider-sense tingles, something's up.

Spider-Man, particularly as drawn by original artist Steve Ditko, is a more tactile hero than Superman or Batman. He clings to buildings, and Ditko clearly relished the opportunity to further skew the perspectives of the city.

Ditko's other creation was Dr. Strange, a mystic master who lived in a great Greenwich Village brownstone. Ditko rendered Strange's ectoplasmic conjurings with peculiar solidity, while in Spider-Man the physical space of the actual city became utterly unstable. Walls became floors and verticality was close to being entirely lost in his swirling circular forms. One small Ditko panel gives us a rear view of Spider-Man in the air over the city. His artificial web snakes slackly through his hands: this is movement in progress, not an arrested bat pose. Two buildings flank his body in the lowest part of the frame, no more than jutting corners against the open space. The superhero's body is marvelous and sinuous, as curved as the web but poised and muscular. No wonder he likes to get out of the house.

More than other heroes, Spider-Man makes me reach for de Certeau's "Walking in the City."[36] "To walk is to lack a place," de Certeau argues in a famous passage. "It is the indefinite process of being absent and in search of a proper. The moving about that the city multiplies and concentrates makes the city an immense social experience of lacking a place." Spider-Man indeed lacks a place. Superman and Batman are guardians of the urban space, but Spider-Man is a trespasser. He is not the master of Metropolis, as is Superman or Luthor; he is not a part of the city's power elite, as is Bruce Wayne. He is not as omnipresent as Batman, and he doesn't own a skyscraper like the Fantastic Four. What de Certeau calls the strategies of institutional control (by governments, for example, or corporations) are not his to command. He is, at best, an interloper, making his own path across the spaces controlled by others (The Kingpin, for example).[37] The tactics of spatial trespass, de Certeau reminds us, constitute the art (the essential art) of the weak.[38]

That same early issue that began with Peter's study break ends with Spider-Man standing, alone, on an isolated chimney, wishing he could simply let everyone know who he really is. "To walk is to lack a place," Certeau writes, but the anonymity implied by one's lack of place is precisely what permits that trajectory across the range of positions that only the city allows.[39]

Crusaders for the City

William Randolph Hearst was more than just a maverick millionaire, publisher, and comics devotée; he also cast himself in the role of social crusader. From an 1887 editorial in his first paper, the *San Francisco Examiner*: "*Examiner* reporters are everywhere; they are the first to see everything, and the first to perceive the true meaning of what they see. Whether a child is to be found, an eloping girl to be brought home or a murder to be traced, one of our staff is sure to give the sleepy detectives their first pointers . . . the *Examiner* reporter is a feature of modern California civilization. His energy, astuteness and devotion make him the one thing needed to redeem the community from the corruption that seems to have selected this period as its peculiar prey." *His energy, astuteness, and devotion*—Hearst's reporters were already superheroes, redeeming the community from corruption (and San Francisco was probably a pretty good place to start).

In a way, then, Superman and his alter ego, crusading journalist Clark Kent, are fighting the same fight using the same methods: ubiquity, speed, enhanced powers of vision and comprehension, and incorruptibility. Early Superman stories often begin with Clark tackling a major social problem—corrupt politicians, slum clearance, racketeering in the taxicab industry—with Superman on hand to confront the danger and solve the problem. Here's an example from *Action Comics* #12:

> *Panel 4*. "Clark telephones the city's mayor—" [a diagonal split screen effect]:
> *Clark*: Why has our city one of the worst traffic situations in the country?
> *Mayor*: It's really too bad—but—what can anyone do about it?
>
> *Panel 5*. "Later, in the privacy of his apartment, Clark Kent dons a strange uniform, transforming himself into the dynamic SUPERMAN—"
> *Superman*: I, for one, am going to do *plenty* about it!

It was almost inevitable that Clark would reappear in the final panels to receive the accolades, get caught in traffic, or strike out with Lois Lane. In a strong sense, Superman *is* the mighty newspaper.

And now we have Spider Jerusalem, the hero of Warren Ellis's postcyberpunk *Transmetropolitan*. Spider is a crusading journalist of another kind—more Hunter S. Thompson than William R. Hearst. He'd been hiding out on a mountain for five years ("Five years of shooting at fans and neighbors, eating what I kill, and bombing the unwary"),[40] but circumstances necessitate his return to the City, a crackling environment of shrill media, downloaded personalities (foglets), revived citizens from the twentieth century (nobody cares), and all manner of streetwise creatures. "This city never allowed itself to decay or degrade. It's wildly, intensely *growing*. It's a loud bright stinking mess. It takes strength from its thousands of cultures. And the thousands more that grow anew each day. It isn't perfect. It lies and cheats. It's no utopia and it ain't the mountain by a long shot—but it's alive. I can't argue that."[41]

It's Spider's endless regard for the noisy plurality of the urban environment that made *Transmet* one of the most romantic comics around (despite its, and Spider's, surface nihilism). The covers repeatedly posed Spider against the background of the city—Geoff Darrow's cover for issue #22 is a particularly fine example: a slightly oblique, somewhat high-angle view of Spider sitting on the edge of a huge electric marquee, laptop ready, a cigarette smoldering between his fingers, toasting us with his second bottle of whiskey, his two-headed cat by his side, smiling out at us. Behind him the city simply exists through the incredible density of detail that is Darrow's hallmark—bumper to bumper traffic, mounds of bagged trash and scattered litter, graffiti on every street-level surface, radioactivity warnings, jumpers, advertisements, and, in one open window, a guy on a couch with his pants open, empty beer cans and leftover pizza strewn about him. This isn't Metropolis, and Spider Jerusalem, armed with his effective "bowel disruptor," is no mild-mannered reporter, even if he sometimes refers to himself as one.[42] His column may be called "I Hate it Here," but he is deeply proud to serve as the voice of "the new scum," the underclass created by The City's new economics, technologies, and moralities.

What is best about *Transmet*, and what it lifted from the best cyberpunk, is its refusal of the city as a totalitarian site of control. Despite the constant mass media bombardment, there is always something more to see, and whenever Spider feels trapped by his new position as crusader, "media element and TV celebrity," he knows just what to do. "Do what I always do. Get the city under my feet. Become alive." In other words, he takes a walk. Michel de Certeau would be proud. I see them strolling the city together, sharing their thoughts: "I only ever experience the city properly on the street," Spider says. Michel agrees: "The act of walking is to the urban system what the speech act is to language. . . . Walking affirms, suspects, tries out, transgresses, respects, etc., the trajectories it 'speaks'. All the modalities sing a part in this chorus, changing from step to step, stepping in through proportions, sequences, and intensities which vary according to the time, the path taken, and the walker. These enunciatory operations are of unlimited diversity." Spider answers, yeah, I know what you mean: "It only ever speaks to me here. . . . Just let it talk, in all its languages.'"[43] Michel continues: "the relationships and intersections of these exoduses . . . intertwine and create an urban fabric . . . placed under the sign of what ought to be, ultimately, the place but is only a name, *the City*."[44]

Journalists aren't the only crusading superheroes. In the early 1980s there was Mr. X, architect of the now-corrupted psychetecture in the city of Somnopolis.[45] "The subtleties of my psychetecture . . . *destroyed*," he laments, as he tries to restore his creation. The shaved head and tinted shades of Mr. X prefigure Spider Jerusalem's basic look: both are outsiders returning to the cities that mark their principle obsessions, becoming what de Certeau called "foreigners at home," trying to negotiate a barely contained chaos.[46] "This city was not meant for people," moans one Radiant City dweller. As an avenging superhero, Mr. X is on a crusade to repair the city, but in *Mr. X* and *Transmet*, such fantasies of megalomaniacal control have become self-evidently outmoded, damaging, and useless, especially in light of Spider Jerusalem's enunciation of urban diversity.

PART THREE: OF MASKS AND CAPES

(Secret) Identities

Superheroes are all about multiple identities and so embody the slippery sense of self that living in the city either imposes or permits. Simmel, of course, set the tone for a pervading ambivalence in his recognition that the quantification of the urban population in terms of productive labor power represented only a very partial accounting of the men and women in the crowd. The city was a place of aspiration and anonymity, a site of failure and rebirth. "It is the function of the metropolis to make a place for the conflict" between a definition of the city dweller as an object of economic relations and as an autonomous, free, and unique being.[47] In the city, "the individual's horizon is enlarged": the crowd becomes you, and you wend your way through the crowd.[48] The instrumentalities of individual capitalism define the human with precision but not completeness. As a place of being, the city offers room to move.

Who reveals this better than the superhero? Whether in their "true identities" as a mild-mannered reporter, a bored millionaire playboy, a crippled paperboy, or a policeman or incarnated in their more spectacular forms, superheroes play a continuous game of deception and duplicity that could only be played out in the city. Admittedly, none of these characters approach the ambiguity of The Shadow of the pulp magazines; his identity as "Lamont Cranston" was itself only another disguise (perhaps). The city is a haven for imposters: by the early nineteenth century, physical mobility had made a mockery of social standing. "One cannot mingle much in society here without meeting some ... mysterious individual, who claims to be of noble birth," James McCabe observed in 1872.[49] The city attracted them all: false noblemen, deceptive charity workers, strange and disguised visitors from other planets.

Clearly, it is the potential for hubristic comeuppance, and nothing else, that forces Superman to don a pair of spectacles, comb his hair, and therefore transform himself into Clark Kent, mild-mannered reporter. In later years, they tried to convince us that Superman made his face vibrate ever so slightly, which was why nobody twigged to his looking a lot like Clark Kent. Yeah, sure. We know that Clark's anonymity was a function of a sturdy pair of eyeglasses and, mostly, the very nature of life in the city. Perhaps, by the twentieth century, it no longer mattered who you really were as long as the mask fit. The Spirit, the resurrection of the seemingly deceased police detective Donny

Colt, dons a small black mask, and no one seems the wiser—no one even seems to care.

The perfect urban hero is, again, probably Plastic Man, a one-time crook who can remold his face and body at will (something to do with some acid). He has used his power not only to forsake crime but to fight it (something to do with a monastery). One could certainly, in the cities of Poe, Doyle, and Batman, imagine the reverse effect. Plastic Man is really more of an "Indian Rubber Man!" as his own comic calls him, but "plastic" is more appropriately modern, more descriptive of a personal malleability: a new man for a new city.

The secret identity of the superhero depends on the mask he wears. In Moore's *Watchmen*, superheroes are generically referred to as "masks." The mask is a perfect synecdoche for the superhero, the mysterious totem that makes everything possible. Masks have their place in the history of modernity, as they do in so many other histories. Bakhtin has labeled it the most complex theme of folk culture, but it accrued still more meanings in Western cultures during the Enlightenment and still more within mass culture in the twentieth century. Terry Castle has observed the "ambiguous philosophical and ethical meanings" so prevalent in narrative appearances of masks in the eighteenth century, but these ambiguities may not be as thoroughly forgotten as she might think.[50] The mask had found its place within the elegant, decadent recreation of the masquerade, a carefully delineated realm of comparative abandon. In the novels of, say, Fielding, things happen under cover of the masquerade: intrigues, scandals, and a refusal of prevailing social mores are all played through. Castle notes a conflation of mask functions in these tales. Bakhtin and Caillois wrote of an "old mask" of "shamanistic ritual and medieval carnival, [that] embodied 'the joy of change and reincarnation'—the spiritual and organic union of opposites," and of the "mask of modern times," which was "no more than a screen, a disguise or 'false front,' evoking new and sinister realms of alienation." Castle continues: "Instead of working marvelous transformations, the mask now 'hides something, keeps a secret, deceives.'"[51]

In English novels of the eighteenth century, these two ideations of the mask intertwine without resolution. The masquerade permits an uncanny return to an earlier animism. Identity is hidden, but upon this act of disguise something of the earlier talismanic power of the mask can again emerge. In Fielding, "the masquerade is that charged topos around which forgotten or subversive possibilities cluster."[52] The mask of the modern superhero is also both a "new" mask of disguise and an older mask of "marvelous transformation."

For Bakhtin, the mask could never be "another object among objects"—it was simply too charged with meanings and functions, whether erotic, magical, or fashionable. In earlier or non-European cultures, masks marked social identity, while the modern use of the mask in the West is intended to conceal difference, protect identity. Castle points out that only after the emergence of a particular notion of the self as unique, individual, and distinct does the concealment of identity take on social significance. To protect the self in modern times, then, modern man had to don the mask, join the crowd. "Whereas the primitive mask expressed an identity to the outside, in fact constructed that identity, the modern mask is a form of protection, a canceling of differences on the outside precisely to make identity possible, an identity that is now individual."[53] Thus, the mask is invisible: for it to function, one cannot be seen to be masked.

I dwell on these ideas of masking and modernity because it seems to me that superheroes partake of some of the ambiguity that Castle ascribes to eighteenth-century English narrative as well as twentieth-century urban concerns with anonymity and the mask that cannot be seen. In their secret identities, superheroes all hide in plain sight. Superman sets the stage but also remains somewhat unique. As Jules Feiffer was among the first to observe, while all the other heroes adopted their colorful alter egos, Superman grew up hiding his true abilities.[54] Superman is disguised as Clark Kent, while Bruce Wayne disguises himself as Batman. Clark Kent, mild-mannered, blue-suited, earnest, hardworking, dolefully dweeblike for most of his history, is a perfect embodiment of the masked figure of modern man. One can read so much into this particular masquerade: Superman's adolescent creators, recognizing the repression endemic to the world of adulthood; Jewish youngsters fantasizing of being both uniquely superhuman and invisibly assimilated; American Everyman as Superman. Meanwhile, Superman is the hero without a mask, his "true" face revealed to the world, at once monumental and generic. Superman becomes us, goes among us, and we might be him. But Clark is about more than assimilation and even about more than geek dreams of godhood. This Everyman in a dependable suit depends on invisibility, the anonymity permitted by a great metropolis. He cannot be visible, and he has a secret. And so Superman and Clark subvert one another: the man who sees everything meets the man who is not seen.

But most of the others hide their faces: they can't wait to pull on the tights, don the masks, and streak out into the bright life of the city. Here masks once again mark a social identity—the costume of the burglar becomes, following Zorro and the Lone Ranger, a sign of the vigilante hero. In their first adventures, Superman and Batman battle ordinary, uncostumed foes. Batman's rogue's gallery moves decidedly toward the grotesque with such villains as the Joker and Two-Face, figures who are never permitted the luxury of hiding what they are (although Two-Face, acid scarred on one side, normal on the other, carries a LOT of symbolic weight). Soon, however, with the advent of costumed and masked villains, the mask becomes less a sign of ethical status than a morally indeterminate "superness."

Both masked heroes and villains tapped back into the history of the mask in "shamanistic ritual and medieval carnival": in comic books, the mask once more embodied something of "the joy of change and reincarnation." Many of these characters are literally or figuratively reborn into their new identities. Jim Corrigan is a cop murdered in the line of duty, but he returns as the domino-cloaked Spectre, a figure of unyielding vengeance. The animistic underside of the rational space of the city is exposed in bold, bright colors.

The Vigilante and the Dandy

The city is a permanent costume party, Koolhaas and Jonathan Raban remind us, and superheroes have the brightest costumes. Their outfits are streamlined amalgams of the machinic, the historical, and the organic, but they always emphasize the (increasingly exaggerated) human musculature beneath. An Alan Moore character of recent vintage actually wears no costume; she simply adjusts her pigments to superheroic patterns. When people find out she's "really" naked, they no longer know quite where to look, but Moore's little joke reminds us that superhero bodies have always been naked bodies exhibited to a very public gaze.

Superheroes are acrobats: their colorful tights are the garb of circus performers. Dick Grayson was a circus performer, one of the Flying Graysons, but he was orphaned when gangsters doctored the trapeze ropes (that damn acid again!). After a little training by Batman (another orphan—these cities attract them) he takes on a new role as "that astonishing phenomenon, that young Robin Hood of today—Robin the Boy Wonder!" Deadman is a reincarnated circus acrobat out to find out who had him assassinated in mid-performance, but really they're all circus performers. There are strong men (Superman, The Thing), aerialists (Batman, Daredevil), clowns (the Joker), acrobats (Nightcrawler), ringmasters (Lex Luthor, The Ringmaster), hypnotists (Mysterio), wild beasts (Catwoman, Wolverine, Hawkman et al.), contortionists (The Elongated Man, Mr. Fantastic), fire acts (The Human Torch), escape artists (Batman, Mr. Miracle), sideshow freaks (Bizarro, The Geek, the X-Men), magicians (Mandrake, Dr. Strange), sharpshooters (Green Arrow), half-men/half-beasts (The Hulk, Swamp Thing), and a big finish (The Human Bomb).

In *Sex and Suits*, Anne Hollander describes several shifts in the history of "civilized" attire. At some point dress began to mark differences of gender, and not simply of class, and the neoclassical moment "put a final seal of disapproval on gaudy clothes for serious men."[55] While the man's suit was a dynamic yet subtle manifestation of bodily power—flexible and flowing, closely shaped to torso and mobile limbs—men's clothing also moved away from flamboyant color and excess. The superhero costume marks a return to earlier modes of male self-presentation by combining Rococo ornamentation (with its flashing colors, flowing capes, epaulets, and talismans) with a classical ideal in which "the hero wore nothing but his perfect nudity, perhaps enhanced by a short cape falling behind him. The nude costume was the one most suggestive of perfect male strength, perfect virtue, and perfect honesty, with overtones of independence and rationality. The hero's harmonious nude beauty was the visible expression of his uncorrupted moral and mental qualities" (87). Purity and performative flamboyance were thus uniquely combined in the superhero's costume. And, if Batman eschewed color to embody instead his heart of darkness, Robin the Boy Wonder was right by his side, accoutered in red tunic, yellow cape, and green booties.

The appeal of classical purity speaks for itself, but flamboyance is the real issue here. Alongside the image of an idealized, classical self, superheroes further embody a male fantasy of flamboyant, performative intemperance, something blocked by the pragmatic, self-controlled economy of a historically constructed masculine cultural identity signified by the visual drabness of his closet. But many of those closets have secret doors opening onto a broader sense of what is appropriate for the boy or man. Our costumed vigilante is perhaps something more a dandy, a flamboyant, flamboyantly powered, urban male, who, if not for his never-ending battle for truth, justice, and the American Way, would probably be ordered to "just move it along." What battles against "crime" and "corruption" really do, it seems, is license the donning of the superhero garb, legitimate the movement out of the home, through the window, and into the secret magic of the urban night. The fantasy, then, is one of dressing up—superheroes don't wear costumes in order to fight crime, they fight crime in order to wear the costumes.[56]

Here it seems that I'm edging up on a homoerotic reading of buff closet queens escaping the mundane world to mingle in secret places with their even more flamboyantly subversive enemies/allies/doppelgangers. But that's been done. Instead, I'd like to soften the reading and spin it somewhat differently by suggesting that the superhero raids *several* closets before swinging out on the town, indulging in the flamboyance of urban fashion, desiring to perform anonymously but in full view, fantasizing of a *present*ness usually assigned to ethnic others. The superhero heads for marginalized sites, sites of nonproduction or spectacular destruction, not to impose order but to participate in, *belong to*, the chaos.

Perhaps the concern with "law and order" should be reconstrued to remove it from a narrow, legalistic definition. After all, the "laws" of physics and biology are more inverted than affirmed by these free-flying figures, and what role can "order" serve with regard to the flamboyant contents of the superhero's closet? Baudelaire referred to dandyism as "an institution beyond the laws," and despite its association with effeminacy Sartre found it more exhibitionist than homosexual at its core. Dandies operate on "their own authority" and, with "the help of wit, which is an acid, and of grace, which is a dissolvent . . . manage to ensure the acceptance of their changeable rules, though these are in fact nothing but the outcome of their own audacious personalities." While superheroes, especially those who wisecrack while in the very midst of battle, seem more witless than witty, their universe is a kind of self-referential and solipsistic realm centered on an audacious performance by a flamboyant figure who is permitted to slip the bonds of conventional behavior and being. In Superman, the transcendent imperatives of the *übermensch* are tempered by the dandy's unseriousness: *Look, up in the sky! Is it a bird?*

Baudelaire connected the dandy to the modern urban landscape, although his analysis of a more self-alienated observer, the flaneur, has received more attention of late than the seemingly blasé but relentlessly committee performance of the dandy. Barbey noted Brummell's "air of elegant indifference which he wore like armore, and which made him invulnerable" or, Barbey quickly adds, "which made him *appear* invulnerable." (If not for my childhood reading of Superman, would I even *know* the word *invulnerable*?) The costume is the sign and source of power, the mark of *grace*.

Norman Mailer's "white Negro" tries to co-opt some of the dandy's projected grace. In Mailer's mythos the white Negro, or hipster, is a kind of racial cross-dresser, performing the perceived existential freedom of the urban black male. Rendered powerless in American society, the black man "lived in the enormous present, he subsisted for his Saturday night kicks, relinquishing the pleasures of the mind for the more obligatory powers of the body." The hipster partakes of this acceptance of death and danger, living as he is in the shadow of the Bomb and the Holocaust. His isolation is willed; Mailer calls it "the isolated courage of isolated people," a fine superhero credo.

Superheroes could be some inchoate version of the same thing. Their sagas are passing narratives—Superman's Midwestern Jewish cocreators cloaking themselves not only in the power of Superman but in the metropolitan anonymity of Everyman Clark Kent. And in his multicolored, flamboyant absurdity the superhero is also a kind of hipster, seeking to swoop down and possess the life of the street. The costume still serves as a mark of difference, but now the superhero signals an abdication of responsibility rather than becoming its exemplary figure.

So this is a fantasy of blacking up—putting on the mask permits an extroversion only in the guise of the other, which is exactly Mailer's critique of the hipster. And, as Garelick argues, "All dandyism hints at a wish for male autochthony"—the woman disturbs the dandy's (and the superhero's?) perfect aesthetic self-containment. The self in motion is also a "reified, immobilized Self."[57]

The foregoing analysis is valid and important, but it is also surely too damning. The dandy, according to Barbey, combines "frivolity, on the one hand, acting upon a people rigid and coarsely utilitarian, on the other, Imagination, claiming its rights in the face of a moral law too severe to be genuine, [producing] a kind of translation, a science of manners and attitudes, impossible elsewhere." Fantasy is, after all, the place for the abdication of responsibility, a place of temporary grace.

One hesitates to play the Nietzsche card, as his name has dominated too many attempts to take superheroes seriously. Superman just doesn't cut the mustard as an *übermensch*. He is to the manner born, so to speak; he doesn't need to *become* a superman. Despite his power, he continues to identify with, and fight for, the values of ordinary men (hence Clark Kent), and thus he is a superman who preserves rather than sabotages the status quo. Superman is the overman domesticated, muzzled, and neutered. There have recently appeared several serious and sustained works that grapple with the Nietzchean connotations of the genre by exploring the darker relations between superhuman morality and social responsibility.[58]

But another aspect of Nietzsche's thought might be more pertinent to our friendly neighborhood superheroes. Central to *Thus Spoke Zarathustra* and *The Gay Science* is the concept of play. Independence, the position of the overman, can only be attained through new modes of thought and thus through new languages that implicitly deconstruct the assumptions of the old. A gay science "is meant to be anti-German, anti-professorial, anti-academic. . . . It is also meant to suggest 'light feet,' 'dancing,' 'laughter'—and ridicule of 'the spirit of gravity.'"[59] Poetry and play, "light-hearted defiance(s) of convention," are the means to a new spirit of investigation: a gay science.

> I would believe only in a god who could dance. And when I saw my devil I found him serious, thorough, profound, and solemn: it was the spirit of gravity—through him all things fall.
>
> Not by wrath does one kill but by laughter. Come, let us kill the spirit of gravity!
>
> I have since learned to walk: ever since, I let myself run. I have learned to fly: ever since, I do not want to be pushed before moving along.
>
> Now I am light, now I fly, now I see myself beneath myself, now a god dances through me.[60]

Thus, the plumage of the dandy is quite in keeping with the playful aspects of Nietzsche's thought and language, although not, one must note, with the philosopher's asceticism, which the dandy would fine tedious. The superhero does have affinities with the overman but not in the Nietzsche Lite version of transcendence that gives the hero powers and abilities far beyond those of mortal men, nor in the movement of the hero beyond good and evil, but rather through a basically light, playful, and performative dance. The superhero is our ally against the spirit of gravity: in rising brightly over our heads, he compels us to look, and look again, and then to exclaim: *Look! Up in the sky.*[61]

"Wish I Could Fly Like Superman"

The challenge in writing about comic books lies in both the dearth of scholarship and the inaccessibility of the actual objects. In many ways, the most valuable historians of the medium have been the creators themselves, in particular those writers, editors, and artists who have continuously revitalized the genre over the last twenty years, who have pushed and prodded the idea of the superhero in all directions.[62] Because of course superheroes are real: they have history and have exerted a material impact on culture for sixty years. Most of us have grown up in a world of superheroes, a world in which the original Superman, jumping his one-eighth mile and chucking cars about, seems, let's face it, like a bit of a wuss. Anything less than planet-shattering power isn't worth the computer-colored paper it's printed on. But some recent comics have begun to settle back to Earth, fueled by the recognition that the real power of the superhero is primarily iconic.

Hence the spate of stories about being, or wanting to be, a superhero. *Watchmen* and *Astro City* are filled with citizens dreaming of superheroes or superheroics, and James Robinson's updating of *Starman* centers on the aging hero's son, who reluctantly takes up the heroic mantle and gravity rod but won't wear the tights. In 2000, DC Comics published its *Realworld* series, in which "fictional superheroes influences all-too-human people to attempt superhuman things."[63] *Realworlds: Batman* gave us a youth who thinks he's Batman. He poses in his homemade costume on the cover, beneath the Bat logo from the 1960s television program, surrounded by Bat paraphernalia of every kind, including a poster of New York he has relabeled "Gotham."[64]

Alan Moore has moved from the darkness of *Watchmen*, in which the fantasy of superheroes was tinged with pathos, to work that emphasizes the playful, colorful grace of the genre. His *Promethea*, a heroine of stories, pulp magazines, and comic books, is physically manifested through those who chronicle her adventures, each time incorporating the persona of her latest "creator." To write about her is to write her into existence. In another Moore comic, the character Supreme hides behind his secret identity as a superhero comic book artist who draws the adventures of "Omniman." ("I mean, you just put on glasses and nobody recognizes you!" gasps his girlfriend. "Is everybody just, like, *stupid* or what?" "I've wondered that myself," Supreme answers.)[65] In *Promethea* and *Supreme*, Moore has incorporated the comic's creator—the mythmaker—into the myth, in a movement that goes beyond postmodern parlor games of reflexivity to a deeper acknowledgement of our own imbrication in the life of our fantasies.

To Be Continued . . .

Superheroes are vehicles of urban representation; they embody perceptual paradigms. Through the vehicle of the superhero, as through cinema and sociology, one recovers the city as new and shifting ground. Urbanism was defined as a way of life by sociologist Louis Wirth in 1938, the year that also saw the appearance of Superman. Superheroes exist to inhabit the city, to patrol, map, dissect, and traverse it. They are surprisingly proper guides to these cities of change: invulnerable yet resilient and metamorphic, they hold their shape. They hold their shape as do the other skyscrapers and monuments of the metropolis, perhaps accreting some fussy ornamentation, some new functionality or relevance, but still managing to embody a dignified history that is occasionally sandblasted back into visibility.

Surely the colors should have faded by now, yet superheroes are still in the air and on the T-shirts on my chest. When I look in the mirror, I see Superman.

NOTES

1. With an occasional "good neighbor" nod toward Montreal, Mexico City, or London.
2. Four titles figured most significantly in a brief explosion of postmodern urban renewal: *American Flagg!* by Howard Chaykin, *Watchmen* by Alan Moore and Dave Gibbons, Frank Miller's *Dark Knight Returns*, and *Mr. X* by Dean Motter and the Hernandez brothers. I discuss some of these, as well as Judge Dredd and the comics of Moebius, in Scott Bukatman, *Terminal Identity: The Virtual Subject in Postmodern Science Fiction* (Durham: Duke University Press, 1993).
3. Interview with Howard Chaykin, "The New Superhero," *Spin* 4.5 (August 1988):49.
4. I have relied greatly on histories of comics by Jules Feiffer, Mike Benton, Jim Steranko, and Les Daniels.
5. Rem Koolhaas, *Delirious New York* (New York: Monacelli, 1994), 104.
6. They included *Little Nemo in Slumberland*, *Polly and Her Pals*, *Gasoline Alley*, *Krazy Kat*, *Tarzan*, and *Prince Valiant* (and these are only a few examples).
7. With some exceptions (Will Eisner, Harvey Kurtzman, Jack Cole, Hergé, and Carl Barks) it wasn't until the later 1960s that the panel was superseded by the page as an explicit unit

of composition in comic books. Panels were increasingly fragmented into diagonal shards, incorporated into larger graphic elements, or generally organized against the grain of a strict linearity. [Other examples predating the late 1960s can also be found. See Joseph Witek's essay "The Arrow and the Grid" in Heer and Worcester, eds., *A Comics Studies Reader* (Jackson: UP of Mississippi, 2009.—*eds.*]

8. Koolhaas, 104.
9. Vivian Gornick, "On the Street: Nobody Watches, Everyone Performs," in *Approaching Eye Level* (Boston: Beacon, 1996): 15.
10. A more effective design would have used the broad avenues to link the rivers, for example.
11. Batman is the fully accessorized superhero, much like Barbie: both are outfitted with clothes, car, dreamhouse, and a useless appendage (Ken, Robin).
12. See Art Spiegelman and Chip Kidd, *Jack Cole and Plastic Man: Forms Stretched to Their Limits* (New York: Chronicle, 2001); as well as three DC Comics' reprint volumes; Jack Cole, *The Plastic Man Archives* (New York: DC Comics, 1999 and 2001).
13. Editor Denny O'Neil allows *Batman* artists to play with the character's iconography, especially his sensuous cape: "We now say that Batman has two hundred suits hanging in the Batcave, so they don't have to look the same" (quoted in Les Daniels, *Batman: The Complete History* [San Francisco: Chronicle, 1999], 159). Nobody has ever drawn more graceful flying figures than 1960s *Green Lantern* artist Gil Kane. His superheroes seemed to float above the page. *Daredevil*'s artist through the 1970s was Gene Colan, whose swirling lines created remarkable kinetic effects, within the frame and across the page. Superman's coloration was a function, and a virtue, of the primitive printing in the earliest comic books.
14. Alan Moore and Curt Swan, *Whatever Happened to the Man of Tomorrow?* (New York: DC Comics, 1997), 17 (reprints material originally published in 1986).
15. Jeph Loeb and Tim Sale, *Superman for All Seasons* (New York: DC Comics, 1999).
16. Peter Fritzsche, *Reading Berlin, 1900* (Cambridge: Harvard University Press, 1996), 1.
17. See David M. Henkin, *City Reading: Written Words and Public Spaces in Antebellum New York* (New York: Columbia University Press, 1998); and Fritzsche.
18. Several of Calvin's other fantasies shrank him to bug size.
19. Susan Stewart, *On Longing: Narratives of the Miniature, the Gigantic, the Souvenir, the Collection* (Durham: Duke University Press, 1993), 60, 67.
20. *Batman: Mask of the Phantasm* (1993).
21. Stewart, 46.
22. Ibid., 56. For Scott McCloud, the flat colors that until recently defined comics also evoke a child's perception by emphasizing the shapes of objects and reveling in "the wonder of *things*." Comics present "worlds fairly glowing with that mystery of first encounters. Any wonder then that comics in America has been so reluctant to 'grow up'?" (Scott McCloud, *Understanding Comics: The Invisible Art* [Northhampton, MA: Tundra, 1993], 188–189).
23. Jack (*Starman*) Knight has a poster for the Fair on the wall of his Opal City apartment.
24. Stewart, 90.
25. Franco Minganti, "1939: Flying Eyes—Flight, Metropolis, and Icons of Popular Imagination," *Storia Nordamericana* 7.1 (1990): 100.
26. Michel de Certeau, "Walking in the City," translated by Steven Rendell, in *The Practice of Everyday Life* (Berkeley: University of California, 1984), 92.
27. Ibid.
28. Le Corbusier, *The City of To-Morrow and Its Planning* (New York: Dover, 1987), 86.
29. Cited in Daniels, 164. The screenplay is credited to Sam Hamm and Warren Skaaren.

A SONG OF THE URBAN SUPERHERO   197

30. Rick Marschall, Foreword to *Batman Archives* (New York: DC Comics, 1990), 1:5.
31. Tom Gunning, "From the Kaleidoscope to the X-Ray: Urban Spectatorship, Poe, Benjamin, and *Traffic in Souls* (1913)," *Wide Angle* 19.4 (1997): 25–61.
32. Terry Castle, *The Female Thermometer: Eighteenth-Century Culture and the Invention of the Uncanny* (New York: Oxford University Press, 1995), 80.
33. Such writers include Frank Miller, Alan Moore, Howard Chaykin, Paul Dini, Dave Gibbons, and Kurt Busiek, among others.
34. And note that Batman is usually accompanied by his brightly attired "sidekick," Robin.
35. Stan Lee and Steve Ditko, "Where Flies the Beetle . . . ," *Amazing Spider-Man* #21 (February 1965). Reprinted in Stan Lee and Steve Ditko, *The Essential Spider-Man, vol. 2* (New York: Marvel Comics, 1997).
36. De Certeau, "Walking in the City."
37. The Kingpin, an enemy of both Spider-Man and Daredevil, set the standard as an Edward Arnold-style ward boss and gangster well before Luthor's makeover.
38. De Certeau, *The Practice of Everyday Life*, 37.
39. New York is also home to Daredevil, another Marvel hero with enhanced senses.
40. Warren Ellis and Darick Robertson, *Transmetropolitan* #1 (1998), 5.
41. Ibid., 14.
42. Warren Ellis and Darick Robertson, *Transmetropolitan* #2 (1998), 2.
43. Warren Ellis and Darick Robertson, *Transmetropolitan* #32 (2000), 5, 6.
44. De Certeau, 103, my emphasis. The City is also the name of the place that the great comic and cartoon hero The Tick has sworn to protect.
45. Motter et al., *The Return of Mr. X* (East Fullerton, CA: Graphitti Designs, 1986).
46. De Certeau, 13.
47. Georg Simmel, "The Metropolis and Mental Life," in *On Individuality and Social Forms*, edited by Donald N. Levine (Chicago: University of Chicago Press, 1971), 339.
48. Ibid, 334.
49. James McCabe, "Imposters," in *Writing New York: A Literary Anthology*, edited by Philip Lopate (New York: Library of America, 1998), 260 (excerpted from James McCabe, *Light and Shadows of New York Life* [1872]).
50. Terry Castle, *Masquerade and Civilization: The Carnivalesque in Eighteenth-Century English Culture and Fiction* (Stanford: Stanford University Press, 1986), 183.
51. Ibid. The internal citation is Mikhail Bakhtin's *The Dialogic Imagination*, translated by Caryl Emerson and Michael Holquist, edited by Michael Holquist (Austin: University of Texas Press, 1991), 39. The text by Roger Caillois is *Man, Play, and Games*, translated by Meyer Barash (New York: Free Press of Glencoe, 1961).
52. Castle, *Masquerade*, 186.
53. Ibid, 37.
54. Jules Feiffer, *The Great Comic Book Heroes* (New York: Dial, 1965), 18–19.
55. Anne Hollander, *Sex and Suits: The Evolution of Modern Dress* (New York: Alfred A. Knopf, 1994), 7.
56. Zorro, Batman, and the Green Hornet *pretend* to be dandies in their "secret identities," but they're all *still* dandies, right? (especially Zorro and Van Williams's TV incarnation of the Green Hornet).
57. Garlick, 19.
58. *Watchmen, Squadron Supreme,* and *The Golden Age* come to mind. I should also mention that recent revisions of the Superman mythos have placed new emphasis on his learning how to live with (and live up to) his superhuman powers.

59. Walter Kaufmann, translator's introduction to Friedrich Nietzsche, *The Gay Science* (New York: Vintage, 1974), 7.
60. Friedrich Nietzsche, "Thus Spoke Zarathustra," in *The Portable Nietzsche*, edited and translated by Walter Kaufmann (New York: Viking, 1954), 153. See also Nietzsche, *Gay Science*.
61. Is it a bird? "The ostrich runs faster than the fastest horse, and even he buries his head gravely in the grave earth; even so, the man who has not yet learned to fly. Earth and life seem grave to him; and thus the spirit of gravity wants it. But whoever would become light and a bird must love himself, thus *I* teach" (Nietzsche, "Thus Spoke Zarathustra," 304).
62. Alan Moore, Howard Chaykin, James Robinson, Frank Miller, Alex Ross, Kurt Busiek, Grant Morrison, John Byrne, Neil Gaiman, Walt Simonson, and Todd MacFarlane are only a few of those who have spun out eloquent and varied alternatives.
63. The title refers to the *Elseworlds* titles, which allowed creators free reign to reimagine DC's classic characters outside the constraints of "normal" series continuity.
64. Other than this, however, the series lacked any sense of irony about its own iconography.
65. Alan Moore, "Suddenly, the Supremium Man!" *Supreme: The Return* #5 (May 2000), 5.

Section Three

CULTURE AND IDENTITY

AS HENRY JENKINS NOTES IN HIS ESSAY ON "DEATH-DEFYING HEROES," WHICH closes this volume, superheroes "have been more or less in continuous publication since the 1930s or early 1940s." "Nowhere else in popular culture," he says, "can you find that same degree of continuity." Comics fandom takes this decades-long history quite seriously, as witnessed by the fact that comics conventions routinely host panels on Golden Age comics, fan publications often feature interviews with industry veterans, and comic book stores usually carry at least a sprinkling of reprint volumes. It makes sense, then, that this *Reader*'s opening section is concerned with the genesis and development of the superhero genre.

Theoretically informed writing on superheroes came later, but has gained significant traction over the past decade or so. This book's second section thus brings together major essays on the tropes, conventions, and embedded discourses of the superhero genre. The field of comics studies has increasingly embraced theoretically sophisticated approaches, and it seems likely there will be a further outpouring of ambitious superhero commentary in the coming years. Recounting plots, recycling anecdotes, and positing vague connections between real-world events and superhero storylines are no longer sufficient, if indeed they ever were. As description has given way to analysis, the bar has been raised. This is a welcome and no doubt overdue development.

Yet the most striking aspect of the superhero genre may be the passions it stirs, not only among core readers, but also within the culture at large. Just as some folks make a point of seeing every superhero movie, visiting their local comic book store on a weekly basis, and attending comics conventions—sometimes in costume—many more disdain the genre, and its attendant subculture, altogether. Superheroes undoubtedly resonate, but they also polarize to an extent that is not quite the case for other mass-market genres. As a result, fan culture stereotypes have become ubiquitous, from *The Simpsons*'s Comic Book Guy to the young scientists on *The Big Bang Theory*. While these caricatures typically construct the superhero audience as male, straight (or sexually ambivalent), Caucasian, and middle class, the truth is more complex, and much more interesting. Superhero comics attract all sorts of readers, and these readers extract all sorts of messages from costumed adventure tales. The multifaceted audience is integral to the larger story of the genre.

As this section makes clear, many essayists and scholars have reflected on the superhero genre from the standpoint of different social locations and subject positions. While superhero storytelling offers a window onto the (recent) past and can provide grist for rigorous, theory-inflected investigation, superhero tales also represent a means by which individuals can interrogate and articulate their own feelings, experiences, and social relations. Granted, the superhero is not the only genre that evokes strong emotions—as Lorrie Palmer and others have pointed out, the Western once occupied a pivotal role in the emotional life of the mass audience—but its tenacious grip on the imaginations of millions of children, adolescents, and adults is worth exploring.

This section's opening essay, by the prominent feminist writer Gloria Steinem, explains how the early adventures of Wonder Woman "rescued" Steinem from the notion that heroism is a male prerogative and that the "ideal life" for women involves "sitting around like a Technicolor clothes horse." While she notes that these stories "are not admirable in all ways"—they strongly implied that women are *essentially*, intrinsically, better than men, and reproduced the aggressive ethnocentrism of midcentury U.S. culture—she also proposes that William Moulton Marston's iconic Amazons provide "psychic evidence" of "stable and peaceful agricultural societies," led by women, that "resisted the patriarchal age."

The following essay, by the late Lillian Robinson, is similarly positioned at the intersection of feminist commitment and superhero storytelling. Her piece explores the "saving irony" associated with the sole female member of the Fantastic Four, Sue Storm, who is otherwise known as Invisible Girl (and, subsequently, Invisible Woman). Robinson's nuanced essay—excerpted from her book *Wonder Women*—deploys an admirably light touch in examining the ways in which "stereotype and innovation work together" in the Silver Age stories of "Marvel's first female superhero."

In "Love Will Bring You to Your Gift," freelance writer Jennifer Stuller explores the relationship between superheroines, love, and "three intertwined themes: redemption, collaboration, and compassion." She pays particular attention to how Xena the warrior princess, Buffy the vampire slayer, and Max Guevara (from television's *Dark Angel*) have all pointed the way toward a more "egalitarian" and "reciprocal" form of heroism than is typically modeled in superhero comics. Acts of compassion, she says, "can change lives, heal past wounds, and even save the world."

Examining the Batman mythos from the standpoint of an "interested outsider," Andy Medhurst makes a bracing case for why he favors the televised,

Adam West version of the caped crusader (1966-68) to "that whole portentous Dark Knight charade." The "incongruities, the absurdities, the sheer ludicrousness of Batman were brought out so well by the sixties version," he says, "that for some audiences there will never be another credible approach." Medhurst, writing from an avowedly gay perspective, celebrates the reading strategies of gay Batman audiences and the campy irony of the television version, which invited queer readings. Finally, he decries the insistent, even homophobic, reassertion of Batman's "straight" identity in subsequent versions of the character.

Adilifu Nama, in an excerpt from his book *Super Black: American Pop Culture and Black Superheroes*, investigates the exploits of superheroes of color in mainstream comic books from the 1970s onwards. Resisting "linear and reductive" readings of comics and racial categories, Nama shows how characters like Black Lightning and John Stewart, the first nonwhite Green Lantern, evolved, as artists, writers, and publishers grappled with "the cultural politics of race in America." He also highlights the "unpredictably complicated" work of Dennis O'Neil and Neal Adams in the landmark *Green Lantern Co-Starring Green Arrow* comics of the early 1970s, which "forever changed the boundaries of the superhero genre."

Jeffrey A. Brown has also written extensively on black superheroes, but here, in an excerpt from his book *Black Superheroes, Milestone Comics, and Their Fans*, he focuses as much on reader reception as character development. Drawing on ethnographic research he conducted in the 1990s, Brown considers how superhero fans distinguished depictions of gender roles in superhero comics published by two high-profile companies that were launched in the early 1990s, Image and Milestone. While Image's comics tended to promote "hypermasculinity," the Milestone line, he suggests, worked to "infuse gentler, more responsible, and more cerebral qualities within the codes of dominant masculinity." While Brown's ethnographic methods presage those of many subsequent studies, his attention to the intersectionality of race and gender remains rare in superhero studies.

Marvel's most famous vigilante, the Punisher, could certainly be characterized as hypermasculine. In her essay on the "revisionist superhero Western," Lorrie Palmer explores the relationship between Jonathan Hensleigh's 2004 film adaptation and the innumerable melodramas, Westerns, and film noirs that laid the groundwork for its gestures, imagery, and "oppositions." The "oppositional structure of civilization versus wilderness," she suggests, "has been rendered through a hybrid blend of genres . . . bringing them all into alignment with this recent example of action cinema." Along with Stuller and Medhurst, Palmer's main interest is in how superhero characters have been portrayed in film and television, rather than in comic books, yet she is talking about comics as well as moving images when she concludes that contemporary lone wolf vengeance seekers are directly descended from "the Western hero."

Finally, Henry Jenkins writes movingly about his lifelong and yet often ambivalent engagement with superhero comics, in particular about the ways in which the genre's "death-defying superheroes helped me to model a process of letting go" as he watched his mother succumb to cancer. While his essay explores the complex relationship between time, history, and superheroes, it also delves into deeply personal territory and helps explain why some of us take the genre so seriously, even though it is steeped in the ephemeral.

Wonder Woman

GLORIA STEINEM

Reprinted by permission of the author from *Wonder Woman* (Bonanza Books, 1972), 2–7.

COMIC BOOKS WERE NOT QUITE RESPECTABLE, WHICH WAS A LARGE PART OF the reason I read them: under the covers with a flashlight, in the car while my parents told me I was ruining my eyes, in a tree or some other inaccessible spot; any place that provided sweet privacy and independence. Along with cereal boxes and ketchup labels, they were the primers that taught me how to read. They were even cheap enough to be the first items I could buy on my own; a customer whose head didn't quite reach the counter but whose dignity was greatly enhanced by making a selection (usually after much agonizing) and offering up money of her own.

If, as I have always suspected, children are simply short people—ancient spirits who happen to be locked up in bodies that aren't big enough or skillful enough to cope with the world—then the superhuman feats in comic books and fairy tales become logical and necessary. It's satisfying for anyone to have heroes who can see through walls or leap over skyscrapers in a single bound. But it's especially satisfying if our worldview consists mostly of knees and tying our shoes is still an exercise in frustration.

The trouble is that the comic book performers of such superhuman feats—and even of only dimly competent ones—are almost always heroes. Literally. The female child is left to believe that, even when her body is as grown up as her spirit, she will still be in the childlike role of helping with minor tasks, appreciating men's accomplishments, and being so incompetent and passive that she can only hope some man can come to her rescue. Of course, rescue and protection are comforting, even exhilarating experiences that should be and often are shared by men and boys. Even in comic books the hero is frequently called on to protect his own kind in addition to helpless women. But dependency and zero accomplishments get very dull as a steady diet. The only option for a girl reader is to identify with the male characters—pretty difficult, even in the androgynous years of childhood. If she can't do that, she faces limited prospects: an ideal life of sitting around like a Technicolor clothes horse getting into jams with villains, and saying things like, "Oh Superman, I'll always be grateful to you." Even as her hero goes off to bigger and better adventures, it hardly seems worth learning to tie our shoes.

I'm happy to say that I was rescued from this plight at about the age of seven or eight. Rescued (Great Hera!) by a woman. Not only was she as wise as Athena and as lovely as Aphrodite, she had the speed of Mercury and the strength of Hercules. Of course, being an Amazon, she had a head start on such accomplishments, but she earned them in a human way by training in Greek-style contents of dexterity and speed with her Amazon sisters. (Somehow it always seemed boring to me that Superman was a creature from another planet, and therefore had bulletproof skin, X-ray vision, and the power to fly. Where was the contest?) This beautiful Amazon did have some fantastic gadgets to help her. An invisible plane that carried her through dimensions of time and space, a golden magic lasso, and bullet-proof bracelets. But she still had to get to the plane, throw the lasso with accuracy, and be agile enough to catch bullets on the steel-enclosed wrists.

Her creator had also seen straight into my heart and understood the secret fears of violence hidden there. No longer did I have to pretend to like the "power and crunch" style of Captain Marvel or the Green Hornet. No longer did I have nightmares after reading ghoulish comics filled with torture and mayhem. Comics made all the more horrifying by their real-life setting in World War II. (It was a time when leather-clad Nazis were marching in the newsreels *and* in the comics. And the blood on the pages seemed frighteningly real.) Here was a heroic person who might conquer with force, but only a force that was tempered by love and justice. She converted her enemies more often than not. And if they were destroyed, they did it themselves, usually in some unbloody accident.

She was beautiful, brave, and explicitly out to change "a world torn by hatreds and wars of men."

She was Wonder Woman.

Looking back now at these Wonder Woman stories from the forties, I am amazed by the strength of their feminist message. One typical story centers on Prudence, a young pioneer in the days of the American frontier. (Wonder Woman is transported there by her invisible plane, of course, which also served as a time machine.) Rescued by Wonder Woman, Prudence realizes her own worth and the worth of all women. "I've learned my lesson," she says proudly in the final scene. "From now own, I'll rely on myself, not on a man." In yet another episode, Wonder Woman says, "I can never love a dominant man who is stronger than I am." And throughout the strips, it is only the destructive criminal woman, the woman who has bought the whole idea that male means aggression and female means submitting—who says "girls want superior men to boss them around."

Many of the plots revolve around evil men who treat women as inferior beings. In the end, all are brought to their knees and made to recognize women's strength and value. Some of the stories focus on weak women who are destructive and confused. These misled females are converted to self-reliance and self-respect through the example of Wonder Woman. The message of the strips is sometimes inconsistent and always oversimplified (these are, after all, comics), but it is still a passable version of the truisms that women are rediscovering today—that women are full human beings; that we cannot love others until we love ourselves; that love and respect can only exist between equals.

Wonder Woman's family of Amazons on Paradise Island, her band of college girls in America, and her efforts to save individual women are all welcome examples of women working together and caring about each other's welfare. The idea of such cooperation may not seem particularly revolutionary to the male reader. Men are routinely depicted as working well together, but women know how rare and therefore exhilarating the idea of sisterhood really is.

Wonder Woman's mother, Queen Hippolyte, offers yet another welcome example to young girls in search of a strong identity. Queen Hippolyte founds nations, wages war to protect Paradise Island, and sends her daughter off to fight the forces of evil in the world. Perhaps most impressive in an age fraught with Freudian shibboleths, she also marshals her queenly strength to protect her daughter in bad times. How many girl children grew to adulthood with no experience of a courageous and worldly mother, except in these slender stories? How many adult women disdain the birth of a female child, believe it is "better" to bear male children, and fear the competition and jealousy they have been conditioned to believe is "natural" to a mother and daughter? Feminism is just beginning to uncover the sense of anger and loss in girls whose mothers had no power to protect them in the world, and so trained them to be victims, or left them to identify with their fathers if they had any ambitions outside the traditional family role.

Wonder Woman symbolizes many of the values of the women's culture that feminists are now trying to introduce into the mainstream: strength and self-reliance for women; sisterhood and mutual support among women; peace, fullness and esteem for human life; a diminishment both of "masculine" aggression and of the belief that violence is the only way of solving conflicts.

Of course, the Wonder Women stories are not admirable in all ways. Many feminist principles are distorted or ignored. Thus, women are converted and saved; mad scientists, foreign spies, criminals, and other male villains are regularly brought to the point of renouncing violence and, more often, of saying, "You're right. Wonder Woman, I'll never make the mistake of thinking women are inferior again." Is the reader supposed to conclude that women are superior? The Wonder Woman stories not only depict women as culturally different (in ways that are sometimes constructive and sometimes not), they also hint that women are biologically, and therefore immutably, superior to men.

Few modern feminists would agree. There are as yet no perfectly culture-free tests to prove to us which traits come from conditioning and which do not, but the consensus seems to be that society, not biology, assigns some human traits to males and others to females. Women have suffered from being taught to develop what society considers the less-valued traits of humanity, but this doesn't mean we want to switch to a sole claim on the "more valuable" ones either. That might accomplish nothing more than changing places with men in the hierarchy. Most feminist philosophy supposes that the hierarchy itself must be eliminated, and that individuals who are free of roles assigned because of sex or race will also be free to develop the full range of human qualities. It's the multitudinous differences in individuals that count, not the localized differences of sex or race.

For psychologist William Moulton Marston—who, under the pen name of "Charles Moulton," created Wonder Woman—females were sometimes romanticized as biologically and unchangeably superior. "Women," he wrote, "represent love. Men represent force. Man's use of force without love brings evil and unhappiness. Wonder Woman proves that women are superior to men because they have love in addition to force." If that's the case, then they were stuck with yet another social order based on birth.

For the purposes of most Wonder Women stories, however, the classic argument of nature versus nurture is a mere intellectual quibble. Just helping women to respect themselves, to use their strength and refuse domination by men is time-consuming enough. Wonder Woman rarely has the leisure to hint at what the future social order ought to be as for men. We do get the idea that they have some hope—even if vague—of collective redemption. "This man's world of yours," explains Wonder Woman, "will never be without pain and suffering until it learns respect for human rights." Put in more positive terms, this does seem to indicate that humanized men will have full membership in the new society.

Some of the Wonder Woman stories preach patriotism in a false way, but much of the blame rests with history. Wonder Woman was born in 1941, just about the time that World War II became a reality for most Americans, and she therefore had to spend much of her time protecting this country from foreign threats. Usually, that task boiled down to proving that women could be just as brave and loyal as men in the service of their country. Even when her adventures took place in other countries or at other times, they still invariably ended with simplistic commercials about democracy. Although Wonder Woman was shocked by America's unjust patriarchal system—a shock she recorded on her arrival here from Paradise Island—she never had much opportunity to follow up on it. A nation mobilized for war is not a nation prepared to accept criticism. In fact, her costume was patterned after the American flag, and her wartime adventures sometimes had highly jingoistic and even racist overtones, especially when she was dealing with Japanese and Germans.

Compared to the other comic book characters of the period, however, Wonder Woman is still a relief. Marston invented her as a counter to the violence and "bloodcurdling masculinity" that pervaded most comic books, and he remained true to his purpose. Wonder Women and her sisters were allowed to use violence, but only in self-defense and only if it stopped short of actually killing someone. Most group conflicts between men and women were set not in America, but in a mythological past. Thus Mars, the god of war, periodically endangered the Amazon community and sometimes tried to disarm Queen Hippolyte through the ruses of love. Mars, of course, was the "heavy." He preached that women "are the natural spoils of war" and must remain at home, the helpless slaves of the male victors. Marston used Mars as the symbol of everything Wonder Woman must fight against, but he also gave the god of war a rationale for his beliefs that was really the female superiority argument all over again. If women were allowed to become warriors like the Amazons, they would grow stronger than men, and put an end to war. What future for an unemployed god?

The inconsistencies in Wonder Woman's philosophy are especially apparent in her love life. It is confused, to say the least. Sometimes her adventures with Steve, the pilot she is supposedly "in love" with, bear a feminist message, and sometimes they simper and go conventional in a way that contradicts everything that has gone before. In her American disguise as mild-mannered Diana Prince (a clear steal from Superman), she plays the classic feminine role: secretary, nurse, and worshipful, unrequited sidekick to Steve. The implicit moral is that, at least as Wonder Woman, she can love only an equal. But an equal never turns up, and sometimes she loses her grip on herself and falls for the masculine notion that there must be a permanent winner and a permanent loser, and conqueror and a conquered. "Some girls love to have a man stronger than they are to make them do things," she muses aloud. "Do I like it? I don't know. It's sort of thrilling. But isn't it more fun to make a man obey?"

I remember being worried by these contradictions. How could Wonder Woman be interested in Steve, who seemed so weak and so boring? Did women really have to live in a community by themselves—a separate country like Paradise Island—in order to be both happy and courageous? The very fact that the ideal was an island—insular, isolated, self-contained, cut-off—both pleased and bothered me. And why, when she chose an earthly disguise, did Wonder Woman have to pick such a loser? How could she bear to be like Diana Prince? Did that mean that all women really had to disguise their true selves in weak feminine stereotypes in order to survive?

But all these doubts paled beside the relief, the sweet vengeance, the toe-wriggling pleasure of reading about a woman who was strong, beautiful, courageous, and a fighter for social justice. A woman who strode forth, stopping wars and killing with one hand, distributing largesse and compassionate aid with the other. A Wonder Woman.

In 1947, William Marston died, leaving his heroine in the hands of writers who didn't really understand his spirit. Gradually, her feminist orientation began to wane. She became simultaneously more submissive to men. I don't remember the transition very well possibly because I myself was on the verge of adolescence and was therefore putting comic books behind me. Or possibly because the comparatively free years of my childhood were at an end. Like Wonder Woman, the full impact of the feminine role was beginning to close around me. Now I was thirteen and made to see that the idea of accomplishing anything on my own was at best eccentric and at worst impossible. Recognition, and status through men, was the best possibility; it was also socially rewarded and socially enforced. Both Wonder Woman and I fell into some very hard times in the 1950s.

Looking at her most recent adventures is even more discouraging. By 1968, she had given up her magic lasso, her bracelets, her invisible plane, and all her superhuman Amazonian powers. She had become Diana Prince, a mere mortal who walked about in boutique clothes and took the advice of a male mastermind named "I Ching." She still had adventures and she had learned something about karate. But any attractive man could disarm her. She was a female James Bond—but far more boring since she was denied his sexual freedom. She had become a simpleminded "good girl."

In 1973, Wonder Woman comics will be born again; I hope with the feminism and strength of the original Wonder Woman—my Wonder Woman—restored. But regardless of her future, the original adventures of the golden forties will remain classics for children, boys as well as girls, and perhaps for many heroine-starved and nostalgic grownups as well. If we had all read more about Wonder Woman and less about Dick and Jane, the new wave of the feminist revolution might have happened less painfully and sooner.

Wonder Woman is a comic book character. She and her Amazon sisters are fictional creations. Indeed, Amazons have generally been considered figments of the imagination, perhaps the mythological evidence of man's fear of woman. Yet there is a tentative but growing body of anthropological and archeological evidence to support the theory that Amazon societies were real;

they did exist. German and Brazilian scientists exploring the jungles of Brazil, for instance, recently came upon the caves of what appears to have been an all-female society. The caves are strikingly devoid of the usual phallic design and theme. They feature, instead, the triangular female symbol. (The only cave that does bear male designs is believed to have been the copulatorium.)

Though the Brazilian research is still too indefinite for conclusions, there are many evidences of the existence of Amazon societies in all parts of the world. Being a writer, not a scientist tied to proven fact, I have fused the sometimes contradictory versions of Amazonia into one amalgam; into a story that sounds right to me in the way that a dream interpretation or a race-memory seems suddenly, thuddingly right as it strikes off our subconscious. Much of it has been proved, but I tell it as a story.

Once upon a time, the many cultures of this world were all part of the gynocratic age. Paternity had not yet been discovered, and it was thought (as it still is in some tribal cultures) that women bore fruit like trees—when they were ripe. Childbirth was mysterious, it was vital and it was envied. Women were worshipped because of it, were considered superior because of it. Men prayed to female gods and, in their religious ceremonies, imitated the act of birth (as many tribesmen still do). In such a world, the only clear grouping was that of mothers and children. Men were on the periphery—an interchangeable body of workers for, and worshippers of, the female center, the principle of life.

The discovery of paternity, of sexual cause and childbirth effect, was as cataclysmic for society as, say, the discovery of fire or the shattering of the atom. Gradually, the idea of male ownership of children took hold. With it came the idea of private property that could be passed down to children. If paternity was to be unquestioned, then women had to be sexually restricted. This was the origin of marriage.

Gynocracy also suffered from the periodic invasions of nomadic tribes. Gynocracies were probably stable and peaceful agricultural societies since agriculture was somewhat more—though not totally—a female occupation. Nomadic tribes survived by hunting, which was somewhat more—though not totally—a male occupation. The conflict between the hunters and the growers was really the conflict between male-dominated and female-dominated cultures.

Restricted by new systems of marriage as well as by occasional pregnancies, women gradually lost their freedom, mystery, and superior position. For five thousand years or more, the gynocratic age had flowered in peace and productivity. Slowly, in varying stages and in different parts of the world, the social order was painfully reversed. Women became the underclass, marked by their visible differences regardless of whether they had children. Often, the patriarchal take-over of female-dominated societies was accomplished violently. Everywhere, fear of goddesses, of women's magical procreative powers, and of the old religions caused men to suppress the old social order very cruelly indeed.

Some women resisted the patriarchal age. They banded together to protect their female-centered culture and religions from a more violent, transient, and male-centered way of life. Men were dangerous, to be tolerated only during periodic mating ceremonies. The women themselves became adept at self-defense.

These were backlash cultures, doomed by their own imbalance, but they did survive in various groupings on every continent for many thousands of years. Why don't they turn up in history? For one reason, most of their existence was lived in those thousands of years dismissed as *pre*history—that is, preliterate. The few records that are available to us were written under the patriarchal assumptions of a much later age. Even archeology and anthropology have suffered from the fundamental, almost subconscious assumption that male and female roles as we see them in the patriarchal age are "natural"; therefore, they must have been the same in the prehistoric past. Only lately have we begun to question and check out those assumptions. Large, strong, and presumably male skeletons from prehistoric sites, for instance, have turned out on closer examination to be female after all.

Mythology is a collective human memory that has, on other occasions, turned out to be accurate about invasions, great floods, and the collision of stars. The Amazon cultures may also one day be proven as fact. Meanwhile, the fascination that brings them up as fantasy again and again may itself be some psychic evidence of their existence.

If so, Wonder Woman becomes just one small, isolated outcropping of a larger human memory, and the girl children who love her are responding to one small echo of dreams and capabilities in their own forgotten past.

Invisible Girl

LILLIAN ROBINSON

Reprinted by permission from *Wonder Women: Feminisms and Superheroes* (Routledge, 2004), 88–94.

WHAT MAY BE CALLED THE NEW MARVEL ATTITUDE BEGINS WITH THE CREATION in 1961 of *The Fantastic Four*, with mutations, internecine insults, ambivalence, and irony all over the text, but drawn in the traditional adventure or detective comics mode. The first major change in artistic style did not occur until well into the 1960s, after the success of Pop Art. I do not insist on this "post-Pop ergo propter Pop" argument, but it seems to me suggestive, not only of a seismic shift in visual approach, but of the growing importance of the visual domain that was later to mark the "Revelation" phase of comic book history in general and the female superhero experience in particular.

Marvel's first female superhero, Invisible Girl, preceded the moment of Wonder Woman's feminist renewal by more than a decade. Invisible Girl was subsequently—and significantly—to become Invisible Woman who, as wife, mother, and superhero, remains one of the Fantastic Four. Along with the other mutants in that group, she was "transformed by an accident in outer space into something much more than human" and has "vowed to use ... [her] awesome power to help mankind chart the unknown" (#357, October 1991). And, as is the case with the other Fantastics, her particular superpower is an extension of her salient premutation qualities. Sue Storm was a distinctly—almost pathologically—shy and retiring girl. Her invisibility, along with some additional powers, enabled her to help "chart the unknown" on behalf of "mankind," and, in the process, vanquish technologically and cybernetically sophisticated villains, who often possessed convoluted motives of their own. These included but were by no means limited to the alien Skrulls and the human Dr. Doom. Her role and powers increased with time and become most interesting in the period from 1968 on. Throughout, Sue's visible dimension, when not in action, includes no signs of exceptional bodily powers, although, like the latter-day Wonder Woman, she evidently frequents a reputable health club.

The accident that gave the Fantastic Four their superpowers was an artifact of the Cold War mentality. Pilot Ben Grimm initially refuses to fly the rocket ship to the stars, because there has not yet been enough research on the effects of cosmic rays. "They might kill us all out in space!" he insists to the brilliant scientist Reed Richards, his former college roommate (#1, November 1961). But Sue Storm, Reed's fiancée, insists on the political necessity of an immediate liftoff. "Ben, we've *got* to take that chance! Unless we want the Communists to beat us," adding, "I—I never thought that *you* would be a coward!" As will happen throughout Ben's subsequent career as the Thing, it is the challenge to his manliness that goads him to accept the assignment, and the four are off. There are four of them because, although only Reed and Ben are required for the mission itself, Sue comes along, explaining to Richards, "I'm your fiancée! Where you go, I go." To which Johnny Storm appends, "and I'm taggin' along with Sis, so it's settled!"

In a reprise of the origins story (#11, February 1963), it is Reed who explains, "We've got to reach the stars before the Reds do!" while Sue chimes in, "Oh, Reed, if only the government had listened to you in time—heeded your warning!" In this version, she tells the reluctant Ben that she and her kid brother Johnny are planning to ride the starship so that Reed will see that at least *they* are not afraid!

It is worth noting that the U.S. moon landing—I mean, forget about the stars!—was nearly eight years in the future. Even more interesting from a political perspective, once the Four were launched as a super heroic team, the first issues contained very few references to the Cold War. The space race is mentioned a couple of times, a Russian villain addresses his simian sidekick as "Comrade Ape," a suspicious device is said to bear "Communist insignia," and Khrushchev himself is caricatured a couple of times yelling at his subordinates or the whole UN in a fashion reminiscent of wartime's comic book Nazis. But, at their worst, the Soviets are never represented as being or even being in league with the real enemy, which threatens the entire planet, with no concern for national borders or identities. As in representations of World War II, the fight is nominally for "democracy," which is constructed as being synonymous with capitalism, but is not the focus of narrative or ideology, since the battle for world domination is being waged on an entirely different plane.

At any rate, Sue's presence on the flight that exposed all those aboard to the cosmic rays was as an appendage of her boyfriend. In the revisionist 1963 version, she also serves an ideological function, as she and Johnny, a callow teenager who perpetually gets on the Thing's nerves, stand in for the proverbial "women and children" that traditional heroes are pledged to defend. But the cosmic rays are an equal-opportunity mutator, so they get endowed with superpowers, too. With an irony that I assume is intentional, Ben, the only space traveler to express his reservations, is the most damaged, and, for many years, the only one of the Four whose mutated, if super-powered identity, his horrible Thing-ness, cannot be switched on and off at will. Meanwhile, open-minded scientist Reed Richards, the Four's leader, becomes Mr. Fantastic, endowed with amazing flexibility, as well as strength; hot-headed young Johnny becomes the Human Torch, and Sue becomes Invisible Girl. "Together," announces Reed, "we have more power than humans have ever possessed!" But it is the ever-truculent Ben who gets to shout out the implications: "You don't have to make a speech, big shot! We understand! We've got to use that power to help mankind, right?"

Although Sue's nonsuperhero role is as an adjunct to Reed, only rarely do we see the shyness that was her defining trait before the accident. One such case, though, is the government's testimonial dinner in their honor, which three of the Four are extremely reluctant to attend. Speaking last, Sue, who went on the starship voyage to show her fearless trust in her beloved, whimpers, "Oh, Reed, I—I'm *afraid* to go! I'm not used to meeting all those important people! I'm liable to get so flustered that before I know it, I might vanish in front of their eyes? If that ever happened, I'd simply die of embarrassment!" (#7, October 1962).

Commenting on a series of frames (*Fantastic Four King Size Special #4*, November 1966) in which, successively, Sue Storm serves coffee, jokes about the clothing bills she's run up, attends a fashion show, and faints dead away, Trina Robbins observes:

> Unlike the insecurities and self-doubts that afflicted male heroes, and which encouraged the reader's identification and evoked admiration when the heroes overcame them, Sue Storm's . . . flaws were almost a caricature of Victorian notions of the feminine, an invisible woman who faints when she tries to exert herself (*The Great Women Superheroes*, 114).

It does not seem to occur to her that, with Stan Lee's characteristic Marvel irony already operating, the caricature may be intentional.

Yet it must be admitted that, in the early issues, Sue assumes a number of stereotyped feminine roles. It is she, for instance, who designs the group's uniforms. When the Thing, with typical self-reflexivity about the comics themselves, fulminates, *"Bah!!* Costumes—tights—that's kid stuff! Who needs 'em?" she is quick on the uptake: "*We* do, if we're in the business of crime fighting for real! If we're a team, we should look like a team!" Even more revealing is her reply when Reed, trying on his suit, praises the design: "Say! This isn't half had, Sue! You ever think of working for Dior?" While adjusting the Thing's mask, she answers, "I've got enough to do acting as nursemaid to you three!" (#3, March 1962).

In the same vein, Sue is in a "chi-chi beauty parlor on Fifth Avenue" when she spots the flaming "4" signal in the sky. Having waited months for an appointment with the exclusive Monsieur Pierre, she is as upset as the coiffeur himself that she has to rush off before he can create her new hairdo. There is a certain wit, as well as girlishness, to her thoughts as she dashes away and transforms at the same time: "Better turn invisible! I can't run thru the streets with curlers in my hair!" (#15, June 1963). More disturbing, because apparently devoid of saving irony, is the moment when Reed finishes his special report for NASA on rocket fuel and goes looking for Sue to type it up. She hastily erases the undersea view-screen on which she has been seeking the Sub-Mariner, the other male in her life, and, once Reed says he wishes that Namor *would* surface again, so she could finally make up her mind, the next caption reads, "And then, after giving Sue the report to type . . ." while the illustration shows him reflecting sadly on his beloved's ambivalence: "Strange how nobody is ever really master of his own fate!" (#14, May 1963). Strange, too (if you ask me), how someone whose fate is in another person's hands thinks nothing of placing those hands on a keyboard to serve him and his work!

Much of this comes to a head in issue #11 (February 1963), in the same feature, "A Visit with the Fantastic Four," that retold the origins story. Reed finishes his narration of the accident and the consequent mutations by saying, "We've come a long way since those early days—and had many almost unbelievable adventures!" His complacency about this history is shattered, however, by Sue's retort: "But they were *your* adventures—the three of you—much more than mine!" It seems that readers have been sending Sue unpleasant letters, charging that she doesn't contribute enough to the team effort and that the others would be better off without her. "She's not exaggerating," says Reed, when he's read some of them. He shouts, "Well—it's time to set the record straight—here and now!" It's Ben, temporarily redeemed from Thing-ness, who, for a change, utters the calming note: "Take it easy, pal! The kids didn't mean any harm—they just don't understand!"

Setting the record straight has two interestingly contradictory parts. On the one hand, says Reed, gesturing toward a handy bust of Abraham Lincoln, the Great Emancipator famously said his mother was "the most important person in the world to him," although she did not, as Ben adds sarcastically, "*do* enough" in the chronicle of his deeds. Once invoked, her role as nurturer of Abe and hence of his accomplishments is presumably self-evident enough that it needs no further elaboration, so they move on to the other half of the argument: Sue does take part in the comics' action dimension. A couple of examples are cited, her brave leap into the middle of their battle with the Skrulls and her rescuing them all from Dr. Doom's airless prison. Only two dramatic events occur in this Special Bonus Feature. First of all, Ben gets so angry as he admonishes Sue's detractors ("If you readers wanna see women fightin' all the time, then go see lady wrestlers!") that he turns back into the Thing. And the Torch sounds an alarm bell summoning the others away from this discussion to a surprise birthday party the three males have prepared for Sue. ("You remembered!") As she cuts the inscribed cake Johnny has "rigged up" for her, she says, "I'm so choked up I don't know what to say." The Thing comments that it's the first time he's ever heard a female make such a statement, while Reed wishes, "Many happy returns . . . to our *favorite* partner!" Once again, stereotype and innovation work together.

In the concluding frame, the editors explain that this episode without a real story—at least, not an adventure story—was produced in response to letters and queries from readers. "From time to time in future issues," they continue, "we shall attempt to pictorially comment on other letters from you—our valued fans!" Whether it really was readers' letters or their own bad conscience, something convinced the creators that it was worthwhile to explain Sue's apparent failure to pull her superheroic weight. The editors and their characters make it clear that they plan to keep Invisible Girl in the series and that she's just fine the way she is. I wonder, myself, if it occurred to any readers to propose giving her an equal part in the action sequences, rather than removing her from the tetrad. Or to any writers to attempt such a move. It certainly doesn't look that way! After all, Sue herself expresses the official position before becoming invisible and hitching onto the evil Mr. Miracle's truck: "One invisible girl can sometimes accomplish more than a battalion!" (#3, March 1962).

Love Will Bring You to Your Gift

JENNIFER STULLER

Reprinted by permission from *Ink-Stained Amazons and Cinematic Warriors: Superwomen in Modern Mythology* (I.B. Tauris, 2010), 87–104.

> Empathy is really the most revolutionary emotion.
> **GLORIA STEINEM**

"LOVE"—A COMPLICATED CONCEPT IF THERE EVER WAS ONE. BUFFY IS TOLD BY her spirit guide that love will bring her to her gift. William Marston's Wonder Woman is made of love, simply because she has the body of a woman. He even wrote that "Man's use of force without love brings evil and unhappiness. But Wonder Woman has force bound by love and with her strength, represents what every woman should be and really is."[1] In Luc Besson's film *The Fifth Element*, the eponymous character finds that the only reason to save our tragic world is for love. And for a time, Xena's companion Gabrielle follows a pacifist philosophy called "The Way of Love."

Often with women, *love* is stressed again and again—making it necessary to wonder about this particular emotion, or ethic, consistently being linked to the source of a female hero's strength. Does love constitute a reimagining of heroism? It's certainly a different motivation from that of a quest for a prize, be it grail, fleece, dragon, or damsel. It is also a break from the "Lone Wolf" model of heroism, which is rooted in traditional uber-masculinity and isolationism.[2]

Does the suggestion of love as strength, or as gift, embrace innately female characteristics? Does it infuse what is "naturally" powerful about women into a liberating archetype? Or does it reinforce stereotypes about how women should behave as self-sacrificing nurturers? The assumption that love is inherent in women, but not in men, is a sticky, even sexist concept, and the idea that a female superhero's greatest gift is her nurturing temperament or her ability to love selflessly certainly has the potential to reinforce stereotypical feminine ideals. But there's evidence that love in the superwoman *does* in fact present a reimagining of heroism. Wonder Woman, Xena and Gabrielle,

Buffy and the Scoobies, and Max Guevara (among others) are compelled by their values, which are in turn reinforced by love—a power greater than any of their physical skills. Their love is the impetus, but becomes integral to their strength, and thus the success of their missions. These superwomen illustrate a new form of heroism for popular culture that is based on loving compassion, and compassion itself is a heroic act.

The connection between "love" and superwomen can at first seem troublesome, as it evokes notions of heroines in the traditional sense—of fair maidens and damsels in need of rescue by the hero of the story. But superwomen are *not* heroines in the traditional sense. Love, as it's used in stories about the female heroes described throughout this chapter, underscores three intertwined themes: redemption, collaboration, and compassion.

Redemption comes through a personal quest to make amends for past wrongs, often with guidance from a partner or a community. This definition of redemption emphasizes the belief that there is an innate good in all of us and allows for second chances. And many superwomen believe that anyone can change and grow into a better person.

In the original *Wonder Woman* series, this is seen as reformation, and in *Buffy* and *Xena*, it is seen as redemption. (The difference between reformation and redemption may seem subtle, but the nuance is crucial when evaluating the evolution of emotional complexity in depictions of superheroes in modern myth.) In the early Wonder Woman mythos, "Redemption" came through imprisonment and "love re-education." Villainnesses were taken to Paradise Island's sister oasis, Transformation Island (originally named *Reform* Island), a place where "bad" women were taught to be "good" women. Here, good is of course equated with loving—in keeping with Marston's theories of the good and beautiful woman who should rule the world with her altruistic love.[3] In the Buffyverse, the individual human or demon in question is provided with the agency to decide what kind of life to live and what kind of person they want to be. (And just about anyone who has met Buffy is indeed influenced by her compassionate example to better themselves.) Along with female power, redemption is one of the overriding themes of the Whedonverse. Writer/director Joss Whedon has said,

> Redemption has become one of the most important themes in my work. . . . I think as you make your way through life it's hard to maintain a moral structure, and that difficulty and the process of coming out the other side of a dark, even psychological time [adolescence] is to me the most important part of adulthood. . . . I think to an extent every human being needs to be redeemed somewhat or at least needs to look at themselves and say, "I've made mistakes, I'm off course, I need to

change." Which is probably the hardest thing for a human being to do and maybe that's why it interests me so.⁴

Choosing to live by a love ethic, writes bell hooks, "ensures that relationships in our lives, including encounters with strangers, nurture our spiritual growth."⁵ Though Xena strives for redemption by helping those in need, a love ethic does not come easily to her. Fortunately, Gabrielle's stalwart morality helps bring Xena time and again to a place where she is capable of acting out of compassion. Indeed, hooks notes that "Those who choose to walk on love's path are well served if they have a guide. That guide can enable us to overcome fear if we trust that they will not lead us astray or abandon us along the way."⁶ Clearly Gabrielle is Xena's guide on the path to redemption. Their mutual admiration is evident in their passionate praise of each other, as well as their sincere declarations of love and friendship, but it was Gabrielle's understanding of right and wrong that informed nearly every step they took. In the series finale, Xena tells her life partner, "if there is a reason for our travels together—it's because I had to learn from you, enough to find the final, the good, the right thing to do."⁷

Gabrielle had studied The Way of Love from a prophet named Eli (Timothy Omundson). In the Season 4 episode, appropriately titled "The Way," he taught her that the only way to end the "cycle of violence that has ravaged the Earth for centuries" is through nonviolence—a practice that is antithetical to Xena's warrior nature. In the same episode, the warrior princess learns from her own spiritual teacher, Krishna, that to fully tap into *her* strength she too must embrace "The Way":

> *Xena*: The Way? I've heard about the way in Greece, Ch'in, Anatoli, and now India. I don't get it. The way is not for people like me.
> *Krishna*: You're wrong. You're very close to the way now. However, missing it by the width of a hair is the same as missing it by the height of a mountain.
> *Xena*: I'm close? I don't think so. I don't have the patience of Gabrielle, the love of Eli, or the serenity of my mentor, Lao Ma. I'm just an angry, ass-kicking. . . .
> *Krishna*: Warrior.
> *Xena*: Yes, a warrior.⁸

Xena learns that "The Way of the Warrior" is a path that is just as valid and necessary as Gabrielle's, and though their paths are different, they walk them together.⁹ When Xena apologizes for a time when she feels she's taken Gabrielle away from *her* truth, Gabrielle reconciles their ways of being. "Don't be sorry," she says, adding, "Xena, do you think I could have understood the power of selfless love if it weren't for our friendship?"[10]

Later, Gabrielle abandons the Way of Love for an even higher power. In "The Ides of March" (4.21), she dispenses with her pacifism when Xena is critically injured. With a violent rage rarely seen in her, Gabrielle destroys a troop of Roman soldiers attempting to finish off the paralyzed warrior princess. Though she is wounded, a horrified Xena feels responsible, thinking she has again caused Gabrielle to walk a spiritually false path: "I made you leave the way of love. It was my fault." Gabrielle reminds her that she had a choice, "do nothing or save my friend." With conviction she adds, "I chose the way of friendship."[11]

As Dana Hlusko rightly noted in an article for *Whoosh!*, compassion is the foundation for the Way of Friendship. She writes that with this concept Gabrielle designed a valid philosophy of life, one that was an even higher developed model than the Way of Love. Hlusko also points out that "These are not mutually exclusive 'ways.' They are tightly integrated in a service oriented, compassionate way of life." Most profoundly she adds, "One cannot live the Way of Friendship if one cannot love."[12]

When we are introduced to Max Guevara of *Dark Angel*, she like Xena is more interested in self-preservation than in helping others. But like *Spider-Man*'s Peter Parker, who initially ignored his uncle's advice that "with great power comes great responsibility," a mistake that resulted in a death Peter could have prevented, so too will Max encounter a life-altering situation that her involvement could have averted. Her military training will cause her to be cautious, defiant even, but she'll also realize that she not only has the power to make a difference, but, like all of us, the responsibility to do so.[13]

As Lorna Jowett observed, in the beginning of the series,

> Max is recognizably the pragmatic, amoral thief who cares only for her own gain.... She initially assists Logan because "a friend of [hers] died on account of the villain of the week (Pilot), in other words, for personal, not political reasons.[14]

But personal reasons are often the motivation for heroic acts. And for Max, especially as a transgenic—or symbolic—Other, the personal will become political.

After Max's initial break-in at Logan's, he tracks her down, hoping to enlist her superhuman assistance. She can't believe that he's interested only in exposing corruption and not, like most everyone else in the post-Pulse States, after the almighty dollar. She asks, "What's your shot in all this? I mean being a famous, underground, pirate cyber-journalist can't be much of a payday." Logan explains that his parents "were loaded," he believes in making a difference, and uses his resources to do so. He encourages Max to use hers, but her response is that she's more interested in riding her motorcycle than giving herself a headache over stuff she can't do anything about. Logan reprimands her, lecturing, "You accept the way things are . . . you're an active participant in making them worse." A defensive Max responds with trademark sass, "Is the social studies class over for today?"[15]

Logan wants Max to protect a key witness in a trial against a man named Sonrisa who had been replacing crucial medicine for war veterans with sugar pills and then selling the real deal for a marked-up price in Canada. The self-protective Max refuses, but when her friend Theo dies as a result of the false treatment, and she catches a news report detailing the kidnapping of the witness's daughter, as Logan is shot and his bodyguard killed, our hero steps up to the proverbial plate. Whether Max is driven by guilt or a desire for social justice is up in the air at this point. She saves Logan from a second assassination attempt and rescues the abducted child. She even executes a plan that takes down Sonrisa and his organization.

Logan thinks that Max's involvement means he's cracked her "bioengineered military-issue armor plating [to find her] beating heart"—and perhaps her sense of social responsibility. But she's wary, telling him she's "not signing up to join the Logan Cale brigade for the defense of widows, small children, and lost animals."[16] He entices her with an offer of exchange—information on the whereabouts of her X-5 siblings (which his clandestine investigations have led him to be aware of) for help with legwork. He produces a file on her brother, Zack, and in the closing narrated voice-over, Max says,

> I knew it. I always knew Zack was out there somewhere, but you know, just my luck this guy Logan had to be the one to find him. Now he figures I'm going to go and do the right thing because I owe him. Like I even care.[17]

Max does care and does do "the right thing." But not because Logan tells her to. (Although more often than not the "right" thing will be determined, designated, and validated by Logan—who has no problem manipulating Max for his own agenda, no matter how socially conscious or righteous it may be.)[18] Much of Max's motivation comes from finding and protecting her family—initially the X-5s she escaped with and later the majority of transgenics bred by Manticore. But she's also consistently faced with situations that allow her to heal the wounds of her own past by helping others move ahead in their lives. For instance, in "Flushed" (1.2), after a series of events lead to her arrest, she encounters Maria, a young woman being sexually abused by the prison's warden. Max, who had lived with a foster family after her escape from Manticore, has long felt guilt over not protecting her foster sister from similar abuse—even when she could have done so with her training. But Manticore's training also taught her that "You engage an adversary only if it is consistent with the overall strategic objective. Failing that, you will initiate a tactical withdrawal."[19] The child Max's objective was self-preservation, doing whatever she could to resist recapture. But she regrets leaving without the abused girl and doesn't make the same mistake twice—rescuing Maria and having Logan connect the young girl with a loving adoptive family. When Max thanks Logan, he reminds her, "You were the one who cared enough about this girl to go in and get her out. You did a good thing, Max." She replies, "Better late than never."[20]

Max will continue to learn that the "objective"—as dictated by her military training—is the last thing that matters. People—*good* friends, friends, family, and the disenfranchised are what're truly important.

Notably, both Max and Buffy Summers reject patriarchal systems of behavior in favor of lived knowledge: experience, gut feelings, friendship, and context-based decision-making. When Max finally reunites with Zack, he chastises her for her emotional attachments. As Jowett observes, "Fairly early the show emphasizes that while staying in Seattle puts Max in danger of recapture by Manticore, over and over she chooses to remain with her various communities." Zack believes Max has allowed her tactical judgment to be clouded by feelings and emotions that will ultimately cost her her freedom. But, like Buffy, her emotions give her power. And so do her friends.

Collaboration with friends, family, or community is common to the female hero—not because she is incapable of succeeding on her own, but because she is more successful when she recognizes, encourages, and utilizes the talents of others. This support system is essential to the evolution of her spirit—which will ultimately make her a better warrior. Additionally, in stories about the female hero, the sidekick—who is traditionally of lesser power than the hero, generally in need of rescue, and often serves the narrative purpose of comic relief—is elevated to the role of hero themselves through collaborative contribution.[21]

Xena was one of the first superwomen to be depicted as having complex and meaningful female friendships and as a participant in female communities. While Gabrielle is the single most important relationship in Xena's life, the warrior princess has also been involved in several mentor/protégée relationships with other women (even more notable because the learning and teaching were reciprocal). These include Helen of Troy, whom in the series's trademark rewriting of myth, Xena and Gabriele liberate and empower; Lao

Ma, a Chinese philosopher and ghost writer for Lao Tzu; and M'Lia, a Gaelic slave who taught Xena "The Pinch."[22] The Amazons also serve as an extended family of sorts, particularly as Gabrielle was gifted with leadership of their nation. In the episode, "Is There a Doctor in the House?," when the pair encounter Ephiny (Danielle Cormack), the Amazon who trained Gabrielle, in labor and alone in the middle of a battlefield, they protect and assist her and reassure her that her friends and family are there to support her.

> *Ephiny*: Family?
> *Gabrielle*: Hey—I'm your sister Amazon, remember? Xena and I will take care of you.[23]

Sherrie A. Inness notes in *Tough Girls: Women Warriors and Wonder Women in Popular Culture*: "Friendships are rare for tough women because such relationships can undermine the cool, aloof attitude of the tough her . . . [but] Xena shows that toughness in women does not have to be antithetical to friendship." The modern superwoman deviates from the Lone Wolf model of heroism by being able to be both independent and part of a community. "The result," Inness writes, "is a new vision of toughness that emphasizes both her physical toughness and her connection to other women."[24] Here, the warrior princess demonstrates her priorities when she declares, "I'm gonna find a safe place for Ephiny to have her baby. And *then* I'm gonna stop this war."[25]

Xena populates her family with a variety of people, from Gabrielle and Joxer (Ted Raimi), to Ephiny and the other Amazons. It could even be argued that the gods, Ares (Kevin Smith) and Aphrodite (Alexandra Tydings), are part of her extended family.

Chosen families also play a large part in *Buffy the Vampire Slayer*, *Angel*, and *Firefly*. Joss Whedon has noted that he is much more interested in the created family than in families of origin, and in telling stories in which the chosen family is depicted as being more lasting and loving.[26] hooks also reflects on the value, and healing power, of such a family:

> If we do not experience love in our extended families of origin (which is the first site for community offered to us), the other place where children in particular have the opportunity to build community and know love is in friendship. Since we choose our friends, many of us, from childhood on into our adulthood, have looked to friends for the care, respect, knowledge and all-around nurturance of our growth that we did not find in the family.[27]

She adds that "Many of us learn as children that friendship should never be seen as just as important as family ties. However, friendship is the place in which a great majority of us have our first glimpse of redemptive love and caring community."[28]

Nowhere in this series is this sentiment more poignantly put than in the Season 5 episode, "Family," in which Willow's girlfriend Tara Maclay—relative newbie to the tight-knit Scooby Gang—approaches her twentieth birthday. Willow's excited for the impending celebration, but the rest of the Scoobies, who admittedly like Tara very much, have yet to get to know her.

Unexpectedly, Tara's father, brother, and cousin arrive in Sunnydale with the intention of taking her back home with them. They've let her attend some college, but maintain that now her duty is to care for the men of her family, rather than dabble in alternative lifestyles. Her proficiency in magic especially alarms them, as they claim that Maclay women turn "demon" on their twentieth birthday. Tara's terrified that if the Scoobies find out about this they will reject her; to keep her secret, she casts a spell that makes them unable to see her demon side. Unfortunately, the spell backfires when it renders the Scoobies unable to see *any* demons, and at the magic shop that Giles owns, they are attacked by what they believe is an invisible enemy.

Buffy, of course, defeats the demons, and as Tara reverses the spell, she apologizes and begins to cry. The Maclays have arrived on the scene:

> *Mr. Maclay*: I don't understand.
> *Buffy*: (*arms folded, looking at Tara*) I'm not sure I do either.
> *Tara*: I'm sorry. I'm s-s-sorry. (*sniffling*) I was, I was trying to hide. I didn't want you to see what I am.
> *Willow*: Tara, what?
> *Buffy*: What do you mean, what you are?
> *Mr. Maclay*: Demon. The women in our family have demon in them. Her mother had it. That's where the magic comes from. We came to take her home before . . . well, before things like . . . (*points at a dead demon*) this started happening.

It's obvious that Tara doesn't want to leave and she and Willow are distraught. Buffy and Giles are disappointed in her seeming betrayal of their trust, but cautiously weigh the circumstances. Every one of the Scoobies has made a life-threatening mistake and been forgiven, protected, and loved.

> *Mr. Maclay*: You're going to do what's right, Tara. Now, I'm taking you out of here before somebody *does* get killed. The girl belongs with her family. I hope that's clear to the rest of you.
> *Buffy*: It is. You want her, Mr. Maclay? You can go ahead and take her. You just gotta go through me.
> *Mr. Maclay*: What?

Buffy: You heard me. You wanna take Tara out of here against her will? You gotta come through me.
Dawn: And me! (*Tara smiles.*)
Mr. Maclay: Is this a joke? I'm not gonna be threatened by two little girls.
Dawn: You don't wanna mess with us.
Buffy: She's a hair-puller.
Giles: And . . . you're not just dealing with, uh, two little girls. (*Tara smiles even more.*)
Xander: You're dealing with all of us.[29]

Tara's father is furious and insists that "you people have no right to interfere with Tara's affairs. *We* are her blood kin! Who the hell are you?"

Giles, Dawn, Buffy, Willow, Tara, Xander, and Anya stand in solidarity, even Spike is included in the background. Buffy states with resolute love, "We're family."[30]

Tara has no demon in her—the accusation was a misogynist ploy by the Maclay men to keep their women oppressed. But it wouldn't have mattered to the Scooby family. As Jes Battis observes in his book, *Blood Relations: Chosen Families in Buffy the Vampire Slayer and Angel*, in Whedon's created families,

> You can be a werewolf, a vampire, an ex-vengeance-demon, a witch, a covert government agent—you can even be queer, which is still a stumbling block for most primetime offerings. Heredity, biology, genetics, appearance, class, gender, sexuality . . . none of these signifiers are crucially definitive within the Buffyverse. Your access to the Scooby Gang is based on your commitment to its mission, and your inherent sense of loyalty. Once you're in, you're loved—it's that simple.[31]

According to Battis, this episode illustrates that for the Scoobies, "blood kin" will never be as powerful as "family." Rather, in the Buffyverse, family is measured by emotional attachment, not heredity.[32] He adds that Buffy reorders the definition of family so that it encompasses members based on compassion rather than genetics and is therefore a perfect example of caring community.[33]

Of heroic collaboration and community, Sharon Ross writes, "while traditional heroes of the past have been made tough via their individualism and their ability to confront obstacles by themselves, modern female heroes such as Buffy, Willow, Xena, and Gabrielle grow as heroes because of their friends."[34] She adds that they "are not heroes *for* other women so much as they are heroes *with* them" (emphasis in original).[35] Of course, on *Buffy*, it's necessary to add that women are also heroes *with* men. Instead of being the "one girl in all the world," Buffy rejects the traditional solitary mission of the Slayer. She chooses to collaborate with her friends, women and men working on equal footing—spiritually and even occasionally physically—forming a symbiotic entity or "group" hero, as in the episode "Primeval" (4.21).[36]

In this final battle of Season 4, Buffy and the Scoobies join together to defeat the "Big Bad" of the season, an uber-enemy named Adam. The group discusses how to extract Adam's power source, a uranium core embedded in his half-human, half-monster body. Willow suggests a magical solution:

> *Willow*: What about magic? Some kind of, I don't know . . . uranium-extracting spell? (Everyone looks at her in disbelief.) I know, I'm reaching. (*Giles stands up.*)
> *Giles*: Perhaps a paralyzing spell. (*He walks over to the bookshelf and pulls a book off.*) Only I can't perform the incantation for this.
> *Willow*: Right. Don't you have to speak it in Sumerian or something?
> *Giles*: I do speak Sumerian. It's not that. Only an experienced witch can incant it, and you'd have to be within striking distance of this object.
> *Xander*: See what you get for takin' French instead of Sumerian?
> *Buffy*: What was I thinking?
> *Xander*: So no problem, all we need is combo Buffy—her with Slayer strength, Giles' multi-lingual know how, and Willow's witchy power. (*Giles looks at him.*) Yeah, don't tell me. I'm just full of helpful suggestions.
> *Giles*: As a matter of fact, you are.[37]

The friends agree to do a "joining" spell so that each of the Scoobies' individual strengths will be embodied in Buffy. In doing this, the Scoobies create the ultimate superhero—and not just on special occasions such as this particular episode, but throughout the series run, though in a more figurative sense. The joining spell in yet another metaphor indicative of the "high school *is* hell" based series that illustrates what we can do heroically with our lives when we have the strength, trust, support, and love of our friends. Buffy may be the heroic vessel, but her friends are her heroic source. As Jana Reiss notes in her book *What Would Buffy Do? The Vampire Slayer as Spiritual Guide*:

> In Buffy's world the most powerful individuals are those with a strong support system—friends and family members who share responsibility and heartache and who encourage one another to fight the good fight. The show doesn't preach about friendship . . . instead, Buffy shows us the power of friendship in action and prompts us to ask ourselves why friendship makes us so much stronger.[38]

The obvious question that follows is, "Why aren't the X-Men and the Justice League of America also examples of this kind of 'group' hero?" The answer is that the JLA are solitary heroes who happen to periodically work together, and though the X-Men are something of a created family, they don't always demonstrate the depth of connection the Scoobies share. These individualistic superheroes don't play off each other's talents and don't seem to be inspired by one another, no matter how much respect they have for their colleagues. In contrast, the Scoobies have a familial love for one another that is fueled by their profound connectivity. Comparing the JLA to the Scooby Gang is like comparing co-workers to soul mates.

Through the Scoobies' enlightened example of collaboration, our traditional understanding of heroic tropes is once again rocked by Whedon. Though old-standard Jungian archetypes are recognizable in the Buffyverse, in Whedon's mythological world, the hero/ine, the sidekick, the lover, the sage, the trickster, and the great mother, all become champions whose unique capacities are of equal heroic importance. They are much more than a team—they are a heroic entity.

Max Guevara also has female friends, though unfortunately they are too often peripheral to the story. Her roommate Kendra disappears midway through the first season of *Dark Angel* when she moves in with her boyfriend, and interactions with Original Cindy are brief. As with Buffy Summers, Max's family is a combination of choice and origin and includes her "Sister Girl" Original Cindy, the X-5s she trained (and escaped) with, *their* children, and Logan Cale. Max's love for her family helps her evolve from a pouty, jaded, uber-sultry, and understandably self-protective girl to a courageous leader—a superwoman. This evolution is hinted at from the very beginning of the series, in Max's initial encounter with Logan when his eye catches the statuette she was in the process of stealing:

Logan: You have good taste. French, 1920s, a tribute to Chitarus.
Max: Whoever that is.
Logan: Oh. So, what? You liked it 'cause it was shiny?
Max: No. Because it's the Egyptian goddess Bast—the goddess who comprehends all goddesses, eye of Ra, protector, avenger, destroyer; giver of life who lives forever.[39]

Bast is depicted as a woman with the head of a lion or in the full form of a domestic cat. It's not a stretch to say that Max is an avatar of this goddess—especially as in Season 2 we see her fully come into her role as a compassionate leader, who protects her family and her communities.

In the beginning of Season 2, when Logan and Max have exposed the location of Manticore, the organization sets fire to the facility without evacuating its transgenic population. But Max arrives and releases her brothers and sisters from what would have been a fiery tomb. Many have never been outside the Manticore groups, most have been trained as soldiers, several have been tortured to madness, and some look so different from humans as a result of their animal DNA that they could only be called "freaks." Survival for many will be difficult: as Max continually points out, people fear what's different.

Contrary to her "like I care" attitude expressed in the pilot, Max takes responsibility for releasing the transgenics into an unfamiliar and unfriendly world. Over the course of the season, she aids transgenics in need and stops those who abuse their power or jeopardize others with exposure. By season's end, when the transgenics have been exposed to the public, and the public responds with bigotry, Max will fight for the rights of her "Freak Nation" to exist.

Max would not have done this, in fact *could not have done this*, without compassion and love, both her own capacity for it and the nurturing support of her family and friends. Echoing Max's namesake, Guevara, who said that "the true revolutionary is guided by a great feeling of love" and that a "love of living humanity will be transformed into actual deeds," hooks has written that "All the great social movements for freedom and justice in our society have promoted a love ethic. Concern for the collective good of our nation, city, or neighbor rooted in the values of love makes us all seek to nurture and protect that good."[40]

Max has become the protector/avenger.

Love is redemptive; it heals and inspires—but so does the ability to forgive and be forgiven, which is made possible by compassion. As bell hooks wrote in *All about Love: New Visions*: "Making amends both to ourselves and to others is the gift compassion and forgiveness offers us."[41] Xena's story is a quest to make amends for the sins of her past, and though the theme is never explicitly called out on *Dark Angel*, Max continually encounters people in need who echo her past mistakes. Her assistance allows her to somewhat absolve her guilt over choices she wishes she'd made differently, if not, at least, to forgive herself for her own regrets.

Compassion is an act of selfless love often born out of empathy and an essential component of the love ethic that drives heroes to action without expectation of reward. Superman acts out of his love for his adopted homeworld, and as that great mantra from the Spider-Man mythos points out, there is an understanding that "with great power comes great responsibility," which underscores that our gifts are to be used for the greater good. They protect because it is just, as do superwomen, but again, the latter take heroic themes to a higher level. Their compassionate actions not only save others, but also *inspire* them to find and perfect the heroic in themselves.

On *Xena, Warrior Princess*, Xena and Gabrielle's long and tragic history with a woman named Callisto serves to show how a pivotal act of compassion can forever affect all lives involved.

When Callisto (Hudson Leick) was a child, her family was killed when Xena's army ravaged her village. Orphaned and alone, she swore revenge on the warrior princess. As an adult she does this in a number of ways: she raids villages in Xena's name to sully her reformed reputation, kills Gabrielle's husband, steals Xena's body, and influences events from beyond the grave that ultimately lead to Xena's and Gabrielle's crucifixion in "The Ides of March" (4.21).

In the Season 5 premiere, "Fallen Angel," the pair are on their way to Heaven when Callisto organizes an attack on them with an army of demons from hell. Xena makes it to Paradise, but Gabrielle is not so lucky. The archangel Michael allows Xena to undergo a purification process and become a higher angel in order to rescue her companion. But he warns her that her capacity for compassion is now heightened and that the suffering she'll see in Hell will break her heart. He adds that if they can't rescue Gabrielle, Xena might be tempted to save her from her pain, and there's only one way to do that: "You would have to take on her guilt, and free her from her suffering—by giving her your light." This sacrifice would release Gabrielle from Hell, but doom Xena to stay there for eternity.

The angels manage to save Gabrielle before she becomes a full demon, but when Xena sees Callisto—suffering, demonic, and full of rage—her heart does break. Callisto seethes and shouts, "I will *never* stop hating you, Xena, do you hear me?! Never! You killed my *family*! My soul! My reason to live and love! And I will spend eternity seeking revenge!" Xena, angelic with tears in her eyes, simply whispers, "No."[42]

When Gabrielle arrives in heaven and her partner is nowhere to be found, Michael informs her that "Xena gave herself up—to save one of the damned." When Gabrielle learns just who Xena sacrificed herself for, she's horrified, turning to Michael and screaming, "This is insane. You call this justice?" Michael answers that "Xena called it justice" and encourages Gabrielle to respect Xena's decision to suffer in Callisto's place.

Callisto has no memory of who she was before she died, and in Heaven she's the kind and gentle spirit she would have been had Xena not killed her family. Gabrielle forgives Callisto for her past misdeeds, and in doing so, becomes an archangel herself. Callisto waits in Paradise as Gabrielle and the archangels attempt to now rescue the warrior princess.

As the angelic Gabrielle battles the now demonic Xena, the Earthly Eli is distraught over his inability to protect his friends. Questioning his way, he receives a vision of Callisto, telling him that "Love *is* the way" and "go to them." With Callisto's heavenly aid, Eli brings Xena and Gabrielle back to life, healing them with both his and Callisto's love. Xena's act of selfless compassion will heal once more; Callisto will later choose to be reborn through Xena, which will bring them both back that which they caused each other to lose—family.

If Xena and Gabrielle are archangels, and Max Guevara is symbolic of Bast, then Wonder Woman and Buffy illustrate a Bodhisattva ideology, as embodied by the Bodhisattva of compassion, Avalokiteshvara, best known by the name Kwan Yin.[43]

Bodhisattvas do not teach; rather they lead by example. Kwan Yin, in all her names, helps others to realize their potential through example and chooses to delay enlightenment in order to walk in the world helping others become the heroes of their own lives.[44] William Moulton Marston created in Wonder Woman a warrior who fought for the greater good of humanity through an altruistic love. He'd felt that the "bloodcurdling masculinity" exhibited by men was detrimental to society, and his belief that women are fundamentally different from men led him to suggest that women should rule the world, precisely because they *are* women. With the character of Wonder Woman, he took the characteristics of love and compassion, which he believed to be natural to women, and made them heroic by giving women a superhero of their own.

Wonder Woman's Bodhisattva nature is realized when she gives up her immortality to help America win the Second World War. Her initial motives for leaving Paradise Island may include an adolescent crush on Steve Trevor, but once in America she inspires women to lead successful lives regardless of whether or not they had men in them. In one issue of the comic book, the Holliday Girls thank Wonder Woman for helping them. They helped themselves, she replies: she only showed them how.[45]

Contemporary superwomen also have a Bodhisattva nature, but Buffy and her companions illustrate more complex notions about heroic example. Although they don't always want to be the hero—a staple of the heroic archetype, according to Joseph Campbell's oft-referenced model—they are compelled to continue down their heroic pathways. For example, even with Buffy's occasional lack of faith in her sacred calling or in the merits of humanity, it is more often her Bodhisattva nature, than her duty as a Slayer, that compels her to continue to exhibit compassion regardless of exhaustion or discouragement.

Buffy's acts of love and compassion are relatively unique not only in the world of superheroes, but also in the world of Slayers. She breaks the mold in her own mythos, rejecting the patriarchal Watchers' Council and trusting her own knowledge and skill, as well as consulting her loved ones in order to make informed and just decisions. As the Slayer, ultimately the course of action is up to her, but she continually utilizes and nurtures the gifts of those around her—even when it may be easier for her to do the job alone. Therefore, it is because of her Bodhisattva, or compassion, example that individuals are inspired to make the choice to realize their full potential as well as to nurture the potential of others.

Yet Buffy is often unaware of the trickle-down effect of her selfless acts. Fortunately, she is occasionally bolstered by profound expressions of sentiment as in the Season 3 episode, "The Prom," when she is given a "Class Protector" award by her peers. They tell her:

> We're not good friends. Most of us never found the time to get to know you, but that doesn't mean we haven't noticed you. We don't talk about it much, but it's no secret that Sunnydale High isn't really like other high schools. A lot of weird stuff happens here. But, whenever there was a problem or something creepy happened, you seemed to show up and stop it. Most of the people here have been saved by you, or helped by you at one time or another.[46]

This recognition of Buffy's compassionate heroism inspires the students to recognize their own heroic nature two episodes later, when she asks them to risk their lives to save the world from yet another apocalyptic threat.[47]

The Bodhisattva of compassion is also useful for illustrating a gender-inclusive model of heroism. This particular Bodhisattva, Avalokiteshvara, is manifested in both female and male forms, just as heroic action born out of compassion is exhibited by both men and women in the *Buffy the Vampire Slayer* series—and for that matter, in the Whedonverse (the tagline of Angel Investigations, the detective agency of *Buffy* spin-off *Angel*, was a humorous, and accurate, "We help the helpless"). Compassionate heroism and its ability to inspire is not a phenomenon specific to superwomen, or limited to the works of Joss Whedon. Kevin Sorbo's Hercules goes from village to village helping those in need, while the late 1970s television version of *The Incredible Hulk* consistently showed David Bruce Banner (Bill Bixby) aiding everyday people. In another mid-1970s television series, *Kung Fu*, Kwai Chang Caine (David Carradine) was also compelled to help others, even if it jeopardized his own safety. In *Lord of the Rings*, the ultimate destruction of the One Ring was made possible by Sam Gangee's love for Frodo Baggins.

But to illustrate the heroic values of loving compassion, friendship, and redemption as the values of a gender-inclusive form of heroism made possible by the modern superwoman, it's useful to revisit *Buffy the Vampire Slayer*. In the climatic scene from Season 6's finale, "Grave" (6.22), Willow has gone on a murderous rampage after the death of Tara and intends to destroy the world to stop the pain and suffering of humanity. But Xander—who has no "mystic" or "super" powers—stops her and saves the world through an act of love.[48]

As the scene begins, Willow stands atop a bluff overlooking Sunnydale. She intends to resurrect the buried temple of a powerful female demon in order to end the world. As Xander approaches, Willow tells him:

Willow: You can't stop this.
Xander: Yeah, I get that. It's just, where else am I gonna go? You've been my best friend my whole life. World gonna end, where else would I want to be?
Willow: (*mockingly*) Is this the master plan? You're going to stop me by telling me you love me?
Xander: Well, I was going to walk you off a cliff and hand you an anvil, but it seemed kinda cartoony.
Willow: Still making jokes.
Xander: I'm not joking. I know you're in pain. I can't imagine the pain you're in. And I know you're about to do something apocalyptically evil and stupid, and hey, I still want to hang. You're Willow.
Willow: Don't call me that.
Xander: First day of kindergarten. You cried because you broke the yellow crayon, and you were too afraid to tell anyone. You've come pretty far, ending the world, not a terrific notion. But the thing is, yeah. I love you. I loved crayon-breaky Willow and I love scary veiny Willow. So if I'm going out, it's here. If you wanna kill the world, well, then start with me. I've earned that.
Willow: You think I won't?
Xander: It doesn't matter. I'll still love you.[49]

The scene continues with Willow physically attacking Xander, wounding him with her powerful magic. Xander stays strong throughout the attacks—after every painful electric bolt he is hit with, he repeats his devotion to his best friend by saying, "I love you." Willow succumbs to the profound power of loving friendship and human compassion as she returns to her true self.

This beautiful and intimate sequence shows us that a compassionate act is a heroic act. Though Willow initially mocks Xander's heroic intention by asking him, "Is this the master plan? You're going to stop me by telling me you love me?," his action has a successful outcome—the day is saved, as is his friend.[50]

In her essay "Love Saves the World," Jean Lorrah notes that it shouldn't surprise us that "only Xander, often considered the weakest of Buffy's cohorts, can reach and persuade Willow" because he and Willow share a lifelong bond of loving friendship.[51] His unexpected heroic deed is partly inspired by his deep affection for Willow, but it's important to note that Xander gets his courage from Buffy. (He's told her that "when it's dark and I'm all alone and I'm scared or freaked out or whatever, I always think, 'What would Buffy do?' You're my hero.")[52] Xander has great respect for female power, and he's not afraid to incorporate traditionally feminine traits into his behavior and actions—no matter how much he may make deflective jokes to the contrary.

As Lorna Jowett points out in her book *Sex and the Slayer: A Gender Studies Primer for the Buffy Fan*, Xander's expressions of "emotion, love, and friendship is part of [Whedon and company's] project of dissociating gender and behavior." Invoking the group ritual in "Primeval," she points out that more conventionally the "heart" of a superfamily would be female.[53] Stephanie Zacharek echoes this sentiment in an article for *Salon* when she writes that Xander's actions "might be Whedon's way of saying that the best traits of men are sometimes those we associate with women."[54]

Compassionate collaboration leads to a realization of potential in the self and in others. The Buffyverse in particular provides a model of heroism that is gender inclusive because the Scoobies show us a world in which men and women work successfully together. Reiss notes that

> For Xander, Angel, Buffy, and other characters, self-sacrifice is not a sign of weakness but of strength: their altruism extends from a desire to see justice accomplished for others as well as themselves. It's not a heroism that is out of reach but an everyday heroism born of compassion.[55]

Kathleen D. Noble envisioned a hero such as Buffy when she wrote in her book, *The Sound of a Silver Horn: Reclaiming the Heroism in Contemporary Women's Lives*, that "the female hero must fuse the best attributes of femininity and masculinity and so create a new archetype of heroism that speaks to both women and men."[56] Buffy's influence on Xander is proof that the Scoobies are this new archetype. The message of an episode such as "Grave" is that heroes act from a place of compassion and that compassion is a heroic act, regardless of sex or gender.

Generosity, kindness, and tolerance, especially when enhanced by love, transcend stereotypically gendered motivations to offer up twenty-first century models of inclusive and resonant heroisms.

The early *Wonder Woman* showed women that they didn't need the love or protection of a man in order to live successful and fulfilling lives—but it also emphasized that women *should act lovingly* in the world. William Marston's concept of "love" is problematic as a feminist ideology because his work advocated a reversal of the existing gender hierarchy rather than an egalitarian society. Additionally, his belief that there are essential sex characteristics is a controversial and unproductive dogma. In his utopian fantasy world, men were expected to lovingly submit to a compassionate feminine authority rather than make sacrifices and work with women on equal footing.[57] bell hooks rightly stresses that such

> sexist thinking obscures the fact that these women [who make everyday sacrifices for others] make a choice to serve [and] give from the space of free will and not because of biological destiny. . . . When anyone thinks a woman who serves "gives 'cause that's what mothers or real women do," they deny her full humanity and thus fail to see the generosity inherent in her acts.[58]

As the superwomen in this chapter have shown, selfless compassion, and a giving of self to others, do not necessitate loss of identity or confinement to a biologically determined persona.

Love, as both concept and action in the Whedonverse, Xena's ancient Greece, and Max Guervera's Freak Nation, is much more egalitarian. The heroisms—for truly there are many ways to be heroic—of Buffy, Xena, and Max are reciprocal; the superwoman inspires others, who in turn inspire her. And love, when motivated by a spiritual interdependency, can show us how an act of compassion—regardless of who acts and who receives—can change lives, heal past wounds, and even save the world.

NOTES

1. Edgar, Joanne. Quoting Marston, William M. "Wonder Woman Revisited," *Ms.* magazine, #1, 1972, 53–54 (emphasis in original).
2. Reynolds, Richard. *Super Heroes: A Modern Mythology*. Jackson, MS: University Press of Mississippi, 1994, 18.
3. This domestication of the "naughty girl" could easily be read as just another example of popular culture working to put women back in their normative place. But it could also be interpreted as a simplistic approach to narrative typical of the black-and-white moral universe of Golden Age comics. Regardless, on Transformation Island, reformation—though well intended—is more forced rehabilitation than enlightened atonement.
4. Whedon, Joss. "Ten Questions for Joss Whedon." *The New York Times*. May 16, 2003.
5. hooks, bell. *All About Love: New Visions*. New York: William Morrow, 2001, 88.
6. Ibid, 161.
7. "Friend in Need II," 6.22. *Xena, Warrior Princess*. Writer R. J. Stewart, director Robert G. Tapert. Original airdate: June 18, 2001.

8. "The Way," 4.16. *Xena, Warrior Princess*. Writer R. J. Stewart, director John Fawcett. Original air date: February 22, 1999.
9. Kathleen Kennedy observes in "Love Is the Battlefield" that "Preserving the purity of Gabrielle's faith in 'the way of love' is one of the most important components of Xena's quest." Kennedy, Kathleen, *Athena's Daughters: Television's New Women Warriors*. New York: Syracuse University Press, 2003, 43.
10. "The Way," 4.16. *Xena, Warrior Princess*. Writer R. J. Stewart, director John Fawcett. Original air date: February 22, 1999.
11. "The Ides of March," 4.21. *Xena, Warrior Princess*. Writer R. J. Stewart, director Ken Girotti. Original air date: May 10, 1999.
12. Hlusko, Dana. "The Way of Friendship Defined." *Whoosh!* #45. Accessed online on March 25, 2008: http://www.whoosh.org/issue45/hlusko07.html.
13. Notably, James Cameron was at one time attached to a Spider-Man film project before *Dark Angel*, so it wouldn't be a stretch to assume there is an influence on Max.
14. Jowett, Lorna. "To the Max: Embodying Intersections in *Dark Angel*." *Reconstruction* 5.4, Fall 2005. Accessed online on March 27, 2008. http://reconstruction.eserver.org/054/jowett.shtml.
15. "Pilot," 1.0. *Dark Angel*. Writer James Cameron and Charles H. Eglee, director David Nutter. Original air date: October 3, 2000.
16. Both quotes are from "Flushed," 1.2. *Dark Angel*. Writer Charles H. Eglee and René Echevarria, director Terrence O'Hara. Original air date: October 17, 2000.
17. "Pilot," 1.0. *Dark Angel*. Writer James Cameron and Charles H. Eglee, director David Nutter. Original air date: October 3, 2000.
18. Sara Crosby convincingly argues in "Female Heroes Snapped into Sacrificial Heroines" in the anthology *Action Chicks: New Images of Tough Women in Popular Culture* that Max takes on her "heroic identity only after she subordinates her physical power to his political goals and literally begins to work for [Logan]." She suggests that accepting Logan's moral judgment causes Max to help him "in his crusade for a renewal of patriarchal privilege" and though *Dark Angel* "sells itself as being all about choice, the choices it gives Max are between patriarchy A [the military] or patriarchy B [Logan's journalistic obsessions]." Crosby does note that the series had potential for the promotion of "feminist and democratic goals more radically and on more levels than any previous superhero show," including feminist social justice issues such as class, race, sexuality, and gender hierarchies.
19. "Flushed," 1.2. *Dark Angel*. Writer Charles H. Eglee and René Echevarria, director Terrence O'Hara. Original air date: October 17, 2000.
20. Ibid.
21. The amazing feats of a Batman or other traditional heroes lead us to believe that there is a separation between heroes and the rest of us and that amazing feats are for those who are special. Modern superwomen show us that we all have the potential to be special with devotion and effort. Like Wonder Woman before them, Buffy, Max, and Xena inspire small armies of people who accomplish feats they never thought they could. Additionally, rather than adopting mentor-ward relationships that illustrate a clear separation of power, superwomen champion the sharing of it, as well as a mutual exchange of knowledge.
22. See "Beware Greeks Bearing Gifts," "The Debt Parts I & II," "A Friend in Need Parts I and II," and "Destiny," respectively.
23. "Is There a Doctor in the House?" 1.24. *Xena, Warrior Princess*. Director T. J. Scott. Original air date: July 29, 1996.

24. Inness, Sherrie A. *Tough Girls: Women Warriors and Wonder Woman in Popular Culture*. Philadelphia: University of Pennsylvania Press, 1998, 168.
25. "Is There a Doctor in the House?" 1.24.
26. "Ten Questions for Joss Whedon."
27. hooks, *All About Love*, 133.
28. Ibid, 134.
29. "Family." 5.6. *Buffy, the Vampire Slayer*. Writer Joss Whedon, director Joss Whedon. Original air date: November 7, 2000.
30. http://www.buffy-vs-angel.com/buffy_tra_84.shtml.
31. Battis, Jes. *Blood Relations: Chosen Families in Buffy the Vampire Slayer and Angel*. North Carolina: McFarland & Company, 2005, 147.
32. Ibid, 147.
33. Ibid, 147–8. The created family is a theme Whedon explores in his *Angel* and *Firefly/Serenity* franchises as well.
34. Ross, Sharon. "'Tough Enough': Female Friendship and Heroism in *Xena* and *Buffy*," in *Action Chicks: New Image of Tough Women in Popular Culture*. Edited by Sherrie A. Inness. New York: Palgrave Macmillan, 2004, 231.
35. Ibid, 232.
36. "Primeval," 4.21. *Buffy, the Vampire Slayer*. Writer David Fury, director James A. Contner. Original air date: May 16, 2000.
37. http://uk.geocities.com/slayermagic/Scripts/Episode77Primeval.html.
38. Reiss, Jana. *What Would Buffy Do? The Vampire Slayer as Spiritual Guide*. San Francisco: Jossey-Bass, 2004, 53–4.
39. "Pilot," 1.0. *Dark Angel*. Writer James Cameron and Charles H. Eglee, director David Nutter. Original air date: October 3, 2000.
40. hooks, *All About Love*, 98.
41. Ibid, 217.
42. "Fallen Angel," 5.1. *Xena: Warrior Princess*. Writer R. J. Stewart, director John Fawcett. Original air date: September 27, 1999.
43. For more detail, see Taigen Daniel Leighton's *Bodhisattva Archetypes*. New York: Penguin, 1998—particularly chapter seven, which explores Avalokiteshvara in detail.
44. Buffy achieves enlightenment in the Season 5 finale, when she sacrifices her life for that of her sister, Dawn. Buffy's spirit guide had told her that "Love is your gift" and that "death will bring you to your gift." On one level, "the gift is that of life to Dawn, but as we learn early in Season 6, it turned out to also be a gift to Buffy. She'd fulfilled her Slayer duty and was at peace in Heaven. When she is forced to return to the world, her enlightenment is again delayed. She walks through the world trying to lead and inspire as before, but for most of the season, she's "just going through the motions."
45. Steinem, Gloria. *Wonder Woman*. New York: Holt, Rinehart and Winston, 1972.
46. "The Prom," 3.20. *Buffy, the Vampire Slayer*. Writer Marti Noxon, director David Solomon. Original air date: May 11, 1999.
47. And it is not just her peers who are motivated or inspired by her Bodhisattva example, but her enemies as well. From Season 4 through to the end of the series, we watch the metamorphosis struggle of the vampire, Spike, whose admiration for Buffy inspires him to become a better man, to seek a soul, and ultimately to sacrifice himself to save humanity.
48. "Grave," 6.22. *Buffy, the Vampire Slayer*. Writer David Fury, director James A. Contner. Original air date: May 21, 2002.

49. Ibid.
50. Again, notice the cyclic nature of Bodhisattva inspiration. Each of the Scoobies is, at one time or another, a hero in his or her own right, but it is always because of each other. Some have pointed out the Christian allegory in this scene. Simply put, Xander, who is by now a carpenter, saves the world through his selfless love. Yet this scene also directly echoes Jean Grey's sacrifice of herself in Chris Claremont's *Dark Phoenix Saga*, as well as the climactic scene in *Return of the Jedi* when Luke Skywalker defeats the evil Darth Vader and restores his father Anakin's humanity with compassion rather than weaponry. The influence of both is evident. Willow is directly referred to as "Dark Phoenix" by another character on the show. And when *SFX* magazine asked Joss Whedon what movie he would have loved to have written, he answered *Return of the Jedi*. Ironically, the climactic scene in the film *X-Men 3: The Last Stand* would cinematically echo the scene between Xander and Willow in "Grave," although the rewriting of the *Dark Phoenix Saga*—especially with Jean's murder rather than sacrifice—would negate all the emotional poignancy that inhabited both the original X-Men story arc, and Whedon's likely appropriation of it.
51. Lorrah, Jean. "Love Saves the World," in *Seven Seasons of Buffy: Science Fiction and Fantasy Writers Discuss Their Favorite Television Show*. Edited by Yeffeth, Glenn. Dallas: BenBella Books, 2003, 167–75.
52. "The Freshman," 4.1 *Buffy, the Vampire Slayer*. Writer Joss Whedon, director Joss Whedon. Original air date: October 5, 1999.
53. Jowett, Lorna. *Sex and the Slayer: A Gender Studies Primer for the Buffy Fan*. Middletown, CT: Wesleyan University Press, 2005, 134.
54. Zacharek, Stephanie. "Willow, Destroyer of Worlds," *Salon*, May 22, 2002. Nancy Holder has written of Buffy that "what was perhaps more interesting than this *Wonder Woman* redux was the fact that *BTVS* redefined male power." She quotes Gail Berman, former president of FOX Entertainment, who said, "We'll have more Buffys when we have more Xanders."
55. Reiss, *What Would Buffy Do?*, 11.
56. Noble, Kathleen, D. *The Sound of a Silver Horn: Reclaiming the Heroism in Contemporary Women's Lives*. New York: Ballantine Books, 1994, 194.
57. According to Les Daniels, Marston gave an interview to the *New York Times* in November of 1937 where he stated that "the next one hundred years will see the beginning of an American matriarchy—a nation of Amazons in the psychological rather than physical sense." Daniels writes that Marston believed "women could and would use sexual enslavement to achieve [political and economic] domination over men, who would happily submit to their loving authority." Les Daniels, *Wonder Woman: The Complete History*. San Francisco: Chronicle Books, 2004, 19.
58. hooks, *All About Love*, 142.

Batman, Deviance and Camp

ANDY MEDHURST

Reprinted by permission from Roberta E. Pearson and William Uricchio, eds. *The Many Lives of the Batman: Critical Approaches to a Superhero and His Media* (Routledge, 1991), 149–163.

> Only someone ignorant of the fundamentals of psychiatry and of the psychopathology of sex can fail to realize a subtle atmosphere of homoeroticism which pervades the adventure of the mature "Batman" and his young friend "Robin."
>
> **FREDRIC WERTHAM**

> It's embarrassing to be solemn and treatise-like about Camp. One runs the risk of having, oneself, produced a very inferior piece of Camp.
>
> **SUSAN SONTAG**

I'M NOT SURE HOW QUALIFIED I AM TO WRITE THIS ESSAY. BATMAN HASN'T BEEN particularly important in my life since I was seven years old. Back then he was crucial, paramount, unmissable as I sat twice weekly to watch the latest episode on TV. Pure pleasure, except for the annoying fact that my parents didn't seem to appreciate the thrills on offer. Worse than that, they actually laughed. How could anyone laugh when the Dynamic Duo were about to be turned into Frostie Freezies (pineapple for the Caped Crusader, lime for his chum) by the evil Mr. Freeze?

Batman and I drifted apart after those early days. Every now and then I'd see a repeated episode and I soon began to understand and share that once infuriating parental hilarity, but this aside I hardly thought about the man in the cape at all. I knew about the subculture of comic freaks, and the new and alarmingly pretentious phrase "graphic novel" made itself known to me, but I still regarded (with the confidence of distant ignorance) such texts as violent, macho, adolescent, and, well, silly.

That's when the warning bells rang. The word "silly" reeks of the complacent condescension that has at various times been bestowed on all the cultural forms that matter most to me (Hollywood musicals, British melodramas, pop music, soap operas) so what right had I to apply it to someone else's part of the popular cultural playground? I had to rethink my disdain, and 1989 has been a very good year in which to do so, because in terms of popular culture 1989 has been the Year of the Bat.

This essay, then, is not written by a devotee of Batman, someone steeped in every last twist of the mythology. I come to these texts as an interested outsider, armed with a particular perspective. That perspective is homosexuality, and what I want to try and do here is to offer a gay reading of the whole Bat-business. It has no pretension to definitiveness; I don't presume to speak for all gay people everywhere.

I'm male, white, British, thirty years old (at the time of writing) and all of those factors need to be taken into account. Nonetheless, I'd argue that Batman is especially interesting to gay audiences for three reasons.

Firstly, he was one of the first fictional characters to be attacked on the grounds of presumed homosexuality, by Fredric Wertham in his book *Seduction of the Innocent*. Secondly, the 1960s TV series was and remains a touchstone of camp (a banal attempt to define the meaning of camp might well start with "like the sixties *Batman* series"). Thirdly, as a recurring hero figure for the last fifty years, Batman merits analysis as a notably successful construction of masculinity.

NIGHTMARE ON PSYCHIATRY STREET

Seduction of the Innocent is an extraordinary book. It is a gripping, flamboyant melodrama masquerading as social psychology. Fredric Wertham is, like Senator McCarthy, like Batman, a crusader, a man with a mission, an evangelist. He wants to save the youth of America from its own worst impulses, from its id, from comic books. His attack on comic books is founded on an astonishingly crude stimulus-and-response model of reading, in which the child (the child, for Wertham, seems an unusually innocent, blank slate waiting to be written on) reads, absorbs, and feels compelled to copy, if only in fantasy terms, the content of the comics. It is a model, in other words, which takes for granted extreme audience passivity.

This is not the place to go into a detailed refutation of Wertham's work, besides which such a refutation has already been done in Martin Barker's excellent *A Haunt of Fears*.[1] The central point of audience passivity needs stressing, however, because it is crucial to the celebrated passage where Wertham points his shrill, witch-hunting finger at the Dynamic Duo and cries "queer."

Such language is not present on the page, of course, but in some ways *Seduction of the Innocent* (a film title crying out for either D. W. Griffith or

Cecil B. DeMille) would be easier to stomach if it were. Instead, Wertham writes with anguished concern about the potential harm that Batman might do to vulnerable children, innocents who might be turned into deviants. He employs what was then conventional psychiatric wisdom about the idea of homosexuality as a "phase":

> Many preadolescent boys pass through a phase of disdain for girls. Some comic books tend to fix that attitude and instill the idea that girls are only good for being banged around or used as decoys. A homoerotic attitude is also suggested by the presentation of masculine, bad, witch-like, or violent women. In such comics women are depicted in a definitely anti-erotic light, while the young male heroes have pronounced erotic overtones. The muscular male supertype, whose primary sex characteristics are usually well emphasized, is in the setting of certain stories the object of homoerotic sexual curiosity and stimulation.[2]

The implications of this are breathtaking. Homosexuality, for Wertham, is synonymous with misogyny. Men love other men because they hate women. The sight of women being "banged around" is liable to appeal to repressed homoerotic desires (this, I think, would be news to the thousands of women who are systematically physically abused by heterosexual men). Women who do not conform to existing stereotypes of femininity are another incitement to homosexuality.

Having mapped out his terms of reference, Wertham goes on to peel the lid from Wayne Manor:

> Sometimes Batman ends up in bed injured and young Robin is shown sitting next to him. At home they lead an idyllic life. They are Bruce Wayne and "Dick" Grayson. Bruce Wayne is described as a "socialite" and the official relationship is that Dick is Bruce's ward. They live in sumptuous quarters, with beautiful flowers in large vases, and have a butler, Alfred. Batman is sometimes shown in a dressing gown. . . . It is like a wish dream of two homosexuals living together. Sometimes they are shown on a couch, Bruce reclining and Dick sitting next to him, jacket off, collar open, and his hand on his friend's arm.[3]

So, Wertham's assumptions of homosexuality are fabricated out of his interpretation of certain visual signs. To avoid being thought queer by Wertham, Bruce and Dick should have done the following: never show concern if the other is hurt, live in a shack, only have ugly flowers in small vases, call the butler "Chip" or "Joe" if you have to have one at all, never share a couch, keep your collar buttoned up, keep your jacket on, and never, ever wear a dressing gown. After all, didn't Noel Coward wear a dressing gown?

Wertham is easy to mock, but the identification of homosexuals through dress codes has a long history.[4] Moreover, such codes originate as semiotic systems adopted by gay people themselves, as a way of signaling the otherwise invisible fact of sexual preference. There is a difference, though, between sporting the secret symbols of a subculture if you form part of that subculture and the elephantine spot-the-homo routine that Wertham performs.

Bat-fans have always responded angrily to Wertham's accusation. One calls it "one of the most incredible charges . . . unfounded rumors . . . sly sneers"[5] and the general response has been to reassert the masculinity of the two heroes, mixed with a little indignation: "If they had been actual men they could have won a libel suit."[6] This seems to me not only to miss the point, but also to *reinforce* Wertham's homophobia—it is only possible to win a libel suit over an "accusation" of homosexuality in a culture where homosexuality is deemed categorically inferior to heterosexuality.

Thus the rush to "protect" Batman and Robin from Wertham is simply the other side to the coin of his bigotry. It may reject Wertham, cast him in the role of dirty-minded old man, but its view of homosexuality is identical. Mark Cotta Vaz thus describes the imputed homosexual relationship as "licentious" while claiming that in fact Bruce Wayne "regularly squired the most beautiful women in Gotham city and presumably had a healthy sex life."[7] Licentious versus healthy—Dr. Wertham himself could not have bettered this homophobic opposition.

Despite the passions aroused on both sides (or rather the two facets of the same side), there is something comic at the heart of this dispute. It is, simply, that Bruce and Dick are not real people but fictional constructions, and hence to squabble over their "real" sex life is to take things a little too far. What is at stake here is the question of reading, of what readers do with the raw material that they are given. Readers are at liberty to construct whatever fantasy lives they like with the characters of the fiction they read (within the limits of generic and narrative credibility, that is). This returns us to the unfortunate patients of Dr. Wertham:

> One young homosexual during psychotherapy brought us a copy of *Detective* comic, with a Batman story. He pointed out a picture of "The Home of Bruce and Dick," a house beautifully landscaped, warmly lighted and showing the devoted pair side by side, looking out a picture window. When he was eight this boy had realized from fantasies about comic book pictures that he was aroused by men. At the age of ten or eleven, "I found my liking, my sexual desires, in comic books. I think

> I put myself in the position of Robin. I did want to have relations with Batman... I remember the first time I came across the page mentioning the 'secret batcave.' The thought of Batman and Robin living together and possibly having sex relations came to my mind...."[8]

Wertham quotes this to shock us, to impel us to tear the pages of *Detective* away before little Tommy grows up and moves to Greenwich Village, but reading it as a gay man today I find it rather moving and also highly recognizable.

What this anonymous gay man did was to practice that form of bricolage which Richard Dyer has identified as a characteristic reading strategy of gay audiences.[9] Denied even the remotest possibility of supportive images of homosexuality within the dominant heterosexual culture, gay people have had to fashion what we could out of the imageries of dominance, to snatch illicit meanings from the fabric of normality, to undertake a corrupt decoding for the purposes of satisfying marginalized desires.[10] This may not be as necessary as it once was, given the greater visibility of gay representations, but it is still an important practice. Wertham's patient evokes in me an admiration, that in a period of American history even more homophobic than most, there he was, raiding the citadels of masculinity, weaving fantasies of oppositional desire. What effect the dread Wertham had on him is hard to predict, but I profoundly hope that he wasn't "cured."

It wasn't only Batman who was subjected to Dr. Doom's bizarre ideas about human sexuality. Hence:

> The homosexual connotation of the Wonder Woman type of story is psychologically unmistakable.... For boys, Wonder Woman is a frightening image. For girls she is a morbid ideal. Where Batman is anti-feminine, the attractive Wonder Woman and her counterparts are definitely anti-masculine. Wonder Woman has her own female following.... Her followers are the "Holiday girls," i.e. the holiday girls, the gay party girls, the gay girls.[11]

Just how much elision can be covered with one "i.e."? Wertham's view of homosexuality is not, at least, inconsistent. Strong, admirable women will turn little girls into dykes—such a heroine can only be seen as a "morbid ideal."

Crazed as Wertham's ideas were, their effectiveness is not in doubt. The mid-fifties saw a moral panic about the assumed dangers of comic books. In the United States companies were driven out of business, careers wrecked, and the Comics Code introduced. This had distinct shades of the Hays Code that had been brought in to clamp down on Hollywood in the 1930s, and under its jurisdiction comics opted for the bland, the safe, and the reactionary. In Britain there was government legislation to prohibit the importing of American comics, as the comics panic slotted neatly into a whole series of anxieties about the effects on British youth of American popular culture.[12]

And in all of this, what happened to Batman? He turned into Fred MacMurray from *My Three Sons*. He lost any remaining edge of the shadowy vigilante of his earliest years and became an upholder of the most stifling small town American values. Batwoman and Batgirl appeared (June Allyson and Bat-Gidget) to take away any lingering doubts about the Dynamic Duo's sex lives. A 1963 story called "The Great Clayface-Joker Feud" has some especially choice examples of the new, squeaky-clean sexuality of the assembled Bats.

Batgirl says to Robin, "I can hardly wait to get into my Batgirl costume again! Won't it be terrific if we could go on a crime case together like the last time? (sigh)." Robin replies, "It sure would, Betty (sigh)." The elder Bats look on approvingly. Batgirl is Batwoman's niece—to make her a daughter would have implied that Batwoman had had (gulp) sexual intercourse, and that would never do. This is the era of Troy Donohue and Pat Boone, and *Batman* as ever serves as a cultural thermometer, taking the temperature of the times.

The Clayface-Joker business is wrapped up (the villains of this period are wacky conjurors, nothing more, with no menace or violence about them) and the episode concludes with another tableau of terrifying heterosexual contentment. "Oh Robin," simpers Batgirl, "I'm afraid you'll just have to hold me! I'm still so shaky after fighting Clayface . . . and you're so strong!" Robin: "Gosh Batgirl, it was swell of you to calm me down when I was warned about Batman tackling Clayface alone." (One feels a distinct Wertham influence here: if Robin shows concern about Batman, wheel on a supportive female, the very opposite of a "morbid ideal," to minister in a suitably self-effacing way.) Batwoman here seizes her chance and tackles Batman: "You look worried about Clayface, Batman . . . so why don't you follow Robin's example and let me soothe you?" Batman can only reply "Gulp."

Gulp indeed. While it's easy simply to laugh at strips like these, knowing as we do the way in which such straight-faced material would be mercilessly shredded by the sixties TV series, they do reveal the retreat into coziness forced on comics by the Wertham onslaught and its repercussions. There no doubt were still subversive readers of Batman, erasing Batgirl on her every preposterous appearance and reworking the Duo's capers to leave some room for homoerotic speculation, but such a reading would have had to work so much harder than before. The *Batman* of this era was such a closed text, so immune to polysemic interpretation, that its interest today is only as a symptom—or, more productively, as camp. "The Great Clayface-Joker Feud" may have been published in 1963, but in every other respect it is a fifties text. If the 1960s began for the world in general with the Beatles, the 1960s for *Batman* began with the TV series in 1966. If the Caped Crusader had been all but Werthamed out of existence, he was about to be camped back into life.

THE CAMPED CRUSADER AND THE BOYS WONDERED

Trying to define Camp is like attempting to sit in the corner of a circular room. It can't be done, which only adds to the quixotic appeal of the attempt. Try these:

> To be camp is to present oneself as being committed to the marginal with a commitment greater than the marginal merits.[13]
>
> Camp sees everything in quotation marks. It's not a lamp but a "lamp"; not a woman but a "woman"... It is the farthest extension, in sensibility, of the metaphor of life as theatre.[14]
>
> Camp is... a way of poking fun at the whole cosmology of restrictive sex roles and sexual identifications which our society uses to oppress its women and repress its men.[15]
>
> Camp was and is a way for gay men to re-imagine the world around them ... by exaggerating, stylizing and remaking what is usually thought to be average or normal.[16]
>
> Camp was a prison for an illegal minority, now it is a holiday for consenting adults.[17]

All true, in their way, but all inadequate. The problem with camp is that it is primarily an experiential rather than an analytical discourse. Camp is a set of attitudes, a gallery of snapshots, an inventory of postures, a modus vivendi, a shop-full of frocks, an arch of eyebrows, a great big pink butterfly that just won't be pinned down, Camp is primarily an adjective, occasionally a verb, but never anything as prosaic, as earth-bound, as a noun.

Yet if I propose to use this adjective as a way of describing one or more of the guises of Batman, I need to arrive at some sort of working definition. So, for the purposes of this analysis, I intend the term camp to refer to a playful, knowing, self-reflexive theatricality. *Batman*, the sixties TV series, was nothing if not knowing. It employed the codes of camp in an unusually public and heavily signaled way. This makes it different from those people or texts that are taken up by camp audiences without ever consciously putting camp into practice. The difference may be very briefly spelled out by reference to Hollywood films. If *Mildred Pierce* and *The Letter* were taken up *as* camp, teased by primarily gay male audiences into yielding meaning not intended by their makers, then *Whatever Happened to Baby Jane?* is a piece of self-conscious camp, capitalizing on certain attitudinal and stylistic tendencies known to exist in audiences. *Baby Jane* is also, significantly, a 1960s film, and the 1960s were the decade in which camp swished out of the ghetto and up into the scarcely prepared mainstream.

A number of key events and texts reinforced this. Susan Sontag wrote her *Notes on Camp*, which remains the starting point for researchers even now. Pop Art was in vogue (and in *Vogue*) and whatever the more elevated claims of Lichtenstein, Warhol, and the rest, their art-works were on one level a new inflection of camp. The growing intellectual respectability of pop music displayed very clearly that the old barriers that once rigidly separated high and low culture were no longer in force. The James Bond films, and even more so their successors like *Modesty Blaise*, popularized a dry, self-mocking wit that makes up one part of the multifaceted diamond of camp. And on television there were *The Avengers*, *The Man from U.N.C.L.E.*, *Thunderbirds*, and *Batman*.

To quote the inevitable Sontag, "The whole point of Camp is to dethrone the serious. . . . More precisely, Camp involves a new, more complex relation to 'the serious.' One can be serious about the frivolous, frivolous about the serious."[18]

The problem with Batman in those terms is that there was never anything truly serious to begin with (unless one swallows that whole portentous Dark Knight charade, more of which in the next section). Batman in its comic book form had, unwittingly, always been camp—it was serious (the tone, the moral homilies) about the frivolous (a man in a stupid suit). He was camp in the way that classic Hollywood was camp, but what the sixties TV series and film did was to overlay this "innocent" camp with a thick layer of ironic distance, the self-mockery version of camp. And given the long associations of camp with the homosexual male subculture, Batman was a particular gift on the grounds of his relationship with Robin. As George Melly put it, "The real Batman series were beautiful because of their unselfconscious absurdity. The remakes, too, at first worked on a double level. Over the absorbed children's heads we winked and nudged, but in the end what were we laughing at? The fact they didn't know that Batman had it off with Robin."[19]

It was as if Wertham's fears were being vindicated at last, but his 1950s bigot's anguish had been supplanted by a self-consciously hip 1960s playfulness. What adult audiences laughed at in the sixties *Batman* was a camped-up version of the fifties they had just left behind.

Batman's lessons in good citizenship ("We'd like to feel that our efforts may help every youngster to grow up into an honest, useful citizen"[20]) were another part of the character ripe for ridiculing deconstruction—"Let's go, Robin, we've set another youth on the road to a brighter tomorrow" (the episode "It's How You Play the Game"). Everything the Adam West Batman said was a parody of seriousness, and how could it be otherwise? How could anyone take genuinely seriously the words of a man dressed like that?

The Batman/Robin relationship is never referred to directly; more fun can be had by presenting it "straight," in other words, screamingly camp. Wertham's reading of the Dubious Duo had been so extensively aired as to pass into the general consciousness (in George Melly's words, "We all knew Robin and Batman were pouves"[21]), it was part of the fabric of *Batman*, and the makers of the TV series proceeded accordingly.

Consider the Duo's encounter with Marsha, Queen of Diamonds. The threat she embodies is nothing less than heterosexuality itself, the deadliest threat to the domestic bliss of the Bat-couple. She is even about to marry Batman before Alfred intervenes to save the day. He and Batman flee the church, but have to do so in the already decorated Batmobile, festooned with wedding paraphernalia including a large "Just Married" sign. "We'll have to drive it as it is," says Batman, while somewhere in the audience a Dr. Wertham takes feverish notes. Robin, Commissioner Gordon, and Chief O'Hara have all been drugged with Marsha's "Cupid's Dart," but it is of course the Boy Wonder who Batman saves first. The dart, he tells Robin. "contains some secret ingredient by which your senses and your will were affected," and it isn't hard to read that ingredient as heterosexual desire, since its result, seen in the previous episode, was to turn Robin into Marsha's slobbering slave.

We can tell with relief now, though, as Robin is "back in fighting form" (with impeccable timing Batman clasps Robin's shoulder on the word "fighting"). Marsha has one last attempt to destroy the duo, but naturally she fails. The female temptress, the seductress, the enchantress must be vanquished. None of this is in the least subtle (Marsha's cat, for example, is called Circe) but this type of mass-market camp can't afford the luxury of subtlety. The threat of heterosexuality is similarly mobilized in the 1966 feature film, where it is Bruce Wayne's infatuation with Kitka (Catwoman in disguise) that causes all manner of problems.

A more interesting employment of camp comes in the episodes where the Duo battle the Black Widow, played by Tallulah Bankhead. The major camp coup here, of course, is the casting. Bankhead was one of the supreme icons of camp, one of its goddesses, "Too intelligent not to be self-conscious, too ambitious to bother about her self-consciousness, too insecure ever to be content, but too arrogant ever to admit insecurity, Tallulah personified camp."[22]

A heady claim, but perhaps justified, because the Black Widow episodes are, against stiff competition, the campest slices of Batman of them all. The stories about Bankhead are legendary—the time when on finding no toilet paper in her cubicle she slipped a ten dollar bill under the partition and asked the woman next door for two fives, or her whispered remark to a priest conducting a particularly elaborate service and swinging a censor of smoking incense, "Darling, I love the drag, but your purse is on fire"—and casting her in Batman was the final demonstration of the series' commitment to camp.

The plot is unremarkable, the usual Bat-shenanigans; the pleasure lies in the detail. Details like the elderly Bankhead crammed into her Super-Villainess costume, or like the way in which (through a plot detail I won't go into) she impersonates Robin, so we see Burt Ward miming to Bankhead's voice, giving the unforgettable image of Robin flirting with burly traffic cops. Best of all, and Bankhead isn't even in this scene but the thrill of having her involved clearly spurred the writer to new heights of camp, Batman has to sing a song to break free of the Black Widow's spell. Does he choose to sing "God Bless America?" Nothing so rugged. He clutches a flower to his Bat chest and sings Gilbert and Sullivan's "I'm Just Little Buttercup." It is this single image, more than any other, which prevents me from taking the post–Adam West Dark Knight at all seriously.

The fundamental camp trick that the series pulls is to make the comics speak. What was acceptable on the page, in speech balloons, stands revealed as ridiculous once given audible voice. The famous visualized sound effects (URKKK! KA-SPLOOSH!) that are, for many, the fondest memory of the series work along similar lines. Camp often makes its point by transposing the codes of one cultural form into the inappropriate codes of another. It thrives on mischievous incongruity.

The incongruities, the absurdities, the sheer ludicrousness of Batman were brought out so well by the sixties version that for some audiences there will never be another credible approach. I have to include myself here. I've recently read widely in post-sixties Bat-lore, and I can appreciate what the writers and artists are trying to do, but my Batman will always be Adam West. It's impossible to be somber or pompous about Batman because if you try the ghost of West will come Bat-climbing into your mind, fortune cookie wisdom on his lips and keen young Dick by his side. It's significant, I think, that the letters I received from the editors of this book began "Dear Bat-Contributor." Writers preparing chapters about James Joyce or Ingmar Bergman do not, I suspect, receive analogous greetings. To deny the large camp component of Batman is to blind oneself to one of the richest parts of his history.

IS THERE BAT-LIFE AFTER BAT-CAMP?

The international success of the Adam West incarnation left Batman high and dry. The camping around had been fun while it lasted, but it hadn't lasted very long. Most camp humor has a relatively short lifespan, new targets are always needed, and the camp aspect of Batman had been squeezed dry. The mass public had moved on to other heroes, other genres, other acres of merchandising, but there was still a hard Bat-core of fans to satisfy. Where could the Bat go next? Clearly there was no possibility of returning to the caped Eisenhower, the benevolent patriarch of the 1950s. That option had been well and truly closed down by the TV show. Batman needed to be given his dignity back, and this entailed a return to his roots.

This, in any case, is the official version. For the unreconstructed devotee of the Batman (that is, people who insist on giving him the definite article before the name), the West years had been hell—a tricksy travesty, an effeminizing of the cowled avenger. There's a scene in *Midnight Cowboy* where Dustin Hoffman tells Jon Voight that the only audience liable to be receptive to his cowboy clothes are gay men looking for rough trade. Voight is appalled—"you mean to tell me John Wayne was a fag?" (quoted, roughly, from memory). This outrage, this horror at shattered illusions, comes close to encapsulating the loathing and dread the campy Batman has received from the old guard of Gotham City and the younger born-again Bat-fans.

So what has happened since the 1960s has been the painstaking reheterosexualization of Batman. I apologize for coining such a clumsy word, but no other quite gets the sense that I mean. This strategy has worked, too, for large audiences, reaching its peak with the 1989 film. To watch this and then come home to see a video of the 1966 movie is to grasp how complete the transformation has been. What I want to do in this section is to trace some of the crucial moments in that change, written from the standpoint of someone still unashamedly committed to Bat-camp.

If one wants to take Batman as a Real Man, the biggest stumbling block has always been Robin. There have been disingenuous claims that "Batman and Robin had a blood-brother closeness. Theirs was a spiritual intimacy forged from the stress of countless battles fought side by side"[23] (one can imagine what Tallulah Bankhead might say to *that*), but we know otherwise. The Wertham lobby and the acolytes of camp alike have ensured that any Batman/Robin relationship is guaranteed to bring on the sniggers. Besides which, in the late 1960s, Robin was getting to be a big boy, too big for any shreds of credibility to attach themselves to all that father-son smokescreen. So in 1969 Dick Grayson was packed off to college and the Bat was solitary once more.

This was a shrewd move. It's impossible to conceive of the recent, obsessive, *sturm-und-drang* Batman with a chirpy little Robin getting in the way.[24] A text of the disturbing power of *The Killing Joke* could not have functioned with Robin to rupture the grim dualism of its Batman/Joker struggle. There was, however, a post-Dick Robin, but he was killed off by fans in that infamous telephone poll.

It's intriguing to speculate how much latent (or blatant) homophobia lay behind that vote. Did the fans decide to kill off Jason Todd so as to redeem Batman for unproblematic heterosexuality? Impossible to say. There are other factors to take into account, such as Jason's apparent failure to live up to the expectations of what a Robin should be like. The sequence of issues in which Jason/Robin died, *A Death in the Family*, is worth looking at in some detail, however, in order to see whether the camp connotations of Bruce and Dick had been fully purged.

The depressing answer is that they had. This is very much the Batman of the 1980s, his endless feud with the Joker this time uneasily stretched over a framework involving the Middle East and Ethiopia. Little to be camp about there, though the presence of the Joker guarantees a quota of sick jokes. The sickest of all is the introduction of the Ayatollah Kohomeini, a real and important political figure, into this fantasy world of THUNK! and THER-ACKK! and grown men dressed as bats. (As someone who lived in the part of England from which Reagan's planes took off on their murderous mission to bomb Libya, I fail to see the humor in this cartoon version of American foreign policy: it's too near the real thing.)

Jason dies at the Joker's hands because he becomes involved in a search for his own origins, a clear parallel to Batman's endless returns to his Oedipal scenario. Families, in the Bat-mythology, are dark and troubled things, one more reason why the introduction of the fifties versions of Batwoman and Batgirl seemed so inappropriate. This applies only to real, biological families, though; the true familial bond is between Batman and Robin, hence the title of these issues. Whether one chooses to read Robin as Batman's ward (official version), son (approved fantasy) or lover (forbidden fantasy), the sense of loss at his death is bound to be devastating. Batman finds Robin's body and, in the time-honored tradition of Hollywood cinema, is at least able to give him a loving embrace. Good guys hug their dead buddies; only queers smooch when still alive.

If the word "camp" is applied at all to the eighties Batman, it is a label for the Joker. This sly displacement is the cleverest method yet devised of preserving Bat-heterosexuality. The play that the texts regularly make with the concept of Batman and the Joker as mirror images now takes a new twist. The Joker is Batman's "bad twin," and part of that badness is, increasingly, an implied homosexuality. This is certainly present in the 1989 film, a generally glum and portentous affair except for Jack Nicholson's Joker, a characterization enacted with venomous camp. The only moment when this dour film comes to life is when the Joker and his gang raid the Art Gallery, spraying the paintings and generally camping up a storm.

The film strives and strains to make us forget the Adam West Batman, to the point of giving us Vicki Vale as Bruce Wayne's lover, and certainly Michael Keaton's existential agonizing (variations on the theme of why-did-I-have-to-be-a-Bat) is a world away from West's gleeful subversion of truth, justice, and the American way. This is the same species of Batman celebrated by Frank Miller: "If your only memory of Batman is that of Adam West and Burt Ward exchanging camped-out quips while clobbering slumming guest-stars Vincent Price and Cesar Romero, I hope this book will come as a surprise. . . . For me, Batman was never funny. . . ."[25]

The most recent linkage of the Joker with homosexuality comes in *Arkham Asylum*, the darkest image of the Bat-world yet. Here the Joker has become a parody of a screaming queen, calling Batman "honey pie," given to exclamations like "oooh!" (one of the oldest homophobic clichés in the book) and pinching Batman's behind with the advice, "loosen up, tight ass." He also, having no doubt read his Wertham, follows the pinching by asking. "What's the matter? Have I touched a nerve? How is the Boy Wonder? Started shaving yet?" The Bat-response is unequivocal: "Take your filthy hands off me . . . Filthy degenerate!"

Arkham Asylum is a highly complex reworking of certain key aspects of the mythology, of which the sexual tension between Batman and the Joker is only one small part. Nonetheless the Joker's question "Have I touched a nerve?" seems a crucial one, as revealed by the homophobic ferocity of Batman's reply. After all, the dominant cultural construction of gay men at the end of the 1980s is as plague carriers, and the word "degenerate" is not far removed from some of the labels affixed to us in the age of AIDS.

BATMAN: IS HE OR ISN'T HE?

The one constant factor through all of the transformations of Batman has been the devotion of his admirers. They will defend him against what they see as negative interpretations, and they carry around in their heads a kind of essence of batness, a Bat-Platonic Ideal of how Batman should really be. The Titan Books reissue of key comics from the 1970s each carry a preface by a noted fan, and most of them contain claims such as "This, I feel, is Batman as he was meant to be."[26]

Where a negative construction is specifically targeted, no prizes for guessing which one it is: "you . . . are probably also fond of the TV show he appeared in. But then maybe you prefer Elvis Presley's Vegas years or the later Jerry Lewis movies over their early stuff. For me, the definitive Batman was then and always will be the one portrayed in these pages."[27]

The sixties TV show remains anathema to the serious Bat-fan precisely because it heaps ridicule on the very notion of a serious Batman. *Batman* the series revealed the man in the cape as a pompous fool, an embodiment of superseded ethics, and a closet queen. As Marsha, Queen of Diamonds, put it, "Oh Batman, darling, you're so divinely square." Perhaps the enormous success of the 1989 film will help to advance the cause of the rival Bat-archetype, the grim, vengeful Dark Knight whose heterosexuality is rarely called into question (his humorlessness, fondness for violence, and obsessive monomania seem to me exemplary qualities for a heterosexual man). The answer, surely, is that they needn't be mutually exclusive.

If I might be permitted a rather camp comparison, each generation has its definitive Hamlet, so why not the same for Batman? I'm prepared to admit the validity, for some people, of the swooping eighties vigilante, so why are they so concerned to trash my sixties camped crusader? Why do they insist so vehemently that Adam West was a faggy aberration, a blot on the otherwise impeccably butch Bat-landscape? What *are* they trying to hide?

If I had a suspicious frame of mind, I might think that they were protesting too much, that maybe Dr. Wertham was on to something when he targeted these narratives as incitements to homosexual fantasy. And if I want Batman to be gay, then, for me, he is. After all, outside of the minds of his writers and readers, he doesn't really exist.

NOTES

1. Martin Barker, *A Haunt of Fears: The Strange History of the British Horror Comics Campaign* (London: Pluto Press, 1984).
2. Fredric Wertham, *Seduction of the Innocent* (London: Museum Press, 1955), 188.
3. Wertham, 190.
4. See, for example, the newspaper stories on "how to spot" homosexuals printed in Britain in the fifties and sixties, and discussed in Jeffrey Weeks, *Coming Out: Homosexual Politics in Britain* (London: Quartet, 1979).
5. Phrases taken from Chapters 5 and 6 of Mark Cotta Vaz, *Tales of the Dark Knight: Batman's First Fifty Years* (London: Futura, 1989).
6. Les Daniels, *Comix: A History of Comic Books in America* (New York: Bonanza Books, 1971), 87.
7. Cotta Vaz, 47 and 53.
8. Wertham, 192.
9. Richard Dyer, ed. *Gays and Film.* (New York: Zoetrope, 1984), 1.

10. See Richard Dyer, "Judy Garland and Gay Men," in Dyer, *Heavenly Bodies* (London: BFI. 1987) and Claire Whitaker, "Hollywood Transformed: Interviews with Lesbian Viewers," in Peter Steven, ed., *Jump Cut: Hollywood Politics and Counter- Cinema* (Toronto: Between the Lines, 1985).
11. Wertham, 192–193.
12. See Barker.
13. Mark Booth, *Camp* (London: Quartet, 1983), 18.
14. Susan Sontag, "Notes on Camp," in *A Susan Sontag Reader* (Harmondsworth: Penguin, 1983), 106.
15. Jack Babuscio, "Camp and the Gay Sensibility," in Dyer, ed. *Gays and Film*, 46.
16. Michael Bronski, *Culture Clash: The Making of Gay Sensibility* (Boston: South End Press, 1984), 42.
17. Philip Core, *Camp: The Lie That Tells the Truth* (London: Plexus, 1984), 7.
18. Sontag, 116.
19. George Melly, *Revolt into Style: The Pop Arts in the 50s and 60s* (Oxford: Oxford University Press, 1989), 193.
20. "The Batman Says," *Batman* #3 (1940), quoted in Cotta Vaz, 15.
21. Melly, 192.
22. Core, 25.
23. Cotta Vaz, 53.
24. A female Robin is introduced in the *Dark Knight Returns* series, which, while raising interesting questions about the sexuality of Batman, which I don't here have the space to address, seems significant in that the Dark Knight cannot run the risk of reader speculation that a traditionally male Robin might provoke.
25. Frank Miller, "Introduction," *Batman: Year One* (London: Titan, 1988).
26. Kim Newman, "Introduction," *Batman: The Demon Awakes* (London: Titan, 1989).
27. Jonathan Ross, "Introduction," *Batman: Vow from the Grave* (London: Titan, 1989).

Color Them Black

ADILIFU NAMA

From *Super Black: American Pop Culture and Black Superheroes*, 9–35, by Adilifu Nama. © 2011. By permission of the University of Texas Press.

> Oh, we can beat them, forever and ever. Then we could be heroes just for one day.
> **DAVID BOWIE**

> Ain't no such thing as Superman.
> **GIL SCOTT-HERON**

SCORES OF READERS HAVE USED SUPERHERO COMICS TO VICARIOUSLY DEFY gravity and bound over skyscrapers, swing through the Big Apple with the greatest of ease, stalk the dark streets of Gotham, or travel at magnificent speeds through the universe on an opaque surfboard. Yet superheroes are more than just fuel for fantasies or a means to escape from the humdrum world of everyday responsibilities. Superheroes symbolize societal attitudes regarding good and evil, right and wrong, altruism and greed, justice and fair play. Lost, however, in the grand ethos and pathos that superheroes represent are the black superheroes that fly, fight, live, love, and sometimes die. In contrast, even the most obscure white superheroes are granted an opportunity to make their way from the narrow margins of fandom to mainstream media exposure. Nevertheless, what black superheroes may lack in mainstream popularity they more than match in symbolism, meaning, and political import with regard to the cultural politics of race in America. Even the omission and chronic marginalization of black superheroes are phenomena rife with cultural and sociopolitical implications.

The lack of black superheroes has served as a source of concerned speculation and critique. Arguably, Kenneth Clark's groundbreaking yet flawed doll experiment from the 1950s is a theoretical cornerstone for the racial anxiety associated with an absence of black superheroes and its impact on both black and white children. Clark's work revealed that when given a choice black children overwhelmingly preferred a white doll to a black doll and often associated negative qualities with the latter. This racial preference was taken as evidence that racial segregation contributed to internalized feelings of inferiority on the part of black kids.[1] The results also implied that black children needed positive black images to help counteract low self-esteem. Against this theoretical backdrop the need to create black superheroes for black children to identify with takes on greater significance as a social problem. On the one hand, black superheroes are needed to counteract the likelihood of black children mentally identifying with white superheroes. On the other hand, the glut of white superheroes could encourage white children to accept notions of white superiority as normal.[2] This type of racial logic is clearly on display in Frantz Fanon's psychoanalytic manifesto *Black Skin, White Masks* (1952). In this book he argued that figures like Tarzan the Ape Man reinforced real racial hierarchies by repetitively depicting whites as victors over black people and chronically portraying blacks as representatives of the forces of evil.

A similar suspicion is detected in the Black Power aesthetic of singer and spoken word artist Gil Scott-Heron. On his album *First Minute of a New Day* Scott-Heron echoed Frantz Fanon's trenchant critique of white superheroes with the terse edict, "Ain't no such thing as Superman." The statement subverts and calls attention to the racial implications embedded in Superman as one of the most iconic figures in American pop culture. In this case a virtually indestructible white man flying around the world in the name of "truth, justice, and the American way" is not a figure black folk should waste time believing in. Gil Scott-Heron was signifying the dubious racial politics of having a strange and powerful white man presented as a figure of awe and wonder. Such a sensibility casts Superman's identity as having less to do with being the last son of Krypton and more to do with symbolically embodying white racial superiority and American imperialism.

In contrast to the concern over the normalization of white supremacy in comics, Fredric Wertham accused the entire comic book industry of being a nefarious influence on American youth of all colors. He pronounced that the graphic depictions of violence, suggestive sexuality, fascist ideology, and homosexual innuendo woven into the images and narratives found in crime, horror, and superhero comic books had negative effects on children and were subversive.[3] Wertham's staunch opposition to comics was eventually successful. By 1954 the comic book industry had succumbed to pressure and adopted a content code to mute vocal critics of the medium and placate public concerns that comics were dangerous because they contributed to juvenile delinquency.[4] The code was put in place to protect readers from subversive and upsetting material even though it was predicated on disputed media effects theories.[5] In fact, the emergence of American youth as a significant consumer market and the increasing packaging of adolescent desire as an advertising method are likely stronger forces cultivating behaviors, desires, and ideas than what is presented in comic books.[6]

Ultimately the fear about media effects on black children who admire white superheroes is overly simplistic and fails to seriously take into account the fact that audience reception is a more complex phenomenon than is suggested by a strict stimulus-response model of media consumption.[7] For example, Junot Diaz, the author of the Pulitzer prize-winning novel *The Brief Wondrous Life of Oscar Wao*, in his youth identified with the white mutant superhero team the X-Men. Because the group were mutants and were treated as social outcasts, as a young Dominican immigrant, Diaz felt an affinity for the characters due to his own marginalized racial status that stigmatized him as an outsider to mainstream America.[8] Diaz's experience speaks to the power of superheroes to deliver ideas about American race relations that stand outside of strict notions of authorial intent and draconian concerns about white superheroes (or black ones, for that matter) depositing negative notions about one's racial identity into the reader or viewer. Consequently, even though superhero figures are predominantly white guys and gals clad in spandex and tights, a strict racial reading of the negative impact white superheroes may have on blacks is too linear and reductive.

Diaz's anecdote also demonstrates how easily entertainment media and the cultural politics of race can converge in an interesting way. Yet the connection between the two realms was not clearly perceived or seamlessly integrated until the late 1960s and early 1970s. During this period the bright line between the popular and the political was obliterated as American pop culture began to shed its escapist impulses and boldly engage the racial tensions that America was experiencing. For example, James Brown's song "Say It Loud, I'm Black and I'm Proud" (1968) did double duty as a dance hit and a racial anthem of uplift and self-esteem. A more subtle but just as powerful illustration of the intersection of the popular and the political regarding race occurred on *Sesame Street*, the pioneering public-television show for children. In the early 1960s Kermit the Frog was one of the show's central characters, and when he sang a lament about how difficult it was being the color green the vignette clearly placed racial prejudice in the center spotlight. Even the most innocuous forms of American pop life were getting in on the trend. In 1971 Coca Cola would launch a successful television ad campaign in which a multiracial throng of young people stood on a hilltop and sang the catchy jingle "I'd Like to Teach the World to Sing (In Perfect Harmony)." On one hand, the commercial could be criticized as the pinnacle of pop drivel for an unsophisticated public to mindlessly consume. On the other hand, by presenting an image of blacks, whites, and third world people of color peacefully standing together singing in unison the commercial was a striking symbolic counterpoint to anxiety over racial unrest at home and the Vietnam War abroad.

Arguably the turn toward increasing racial and political relevance in American pop culture was spurred by the baby boomer generation coming of age at the height of American racial unrest and political turmoil. The formulaic and commercial appeal of traditional forms of American pop culture faced severely diminishing entertainment value for the baby boomers. Bloated musical spectacles like *On a Clear Day You Can See Forever* (1970) were virtually ignored, westerns with their high-noon shootouts and sanitized violence were replaced by operatic depictions of bloodshed in spaghetti westerns, and a Blaxploitation movie craze provided a new round of two-dimensional black characters that misled many to believe that racial diversity and the Hollywood film industry were synonymous. Alongside these multiple shifts in content and style, superhero comics also experienced a profound transformation. Marvel Comics was first to adjust. The paradigmatic "perfect" superhero was recreated as emotionally flawed and conflicted, a sensibility that mirrored the adolescent angst and ideological identity crisis that had taken hold throughout America as the turbulent 1960s gave way to the early 1970s.[9] Reluctant superheroes such as Spider-Man, the Fantastic Four, and the Incredible Hulk represented a new typology of superhero: troubled, brash, brave, and insecure. Not to be outdone, however, were the subsequent reimagining of DC Comics's Green Arrow and Green Lantern.

Dennis O'Neil and Neal Adams's *Green Lantern Co-Starring Green Arrow* (1970–1972) comic book series dramatically recast superheroes, and shaped the superhero comic book as a space where acute social issues were engaged. On one hand, Green Lantern embodied President Richard Nixon's no-nonsense dictum of "law and order" in the face of race riots and student protests. On the other hand, Green Arrow was the symbolic representative of activist youth, the working class, and the oppressed. Over at Marvel Comics, Stan Lee and Jack Kirby successfully tampered with the makeup of the superheroes. In contrast, Dennis O'Neil and Neal Adams changed the nature of the superhero genre by erasing the boundaries of what comics could discuss to such an extent that it had an impact on the genre for decades.

Prior to O'Neil and Adams, superheroes were quite predictable in that they mainly battled intergalactic threats or various types of villains commuted to the most grandiose schemes often involving a quest for global domination. What made *Green Lantern Co-Starring Green Arrow* unpredictably complicated was that a significant part of the stories addressed topical and pressing social issues: poverty, racism, overpopulation, and drug abuse. The comic symbolically pitted the conservative politics of the "law and order" elites against the "Age of Aquarius" ideals of youth activists who championed changing the world by challenging the status quo. The magnitude of the social issues Green Lantern and Green Arrow confronted along with the audaciousness of having make-believe figures confront real and troublesome social issues turned the superhero tandem into charismatic characters and politically charged symbols. In the inaugural issue, "No Evil Shall Escape My Sight," the pair confronts American racism. Across several panels an elderly black man is depicted questioning Green Lantern's commitment to racial justice when he voices this short soliloquy: "I been readin' about you. . . . How you work for the Blue Skins . . . and how on a planet someplace you helped out the Orange Skins . . . and you done considerable for the Purple Skins! Only there's skins you never bothered with! The Black Skins! I want to know . . . how come?! Answer me that, Mr. Green Lantern!" With stooped shoulders and his head hung low, the ring-slinger responds with a feeble, "I . . . can't."[10]

Although the elderly black man is drawn as a decrepit and unappealing figure and expresses his concern in an unconvincing black dialect, the exchange between the two is profoundly engaging. Their conversation forever changed the boundaries of the superhero genre. Superheroes were no longer constrained to fighting imaginary creatures, intergalactic aliens, or Nazis from a distant past. Now they would grapple with some of the most toxic real world social issues that America had to offer. In their respective civilian identities as Hal Jordan and Oliver Queen, the two superheroes take off in a truck together and hopscotch their way across the country to experience the real America and find their true place and purpose in it. With their existential quest interrupted by personal dilemmas that are proxies for real life social issues, the series reads like a superhero version of Jack Kerouac's novel *On the Road* (1957). By shifting the focus from villainous spectacle to real world problems plaguing the nation, Green Lantern and Green Arrow were transformed from a pair of mediocre superheroes to robust symbols of the political tensions of time. In this sense, both characters were ideological foils for the other, fusing their comic book dialogue with real-world resonance. Interestingly, racism was a central part of the plots of the Green Lantern and Green Arrow series and was a source of superhero reflection.

For example, in a subsequent panel from "No Evil Shall Escape My Sight," Green Arrow underscores the immorality of racism by invoking the political assassinations of Dr. Martin Luther King and Bobby Kennedy. This point is clearly expressed by a poignant image of Green Arrow standing in the foreground of outlined images of Dr. King and Bobby Kennedy. The picture is underscored by a caption that states, "On the streets of Memphis a good black man died . . . and in Los Angeles, a good white man fell. Something is wrong! Something is killing us all! Some hideous moral cancer is rotting our very souls!"[11] In retrospect, it is easy to look at such writing as maudlin and crudely didactic. Arguably, however, because Green Lantern and Green Arrow were addressing such immense social issues, both characters required grand language and imagery to match the sweeping cultural fallout and the emotional trauma the American psyche suffered from witnessing a spate of political assassinations on American soil. Green Arrow and Green Lantern functioned as elegant cultural ciphers that openly questioned the crisis of meaning and identity that Green Arrow expresses in his lament over the assassinations. Despite the ham-fisted dialogue, the *Green Lantern Co-Starring Green Arrow* comic book series was symbolically sophisticated when confronting white privilege and racial injustice in America.

For instance, in another issue titled "A Kind of Loving, a Way of Death," racial privilege is confronted whereby avowedly anti-racist whites are implicated in supporting a racial hierarchy. In the story, the white female superhero Black Canary is hypnotized by a white supremacist named Joshua.[12] Joshua plans on using her as an agent to instigate a race war, and one of her first tests is to kill Green Arrow. Although she fails to follow through on her task, Green Arrow speculates that Joshua's racist mind control was successful on her to a certain extent because the racial hatred the villain preached struck a chord deep inside of her. Black Canary responds to Green Arrow's insight by subsequently volunteering at an Indian reservation and engaging in deep self-reflection. Unquestionably this narrative tried to address the sociopsychological aspects of racial prejudice as a personal, even subconscious, problem, while the Black Canary easily symbolized white guilt. To the series's credit, "A Kind of Loving, a Way of Death" suggested that racist villainy was just as likely found by looking in the mirror as it was by scouring the countryside for Klansmen. However, the narrative was not without weaknesses. By having Black Canary delve into the recesses of her own heart and mind to root out racist motivations, her action implied that personal reflection was an equal or possibly more important and effective step toward eliminating racism than organized political confrontation of institutional racism.

As well intentioned as this type of personally transformative pop psychology may have been, it signaled that a personal pursuit of individual transformation was the true testament of change rather than the social and institutional quest for racial justice that proponents of civil rights and Black Power movements advocated. As a real-world strategy to eliminate racism, the former approach is debatable, but as a narrative device in "A Kind of Loving, a Way of Death" it was pure genius. It demonstrated that racial bigotry could appeal to even the most respectable and fair-minded whites and that even humans vested with superpowers were impotent to deliver America from racism. As a result, instead of Green Lantern, Green Arrow, and Black Canary leading the charge to end racism as superheroes, they symbolized the need for whites to take ownership of their white privilege, acknowledge the feelings of guilt, and most importantly strive for personal transformation. Ultimately the comic suggested that the most viable solution for ending racism in America was for its white citizenry to become introspective and mindful of their racial prejudices, a solution that did not require one to possess superhuman powers.

It is quite apparent that the *Green Lantern Co-Starring Green Arrow* series was ambitiously dialoguing with real-world issues and trying to tackle some of the most vexing social problems facing American society. Nevertheless, reactionary impulses are also clearly present when the emerald duo confronted the color line. During the two-year run of the comic, the ideological debates and political polemics spoken by Green Lantern and Green Arrow at times lapsed into awkward renderings of American race relations. Increasingly, the idea of racial revenge crops up. For example, the cover of the "Ulysses Star Is Still Alive" issue depicts Green Lantern tied to a Native American totem pole, as if he is being crucified. Green Arrow is adorned with a full Native American ceremonial feathered headdress as he stands in the foreground aiming his bow and arrow at the ring-slinger and declares, "My redskin brothers find you guilty! And I am your executioner!"[13] This type of attention-grabbing cover tilted dangerously towards racial pulp politics. The narrative for this issue was not lacking in racial histrionics, either. With classic lines like, "They've been under the white man's heel for so long they've lost faith in themselves," the comic demonstrated how pugnacious the racial politics of the series could periodically become. Despite these shortcomings, the series was significant for another noteworthy element: the introduction of John Stewart, the original Black Lantern.

Until John Stewart, Green Lantern and his successor, Guy Gardner, were all white men. When Gardner becomes injured and another Green Lantern reserve is needed to fill the position, the Guardians of the Universe choose John Stewart, an African American.[14] Initially, Hal Jordan objects to John Stewart as his backup even though Stewart possesses the requisite courage and honesty essential to activating the green power ring. Hal views Stewart as too angry to justly wield it. The critique of Stewart easily played to the racial archetype of the "angry black man," political shorthand for reducing Black Power advocates to mad men determined to exact revenge on white America with self-destructive violence and intimidation. John Stewart's appearance as the Black Lantern on the cover of the first issue suggested a similar sensibility. The Green Lantern is shown lying at the feet of a fully costumed and outraged Stewart who declares, "They whipped the Green Lantern. Now let 'em try me!" The caption, "Beware My Power," is placed toward the bottom of the page.

The striking cover art and rage-filled declaration of revenge telegraphed a sensational racial drama inside the comic book. John Stewart's first mission as a superhero was to protect a white politician who is an overt racial bigot. The politician plans to stoke racial hostilities by having a white police officer killed as a result of a phony attempt on the politician's life by a black gunman. John Stewart begrudgingly accepts the assignment to save the racist from harm and later foils the nefarious scheme to instigate a race riot. As a result, Stewart gains Hal Jordan's respect and trust. If ever there was an origin narrative that was overdetermined by race, this is truly the one. Rather than having John Stewart use his power ring on his first mission to defeat some generic monster-alien or save a bus load of tourists from plummeting off a broken bridge, he had to protect a comic book version of George Wallace from harm. In his debut, unfortunately, his character was buried under a mound of racial rhetoric and anxiety concerning the type of Black Power politics John Stewart symbolized in the beginning of the story. Early in the issue when Stewart first dons his Green Lantern costume, Stewart informs Hal that he better be called "Black Lantern," and he rejects wearing a mask because, "This Black man lets it all hang out! I've got nothing to hide!" Stewart is a cocky, anti-authoritarian, angry, and race-conscious figure. Near the end of the truncated origin narrative, however, Stewart proclaims that color is not an important criterion for judging character. His change of heart is clearly an ideological nod toward Dr. Martin Luther King's axiom that people should be judged by the quality of their character and not the color of their skin. In keeping with that approach, the Black Lantern moniker is rejected and he is subsequently referred to as John Stewart.

Admittedly, the overt hostility toward white authority that Stewart initially expressed and the racial melodrama his story represented were crude and sensationalistic. Yet the reliance on racial antagonism as the driving force for John Stewart's origin reflected a broader trend. During the early 1970s, films such as *Sweet Sweetback's Badass Song* (1971), *Super Fly* (1972), and *The Spook Who Sat by the Door* (1973), to name only a few, exemplified how Blaxploitation cinema was often a sexually gratuitous and bloody referendum on white authority. Of course by showing blacks killing, fighting, humiliating, loving, and winning against whites, many mediocre movies were able to make good economic sense. In the process, Blaxploitation films increasingly relied on sensationalistic depictions of racial strife, wherein crazed and corrupt whites appeared to live only to plot for the black protagonist's death and, by symbolic extension, black peoples' defeat in the struggle for racial justice. Unfortunately, real racial issues were increasingly presented as spectacle, and various social movements of the period had degenerated into political theater and posturing.[15] A similar impulse cropped up with Dennis O'Neil and Neal Adam's *Superman vs. Mohammed Ali* (1978) comic. The cover was exquisitely evocative of deep-seated yet familiar racial antagonism present in the American body politic.

Although the narrative inside the comic has Superman temporarily forfeit his powers to Ali, combined with a feel-good racial reconciliation message, the magnitude of the racial symbolism presented on the cover dwarfs any concessions concerning Superman's abilities.

Displayed on the cover of the oversized comic book are Superman and Muhammad Ali, wearing boxing gloves, facing each other at the center of the ring, and preparing to throw the first devastating punch with a massive crowd of superheroes, celebrities, and everyday folk as spectators. Ostensibly the Superman vs. Muhammad Ali bout concerns the fate of the planet, as the winner will have to box the representative of an alien race to defend Earth. But symbolically the cover was a potent signifier of American race relations, given that the heavyweight-boxing tournament has historically functioned as a public staging ground for dubious notions and desires concerning race to play out when one opponent is white and the other is black.

In 1908 Jack Johnson became the first black heavyweight boxing champion, which inspired the distinguished American writer Jack London to call on a great white hope to reclaim the title from Johnson. In response, James Jeffries, a former undefeated heavyweight champion was urged to come out of retirement to restore the heavyweight championship title to its previous luster. Billed as the fight of the century, the boxing contest was a racial spectacle that inspired black celebration and white violence in the wake of Johnson's victory.[16] Unfortunately, subsequent titleholders inherited this racial subtext virtually anytime a black fighter and a white fighter were matched against one another. Take for example, Joe "the Brown Bomber" Louis's two heavyweight bouts with Max Schmeling in 1936 and 1938, where Adolf Hitler's perverse ideas about Aryan racial supremacy and Nazism underscored the boxing contests between the two. Four decades later, when the Irish slugger Jerry Quarry faced Muhammad Ali the former was dubbed a "great white hope," and the same theme appeared again when Gerry Cooney boxed Larry Holmes in 1982 for a shot at the heavyweight title.

For decades in America, no matter if the contestants embraced or rejected the racial roles they symbolized when a white and black boxer faced one another in the ring, racial anxieties and personal prejudices were projected onto each fighter as representatives of their respective race. Accordingly the *Superman vs. Muhammad Ali* comic book cover signaled not only the spectacular nature of a fight between two American icons but easily drew on the potent racial history associated with heavyweight championship fights that had occupied America's public imagination for nearly seventy years. On one hand, the cover easily reads as a comic book clash between two titans, a contest that pits the "Man of Steel" against "the Greatest of All Time." On the other hand, an epic battle between a white man that represents "truth, justice, and the American way" and a black Muslim who refused to fight in an American war he was drafted to serve in dredges up deep racial anxieties not fully settled or forgotten since Jack Johnson's heyday, much less Ali's recent racial past.

A decade before the release of *Superman vs. Muhammad Ali*, Ali was a vocal member of the Nation of Islam, a controversial black nationalist religious organization. The "Louisville Lip" rose to fame as a loudmouth heavyweight-boxing champion, but his personal convictions, as a follower of the Honorable Elijah Muhammad and later a voice of poetic dissent regarding the Vietnam War, made Ali a despised figure for many white Americans. By the time the *Superman vs. Muhammad Ali* comic was released, Ali was less of a political lighting rod. He had regained his title as the heavyweight champion of the world which, for the most part, supplanted his past status as a black Muslim and draft resister. Yet his radical black nationalist past remained resonant if not as equally recognized as Ali's status as "the greatest of all time." In this sense, the cover illustration of a white superhero that trumpets "the American way" combating a black man that was a vocal critic of America signified a colossal confrontation of epic racial proportion. Ultimately, however, the *Superman vs. Muhammad Ali* comic book is best framed as marking the beginning of the complete transformation of Muhammad Ali from one of the most despised black athletes in America to one of the most beloved icons in American popular culture.[17]

Arguably the fact that Ali stuck to his principles in the face of severe professional sacrifice and regained the heavyweight title as an underdog challenger to George Foreman helped remake his image and paved the way for his acceptance as a mainstream and tremendously popular American icon. The American public values the underdog narrative of the little guy winning against the odds, and more than anything Ali's triumphant comeback dovetails with a cornerstone of all superhero narratives: meeting harsh resistance and overwhelming odds with integrity and perseverance. Ali, like most superheroes, succeeds not because of superior strength but by moral determination in the face of severe opposition.[18] In this sense, the re-release of the *Superman vs. Muhammad Ali* comic book fits with Ali's transformation into a mainstream hero who upholds American values, a theme that was signaled in the original narrative but that can now be fully embraced, thirty years later, with a story about Superman and Ali working together to save the Earth against alien invaders.

By the late 1970s the kind of socially relevant and racially engaged superhero figures that O'Neil and Adams had created had nearly disappeared. Admittedly their work was not perfect, but it spearheaded a transformation for how superhero comics were written and thought about. Comics were no longer just for the kiddies, and were increasingly recognized as another medium where ideas concerning American racial morality and the cultural politics of a society trying to come to grips with dramatic societal shifts were also seriously engaged. As the end of the 1970s approached, DC Comics introduced a new black superhero that loosely represented a continuation of the superhero social relevancy tradition established by O'Neil and Adams. Black Lightning was the first black superhero in the DC Comics universe to get his own title series, and as a result he could not avoid symbolizing black self-determination or serving as a symbolic reminder of racial tokenism.

Black Lightning is Jefferson Pierce, a former Olympic athlete and a teacher in Suicide Slum, one of Metropolis's toughest areas. When danger appeared or when justice was needed, Jefferson would don an Afro wig attached to a mask, squeeze into a bluish body suit accented with lightning bolts, slide on his buccaneer boots, check his power belt, and then hit the streets as Black Lightning.[19] Dressed to impress, Jefferson would proceed to kick and shock various henchmen and their crime lords into submission. Despite his nearly laughable disco-chic look and the embarrassingly awkward black jargon Jefferson used when he became Black Lightning, he articulated a serious set of class and racial politics. Jefferson Pierce was a striver, a black guy who fought his way out of ghetto squalor to become an accomplished athlete, a successful educator, and, finally, a ghetto superhero. Black Lightning's upward-mobility narrative registered subtle elements of Black Power politics concerning self-determination and black social responsibility, but his black middle-class status was also a source of multiple anxieties. His black bourgeois sensibility clashed with a superhero persona that delivered affected black dialect, a crude racial signifier that attempted to demonstrate that Black Lightning was an authentic black hero not alienated from the inner-city streets he swore to protect.

Despite Black Lightning lapsing into stock phrases to convey his blackness, he communicated several interesting points about black agency. Here was a black superhero situated in the same city as Superman who decides to dedicate his life to single-handedly fighting the rampant crime, drugs, and delinquency that threaten to take over his neighborhood. Moreover, by having Black Lightning combat symbols of white oppression, like Tobias Whale, a white fish-headed crime boss, the comic articulated an acceptable (albeit formulaic) version of Black Power politics as black social responsibility.[20] Even if *Black Lightning* was a comic book holdover from the Blaxploitation-film era, he was a subversive repackaging of Black Power notions, like community control and black middle-class anxieties over economic empowerment and racial authenticity.

Black Lightning symbolized a critique of black Americans who had joined the American middle class in the wake of the civil rights and Black Power movements but abandoned their less fortunate brethren still stranded in black ghettoes across America. Regardless of his successful socioeconomic upward mobility, Jefferson Pierce as Black Lightning was going to take his fight to the streets, keep it there, and do it on his own terms, a theme strikingly rendered on a cover of the *Justice League of America* comic book.[21] The cover illustration depicts Superman inviting Black Lightning to officially join the ranks of the "World's Greatest Superheroes." Black Lightning adamantly rejects the invitation. Eventually, however, Black Lightning becomes a reluctant member of the JLA and serves periodic stints as a member of a loose consortium of superheroes fittingly named the Outsiders.

In retrospect *Black Lightning* arguably tried to incorporate the quest for social relevance concerning race in the same style that O'Neil and Adams pioneered in the *Green Lantern Co-Starring Green Arrow* series. After a mere eleven issues, however, *Black Lightning* folded. The character subsequently became a sporadic guest star in other superhero titles and has periodically regained a solo title several times since. Along the way his look and his powers were constantly revamped, he became increasingly driven by more interior struggles and eventually Black Lightning was rebooted for the new millennium.[22] But for me, the original, late 1970s version is the most dynamic because it showed Black Lightning rejecting membership in the JLA and joining a group of superheroes called the Outsiders, a clear racial critique of black tokenism. Ultimately Black Lightning was a black superhero that symbolically stressed self-reliance, critiqued tokenism, and most importantly symbolized how African Americans were simultaneously insiders and outsiders in American society.

For a brief moment, O'Neil and Adams's socially relevant and thought-provoking material captivated the comic book world by having imaginary superheroes tackling real social issues. Instead of serving as escapist fodder for an increasingly jaded youth market, superheroes provided a more complex and messy morality for readers to consider without totally abandoning the ethical high ground usually associated with the American superhero. O'Neil and Adams's groundbreaking approach to superhero comics also provided a framework for comic book professionals like Frank Miller and Kurt Busiek to create gritty, emotionally unsettled, self-reflective, and socially provocative comic book superheroes and characters. Nevertheless, this type of symbolic and literal exploration of social ills, like the racism witnessed in both the Green Lantern and Green Arrow series and, to a lesser extent, *Black Lightning*, went out of fashion. Consequently, O'Neil and Adam's significance to the comic book field has overwhelmingly been consigned to the past. Often overlooked is the fact that Dennis O'Neil and Neil Adams laid the foundation for a black man to vigorously compete with his white predecessor for center stage in the contemporary American public imagination as the definitive Green Lantern.

Accepted wisdom links the Blaxploitation-film fad to the emergence and stylistic cues present in black superheroes. Ironically, during a later period, in which Blaxploitation no longer existed, the African American Green Lantern became the lead character in a major superhero comic book series. For roughly two years, from 1984 to 1986, John Stewart held the Green Lantern title and in doing so became an important outpost for black representation. Certainly John Stewart's stint as Green Lantern in the mid-1980s appeared to symbolically express contemporary white anxieties about unqualified blacks replacing whites in the workplace as a function of affirmative action. Stewart's early tenure as the black replacement for the white Green Lantern appeared to mimic such racial paranoia because he was a tentative and mistake-prone superhero that inspired doubt and indifference.[23] This changed, however, when Stewart was teamed with the exotic, auburn-colored alien female Katma Tui.[24] Their pairing provided an emotional complexity and dramatic arc to Stewart's reign as Green Lantern. Katma is a Green Lantern guide, partner, and Stewart's future wife. The blossoming romance was unique among their superhero peers. Up to that point, black superheroes rarely had a female superhero counterpart as the object of their interest and affection. Superhero coupling of that sort was traditionally reserved for white superheroes, like Mr. Fantastic and Sue Richards, the Wasp and Hank Pym, Scarlet Witch and Vision, Cyclops and Jean Grey, along with Green Arrow and Black Canary.

The animated television series *Justice League/Justice League Unlimited* (2001–2006) provided a similarly complex version of John Stewart. In the *JL/JLU* series, Stewart was one of several members of the superhero team, yet his character was fully fleshed out due to the brilliant foresight and writing of Dwayne McDuffie. He was even given a signature characteristic: Stewart's eyes have a green glow as a consequence of heavy exposure to the radiation emitted from the green power ring. Across sixty-odd episodes, considerable screen time, story arcs, and character development are devoted to Stewart's Green Lantern. He is also shown with several different love interests: his past relationship with Katma Tui is revisited, and he gets tangled in a love triangle with Vixen and Hawkgirl. This type of character development remains extremely rare for a black superhero sharing the narrative spotlight with other prominent white superheroes. For example, in the long-running animated series *Super Friends* (1973–1986), figures like the laughable Black Vulcan and the poorly developed Cyborg are rarely included in any superhero adventures. Accordingly, compared to the Super Friends, John Stewart's tenure as the lead Green Lantern in the comics and animated television series was quite refreshing. The *Green Lantern: Mosaic* (1992–1993) series is arguably the only other version of John Stewart that was dynamic and interesting. This incarnation of John Stewart was one of the most experimental expressions of superhero blackness ever represented.

The black ring-slinger of the *Mosaic* series was literally light years away from the original John Stewart in style and the field of action. In *Mosaic*, Stewart did not just occasionally venture into space—he relocated there, on the planet Oa, located at the center of the universe. There he battles with various alien creatures to save worlds. Later he becomes a Guardian of the Universe, a godlike entity responsible for protecting life. Although the intergalactic nature of these narratives placed Stewart in various alien milieus and distant planetary locations, the series reads like an existential meditation on black racial identity in America. The inaugural issue and the impressively complex and compelling fifth issue are notable for how they poignantly dialogue with the wonderfully peculiar burden of being a black man in America.[25] The latter has Hal Jordan engage in an epic battle inside Stewart's mind, confronting the various interdependent racial identities that are part and parcel of Stewart's real self. The *Mosaic* title only ran for eighteen issues, but each one reads like a chaperoned acid trip through a wonder world of Dadaist imagery and beat poetry. The beautifully bizarre *Mosaic* presented one of the most daring and complex representations of Afrofuturistic blackness of the time and arguably since. On this distant terrain John Stewart is a cosmic version of the prodigal son, a black star-child returning to his galactic beginnings.

Notwithstanding the avant-garde version of the *Mosaic* John Stewart, his character is also significant in a very traditional sense. Stewart affirms the Green Lantern mythos. In the DC Comics universe, the Green Lantern Corp exists as an intergalactic force comprised of various types of life forms that patrol and protect various sectors of the cosmos. They are governed by a group of diminutive old men with white hair called the Guardians of the Universe. Most importantly, various Green Lanterns of humanoid and alien forms all work together to serve the general good of all living beings under their overarching organization. In this sense, the Green Lantern Corps offers a model for how racial and ethnic diversity should function in America. Admittedly the type of utopian diversity signaled in the Green Lantern Corps is not completely unique. Most notably the original *Star Trek* television series, along with subsequent television and film spin-offs, pioneered the type of science fiction multi-species and racial unity suggested in the Green Lantern comic books.[26] Similarly, the interspecies makeup of the Green Lantern Corps symbolized a utopian form of cultural pluralism. Yet the intergalactic morality and multi-species membership suggested by the Green Lantern Corps is fully realized in terms of race and is anchored in the real world with the inclusion of a black man in their ranks. In this manner, Stewart's racial symbolism has remained fairly stable since his mid-1980s manifestation, and the character basically articulates an integrationist, albeit culturally pluralistic, ethos.

The aggressive and strident Black Power identity politics Stewart originally symbolized and the contemplative racial existentialism he embodied in *Mosaic* have faded into relative obscurity. But the John Stewart character of the comics and animation series has become one of the most traditional and successful symbols of racial diversity, and can be considered a mainstream superhero. A testament to Stewart's foothold in the mainstream is the fact that several different versions of his toy action figure were made, a difficult test for any black superhero. Nonetheless, the white Green Lantern has mounted a definitive comeback.[27] Not only has Hal Jordan regained his power ring in the comic book universe, but a film adaptation of *Green Lantern* looms on the horizon, which is sure to establish the original white character as the definitive emerald knight.

John Stewart and, to a lesser extent, Black Lightning owe their emergence to the narrative gamble that the *Green Lantern Co-Starring Green Arrow* title represented. Unfortunately, they were not paired to take on various social issues like their predecessors. Instead, they symbolically engaged broader racial issues on their own. But imagine if John Stewart and Jefferson Pierce had teamed up like O'Neil and Adams's Green Lantern and Green Arrow of the early 1970s. Stewart and Pierce together in one comic book would read like a superhero version of Chester Himes's Harlem detective duo Coffin Ed Johnson and Gravedigger Jones. John Stewart would symbolize black integration into the mainstream, and his Black Lightning peer would take a more strident position about American race relations, in line with a black nationalistic set of cultural and political talking points. Stewart and Pierce would traverse the American urban landscape fighting bad guys, engaging in deep discussions about the black community, commenting about discrimination in their civilian identity, and arguing over their tastes in music, women, and sports.

Despite existing in separate realms, when John Stewart and Black Lightning are contrasted, a very striking picture still emerges concerning what they communicate about race. Both the black Green Lantern and the campy Black Lightning of the late 1970s were symbolic signposts that respectively masked continuing racial anxieties born of Black Power and affirmative action. In the end, however, John Stewart, the African American Green Lantern, moved significantly away from the overt racial symbolism that Black Lightning continues to articulate. The narrative arc of the former easily dovetails with a post-civil rights sensibility, or possibly a post-racial sensibility, despite that label being carelessly bantered about in the America of today. To the character's credit, however, the racial transcendence, ascension, and acceptance of John Stewart as a formidable Green Lantern symbolically suggest a desire for the destruction of rigid notions of racial hierarchies in American society. Paradoxically, in the DC Comics universe, such racial transcendence only appeared viable in the far reaches of other galaxies, a setting John Stewart is constantly navigating as a member of the Green Lantern Corps. I suspect, however, if O'Neil and Adams had their way, he would be headed back home to Earth in a hurry.

NOTES

1. Gina Philogene, ed. *Racial Identity in Context: The Legacy of Kenneth B. Clark* (Washington, DC: American Psychological Association, 2004).
2. See William H. Foster III, *Looking for a Face Like Mine* (Waterbury, CT: Fine Tooth Press, 2005); Jeffrey Brown, *Black Superheroes, Milestone Comics, and Their Fans* (Jackson, MS: University Press of Mississippi, 2000), 3–4; and see Frantz Fanon, *Black Skin, White Masks* (London: Paladin, 1970), 145–146, for a severe appraisal of the power that comics and film have to promote and inculcate the audience as to the appropriateness of white racial supremacy as a mode of social organization. In his psychoanalytical manifesto on race, Fanon mentions how the superhero figure of Tarzan the Ape Man and various comics function to reinforce real racial hierarchies in the world in which whites repetitively imagine victory over the forces of evil, often represented by blacks and other racial minorities.
3. See Bart Beaty, *Fredric Wertham and the Critique of Mass Culture* (Jackson, MS: University Press of Mississippi, 2005); and see Bradford W. Wright, *Comic Book Nation: The Transformation of Youth Culture in America* (Baltimore: Johns Hopkins University Press, 2001), 159–160, for a thorough examination of the power and place of superhero comics in American society and a detailed discussion of Dr. Wertham's impact on the comic book industry.
4. Wright, *Comic Book Nation*.
5. Jacques Ellul, *Propaganda: The Formation of Men's Attitudes* (New York: Vintage, 1973); Joseph Klapper, *The Effects of Mass Communication* (New York: Free Press, 1960); Shearon A. Lowery and Melvin L. DeFleur, *Milestones in Mass Communications Research: Media Effects* (New York: Longman, 1995).
6. Don Slater, *Consumer Culture and Modernity* (London: Pluto Press, 1999), 164.
7. Stuart Hall, "Encoding/Decoding," in Simon During, ed. *The Cultural Studies Reader* (New York: Routledge, 1999), 507–517; Ian Ang, *Desperately Seeking the Audience* (London: Routledge, 1991).
8. E. Danticat, "Interview with Junot Diaz," *Bomb Magazine* #101 (Fall 2007), 88–95.
9. Wright, *Comic Book Nation*, 224–251.
10. *Green Lantern Co-Starring Green Arrow* #76 (New York: DC Comics, April 1970).
11. *Green Lantern Co-Starring Green Arrow* #76 (New York: DC Comics, April 1970).
12. Dennis O'Neil and Neal Adams, "A Kind of Loving, a Way of Death," in *The Green Lantern Co-Starring Green Arrow Collection Volume I* (New York: DC Comics, 2004), 57–81.
13. Dennis O'Neil and Neal Adams, "Ulysses Star Is Still Alive," in *The Green Lantern Co-Starring Green Arrow Collection Volume I*, (New York: DC Comics, 2004), 82–104.
14. *Green Lantern Co-Starring Green Arrow* #87 (New York: DC Comics, January 1971).
15. For a discussion of this trend in American political life that ranges from historical analysis to high theory see: Todd Gitlin, *The World Is Watching: Mass Media in the Making and*

Unmaking of the New Left (Berkeley: University of California Press, 1980); Guy Debord, *Society of the Spectacle* (Oakland CA: AK Press, 2006), and Chris Hedges, *Empire of Illusion: The End of Literacy and the Triumph of Spectacles* (New York: Knopf, 2009).

16. Geoffrey C. Ward, *Unforgivable Blackness: The Rise and Fall of Jack Johnson* (New York: Vintage, 2006).
17. Mike Marqusee, *Redemption Songs: Muhammad Ali and the Spirit of the Six*ties (New York: Verso, 1999).
18. Richard Reynolds: *Super Heroes: A Modern Mythology* (Jackson, MS: University Press of Mississippi, 1994), 41.
19. *Black Lightning* #1 (New York: DC Comics, April 1977).
20. *Black Lightning* #3 (New York: DC Comics, July 1977). Tobias Whale is an African American albino, but his whiteness has symbolic worth for signifying white authority.
21. *Justice League of America* #173 (New York: DC Comics, 1979).
22. *Black Lightning: Year One* #1 (New York: DC Comics, March 2009).
23. *Green Lantern* #185 (New York: DC Comics, June 1985); *Green Lantern* #187 (New York: DC Comics, June 1985).
24. *Green Lantern* #187 (New York: DC Comics, June 1985).
25. *Green Lantern: Mosaic* #1 (New York: DC Comics, June 1992) and *Green Lantern: Mosaic* #5 (New York: DC Comics, October 1992).
26. Daniel Bernardi, *Star Trek and History: Race-ing Toward a White Future* (New Brunswick, NJ: Rutgers University Press, 1998).
27. See *Green Lantern: Rebirth* (New York: DC Comics, 2007) for Hal Jordan's inspired comeback.

Comic Book Masculinity

JEFFREY BROWN

Reprinted by permission from *Black Superheroes, Milestone Comics, and Their Fans* (University Press of Mississippi, 2001), 178–188.

IF COMIC BOOK SUPERHEROES REPRESENT AN ACCEPTABLE, ALBEIT OBVIOUSLY extreme, model of hypermasculinity, and if the black male body is already culturally ascribed as a site of hypermasculinity, then the combination of the two—a black male superhero—runs the risk of being read as an overabundance, a potentially threatening cluster of masculine signifiers. In fact, prior to the emergence of Milestone, the dominating image of black superheroism was the often-embarrassing image of characters inspired by the brief popularity of Blaxploitation films in the mid 1970s. Such comic book heroes as Luke Cage, Black Panther, Black Lightning, and Black Goliath, who emerged during the Blaxploitation era, were often characterized in their origins, costumes, street language, and antiestablishment attitudes as more overtly macho than their white-bread counterparts. In many ways the Milestone characters have functioned for fans as a redressing of these earlier stereotypes, providing a much needed alternative to the jive-talking heroes of yesterday, as well as on occasion spoofing the Blaxploitation heritage and placing it in an acceptable historical context.

Yet, even today, black superheroes seem to oversignify masculinity to the point of being repositioned for the general public as humorous characters. Recently, white comic book superheroes have been seriously and faithfully adapted for such successful feature films as the *Batman* series (1989, 1992, and 1995), *The Mask* (1994), and *The Crow* (1994). Unfortunately, the same cannot be said for black superheroes. Instead of the grim, serious neo-noir success of other comic books turned into films, the only black entries in this ever-expanding movie genre have been the comedies *Meteor Man* (1993) and *Blank Man* (1994). Rather than legitimate superpowered heroes, Meteor Man and Blank Man, as enacted by Robert Townsend and Damon Wayans, respectively, are bumbling spoofs. Although well-intentioned films, with ultimate true heroism from the comedic protagonists, they are overwritten by the image of the black-costumed hero as a failure, as a buffoon incapable of exercising real power. Even the short-lived television series *Mantis* (1994), starring Carl Lumbly as a crippled black scientist who fights crime with the aid of his exoskeleton-reinforced Mantis costume, was done on such a low budget that it was considered a comedy for most comic book readers when in fact it was meant as serious science fiction drama.

Many of Milestone's most popular characters face the difficult task of playing it straight as black superheroes at the same time that they emphasize their intelligence as one of their most significant attributes, all without diminishing the masculine power fantasy so important to fans of the genre. In direct comparison to the typical Image hero, Milestone heroes are much more realistically depicted, both narratively and in portrayal of the muscular male body. "I really like the Milestone titles for what they're not, namely, Image books," a thirteen-year-old African American comics fan claimed while organizing his purchases just outside the dealers' hall of a local comic book convention. "Static and Hardwire and even Icon are a lot more realistic, not so cartoony. I mean . . . I know they're comic books but come on, look at those guys [in the Image books]; they're fucking *huge*! At least the characters at Milestone look like they could fit through a doorway." I should point out that some of the readers I have studied related to the Milestone books primarily as an alternative or a variation on the theme of black superheroes as presented in the earlier Blaxploitation-style comics of the 1970s and/or the contemporary Afrocentrist and more politically extreme books personified by the Ania publications. But the reading formation I am primarily concerned with here is the way in which many fans, both black and white, understand the Milestone line as it stands in relation to the dominant Image-style emphasis on hypermasculine/hypermuscular bodies and underdeveloped narratives featuring what one comics dealer called "brainless brawl after brainless brawl."

What Milestone comic books do is put the mind back in the body, the Clark Kent back in the Superman. Milestone does this so often with black superheroes that this allows them to develop the image of powerful black men as much more than hypermasculine brutes—"tough, but not too tough." When the conclusion to Milestone's third crossover event, "The Long Hot Summer," was published, many of the readers I had spoken with were eager to point out that the surprisingly peaceful resolution to an amusement park riot was indicative of the company's approach to brains-over-brawn. "Man, just when you thought everything was going to get really, really bloody," a fan in his early twenties explained. "Wise Son [leader of the Blood Syndicate, Milestone's multicultural supergang] gets to the park's communication systems and simply talks people out of hurting each other . . . basically shames them into being responsible for their actions."

Likewise, one fan who was a senior university student was able to recall, almost word for word, his favorite bit of dialogue from *Hardware* #9, a series featuring a black scientific genius who dons his self-constructed superarmor to fight crime. "Hardware is fighting this Alva Technologies-created female version of himself called Technique," the student recalled, "when he loses his jet pack and is falling from thousands of feet up. He grabs his pack and tries to fix it while falling, thinking, 'So here's where I find out if I'm the genius that my IQ tells me that I am.' When the pack works again, moments before becoming street pizza, he says, and this is a great line, 'Worked like a charm! Who says those tests are culturally biased?'" One especially enthusiastic and thoughtful black fan in his late teens remarked, "It's nice to see cool brothers in the comics who can think their way out of a rough spot. You know, Icon's a lawyer, Hardware's an all-purpose science supergenius, and Static, well, he's just a high school kid but he's the coolest, and I think the smartest, of all them. Yeah, I'd stack Static up against any other superhero any day. He's the man." Other readers seemed to agree: "Oh yeah, Static, he's got the best sense of humor and the thing is everybody thinks he's just this kid with wimpy lightning powers, but he's the smart one, always putting down guys bigger than him by being smarter." As an example of the preferred Milestone brains-over-brawn style, several fans chose one of Static's earliest adventures as among their favorites.

The story entitled "Pounding the Pavement," written by Robert L. Washington and Dwayne McDuffie, appeared in the August 1993 issue *Static* #3. The tale features the first appearance of a powerful new villain, Tarmack, in Milestone's fictional setting of Dakota City. As the characters in the book point out, Tarmack looks and acts like a black version of the evil, liquid metal T2000 from the popular movie *Terminator 2: Judgment Day* (1992). Essentially he is a shape-shifting mass of, well, tarmac. Usually configured in the shape of a large and muscular black male body, Tarmack can transform himself into a liquefied state or change his appendages into whatever weapon he desires, including knives, hammers, and anvils. One of Virgil (Static) Hawkins's friends describes Tarmack as "a six-foot blob of silly putty that turns into Riddock Bowe whenever it wants to." The problem is that Tarmack has his sights set on making a name for himself as the guy who takes down Static. He first tries to challenge Static to a fight by destroying a local high school hangout. Unfortunately, Static, who was tied up washing dishes at his part-time job in a nearby burger franchise, arrives too late to fight but in time to rescue bystanders trapped in the building's rubble.

At school the next day, while Virgil is asking his friends to describe Tarmack, word comes out that "the guy who trashed Akkad's is at the playground calling Static out!" Tarmack taunts Static's masculinity, calling him a coward unless he shows up to fight. "Static! Are you deaf, or just afraid?" Tarmack bellows while tearing up all the rides at the playground. "Hidin' behind yo' ugly *momma* won't help boy!" Making up an excuse about having asthma and the excitement being too much for him, Virgil sneaks off to change into his Static costume and returns to confront Tarmack with his usual wit. "Hey, Hatrack," Static calls, "let's work this out over coffee, some cappuccino for *me* . . . a nice cup of silt for *you!*" They proceed to battle for a while with neither gaining the upper hand, then, when Static proves more concerned about the safety of innocent bystanders than with the contest, Tarmack dares Static to show up at a deserted parking lot at midnight in order to decide who's the toughest.

While riding the subway home after school, Virgil and his friends debate what will happen in the final showdown between Static and Tarmack. "I think the high 'n' mighty Static is gonna get his ass handed to him," argues Larry. "Tarmack has all the *Terminator 2* moves! Hammerhands, spike hands whatever! He can melt whatever he touches!" "Well, I think Static's gonna kick butt!" Virgil argues back, a little defensive, a little nervous. "I think you're both wrong," interrupts Frieda, the only one of Virgil's friends who knows his secret identity. "Static's too smart to fall for such an obvious trap."

"That guy's too dumb to set such an obvious trap, or any trap. Static'll fade 'im," Virgil counters good naturedly. "You think ol' stinky goo head is out of Static's league?" "He's older! And Bigger! Static should leave him to Icon!" Frieda warns. "Listen," Virgil confides to Frieda under his breath. "I know it's dangerous. I'm not buying into this anymore than you. But I've got two things he doesn't. A brain . . . and a plan."

Later that night, in the Avalon Mall parking lot, a lone and angry Tarmack bellows, "Static! It's ten after midnight! If you're hidin', you best come out now!" Tarmack spins around just in time to see a trench coat-clad figure surf to the ground on electrical currents. "That's better! Turn around! I want to see your face when you die!" Tarmack screams as he winds up a massive hammerhand punch. "Have it your way toyboy . . . wha!?" As Tarmack delivers his blow the body bursts in a spray of water. Tarmack is left soaked and clutching a deflated plastic clown. "What the @#&* is this?"

"Kawarim!!!" the real Static replies from the shadows as he shoots a powerful charge of electricity through Tarmack. "Ancient Ninja art of misdirection. All you need is something some idiot could mistake for you and . . . some idiot. Guess which one you are." Angrier than ever, Tarmack chases Static across the parking lot. Suddenly, Static turns and uses his electromagnetic powers to wrap a wire fence around Tarmack. "How do you do it, you may ask. How do I stay one jump ahead of you?" Static taunts. "How you want to *die*, is all I'm askin'!" Tarmack yells, as his body begins to liquefy and escape through the links in the fence. "It's easy. You're a moron." Static continues in a fake British accent. "Also, I was here early. Several hours, in fact. Been shoppin.'"

"What're you dumping into meee!?" screams Tarmack as Static throws several canisters into the now completely liquid villain. "Old aerosol cans," Static explains. "Got 'em on sale. Freon, don't you know. Amazing what you can find in a bargain bin, huh. Wanna see what else I got?" All Tarmack can do is howl in pain and frustration as Static hurls flashbulbs and dry ice onto the quickly solidifying form lying on the ground. "Sheesh! I gotta get a better class of supervillain," Static scoffs as he spells out his plan for Tarmack. "See, I figured your liquid body and all that heat went hand in hand. So if you went through some changes, you'd burn up."

"Sslowwinn' downnn . . . brrr," Tarmack gasps. "Brr? You actually say brrr? I don't be-*lie*-ve it!" Static jokes as he pours a canister of freezing liquid oxygen over the now-defeated Tarmack. And as a final insult, Static climbs aboard a steamroller from a nearly construction site and proceeds to literally flatten Tarmack. "You are solely in need of a name change, dude. That 'Mack' thing is so 70s . . . I know what . . . how about I paint a stripe down your middle and . . . Presto! Ta-da! 'I-75, the Living Interstate!'"

Static #3 ends with the humiliating defeat of Tarmack and the arrival of Holocaust, a bigger and badder villain for Static to deal with in the next issue. On one level it is tempting to develop the case that this issue of *Static* critiques an outdated model of black masculinity. But for the Milestone fans who pointed to this specific book as a favorite, it is the story's difference from the current hypermasculine and "brainless" Image comics that makes it important. The message of "Pounding the Pavement" is clear: brains win out over brawn. Nor is this message an isolated incident. *Static* storylines have repeatedly portrayed the teenage hero as victorious because of his quick thinking. Numerous bragging and swaggering supervillains have faced Static, most of whom are clearly more powerful than him and boastfully macho about their intentions to beat him up. Yet time and again Static outthinks the baddies.

Other examples cited by readers include Static's capture of a superpowered car thief, Joyride, by pretending to lose a drag race, thus playing on the villain's ego and tricking him into stepping out of his car, whereby he loses all his powers; or Static's continual outsmarting of the recurring villain Hotstreak, who is too stupid to realize that the new hammer he wields so proudly is made of metal and thus can be controlled by Static's electrical currents. Static's form of intelligent victories is clearly read by some Milestone readers as a positive alternative to the standard formula found in the market-dominating Image-type books. "You'd never really see an Image hero winning a fight by being funny and smart enough to know dry ice and aerosol cans could knock out a serious bad guy," a thirteen-year-old *Static* fan explained. "In other comic books they're much more likely to just keep on pounding each other until the good guy rips the villain's head off, or something crazy like that."

By emphasizing the brains-over-brawn as a fundamental problem-solving technique in many of their stories, Milestone comic books suggest acceptable variations of the masculine ideal for their readers. Rather than espousing the reductionist hypermasculine might-makes-right norm of the Image books, Milestone's series continually depict heroism as a matter of intelligence first and power second, showing that, in fact, intelligence *is* the greatest power of them all. For black readers, and for nonblack readers sensitive to minority concerns, the alternative depiction of *black* masculinity bearing the attributes of both mind and body is, as one fan declared, "progressive, realistic, radical, and a much needed reworking of the African American image in the media." Although it is clear how the Static tale recounted here stresses the reincorporation of "a brain . . . and a plan" as more significant than muscles and brute force, its typical comic book superhero*ish* narrative might seem to undercut any claims made about it representing new forms of masculine ideals. It is, after all, still a relatively straightforward comic book story about two superpowered, costumed characters fighting it out. But when carried to its furthest extreme, Milestone's narrative style, which is interpreted by many readers as antithetical to the dominant hypermasculine Image style, offers alternative models.

The most apparent revisionist models are usually presented within the pages of Milestone's flagship title *Icon*. Unfairly derided by several other African American publishers as nothing more than a chocolate-dip Superman, this popular series follows the adventures of Icon (aka Augustus Freeman IV), an alien with enormous powers (yes, much like Superman's) who has lived in the form of a black man since crashing on a slave plantation over 150 years ago, and his teenage sidekick, Rocket (aka Raquel Irvin), who can fly and redirect vast amounts of energy thanks to the alien technology of her power belt. With Icon's enormous powers and incredibly straight-arrow persona, and Rocket's passion and social conscience, the series is Milestone's most emblematic affirmation of black heroism.

"They can be a little preachy sometimes," a fourteen-year-old told me when I noticed him reading an issue of *Icon* in a shopping mall's food court, "but it's really my favorite book right now. The characters are well done, and the art is usually first rate. And," he looked around a little sheepishly, "I like the stories where they show how Icon has affected normal people in Dakota, you know, inspired them." In his hands was a particularly clear example of Icon's inspiration as a promotion of how readers might pursue masculine ideals built on well-rounded self-improvement rather than the one-dimensional pursuit of hypermasculine power fantasies. *Icon* #32, "Learning to Fly," written by Greg Middleton and illustrated by Elim Mak, is really the story of Lenny, a black youth from the same projects as Icon's partner, Raquel (Rocket) Ervin. Lenny was with Raquel and the others on the night they tried to rob the house of Augustus Freeman, who, under pressure from Raquel, would later become Icon. Years after that first incident, Raquel arranges for Icon to meet and counsel Lenny, who has had trouble staying on the "straight and narrow" since that fateful night.

"I told you, you changed my outlook," Lenny tells Icon as they stroll along the city's waterfront. "But now the funds ain't what they used to be, so me and my girl Susan has been fighting. I found out she's seeing Caesar, down the block. He's *not* 'on-the-straight-and-narrow.' Of course we broke up, but . . . I don't know, man. The so-called *right thing* ain't so easy."

Icon tells Lenny a little about his own past experiences—opportunities lost, loves lost. "Uh-huh. What's your point?" Lenny asks. "Life on Earth is too brief to let us lick our wounds," Icon explains. "Only by confronting this sort of problem will you overcome it." "Ha! You can say that . . . you got *everything* going for you. I'll bet life never sneaks up on *you*. You told us to have faith in our abilities, but one rich man who can fly don't mean I can fly too," replies Lenny. "You know better than that," Icon responds. "There are enough hardships for each of us. I've had first hand experience. But we were discussing *your* abilities, and what you make of them. I can only encourage you to live up to your own potential." "Hey, I'm not going back to my old habits, if that's what you mean," a dejected Lenny says. "It's just . . . not easy . . . ya know."

A couple of pages later we see Lenny trying to live up to his own potential. A collage superimposed over Icon's masked face shows Lenny being all he can be—a virtual one-page self-help manual for readers. We see Lenny resisting the lures of gang life, excelling in school, caring for younger children, developing his body in the gym, playing wholesome sports, and even helping a little old lady with her groceries. "It ain't easy," Lenny narrates over the following pages. "Here I am, an upstanding, Icon inspired, strong black man . . . but staying on the right track helps keep my mind off my problems." Eventually, Lenny is applauded as a hero when he helps Icon and Rocket save a little girl trapped in a burning building.

Back along the waterfront, Icon tells Lenny. "I'm proud of the way you've been handling yourself. Your community is looking up to you . . . for all the right reasons. I wouldn't hesitate to say that you are something of an 'Icon' yourself." "Listen, I got a date with a new lady," Lenny says. "So all I wanted to say was . . . thanks for being there." "You deserve all the credit," Icon smiles as he shakes Lenny's hand. Lenny smiles proudly. "Be good brother."

Despite the Milestone founders discussed for avoiding the *ABC Wednesday after School Special* type of preachiness in their comic books, Icon stories such as the one recounted above veer dangerously close to this pattern. Other issues of *Icon* have dealt just as directly with issues of social responsibility, from a child's hero worship to teenage pregnancy. That these stories can be recognized by many fans as "a little preachy sometimes" but still enjoyed is the strength of the Milestone books. I do not want to suggest here that the Milestone message is incredibly well-concealed propaganda that serves a specific agenda, rather I believe that it forthrightly admits—and is recurringly interpreted as—an alternative to the traditional patriarchal masculine norm that has recently, in other comics and other media, become increasingly skewed toward absurd heights of masculinity. That these books also so consciously use black heroes as simultaneously masculine and thoughtful characters further emphasizes the novel reconstruction of masculinity and ethnic identity based on less traditional notions of gender roles and limiting racist stereotypes.

Although the Milestone line of comic books is read by many fans as an alternative depiction of masculinity in comparison to the Image books and by others (particularly those from minority backgrounds) as "a thinking black man's heroes," they are by no means the sole voices of change present in contemporary culture. Outside the superhero genre, several other comic book series, including *The Sandman*, *The Books of Magic*, *American Splendor*, and *Maus*, have offered much less hyperbolic models of masculinity. Unfortunately, unlike the Milestone books, most of the other revisionist types of comic books are classified as "Mature Reader" titles and are clearly not geared toward the traditional preadolescent consumer. Likewise, less hypermasculine, less "cool pose"-informed images of black men occasionally emerge through the cracks of popular culture. As bell hooks concludes in her chapter on reconstructing black masculinity, "Changing representations of black men must be a collective task" (*Black Looks: Race and Representation*, Toronto: Between the Lines Press, 1992: 113). For true change to take place, for stereotypes (both imposed and internalized) to be broken, alternative representations of blackness in relation to masculine ideals must come from not only comic books but also the realms of music, film, literature, education, and politics.

One of the most often cited alternative visions of black masculinity is put forth by Mitchell Duneier in *Slim's Table: Race, Respectability, and Masculinity* (1992), his acclaimed ethnography about the elderly black men who frequent Valois, a Chicago diner. The men of Valois have constructed for themselves what Duneier describes as a "community of caring." A world apart from the conventional understanding of black men caught up in masculine protests of violence, misogyny, and social alienation, these elderly men are unconcerned with—indeed, outrightly scornful of—displays of masculine posturing.

Instead, the men profiled in *Slim's Table* spend their days offering support, respect, and love for each other in social and personal matters ranging from finances to sexual relationships. Susan Bordo accurately sums up the vision of masculinity revealed in Duneier's work when she writes,

> the oppositions soft/hard, masculine/feminine have no purchase on their sense of manhood, which is tied to other qualities: sincerity, loyalty, honesty. Their world is not divided into the men and the wimps, but between those who live according to certain personal standards of decency and caring and those who try to "perform" and impress others. They are scornful of and somewhat embarrassed by the "cool pose" that has been adopted by many younger black men ("Reading the Male Body," *The Michigan Quarterly Review* 32.4: 696–737).

But whereas Duneier, Bordo, and hooks see gentle, caring men of an older generation, like those who bide their time at Valois, as an ideal that might transform a younger, disillusioned generation, today's youth are likely to find little purchase in this ideal. Although these older men have certainly lived their lives in resistance to racism and other social pressures, young men today—young black men—live in an environment where the standards of hard versus soft and masculine versus feminine are an intricate and unavoidable fact that they must come to terms with. It is here that I think Milestone's reworked image of heroic black masculinity might prove uniquely helpful.

Unlike the communal response documented in *Slim's Table*, the Milestone books do not reject the properties of the cool pose and the dominant binary logic of our culture's key masculine-feminine gender distinction. Rather, it is a *reworking* that allows pervasive and popular conceptions of gender and race to be expanded by incorporating previously disassociated concepts of softness *with* hardness, of mind *with* body. Instead of merely championing the Clark Kent side of masculine duality as a legitimate role in and of itself, the Milestone books work to infuse gentler, more responsible, and more cerebral qualities within the codes of dominant masculinity. As the Milestone principals are well aware, images of cool black characters ("cool" as measured against existing definitions of what it means to be both black and a man in Western culture) and preadolescent fantasies of superhuman abilities are undeniably ingrained in anyone who might pick up a comic book and are powerful forms through which individuals must learn to negotiate their own lives.

Rather than trying to ignore or eradicate the influential reality of existing norms of gender and race-informed patterns of behavior, the Milestone books seem to work most effectively for many of their readers by providing alternatives from within the dominant modes of discourse, by maintaining many of the fundamental conventions of comic book heroism at the same time that they expand the traditional definitions of the medium. "They're still great superhero stories," a young boy explained while his older brother waited for him at the cash register. "But they're different, ya know, and not just because of the color of their skin."

The Punisher as Revisionist Superhero Western

LORRIE PALMER

Reprinted by permission from Terrence R. Wandtke, ed. *The Amazing Transforming Superhero! Essays on the Revision of Characters in Comic Books, Film and Television* (McFarland, 2007), 192–208.

THE MAN IN BLACK WITH VENGEANCE IN HIS HEART HAS COME ROARING ONTO our movie screens in many guises, across eras and vastly different pop-culture landscapes. Whether he is a cowboy, a Jedi knight, or a comic book character, he answers some urge in us to see both darkness and light in our heroes. With two film adaptations, the Punisher, in his evolution, and with his genre roots buried deep in our collective cinematic myths, is worth a closer look. As a character, the Punisher first appeared in *The Amazing Spider-Man* #129 in 1974. Starting out as a foil for Spider-Man, he gradually evolved into a post-Vietnam anti-hero in the vein of cinematic vigilantes like the ones in *Dirty Harry* (1971) and *Death Wish* (1974). He had no superpowers or hi-tech gadgets, just his specialized Marine Corps training and his own implacable determination to right society's wrongs by eliminating the villains who perpetrated them.

The director of the 2004 film version of *The Punisher*, Jonathan Hensleigh, is mindful of a plotline "straight out of Othello" (Hutchins) which partially aligns the film's protagonist, Frank Castle, with Iago because he shrewdly plays on the jealousies of his enemy, instigating the action of the story. Both the comic and film versions revise Shakespeare's villainous prototype as an anti-hero, leaving his dark impulses intact. The film's producer talks about the character as one who has to pick up the mantle of justice when regular law enforcement fails: "It has to do with this whole system in which he has been a willing soldier not giving him the justice that he feels is deserved when killers walk free" (*Comics2Film*). Therefore, the filmmakers looked at not just action films but "crime sagas and westerns made between 1960 and 1978" (*Cinema Review*), an indication of the intricate ancestry that can be claimed by *The Punisher*. Hensleigh was inspired by the dark action films of the 60s and 70s made by directors such as Sergio Leone, Clint Eastwood, and Sam Peckinpah. Likewise, comic book writer Garth Ennis, born in Belfast and raised on John

Wayne westerns, further expands the character's genre influences in his graphic novel through violent shoot-outs enacted by an increasingly tortured, solitary hero. This author's work (along with that of the other Punisher comic book writers and artists) shapes a character arc in the Punisher that mirrors the iconography and evolution of the Western's complex protagonist.

The Western has been said to descend from multiple sources, including Victorian melodrama, an idea that lends itself to the built-in hybridity of the genre. Melodrama, in these early incarnations, was known for "its aspect of excitation, its display of violent action" and the fact that its emphasis on excitation tied melodrama to urban modernity" (Singer 149). Kenneth MacKinnon describes recent "male-oriented family melodramas" (87) such as *The Godfather* and their portrayals of the "varieties of male power within patriarchy, right down to what is clearly male powerlessness" (97). These are concepts well suited to genres that depict males in conflict with each other, as they effectively cross generic boundaries. Films in the noir tradition, such as *The Big Heat* and *Desperate Hours*, as well as quintessential Westerns, such as John Ford's *Stagecoach*, *The Searchers*, and *The Man Who Shot Liberty Valance*, are keen examples of melodramatic masculinity functioning within those thematic structures so inimical to the Western.

In *The Big Heat*, Dave Bannion, although initially allied with the forces of law and order (much like Frank Castle), becomes increasingly similar to the villains he pursues after they murder his family. Seeking vengeance, he breaks with traditional police procedure and steps into the dark, urban world they inhabit as well as into their moral ambiguity. Likewise, when the mild-mannered patriarch Dan Hilliard and his family are threatened by the violent psychopath Glenn Griffith in *The Desperate Hours*, he must find his own dark nature within that dangerous proximity. In his retaliation, he circumvents the police (who gather impotently outside), learns to use uncharacteristic psychological cruelty to inflict pain, and ultimately sends a man to his death without flinching.

In *Stagecoach*, *The Man Who Shot Liberty Valance*, and *The Searchers*, the western frontier frames similar struggles in which men enact pursuit, revenge, individualistic expressions of rough justice, and battles for family. The Ringo Kid in *Stagecoach* seeks the murderers of his father and brother. In *Liberty Valance*, Tom Doniphan (again, John Wayne) must personally dispatch the villain when the politicians, the press, and the frontier authorities only talk about a better world.

In *The Searchers*, Ethan Edwards obsessively tracks down the Comanche tribe that wiped out nearly his whole family. Ethan Edwards is a bleaker, revisionist version of the straightforward pursuit of justice sought by Ringo. Like Frank Castle, he loses part of his own better nature and flirts with true madness on his bloody trek through enemy territory. This is especially true in the Garth Ennis graphic novel *The Punisher: Born*, as Frank Castle deliberately endures three tours of duty in Vietnam because he begins to crave the violent quest, the brutality of the killing fields, and the unleashing of his internal demons. He also believes that the connection he has to his family is his only hope of being rehumanized. The codes of the Old West, self-sufficiency and personal action, thread through all these narratives and continue on, within parallel themes, in the film version of *The Punisher*. In each case, traditional forces of authority are inadequate, leaving the protagonist to enter into direct confrontation with the hostile foes arrayed against him (and a society unable to do so on its own). He must negotiate the shifting dynamics of male power and often adapt the villain's dark modus as his own in order to defeat him and gain vengeance and justice. This formula links melodrama, film noir, and the Western to each other and Frank Castle's story to them all.

In *Super Heroes: A Modern Mythology*, Richard Reynolds describes the origins of comic book characters in a way that often parallels those of the Western protagonist. For instance, he writes that "the hero is marked out from society" and that his "devotion to justice overrides even his devotion to the law" (16). Furthermore, the superhero, like the Western hero, suffers through personal issues involving family, vengeance, and guilt—especially as personified by characters like Batman, Spider-Man, Daredevil, and the Punisher. Reynolds also notes that a superhero's world "is one of mirror images and opposites" (68), a critical similarity to the movie cowboy (and his relationship with the villain) as I discuss here. Through my close reading of *The Punisher* and my simultaneous, parallel examination of the characters and storylines of several influential Westerns, I will show how key aspects of the modern superhero are prefigured in the Western film genre as well as how other generic elements from melodrama and film noir, through their own links to the Western, also color this increasingly nuanced figure.

For instance, a direct comparison in the motivation and character of both Ethan Edwards and Batman gives us an insight into the connection between the superhero and the Western hero. Reynolds could be describing both men when he says that "madness is part of Batman's special identity, and that the protagonist's obsessive character links him with his enemies in a more personal way" (67). Thus is Ethan paired with Scar, and Batman with his own antagonistic doubles such as the Joker.

Exploring film genre, Thomas Schatz writes that "the Western represents a basic story, which is never completely 'told' but is reexamined and reworked in a variety of ways" (37). Philip French speaks to the universality of this genre: "There is no theme you cannot imagine in terms of the Western, no situation which cannot be transposed to the West" (23). Throughout the history of the narrative arts, theater, literature, and myth, an oppositional structure has been the overriding method of storytelling. "The Western's essential conflict ... is expressed in a variety of oppositions" (Schatz 45). The most predominant of these was defined when Jim Kitses adapted "Lévi-Strauss's structural analysis of myth" into a "central antithesis between wilderness and civilization, from which all other conflicts derive" (Buscombe 292). Thus, the Western, with its eternal syntax of good versus evil, and especially with the moral ambiguities of later incarnations, provides a framework by which so many unexpected narratives may be examined.

The oppositions that are visible in the Western traveled forward through successive genre developments. The gangster genre of the 1930s, along with the "hard-boiled detective film" of the 1940s (Schatz 111) and the resulting evolution of 1950s film noir all build on the basic mythology of the Western as one in which a "strong hero" (Wright 138) is "divided between two value systems" (Altman 220). In most cases, "he tends to generate conflict through his very existence. He is a man of action and of few words, with an unspoken code of honor that commits him to the vulnerable ... community and at the same time motivates him to remain distinctly apart from it" (Schatz 51). Our ingrained cultural notions of the Western hero as a man apart are echoes when the Punisher is described in a graphic novel as a man "above all laws, all codes, but his own" (Goodwin). His counterpoint is the villain, who can be both functional and symbolic, and who does "harm to the hero and to the society ... with impunity as far as the legal institutions of society are concerned" (Wright 65). These characters balance the narrative even when "the hero becomes very much like the men he is chasing" (Wright 156) by moving outside traditional authority and breaking the law himself. "Genre films regularly depend on ... dualistic structures" and "intertextual references" (Altman 24–25); it is through these that archetypal characters like the lone, laconic hero who slips over the line and the villain who frequently reflects that hero's darker self are threaded through our literature, our myths, and our movies. Therefore, we can follow a structural and thematic connection from Shakespeare to nineteenth-century melodrama to Westerns to film noir to present-day action films (and graphic novels along the way), right up to and including *The Punisher*.

When George N. Fenin and William K. Everson use the phrase "Le Western Noir" in their book, *The Western*, they are talking about Anthony Mann, a director "brought up on hard-bitten city thrillers" (278) who also directed several films that are considered key examples of noir-ish Westerns of the 1950s. Thomas Schatz describes how "[John] Wayne's stoic machismo and [James] Stewart's 'aw shucks' naiveté are effectively inverted to reveal genuinely psychotic, antisocial figures" (40). The result is our understanding that genre can be as unfixed as any characters wandering across a movie screen. Revisions in classic generic characterizations are what keep the form alive. And in whatever genre he comes, a film hero has a relationship with the natural world and with community in some form, and must confront the oppositions contained in these relationships. The Punisher moves within two worlds: one is the natural world, the family and its rituals, civilization. The other is the wilderness, the city, savagery. Genres such as the Western, film noir, and the melodrama contain the same oppositions, whether they are expressed through the use of a literal wilderness, an urban setting, or within domestic family space. In addition, there are often elements depicting varying expressions of ritual, along with masochism, sadism, and fetishism, within the narrative to bring deeper meaning to the relationship between the villain and the hero: to link them along an ambiguous moral spectrum and to situate them within multiple thematic oppositions. Through the use of iconic imagery, Westerns and film noir can merge with graphic novels into a single film grammar that establishes a fluid hybridity between them.

When *The Punisher* opens, it is with the flourish of a spaghetti Western. The graphics, stark white letters on a black background, are soon riddled with bullet holes as the sound of a lone trumpet dominates the score. The writer and director, Jonathan Hensleigh, thus sets up his film with cues about its origins and its influences. The surname of the protagonist, Frank Castle, is itself a dualistic element that connotes both civilized community and militaristic fortification. In order that his ultimate identity as the Punisher, a man with "antisocial status" (Schatz 49), makes more of an impact, the film first shows us his life as a happy family man who has a successful career with the FBI. He has just finished his last undercover job, a sting operation to halt the sale of an illegal arms cache in Tampa, Florida. During the mission, Bobby Saint, son of local businessman Howard Saint (played by John Travolta), is killed. It is made clear that Bobby is presented with full knowledge of the illegality of his actions. His death, however, is accidental, and Castle expresses anger afterwards at the unnecessary tragedy. He is then feted by his fellow officers in a retirement send-off before his departure for home.

Thomas Schatz describes the use of a critical doorway in *The Searchers* as a "visual motif" (76) indicating a character's relationship with civilization. Both this film and *Shane* frame their protagonists with the symbolic access points, like doors and windows, of a family space. In *The Searchers*, Ethan Edwards is filmed approaching an open door from the outside (in the film's most iconographic image) and walking away from it in the opening and closing scenes. In the latter, the mysterious gunfighter, Shane, stands outside the window of the Starrett homestead as he converses with Marian, a wife and mother who, despite their mutual attraction, he can never have, in a life he can never be part of. These scenes highlight "the hero's basic inability to pass through that doorway and enjoy civilized existence" (Schatz 76).

Frank Castle's relationship to the domestic sphere is a revision of this theme. He is initially framed, lit by bright overhead rays beaming down, in the open doorway of his family home, and, unlike the characters in the previous examples, he can enter through it comfortably. In both his working environment and his home, he is shown in these opening sequences to be a part of the world of family, institutions, and community. "He is upright, clean-living, sharp-shooting, a White Anglo-Saxon Protestant who respects the law, the flag, women and children" (French 48). He has loving relationships with his wife and young son and is looking forward to a long-awaited reunion with his extended family in Puerto Rico.

The dialectical relationship between civilization and savagery is explored in *The Punisher* through three family groups within the society depicted in the film. The Saints "represent unbridled market self-interest" (Wright 140) and yet are, on the surface, respectable. They are highly visible and wealthy; the Saint building, with its towering, cathedral-like roof, marks the city skyline as a distinctive symbol of power. Howard, his dark-haired wife, Livia, his two sons, his business associates, and his employees are shown nearly always dressed in black, which is also the color of his car. Like the Western villain, then, "he dresses in black, rides a dark horse and is doomed to die" (French 48). Thomas Schatz further describes a noir version of the Western villain, the gangster, who "must ultimately lie dead in the streets" (90), and who shows "irrational brutality . . . enterprising business mentality" (87), and a "perverse devotion to his family" (88).

This last point is evident in the dark undercurrents of the Saint family, as it is revealed that Howard jealously covets his wife, despite their genuine affection. At the first sign of something amiss, he investigates behind her back rather than simply asking her for the truth, a fatal flaw that will be exploited by Castle. This family is about status. A pair of Harry Winston diamond earrings carries a nearly Hitchcockian object power. Castle delivers his first message to Saint on the golf course of his private country club. Howard Saint's remaining son, Johnny, who was one of the assassins of the Castle family, is shown coming out of a door with a sign above it that proclaims it to be "The Best Nude Bar" in the city. Along with his deceased brother, Bobby, he is clearly not a member of the upstanding working class that Frank Castle's family is shown to be. Family life at the Saint mansion is conducted through layers of security, with bodyguards and paid lackeys at each successive perimeter that surrounds them, proving, in addition, that "the bad guys are much richer than the good guys" (Wright 139–140). They are seldom shown outdoors, especially in daylight.

The Castle family is more casual and more ordinary: picnicking, swimming, walking on the beach in the idyllic setting of Aguadilla Bay in Puerto Rico. They also have a military tradition, with both Frank and his father having served. Frank's service, his power, has remained invisible to mainstream society through his involvement with Special Operations and a Counter Terrorism Unit. He and his blonde wife, Maria, are dressed in white clothes during a romantic beach scene in which they discuss how lucky they are to have each other, to have their family. The next morning, they talk about having another child as they watch their son, William, sleep. This family is about simple pleasures. During the family reunion, which takes place on the beach in front of his parents' modest island home, kids enjoy vanilla ice cream cones, couples dance in slow motion, Frank sits quietly, tilting his head back and breathing deep, the picture of contentment, while Maria and his son explore the wildlife near the surf.

The final family structure in the film is made up of the "social outcasts" (Schatz 50) that adopt Frank after his family's death, despite his deliberate attempt to remain apart. Just as there are "three mediating figures in *Liberty Valance*," there are three characters who inhabit the isolated, run-down tenement apartment building "on the periphery of the community" (Schatz 50) that become his urban family. This dwelling is like "the Western fort manned by misfits" (French 20) and Joan, Mr. Bumpo, and Spacker Dave, like the microcosm of characters thrown together in *Stagecoach*, form a group that "represents a range of social issues" (Schatz 50) and, further, are all depicted as belonging to the working class. Joan is a waitress (like Hallie in *Liberty Valance*) who is trying to overcome an addiction to alcohol and abusive boyfriends. When we first see her, she is bent over a sewing machine working on the apron for her uniform and there is a jar of saved pennies in front of her. She is a "bruised and intelligent woman" who later speaks earnestly to Frank about a "commitment to reality" (French 143) when she points out that, in his quest for violent vengeance, he is no different than his enemies.

The heavyset Mr. Bumpo is an example of soft masculinity, with his penchant for preparing (and definitely eating) desserts while singing along to "La Donna è mobile" from Puccini's *Rigoletto*—food and opera as escape mechanisms. Dave, on the other hand, displays the badge of alienated youth, with multiple facial piercings on his eyebrow, his nose, his lower lip, and his tongue. He is estranged from the traditional support systems of parents and school. In his first scene, he is playing a computer game, scolding a figure on the screen for being a coward as well as a grave disappointment to his mother and father, hinting at personal experience. He is also the most benign example of masochism to be found in *The Punisher*.

This family is about sanctuary and, despite their outsider status, provides a human element to the nearly machine-like Frank Castle. They are comic relief, music, food, and loyalty in his cold world, whether he wants them or not. Furthermore, as in *Stagecoach*, they prove that "those who display the most nobility are the social outcasts" (Fenin 238). When Castle is in trouble, it is this new family that comes to his rescue, a revision of both the "classic" and "vengeance" hero in Westerns who "can take care of himself . . . and needs no one" (Wright 138).

Thus, these three family groups embody the Western's "essential conflict between civilization and savagery" (Schatz 48), with the Saint family on the savage side and the two families of Frank Castle on the civilized side. The urban setting of Tampa is the wilderness, the "contested space where forces of social order and anarchy" (Schatz 83) collide, and it contrasts with the natural world specifically associated with Frank Castle and his family structures. In the first scene with his son, he talks to him in the lush, green back yard of the family home. Later, there is the seaside family reunion. Finally, when he first drives up to the ugly tenement building where he will be living, the master shot reveals it to be located in a bleak, underdeveloped neighborhood next to a sad and scraggly empty lot. However, in the next shot, Joan is shown digging in the dirt, planting flowers, surrounded by a verdant patch of green next to the brick edifice of their home, as she turns to watch his car pull in. The city, as wilderness, is emphasized by long shots of the skyline dominated by towering vertical structures that bring to mind John Ford's favorite shooting location in Arizona's Monument Valley, "where awesome stone formations reach up to the gods but the desolate soil around them" (Schatz 47) is not arable enough to support the community that lives there. This isolated building is like the hardscrabble little settlement that tries to coax a living from the edge of the wilderness.

These oppositions are further demonstrated through the concept of high culture versus low culture. The strains of a Puccini opera accompany the most elaborate fight scene in *The Punisher* when Frank is nearly pummeled to death by a 6'11", 310–pound character known as "the Russian," a villain hired by Saint to kill him in a scene first enacted in Garth Ennis's "Glutton for Punishment" chapter of *Welcome Back, Frank*. Good guys in both *Tombstone* (1993) and *The Man Who Shot Liberty Valance* recite the same ideas in the "St. Crispin's Day" speech from Shakespeare's *Henry V*, with all these scenes serving to associate the forces for good with high culture. In a contrasting example, Howard Saint calls in a professional hitman, Harry Heck, from Memphis (played by country singer and actor Mark Collie) who shows up at Joan's diner with an ominous guitar case in hand. He opens it, looking directly at Castle, who is seated nearby and whose hand goes for his gun just in case the black-clad stranger does not pull out a musical instrument. Surprisingly he does and begins to sing a mournful and threatening country song that speaks of a time when Frank's time won't be his own anymore. This hired gun sports black nail polish and a tattooed teardrop by his right eye, affectations that place him squarely in the bad guy camp, and before he leaves the diner he tells Frank that he will sing the song at his funeral.

In *The Punisher*, it is through the elements of ritual, along with masochism, sadism, and fetishism, that further connections to the Western (and its generic offspring) are discernible. Ritual is depicted most notably in scenes of family meals and food that are inextricably linked with notions of family and community. The Castle family, even in so brief a period as they are onscreen, is shown sitting down to two large, communal dinners. There are toasts offered to family, the long tables are loaded with plates of food, and when assassins arrive on the scene, there is a shot of bullets shattering a large bowl of salad as the outdoor barbecue pit explodes. There are two later scenes that transfer the dining ritual to Frank's new situation. In the first, he is eating alone at a window table in the diner where Joan works and the only other patrons are Dave and Bumpo, who are eating at the counter. In the second, to show his gradual (if temporary) integration into the small group, he is interrupted in his solitary consumption of canned sardines by the invitation to have some real food with his neighbors. They sit down at a small dinette set to a regular meal of meat, vegetables and iced tea, all of which are served in retro kitchenware (frosted glasses and serving bowls in blue, yellow, and, most tellingly, tangerine and avocado) that harkens back to an old-fashioned era of nuclear families. Joan and Frank are like the parents of the two younger participants, as they all sit down at the dinner table and say what they are thankful for after such a satisfying supper.

Raising a new church in *My Darling Clementine*, the opening meal from *The Searchers*, and the predominance of the kitchen (and some extremely large plates of food) in *The Man Who Shot Liberty Valance* all speak to the presence and importance of ritual human behavior in Westerns. In contrast, the Saints are never shown eating together. After Bobby is killed, Howard, Livia, Johnny, and the family capo, Quentin Glass, sit around a glass table and toast their missing member, but there is no food in sight. They do not partake in traditional family rituals and the setting of this one table scene takes place in their nightclub, called Saints & Sinners (an appropriate expression of genre dialectics), where they are surrounded by bodyguards and strangers. It is primarily the fringes of their home that appear onscreen: the balcony, the patio, the foyer, never a kitchen area, and, aside from Bobby's burial, their own forms of ritual are done individually, not as a family. Howard goes to the office at precisely the same time every day and Livia spends every Thursday night working out at the gym, getting her nails done, and going to the movies. Each one of them performs these routines like clockwork, providing Castle with the tools he needs to destroy them. Such negative connotations of ritual, therefore, emphasize the stark difference between the Saints and the more civilized family in the tenement.

There has always been a "strong undercurrent of masochism" (French 16), along with sadism and fetishism, in Westerns, as well as film noir and melodrama. For example, in the Western films directed by Anthony Mann, the "heroes are frequently wounded in painful ways which go far beyond the obvious purpose of providing a revenge motive" and beatings are often administered "at the hands of sadistic enemies" (French 118), which is clearly the case in John Ford's film when Liberty Valance repeatedly hits, kicks, and humiliates James Stewart's Ransom Stoddard. The horse head scene in *The Godfather*, is a perfect blend of gangster sadism and Western semantics within a melodramatic family saga. In *The Punisher*, Howard Saint kicks at the prostrate lackey who led his son Bobby into the trouble that got him killed, then shoots a leg out from under another employee before killing him with two additional bullets. Livia Saint passes the decree that, not just Frank Castle, but his entire family, is to be killed to avenge Bobby's death. Later, after Castle has planted some incriminating evidence, Howard draws out the murder of his best friend and closest associate, Quentin, by slapping him, cutting his arm, and stabbing him several times as the man begs to know why. Furthermore, he invokes the name of Jim Bowie, who died at the Alamo, as he copies that frontiersman's ritual of kicking aside the furniture before a fight. Later, as lightning crashes, he is equally cruel to his wife for her perceived affair with Quentin (who, unbeknownst to her husband, was gay) before he throws her off a bridge to land in front of an oncoming train (a twist on the old melodramas where a righteous woman is on the railroad tracks). For his part, Quentin tortures young Dave by pulling out all the studs and small hoops that adorn his face in an effort to get him, or Bumpo, to tell them Castle's location. In their determined silence, with Joan hiding an unconscious Frank in a freight elevator beneath their feet, the makeshift family proves as heroic as any western hero.

Frank, through the bullet scars and the superhuman beatings he endures throughout, is a figure with both literal and "symbolic wounds" (French 118) that position him "between subject positions of mastery and being mastered, sadism and masochism—and thus between traditional masculinity and femininity" (MacKinnon 86). This dualism leads logically from the division of "nineteenth-century stage melodrama into 'melodrama of action' and 'melodrama of passion'" (MacKinnon 94) to a film such as *The Punisher* in which both of these elements play out. Likewise, in the graphic novel *Welcome Back, Frank*, writer Garth Ennis has a drunken doctor (shades of Doc Boone in *Stagecoach*) work on Castle after a brutal shoot-out. The doctor itemizes the weaponry and the wounds: "Six magnum loads . . . Massive tissue damage, punctured lung, three broken ribs, fractured sternum, more blood out of you than in" (Ennis). The specificity of pain here points to Frank's doubled status as both a vulnerable, broken body and a nearly invincible warrior—a living embodiment of action and passion.

The body of Thomas Jane, in the character of the Punisher, is fetishized in this film adaptation, along with his weapons and his car. He is frequently filmed in fragments, with his biceps, his thighs, his lean waist, shown in various poses as he wraps himself around the engine of his car while rebuilding it or as he straps on various weaponry. He is shown to wear guns, virtually clothing himself in them in the way that female characters are often filmed putting on suggestive attire. The camera tracks slowly over his collection of military ordnance: grenades, arrows, shells, a high-tech bow, and multiple guns. He is equated with all this hardware, even with machines, as close-ups of his arms and hands combine with both engine and weapon components to fill the frame. Likewise, in the comic book *The Punisher: War Zone*, Frank Castle's body is emphasized, depicted as overtly male, even homoerotic, sitting on his unmade bed clad only in underwear. His biceps are flexed, his calf muscles bulging, and his chest, back, and arms are covered in hair. The warrior's body, then, is a fetish symbol just like his weapons, especially every possible permutation of the gun. As a visual medium, the Punisher graphic novels are able to foreground the image of the gun through the exaggerated perspective found, for instance, in the artwork of Tim Bradstreet and Steve Dillon. Castle's guns are often drawn as they thrust toward the reader, enlarged and at a downward angle, emphasizing the Punisher's dominant stature. They are prominent in both the text and the art, clearly designated as fetish items.

The naturalness of Castle's earlier associations and his penultimate involvement with weapons and battle as "an archangel without wings, a superman whose main interest on this earth is to redress wrongs" (Fenin 30), comes down to a key opposition. "Because the Westerner exists on the periphery of both the community and the wilderness, he never loses touch with either world" (Schatz 51). The way Ethan understands Indian burial rituals in *The Searchers*, and the way that Bannion's capacity for violence comes to rival that of Vince Stone's in *The Big Heat*, is paralleled here with the symbolic ability possessed and utilized by Frank Castle. When he arrives in Saints & Sinners for his final showdown with Howard Saint, he spends several minutes in the woods nearby, a natural, outdoor space, fitting himself with guns, explosive devices, and a bow and arrow. Like the Indians in Westerns, he is skilled at this most stealthy of attacks. And like many examples of the Western genre, we hear the *phsst* of the arrow before we see it strike its first target, a guard outside the club. As he falls downward, out of the frame, we see Castle in the far distance firing his weapon from an elevated position, as Native Americans were often depicted doing from the bluffs and mountains of the Old West.

Interestingly, the second shot of Castle shooting his bow and arrow is done using the kind of iconographic pose one would associate with Robin Hood, not an inappropriate comparison because he later leaves behind money he has stolen from Saint's business for his three low-income neighbors. Iconography plays a large part in our relationship with genre films, especially as it regards the Western hero with "his horse, his gun" (Buscombe 286) and the tense shoot-out on Main Street. The composition of the shots in *The Punisher* depicting two showcase shoot-outs copies those used in virtually every example of the scene ever filmed. Castle, wearing a long black duster, pulls back the edge of his coat over his holster: "he wears a gun on his thigh" (Buscombe 203) and his hand is shown in close-up, hovering over it, ready to draw. The two men facing him do the same and there is a series of head shots and eyeline matches as they assess each other. When Castle gets the draw and fires two guns at once, spent shell casings are ejected past his head in a flurry of firing and his enemies are lifted off their feet in slow motion photography that is "as stylized, graceful and artfully choreographed as a ballet" (French 116), an effect that has been part of cinematic screen violence since Arthur Penn's *Bonnie and Clyde* and Sam Peckinpah's *The Wild Bunch*. Gangsters and cowboys tend to die well on film.

It is through iconographic symbols that further thematic connections can be made within the combined Western-superhero canon. For example, the set design in *The Punisher* forms a link to another, more mainstream superhero. In one of the nightclub scenes, there is a live band playing and behind them is a replica of the rotating double rings that are used in the trial scenes on Krypton in *Superman* and *Superman II*. These rings are the site of judgment, of justice, in *Superman* and, in their echo here at Saints & Sinners, ultimate evoke a similar image. Meaning-through-symbolism abounds in Westerns through icons such as the white hat (the good guy), the horse (the Old World), and the train (the New World, intruding).

In *The Punisher*, Frank Castle wears a t-shirt that his son gave him on the day he died. It is black with a white skull face on the front, which comes to symbolize the part of him that died with his family as well as his own eventual status as a bringer of death to those he hunts. Young William told him that it would "ward off evil spirits" and it becomes his dark identity when he goes into battle. In Ennis's *The Punisher: Born*, the white skull illustrates this duality by speaking to Frank Castle as an external voice, Death itself, and at the same time represents his own internal darkness. The film adaptations of other comic book heroes also use distinctive symbols such as the illuminated Bat signal in *Batman* and the flaming avian outline left behind by *The Crow* (both are, likewise, vengeance narratives). These later superhero films illustrate a shift from idealistic heroes with simple, more ideological goals ("Truth, justice, and the American way" in *Superman*) to personal, darker-themed, revisionist revenge tales. This transition mirrors the one that occurred in the Western film genre, as embodied in the character arcs found from *Stagecoach* to *The Searchers* and on through the nihilism of the Western's later cycle found in *The Wild Bunch* and *High Plains Drifter*.

This dark evolution of the Western genre is described by Thomas Schatz when he writes that legendary Western director John Ford "deconstructs and critiques" (77) the myths of the frontier, myths that he himself helped create in early Westerns like *Stagecoach*. Gung-ho Manifest Destiny and jingoistic ideologies gave way to cynicism and a fragmentation of Western heroes as they began to fight against even their own mythic identities. The cowboys themselves grew darker, more violent, and more divided within themselves in just the same way that comic book vigilantes, like the Punisher, would. Thus, the public personas and the secret identities of superheroes are the modern enactment of this evolving cultural representation.

In the same way that so many of these film genres are connected, so too are questions of fetishism and iconography to style, and they all find their culmination in visual aesthetics. "Really, it is not violence at all which is the 'point' of the Western movie, but a certain image of a man, a style, which expresses itself most clearly in violence" and "to work out how a man might look when he shoots" (Warshow 203). There is an element of this idea playing out when Travis Bickle practices pointing his gun at a mirror in *Taxi Driver*, itself a hybrid of influences which include film noir and Westerns, most notably *The Searchers*. In Amy Taubin's comprehensive exploration of *Taxi Driver*, she describes screenwriter Paul Schrader's and director Martin Scorsese's conscious, deliberate use of John Ford's Western as "the ur-text" for their film (19). When Travis points his gun at the mirror, examining how he looks in that pose, he is linked to the John Wayne character: "Ethan, the lone wolf, becomes Travis, the psychopath, trying to work out on his own what it means to be a man" (Taubin 20). The legacy of the Western gunslinger is fragmented within Travis, "who has problems with boundaries and with splitting" (Taubin 22) in his identification so that his own reflection is part pure image and part meaning, to him and to us. In other words, through the genre conventions of the Western and our own expectations as honed by those conventions, the image of a man with a gun is imbued with cultural, historical meaning. He, as a character, is made mobile across multiple genres and, in the case of the graphic novel, multiple media as well. Artist Steve Dillon, in *Welcome Back, Frank*, draws the Punisher in such a way that we see the Western hero, deliberately and clearly. In a Chapter 1 panel, he stands alone in the frame, wearing a long duster coat, with a holster strapped to each thigh, and a gun in his hand. All at once, we are looking at a revisionist cowboy.

Finally, *The Punisher* evinces a lineage to film noir through several elements, most notably through the use of deep space, glass imagery, wet surfaces, and oblique lines. In the aforementioned Robin Hood–inspired shot which takes place in the nightclub, there is deep horizontal and vertical space behind Frank Castle as he pulls back his bow; when we see Howard Saint enter the club, he is filmed through a wire railing that is rendered as oblique lines cutting across our field of vision. The walls and ceiling of his upstairs lounge area are composed entirely of a grid-like design of lines that also appears oblique from our perspective. "Obliquity adheres to the choreography of the city [and these] oblique lines tend to splinter a screen, making it restless and unstable" (Schrader 219). The 1988 film *Die Hard* provides a visual model for this, as it effectively transplants the technique so prevalent in '50s film noir into a modern action hybrid. *Die Hard*, itself evoking a classic Western by situating its isolated hero within a confined space where he is forced to shoot it out against a superior force, depicts a world of oblique lines in the walls, elevator shafts, ductwork, a zig-zagging conference table, and stairwells that fill the frame throughout. Likewise, in *The Punisher*: outside the building, where Castle and Saint have their final confrontation, each man stands at the narrow end of key oblique lines in the pavement, which is wet. In fact, in nearly every scene shot in the city, the streets are wet (though we never see rain) as they glisten with reflections. The theme of glass furthers this noir tendency to emphasize water and reflective surfaces. Frank smashes through a glass display case to get his deceased father's guns, the glass that he has been drinking copious amounts of Wild Turkey out of drops from his hands to the floor (and falls toward the camera), the Saint building is a glass skyscraper, and Quentin's last name is "Glass." By the time the explosions and gunplay of the final battle are over, all of these ingredients have come into play as the villain lies dead in the street; an urban frontier justice has been served and decades of film language have spoken.

The oppositional structure of civilization versus wilderness has been rendered through a hybrid blend of genres, such as melodrama, film noir, and the Western, bringing them all into alignment with this recent example of action cinema. Furthermore, distinct visual iconography and psychological undercurrents emerge from all these genres through the use of symbols and in various depictions of sadism, masochism, and fetishism, expressed through the *mise en scène* and plot of *The Punisher* as it explores divergent forms of family and ritual. These characterizations of men who suffer familial loss and issues of guilt, who seek vengeance when traditional forces of authority prove unable to attain justice, who ultimately life apart from the society they protect—also enacted within the narratives of Superman, Spider-Man, Batman, and The Crow—show that the modern comic book hero is the descendent of the Western hero. Frank Castle fits the mold of a man who negotiates both society and the anarchic wilderness surrounding it. That he experiences both the intimacy of family and the violence of solitary vigilantism is a revision of the Western archetype who can only observe hearth and home from the outside. The former trait, in fact, allies him with comic book characters like Clark Kent and Peter Parker who are part of strong familial structures (despite Frank Castle's later departure from society). With the film's modern weaponry and contemporary urban setting, it further revises those found in Westerns; however, the basic narrative impetus, a search for justice, remains the same. In both cases, it is the individual, not the institutions of society, that must act to see this justice done.

Finally, the last scene in *The Punisher* provides visual and thematic cues to the film's evocative generic lineage. Castle stands alone, armed, with his car at his side on Tampa Bay's Sunshine Skyway. In voice-over, he gives notice to evildoers everywhere that they will come to know him well, not as Frank Castle who died with his family, but as the Punisher. As the screen begins to fade to black, we realize that there is a brilliant sunset behind him. Calling up all our genre experience with classic Westerns, we imagine that we can hear the beat of a horse's hooves pounding in the distance and, if we squint our eyes, the diagonal steel cables of the bridge, soaring into the peaks above him, almost look like mountains.

WORKS CITED

Altman, Rick. *Film/Genre*. London: British Film Institute, 1999.
The Big Heat. Dir. Fritz Lang. Columbia Pictures, 1953.
Bonnie and Clyde. Dir. Arthur Penn. Warner Bros., 1967.
Buscombe, Edward. "The Western." *The Oxford History of World Cinema*. Ed., Geoffrey Nowell-Smith. New York: Oxford University Press, 1996.
The Crow. Dir. Alex Proyas. Miramax Films, 1994.
Desperate Hours. Dir. William Wyler. Paramount Pictures, 1955.
Die Hard. Dir. John McTiernan. 20th Century-Fox, 1988.
Dixon, Chuck. *Punisher: War Zone*. New York: Marvel Comics, 2002.
Ennis, Garth. *The Punisher: Welcome Back, Frank*. New York: Marvel Comics, 2000.
Fenin, George N., and William K. Everson. *The Western: From Silents to the Seventies*. New York: Grossman, 1977.
French, Phillip. *Westerns*. New York: The Viking Press, 1973.
The Godfather. Dir. Francis Ford Coppola. Paramount Pictures, 1972.

Goodwin, Archie. "Marvel Super Action featuring The Punisher, #1." *The Essential Punisher, Vol. 1*. New York: Marvel Comics, 2004.

High Plains Drifter. Dir. Clint Eastwood. Universal Pictures, 1973.

Hutchins, John. "Jonathan Hensleigh, Writer/Director of *The Punisher* Interview." *Under Ground Online*. December 6, 2004. Ugo.com/channels/filmtv/features/thepunisher/jonathanhensleigh.asp.

MacKinnon, Kenneth. *Love, Tears, and the Male Spectator*. New Jersey: Associated University Presses, 2002.

The Man Who Shot Liberty Valance. Dir. John Ford. Paramount Pictures, 1962.

My Darling Clementine. Dir. John Ford. 20th Century-Fox, 1946.

"Production Notes: The Punisher." *Cinema Review 2004*. December 6, 2004. www.cinemareview.com/production.asp?prodid=2488.

The Punisher. Dir . Jonathan Hensleigh. Lions Gate Films, 2004.

"Punisher Movie Update." *Comics2Film*. October 17, 2003; December 6, 2004. www.cinemareview.com/production.asp?prodid=2488.

Reynolds, Richard. *Super Heroes: A Modern Mythology*. Jackson, MS: University Press of Mississippi, 1994.

Schatz, Thomas. *Hollywood Genres: Formulas, Filmmaking, and the Studio System*. New York: McGraw-Hill, 1981.

Schrader, Paul. "Notes on Film Noir." *Film Genre Reader II*. Ed. Barry Keith Grant. Austin: University of Texas Press, 1995.

The Searchers. Dir. John Ford. Warner Bros., 1956.

Shane. Dir. George Stevens. Warner Bros., 1956.

Singer, Ben. *Melodrama and Modernity: Early Sensational Cinema and Its Contexts*. New York: Columbia University Press, 2001.

Stagecoach. Dir. John Ford. United Artists, 1939.

Superman II. Dir. Richard Lester. Warner Bros., 1980.

Superman: The Movie. Dir. Richard Donner. Warner Bros., 1978.

Taubin, Amy. *Taxi Driver. BFI Film Classics*. London: British Film Institute Publishing, 2000.

Taxi Driver. Dir. Martin Scorsese. Columbia Pictures, 1976.

Warshow, Robert. "Movie Chronicle: The Westerner." *Partisan Review* 21 (1954): 190–203.

The Wild Bunch. Dir. Sam Peckinpah. Warner Bros, 1969.

Wright, Will. *Sixguns and Society: A Structural Study of the Western*. Berkeley: University of California Press, 1973.

Death-Defying Heroes

HENRY JENKINS

Reprinted with permission from *The Wow Climax: Tracing the Emotional Impact of Popular Culture* (New York University Press, 2006), 65–74.

MEDIA SCHOLARS DRAW AN IMPORTANT DISTINCTION BETWEEN MASS CULTURE and popular culture. Mass culture is mass-produced for a mass audience. Popular culture is what happens to those cultural artifacts at the site of consumption, as we draw upon them as resources in our everyday life. Many scholars have focused on how the same mass-produced artifacts generate different meanings for different consumers. Less has been said about the ways our relationships to those artifacts change over time, and the ways that what they mean to us shifts at different moments in our lives. This essay is an autoethnography of my relationship to superhero comics. What I have to say here is shaped by my experience of grief over the death of my mother six months ago. I had checked her into the hospital complaining of indigestion, only to discover what turned out to be a tumor in her kidney already so advanced it was no longer possible to operate. All we could do was keep her comfortable and wait for the inevitable.

I bought the comics on the way to the hospice. They were selected hastily, and even then, I felt guilty about the time it took. I was looking for something banal, familiar, and comforting at a time when my world was turning upside down. I read them intermittently as I and the other family members sat on deathwatch, the experience of the stories becoming interwoven with old family memories and the process of letting go of my mother. Retreating from the emotional drama that surrounded me, I found myself staring into the panic-stricken eyes of a young Bruce Wayne, kneeling over the freshly murdered bodies of his parents. I have visited that moment many times before, but this time, our common plight touched me deeply.

A year ago or a year from now, I would have written a very different essay, but for the moment I am trying to work through what comics might have to say to me about death, aging, and mortality.

I am hardly the first to draw such connections. In his essay "The Myth of Superman," Umberto Eco describes the monstrous quality of the superhero who is not "consumed" by time, who never grows older, who is always cycling through the same kinds of experiences, never moving any closer to death. Eco approaches this question formally; describing how the iterative structure of comics creates its own kind of temporality, which he contrasts with the always already completed action of myth or the unique events of the novelistic: "He possesses the characteristics of timeless myth but is accepted only because his activities take place in our human and everyday world of time."

The fan boy in me wants to point out all of the exceptions and qualifications to Eco's claim, starting with the fact that a whole generation of revisionist comics have sought to reintroduce death and aging into the superhero universe. The images of aging Batman and Superman duking it out in Frank Miller's *The Dark Knight Returns* comes immediately to mind, but most of these books came after Eco's essay was published and might well have been responding to his argument. Regardless, Eco understates the importance of continuity and, thus, of specific series history; to comics readers the same events may unfold again and again, but there is something distinctive about each issue, and mastering those distinctions is part of what separates comics fans from more casual readers. From time to time, the franchises build up such complex histories that they need catastrophic events—such as the Crisis of Infinite Earths—to wipe the slate clean again and allow a fresh start. Yet, such reservations aside, Eco's formal analysis hits on some core psychological truth that I want to explore on an autobiographical level.

One could understand the reading of comics as entering into a psychological space that similarly denies death and mortality, that encourages a nostalgic return to origins. Most of our stereotypes about comics fans start from the idea of arrested development, that is, that the fans have somehow sought to pull themselves out of life processes and to enjoy the same kind of iterative existence as the guys and gals in tights. Yet, I want to suggest that we cannot escape or forestall such dreaded feelings altogether, and that in their own way, both as texts and as artifacts, comics become reflective objects that help us think about our own irreversible flow toward death. In short, this is an essay about what it means to consume and be consumed by superheroes.

I am frequently so tired after the demands of my job that when I crawl into bed at night, I fall asleep too fast if I try to read prose. I move through novels at such a sluggish pace that I lose interest well before I reach the conclusion. I had found that I could maintain consciousness, however blurry my perceptions, long enough to make it through an issue of a comic. There is something energizing in the shift between text and images and in the larger-than-life stories so many comics tell. The repeated formulas of the superhero saga mean that each issue is in a sense predigested, but the most interesting contemporary writers—Brian Michael Bendis, Mark Waid, Greg Rucka, Ed Brubaker, Geoff Johns—bring a distinctive perspective or unique voice to those characters, offering me what I need to sustain my interest in these familiar characters over time.

Comics are the site of enormous diversity, innovation, and experimentation, and many of the titles I am reading this month weren't even being published a year ago; but a healthy portion of the books I buy were those I read as a kid. Nowhere else in popular culture can you find that same degree of continuity. *Star Trek*, currently the longest-running franchise on American television, goes back to the mid-1960s. The James Bond movies, currently the longest-running franchise in American cinema, go back to the early 1960s. Superman, Batman, Wonder Woman, and Captain America have been more or less in continuous publication since the 1930s or early 1940s—always fighting for truth, justice, and the American way, despite generations of readers and writers growing up, growing old, and, yes, dying in their company [Captain America disappeared in 1949, was revived briefly in 1953–54, and then again in 1963–64—*eds.*]. There are, to be sure, enormous variations in the way these characters get interpreted across those various generations, dramatic shifts in styles, successive waves of revisionism, various stabs at relevance or topicality, which mean that the comics are never in a literal sense timeless. Yet, you can go away for decades on end, find your way back to a DC comic, and get reintroduced to the protagonists more or less where you left them. It is often this hope of rekindling something we once felt that draws us aging comic fans back to these titles. It is almost as if we would lose something important in ourselves if watching Batman stalk across a darkened alley or Spider-Man swing from building to building no longer made our hearts beat a little faster.

When I remember my personal history of comics, so much of what I remember are iterative events, the routine patterns that surround comics consumption, rather than specific storylines or particular life experiences.

Curiously enough, my earliest memories of comics tie me back to my mother. When, as a fourth or fifth grader, I would stay in bed with a fever; my mother would go to the local druggist in search of Coca-Cola syrup, which according to southern folklore, was supposed to have remarkable curative powers. In this era before specialty shops and comics "subs," she would return carrying an armload of comics, selected from a large spinning rack at the center of the store. She bought more or less what she could find, so sometimes she would return with a selection of kids comics (*Baby Huey*, *Donald Duck*, or perhaps *Archie*), other times with issues of *Classics Illustrated*, and still other times with DC superheroes. I came to associate comics with the sound of my mother's voice singing me to sleep or her hands feeling my forehead. And I suspect that's why I return to them now at moments of stress.

It is hard to remember when superheroes first entered my life. I suspect it must have been 1966, the year that *Batman* first appeared on television. I was seven or eight. The series rapidly became an obsession among the neighborhood kids. One of my aunts had given me a recording of the theme music, which my playmates and I played at full volume, bouncing up and down on the bed, biffing and powing each other, and tumbling backward into the pillows. Mother had given me an old leotard, sewed a cape and cowl, and cut me a batarang out of plywood. We didn't always understand what we saw. Once we heard an announcement for a forthcoming appearance of King Tut and thought the announcer had said King Duck, and so we spent a week battling it out in the backyard with web-footed foes before discovering that there was this Ancient Egyptian guy. Who knew? My father would peer out from behind his newspaper, expressing mock horror to have discovered that Batman and Robin had died that very day—frozen to death in a giant snow cone or in some other death trap. And every time, I would fall for his joke, bursting into tears, since I could never make up my mind which side of the dividing line between fantasy and reality *Batman* stood. I suspect it bred in me both an intense desire to be able to read the paper myself and some lingering suspicion that the journalists were pulling my leg.

Some of the boys in the neighborhood formed a superhero club. I remember us swearing an oath of loyalty over a stack of comics in my treehouse. We each chose the persona of one of the members of DC's Justice League. The guy who lived across the street was unnaturally big and strong for his age and was quickly cast as Superman. The kid next door was small, wiry, and fast on his feet, and he became the Flash. I had tired of Batman by this point and aligned myself with the Green Lantern for reasons long forgotten. We each spent our weekly allowance on comics and would pass them around. I have reread some of the stories of the era, only to be disappointed. We had fleshed out their personalities through our play, and most of what I recalled so fondly wasn't to be found on the printed page. A few contemporary writers add some of that clubhouse camaraderie into their books, and for a few moments I feel as if I were back with the old gang, drinking Kool-Aid and trying to second-guess the Joker's perplexing secret code, which almost always turned out to be something you could read if you held your comic up to the mirror.

Most of those kids have disappeared from my life and rarely reenter my thoughts. One of them (Superman) tracked me down on the Internet; we got together recently. We talked in big breathless gulps about boyhood days and then suddenly, silence fell over us. We looked at each other blankly as if we were suddenly confronting not the boys we were but the middle-aged men we had become, and we ended the evening early. Neither of us has called the other since. But, we both still read comics.

As I sit down to write this, I am haunted by a curious memory—one of the few memories of comics that centers on a unique event rather than a pattern of repeated experiences. It is early summer and I am sprawled out on the floor of my family's cabin in the north Georgia mountains coloring a picture of Batman as my mother watches television across the room. I have spent most of the day thrashing about in the water pretending to be Aquaman and am now awaiting bed, when a news report interrupts the show my mother is watching to tell us that Robert F. Kennedy has been shot. Why are my memories of my mother's tears over Bobby's death so firmly linked to my memories of super-hero coloring books and fantasy play? Is it because at such a moment—which would have come when I was in sixth grade—I suddenly realized that a line separated the silly plots of the campy television series from the harsh realities of adult life? What had it meant to me as a boy to see my mother crying and not know how to comfort her?

You could say that what drew me to comics the week my mother died was nostalgia—which Susan Stewart describes as a desperate hunger to return to a time and place that never really existed, a utopian fantasy through which our current longings get mapped onto the past. Comics were comfort food, like the southern cooked vegetables my mother used to fix for me when I came home for holidays. Yet, these comics offered me little comfort. I hurt every place my mother had ever touched me and I found myself unable to separate out the comics from the memories they evoked. If comics brought me back to boyhood, then they brought me closer to an age when my mother's love had been the most powerful force in my life.

It is silly to try to explain why I read comics that week. I had been reading comics every week for some years running. I returned to comics sometime in my mid-thirties—searching for something I couldn't name at the time. A few years later, when I was diagnosed with gout, and suddenly faced the realization that I was not indestructible and inexhaustible, I found myself drawn passionately back into the world of the Flash and the Green Lantern. My recognition of my own approaching mortality drew me into the death-defying world of the superheroes, who, unlike me, never grew older, never had bodies that ached. The comics function for me as the reverse of Dorian Gray's portrait—they remain the same while my body ages and decays. And as such, they help me to reflect on the differences between who I am now and who I was when I first read them.

Again, it's not quite that simple because comics kept coming in and out of my life. To tell the story that way would be to skip over my various attempts to get my own son engaged with comics, all doomed to failure; or the way the release of the Batman films rekindled my passion for that character for a while; or my periodic raids on the comic shops to examine some title that a student brought to my attention. True that there are huge gaps in my knowledge of any given character—and whole series that came and went without my awareness—but I never really left comics. It just took me a while to admit that I wasn't wandering into the shop now and again to see what was new; I was going there every week and coming away with bags full.

I wasn't ready to come out as a comics fan. Even though my own work had debunked many stereotypes about science fiction fans, there was a side of me that still believed the clichés about middle-aged comic book readers. That stigma kept me from going down to the local comic shops and setting up my own subs folder, even though doing so would get me a significant discount on my purchases. It also prevented me from bagging, or even organizing, my comics, even though doing so was the only way to combat the clutter of having that many random issues lying around our apartment.

If I have an origin story for my passion for superheroes, I also have an origin story for my fear of becoming a comics fan. And it begins in Tom's smelly basement when I was in seventh grade and had decided I was too old for comics and ready to move on to more mature reading matter, like *Mad* or *Famous Monsters of Filmland*. Tom was a somewhat pudgy kid who lived down the street from my grandmother, and we became friends initially out of geographic accident and emotional necessity—his house was a place to go when I wanted to escape being cooped up with someone who was constantly complaining about her aging and ailing body.

Tom had just moved to Atlanta from Michigan. He read almost exclusively Marvel comics at a time when all of my other friends were committed to DC. (Tom had the last laugh since history has vindicated his tastes over ours.) We would sit in his basement and rummage through this huge mound of yellowing comics, reading late into the night by flashlight, as his two cocker spaniels snorted somewhere in the dark void around us. Every so often when we would explore his basement, we would come upon the fossilized dog turds that gave the space its pungent odor. And to this day, when I go into the dank, dark subterranean shops where comics are mostly sold, I think about Tom's basement and wonder what my foot is going to land on if I linger too long over a box of back issues.

One day in seventh grade, as we were flipping through *Incredible Hulk* comics, he told me that he thought he was gay. The next day, I blurted it out around a picnic table on a school field trip to a bunch of the other guys; and from that moment on, our friendship began to unravel until we were punching each other on the playground and getting sent to the principal's office for squirting each other with milk. I was racked with guilt about betraying his secret identity, even though I wasn't ready to come to grips with what that secret really meant—and in any case, it turned out to be a false alarm. Somehow, in a few short years, the nature of friendship had gotten much more complicated.

When I was an undergraduate, those comic-geek stereotypes got reinforced through encounters with two friends who were both comics collectors, both guilt-ridden Catholics, and both named Mark. One of the Marks was a square-jawed fellow who wanted to be Clark Kent—not Superman, just Clark Kent. What he wanted, above all else, was to be as normal as possible, to hold at bay anything unpredictable or uncontrollable. He wasn't just dull—he was desperately dull. Somehow, for him, memorizing as many facts as he could from superhero concordances was one of the ways he could bring his corner of the galaxy more fully under his control. Years later, when I began to collect comics seriously, my wife bought me some reference books at a used book sale. When we examined them more closely, we discovered Mark's name scrawled on the inside front cover. I am not sure what surprised me the most—that Mark had finally gotten rid of those books or that my interest had grown to the point that I saw a value in owning them. Was I becoming the guy I dreaded in college?

The other Mark took me to his apartment one time and showed me an entire room full of steel boxes, containing thousands of individually bagged comics backed with acid-free cardboard, and gave me a speech about how his comics would be safe and secure long after he was dead. Years later, I visited Mark in Brooklyn and sure enough, he still had all of those boxes of comics and many more. By that time, however, I wanted nothing more than to sit up all night asking him for recommendations or flipping through back issues. The mausoleum had become a library.

I fear that I have reduced Tom and the two Marks into fan boy clichés—not ready to confront the challenges of adult life, obsessed with trivia, determined to preserve their comics at all costs, and vaguely distasteful. And for a long time, those associations colored my memories and fed my own anxiety about admitting that comics were such an important part of my life. Those stereotypes are powerful forces shaping the ways we express and act upon our tastes. Yet, I have come to realize that Tom had shown better taste in comics than I did. Mark 1's encyclopedias were useful in sorting through more than forty years of encrusted DC continuity; and, as for Mark 2, collecting comics wasn't terribly different from collecting any other kind of book.

But there is a key difference. Unlike, say, leather-bound books, comics were not made to last. They were printed on cheap paper with bad ink on the assumption that they would be read and discarded. No one ever thought that people would still be reading them decades later, any more than one imagined holding onto old newspapers. Superheroes may be invincible, but comics rot. What makes old comics valuable for collectors is that so many of them have been destroyed. Every mom who threw away her son's comics increased the fortunes of those who were lucky enough to hold onto theirs. Many fans spend their entire lives—and much of their incomes—trying to recover the issues they had once discarded so casually. And so, fans become preoccupied with the challenges of preserving their collections, with forestalling their ultimate destruction.

To her credit, my mother never threw away my comics. She took them up to the lake house and left them in a drawer. Over the years, they were literally read to death. Young visitors would paw through them with peanut butter-covered fingers. Mice, emboldened by the long months when the cabin was unoccupied, would rip them apart seeking material for their nests. The staples came undone and pages would come off when you tried to read them one last time. The humidity meant that the pages got more and more waterlogged and mildewed. The sun bleached the lurid covers if you left them lying on a window ledge too long. And in the end, not a single one of the superhero books made it past my adolescent years. The *Classics Illustrated* comics were more expensive than the rest—and came with the aura of high culture—so mom treated them as sacred and eternal, not unlike the way she dealt with *National Geographic* magazines. Interestingly enough, they are the only comics from my childhood that I still possess. Despite my horror in recalling how many Jack Kirby books got ripped up when a Boy Scout troop got rained in one weekend at our cabin, I still tend to loan out my comics to my students rather than worrying about keeping them in pristine condition. I have refused to take that last step into fan boy culture. For the moment, I am more interested in reading and sharing comics than in keeping them out of harm's way. I know nothing lasts forever and you are better off really enjoying the things you love while you can.

These are simply some of the memories that passed through my head as I sat on my deathwatch. I had pushed aside *Batman*, not ready to face young Bruce's angst, and turned instead to *Spider-Man*, only to discover that this particular storyline dealt with the memories stirred up by the anniversary of Uncle Ben's death. Eco is right: Superheroes don't move closer to death; they move further away from it. Yet, death still defines the cycles of their lives; it seemed that almost every one of the comics I brought to the hospice dealt—at least in part—with childhood trauma and loss. If comics provide youthful fantasies of empowerment and autonomy, they do so by severing the ties between the superheroes and their parents. Batman takes shape in Bruce Wayne's mind as he vows vengeance over his parents' tombstones. Superman's parents send him away from a dying planet. Peter Parker, not yet aware that with great power comes great responsibility, is too self-centered to stop a crook that runs across his path, allowing him to escape and kill his Uncle Ben. What separated the villains from the heroes wasn't the experience of loss, but what they did after that loss, how it shaped their sense of themselves and their place in the world. Some were strengthened by loss, others deformed.

Most of the literature of childhood has at its heart a kind of emotional violence: we expose children through fiction to the very forces from which we seek to shelter them in real life. Whether in comics or in traditional children's literature, the most powerful theme is almost inevitably the death of or separation from one's parents. Literature helps us to cope with those fears at one level removed. Comic books help us to confront those separation anxieties by depicting their protagonists as moving beyond their initial vulnerabilities and gaining some control over their lives after such losses.

It isn't that these events occur one time in the distant past; they crop up again and again in comics, because these images of death and mourning define the character's identities. And this cycling through the moments of death rings psychologically true. In the months that followed my mother's death, I found myself returning, almost involuntarily, to memories of her final days, the way that a tongue seeks out and presses against a loose tooth—to see if it still hurts. I came away with a new understanding of why the superheroes hold onto their grief, their rage, their anguish, and draw upon it as a source of strength. At one point in my life, I read those stories to learn what it was like to have the power and autonomy of adulthood. Now, I read them to see how you confronted death and came out the other side, how mourning forces you to reassess who *you* are and what your goals are and what you owe to the people who brought you into the world. My mother's death made no sense to me; I felt only the injustice of seeing her die so much younger than I had expected; I saw only my longing to be able to communicate with her. The comics didn't take away that pain; they helped me to make meaning of it. Some parts of what I read touched places in me that were too raw to endure. The reality of my mother's death had resensitized me to fantasy violence, making it hard to pull back from what the protagonists were feeling. Yet, at the same rime, reading those books helped me to realize the common human experience of loss and recovery.

Comics are made to rot and decay. They are such a vital part of our developing imaginations that we try to preserve them forever, but despite our best efforts, they slip through our fingers. The comics of our childhood are impossible to recover. Even if you hold onto your comics, the stories on the page are not the same ones you remember, because our memories are so colored by the contexts within which we encountered them, and especially by the ways we reworked them in our imagination and our backyard play. Eco's claim that superheroes are not "consumed" by death helps to explain why we imagine them as a point of return to bygone days. Yet, even though we change and they don't, we find something new and different each time we come back to these stories. In this case, the death-defying superheroes helped me to model a process of letting go.

CONTRIBUTORS

WILL BROOKER is director of research, film, and TV at Kingston University, London. He is the author or editor of eight books on popular culture, cultural context, and audience. *Batman Unmasked: Analysing a Cultural Icon* (2000) is continued in *Hunting the Dark Knight: 21st Century Batman* (2012).

JEFFREY BROWN is an associate professor of popular culture at Bowling Green State University, where he serves as the coordinator of graduate studies. He is the author of *Black Superheroes: Milestone Comics and Their Fans* (2000).

SCOTT BUKATMAN is an associate professor of art history at Stanford University. His books include *Terminal Identity: The Virtual Subject in Postmodern Science Fiction* (1993), *Blade Runner* (1997), and *Matters of Gravity: Special Effects and Supermen in the Twentieth Century* (2003).

JOHN G. CAWELTI taught literature at the University of Chicago for many years, where he helped pioneer the scholarly study of popular culture. His books include *The Six Gun Mystique* (1971), *Adventure, Mystery, and Romance: Formula Stories as Art and Popular Culture* (1976), and *Mystery, Violence, and Popular Culture* (2004).

PETER COOGAN is the founder and director of the Institute for Comics Studies, as well as the cofounder and co-chair of the Comic Arts Conference. He is the author of *Superhero: The Secret Origin of a Genre* (2006).

JULES FEIFFER is a cartoonist, playwright, screenwriter, novelist, children's book author, and cultural journalist. He was the first cartoonist commissioned by the *New York Times* to create comic strips for their op-ed page. His books include *Passionella* (1957), *Harry the Rat with Women* (1963), *The Great Comic Book Heroes* (1965), *Tantrum* (1979), and *Backing into Forward: A Memoir* (2010).

CONTRIBUTORS

HENRY JENKINS is professor of communication, journalism, and cinematic arts at the University of Southern California. His books include *Fans, Bloggers, and Gamers: Media Consumers in a Digital Age* (2006), *The Wow Climax: Tracing the Emotional Impact of Popular Culture* (2007), and *Convergence Culture: Where Old and New Media Collide* (2008).

ROBERT JEWETT is visiting professor of New Testament at the University of Heidelberg, and the coauthor (with John Shelton Lawrence) of *The Myth of the American Superhero* (2002) and *Captain America and the Crusade Against Evil: The Dilemma of Zealous Nationalism* (2003).

GERARD JONES is a freelance comic book writer and author. His books include *The Comic Book Heroes: The First History of Modern Comic Books* (1996), *Killing Monsters: Why Children Need Fantasy, Superheroes and Make-Believe Violence* (2003), and *Men of Tomorrow: Geeks, Gangsters, and the Birth of the Comic Book* (2005).

GEOFF KLOCK is an assistant professor of literature at the Borough of Manhattan Community College. He is the author of *How to Read Superhero Comics and Why* (2002) and *Imaginary Biographers: Misreading the Lives of the Poets* (2007).

KARIN KUKKONEN is a postdoctoral research fellow at St. John's College, Oxford University. Her research focuses on the interactions between literature and the human mind. She is the author of *Storytelling beyond Postmodernism: Fables and the Fairy Tale* (2010).

ANDY MEDHURST is a senior lecturer in media, film, and cultural studies at the University of Sussex. His books include *Lesbian and Gay Studies: A Critical Introduction* (1997), *A National Joke: Popular Comedy and English Cultural Identities* (2007), and *Coronation Street* (2008).

ADILIFU NAMA is associate professor and chair of the African American Studies Department at Loyola Marymount University. He is the author of *Black Space: Imagining Race in Science Fiction Film* (2008) and *Super Black: American Pop Culture and Black Superheroes* (2011).

WALTER ONG (1912–2003) was a Jesuit priest, a professor of literature, and a philosopher. He served as the president of the Modern Language Association in 1978–1979. His books included *Frontiers in American Catholicism* (1957), *The Barbarian Within* (1962), and *Rhetoric, Romance, and Technology* (1971).

LORRIE PALMER is a PhD candidate in the Department of Communication and Culture at Indiana University-Bloomington. Her research interests include movie genres, global cinema, and representations of masculinity.

RICHARD REYNOLDS is a senior lecturer at the Central Saint Martins College of Art and Design in London. He is the author of *Super Heroes: A Modern Mythology* (1994), as well as a number of academic papers and non-academic works on comics and other aspects of contemporary culture.

TRINA ROBBINS is a comics artist and writer, and cultural historian. Her first comics appeared in the *East Village Other*, and she helped establish the first all-woman comic book, *It Ain't Me, Babe Comix*, in 1970. Her books include *Women and the Comics* (1983), *A Century of Women Cartoonists* (1993), *The Great Women Superheroes* (1997), and *The Brinkley Girls: The Best of Nell Brinkley's Cartoons from 1913–1940* (2009).

LILLIAN ROBINSON (1941–2006) was the principal of the Simone de Beauvoir Institute and a professor of women's studies at Concordia University. Her books included *Sex, Class, and Culture* (1978), *Modern Women Writers* (1996), and *Wonder Women: Feminisms and Superheroes* (2004).

ROGER B. ROLLIN taught literature and popular culture at Clemson University for many years. He is the author of *Robert Herrick* (1992). He served as the president of Popular Culture Association of the South, and president of the American Culture Association.

JOHN SHELTON LAWRENCE is professor emeritus of philosophy at Morningside College. He is the coauthor (with Robert Jewett) of *The Myth of the American Superhero* (2002) and *Captain America and the Crusade against Evil: The Dilemma of Zealous Nationalism* (2003).

GLORIA STEINEM is an internationally renowned feminist, journalist, and political commentator. She cofounded *Ms.* magazine in 1971 and was inducted into the National Women's Hall of Fame in 1993. Her books include *Outrageous Acts and Everyday Rebellions* (1983), *Marilyn: Norma Jean* (1986), and *Moving beyond Words* (1993).

JENNIFER STULLER is a professional writer and critic, specializing in gender and sexuality in popular culture. She is the author of *Ink-Stained Amazons and Cinematic Warriors: Superwomen in Modern Mythology* (2010).

CONTRIBUTORS

FREDRIC WERTHAM (1895–1981) was a German-American psychiatrist who wrote for both scientific journals and the popular press. He authored several widely reviewed books, including *The Brain as an Organ* (1934), *The Circle of Guilt* (1956), *A Sign for Cain: An Exploration of Human Violence* (1968), and *The World of Fanzines: A Special Form of Communication* (1973). His best-known book was, of course, *Seduction of the Innocent* (1954).

PHILIP WYLIE (1902–1971) was a best-selling midcentury author whose books included *Gladiator* (1930), *When Worlds Collide* (1933), *A Generation of Vipers* (1942), and *An Essay on Morals* (1947). He was a prolific novelist, short story author, screenwriter, and essayist.

Editors' Bios

CHARLES HATFIELD is an associate professor of English at California State University, Northridge. He specializes in word and image studies, comics and graphic novels, children's literature and culture, popular culture, and the literature of the fantastic. He has published widely on various aspects of comics and cartoons, for such journals as *ImageTexT*, *English Language Notes*, the *Children's Literature Association Quarterly*, *Transatlantica*, and the *Comics Journal*. He is the author of *Alternative Comics: An Emerging Literature* (2005) and *Hand of Fire: The Narrative Art of Jack Kirby* (2011). He is currently working on a study of the graphic novelist Eddie Campbell.

JEET HEER is writing a doctoral thesis on the cultural politics of *Little Orphan Annie* at York University in Toronto. He is the coeditor of *Arguing Comics: Literary Masters on a Popular Medium* (2004) and *A Comics Studies Reader* (2009). With Chris Ware and Chris Oliveros, he is editing a series of volumes reprinting Frank King's *Gasoline Alley*, four volumes of which have been published by Drawn and Quarterly. He is also the editor of Clare Brigg's *Oh Skin-nay* and is writing the introductions to a multivolume series reprinting George Herriman's *Krazy Kat*. His essays have appeared in the *Virginia Quarterly Review*, the *Literary Review of Canada*, the *Boston Globe*, Slate.com, and numerous other publications.

KENT WORCESTER is a professor of political science at Marymount Manhattan College. With Jeet Heer, he is the coeditor of *Arguing Comics: Literary Masters on a Popular Medium* (2004) and *A Comics Studies Reader* (2009). He is also the author of *C.L.R. James: A Political Biography* (1996), and a longtime contributor to the *Comics Journal*.

INDEX

Aarn Munro, 9
Abel, Robert, 98
Abomination (character), 141
Abrams, M. H., 98
Academy of Comic Arts and Sciences, 62
Ace Comics, 15
Action Comics, 15, 53–54, 75, 100, 102, 104, 106, 114, 125, 134, 179, 182, 185
Adams, Neal, xvii, 101, 114, 121, 142, 201, 255, 259, 261–63, 266
Adkins, Dan, 67
Adventures of Patsy, The, 10
Akira, 176
Alfred the Butler, 64, 116, 239
Alice in Wonderland, 10, 56
All in Color for a Dime, 58
All Our Yesterdays: An Informal History of Science Fiction Fandom in the Forties, 83
Alley Oop, 8–9
All-Star Comics, 54, 113, 140
Alter Ego, 62
Amazing Fantasy, 114
Amazing Spider-Man, 114, 139, 197, 279
Amazing Stories, 17, 19
Amazing Transforming Superhero! Essays on the Revisions of Characters in Comic Books, The, xvi, 279–94
American Born Chinese, xiv
American Flagg!, 176, 195
American Monomyth, The, 74
American Splendor, 276
Anatomy of Criticism, 74, 88, 98
Anderson, Murphy, 65
Andrae, Thomas, 14, 70
Angel, 175
Angel/Angel, 222, 230, 232, 235

Ant-Man, 177
Archie, 170, 297
Arguing Comics: Literary Masters on a Popular Medium, xix
Arkham Asylum/Arkham Asylum, 69, 118, 249
Arrow, 100, 113
Asimov, Isaac, 168
Astro City, xvii, 170, 194
Atom, The, 63, 177
Authority, The, 133
Avengers, The (tv series), 244
Avengers/The Avengers, 68, 106, 114, 134

Baby Huey, 297
Bails, Jerry, 62–63
Bakhtin, Mikhail, 188–89, 197
Bankhead, Tallulah, 245–47
Barbara Gordon, 67–69
Barker, Martin, 238, 250–51
Barks, Carl, 195
Baron Mordo, 141
Barreaux, Adolphe, 12
Barrier, Michael, 114
Barthes, Roland, 70, 112, 115
Batgirl, 69, 242, 248
Batman: The Complete History, 133
Batman: The Dark Knight Returns, 68, 76, 116–35, 182–95, 296
Batman/Batman/Bruce Wayne, xvii, 9, 39, 48, 54, 58, 61–71, 74, 80, 84–86, 88, 90–91, 93–95, 97, 99–101, 107–15, 116–35, 140, 155, 164, 170–71, 175, 177–78, 181–84, 188–91, 194–97, 200–201, 234, 237–51, 269, 281, 291, 293, 296–300, 302
Batman and Me, 70, 115
Batman and Robin, 69

309

Batman Unmasked, 134
Batmania, 62
Battis, Jes, 224, 235
Batwoman, 242, 248
Baudelaire, Charles, 192
Becker, Stephen, xix
Bendis, Brian Michael, 297
Benton, Mike, 14, 195
Beowulf/Beowulf, 74, 84, 89–94, 98
Bergman, Ingmar, 246
Big Bang Theory, The, 199
Billy Batson, 59, 80
Birth of a Nation, The, 82
Bizarro, 190
Black Adam, 140
Black Canary, 257, 264
Black Cat, The, 135
Black Goliath, 269
Black Lightning/Black Lightning/Jefferson Pierce, 201, 262–63, 266, 268–69
Black Superheroes, Milestone Comics, and Their Fans, 201, 267, 269–78
Black Terror/Black Terror, 36–37
Black Vulcan, 264
Black Widow, 245–46
Blackbeard, Bill, 13
Blondie, 40
Blood Syndicate, The, 270
Bloom, Clive, 134
Bloom, Harold, 75–76, 117–19, 131–35
Blue Beetle/Blue Beetle, 36–40
Bob Scully, Two-Fisted Hick Detective, 22
Bogey Man (character), 36
Bolland, Brian, 69
Books of Magic, The, 276
Bordo, Susan, 277
Bradstreet, Tim, 289
Brain Wave, 140
Brave and the Bold, The, 114
Brickner, Richard M., 39
Bridwell, F. Nelson, 63
Brooker, Will, xvi, 5, 134
Broome, John, 65–66
Brown, James, 254
Brown, Jeffrey, 201, 267
Brubaker, Ed, 297

Buck Rogers, 22
Buffy the Vampire Slayer/Buffy Summers/Buffyverse, 13, 200, 216–17, 221–26, 229–36
Bukatman, Scott, xiii, 77
Bullet Man, 36
Burroughs, Edgar Rice, 17
Burton, Tim, 181–83
Busiek, Kurt, xvii, 170, 197–98, 263
Byrne, John, 107
Byrne, Ruth, 161, 167

Cahiers du Cinéma, 66, 85
Caillois, Roger, 188
Calendar Man, 123
Campbell, Frances Stuart, 37
Campbell, Joseph, xii, 37, 74, 229
Caniff, Milton, 30, 86–87
Capp, Al, 43
Captain America/Captain America, 37, 80, 100–101, 107–8, 114, 134, 297
Captain America and the Crusade against Evil, xiv
Captain America and the Struggle of the Superhero, xvi
Captain America Complex, The, 74
Captain and the Kids, The, 41
Captain Easy, 15
Captain Marvel/Captain Marvel, 9, 53, 59, 80–81, 107, 114, 140, 175, 204
Captain Midnight, 36, 108, 115
Carnage (character), 141
Carroll, Lewis, 56
Cassaday, John, xvii
Castle, Terry, 182, 188–89, 197
Catman, 36
Catwoman, 116, 190, 245
Cawelti, John G., 73–74
Cerebus, 14
Certeau, Michel de, 180–81, 184, 186, 196–97
Chandler, Raymond, 118, 171
Chaykin, Howard, 171, 176, 195, 197–98
Childe Roland, 131–32
Cinderella, 36
Civil rights/human rights, 126, 135, 206, 266
Clark, Kenneth, 252–53

Classics Illustrated, 297, 302
Clayface, 123
Clock, The, 11
Coast City, 183
Cold War, xvi, xx, 130, 137, 140, 149–50, 212
Cole, Jack, 175, 195–96
College English, 73, 84
Comic Art, 61
Comic Book Heroes, The, 61, 70
Comic Reader, The, 62
Comic Strip Century: Celebrating 100 Years of an Art Form, The, 13
Comicollector, The, 62
Comics: An Anatomy of a Mass Medium, 15
Comics Code/Comics Code Authority, 100–101, 128, 137, 149–50, 241, 253
Comics Journal, The, 113–14
Comics Magazine, The, 10
Comics of the Golden Age: The Illustrated History, 14
Comics Studies Reader, A, xviii, xix, 196
Comix: A History of Comic Books in America, xix, 59
Commissioner James Gordon, 116, 121, 130, 132, 135, 245
Connie, 56
Consolidated Publishing Company, 22
Contemporary Comic Book Superhero, The, xvi
Continuity, 68–69, 76, 138–39, 144, 152–53, 155, 157, 160, 198–99, 296–97
Coogan, Peter, 3–4
Cooper, Gary, 93
Corbusier, Le, 180–81, 196
Costello, Matthew J., xvi
Crime Comics, 46–52, 100–101
Crisis on Infinite Earths, 156–57, 161–63, 165, 296
Crow, The/The Crow, 291, 293
Crypt of Terror, 114
Cyborg (character), 264
Cyclops (character), 264

Daily Planet/Daily Star, 103, 179
Daniels, Les, xix, 14, 59, 133, 195–96, 236, 250
Daredevil/Daredevil, 118, 175, 190, 196–97, 281
Dark Angel, 200, 219, 226–27, 234

Dark Knight Rises, The, 70
Dark Knights: The New Comics in Context, 134
Darkseid, 151
Darrow, Geoff, 185–86
Davis, Guy, xvii
DC Comics/DC universe, xiii, 5, 12, 53, 61–71, 101–2, 107, 127, 130, 134, 139, 150–52, 156–57, 161–62, 167, 194, 196, 255–56, 262, 264, 267, 298, 300–301
De Haven, Tom, 138
Deadman, 190
Death in the Family, A, 248
Detective Ace King, 22
Detective Comics, 53, 64–71, 113, 240–41
Detective Dan, 22
Devitt, Amy, 153
Diaz, Junot, 254
Dick Tracy, 22, 40, 181
Dillon, Steve, 289, 292
Dini, Paul, 197
Dirty Harry, 74, 80
Disney Corporation, xiii
Ditko, Steve, 63, 141, 183, 197
Do the Gods Wear Capes? Spirituality, Fantasy, and Superheroes, xvi
Doc Savage, 21–22, 108, 115
Doctor Doom, 109, 112, 140–41, 211, 215
Doctor Occult, 10–11
Doctor Octopus, 140–41
Doctor Strange, 141, 184, 190
Donald Duck, 297
Donaldson, E. Talbot, 90
Donenfeld, Harry, 12, 53, 107
Dooley, Dennis, 114
Douglas, Mary, xiii
Doyle, Arthur Conan, 188
Dozier, William, 61
Dr. Kildare, 143
Duneier, Mitchell, 276–77
Dyer, Richard, 241, 250–51

Earhart, Amelia, 57
Eastwood, Clint, 74, 126, 279
Eble, Kenneth E., 90
E.C. (Entertaining Comics), 100–101, 114
Eco, Umberto, 119, 137–39, 162, 296, 302–4

Eisner, Will, 4, 195
Elder, Will, xvii
Ella Cinders, 41
Ellis, Havelock, 16
Ellis, Warren, xvii, 156, 163–64, 185, 197
Elongated Man, 65–66, 190
Engle, Gary, 114
Ennis, Garth, 279–81, 286, 289–90
Eternals, The, 137
Everson, William K., 282

Faerie Queene, The, 84–90, 93–98
Famous Monsters of Filmland, 300
Fanon, Frantz, 253
Fantastic Four/Fantastic Four, 101, 109, 114–15, 139–49, 175–76, 184, 190, 200, 211–13
Fantom of the Fair, The, 178
Fascism/fascist/fascistic, xv, 76, 107, 125, 127, 129–30, 133, 135, 171
Fawcett Comics, 53, 107, 140
Feiffer, Jules, xvi, xix, 4, 59, 83, 98, 114, 189, 195, 197
Feminism/feminist, xxi, 200, 203–10, 211–15, 216–36
Fenin, George N., 282, 286, 289
Fielding, Henry, 17, 188
Fine, Jerry, 21
Finger, Bill, 63, 109–10, 115, 177
Finnley Wren, 17
Firefly/Serenity, 222, 235
First International Science Film Convention, 83
Flash/Flash/Barry Allen/Jay Garrick/Wally West, 9, 53, 65, 80–83, 101, 114, 156, 162–63, 167–68, 175, 298–99
Fleming, Ian, 79, 85, 91
Folklore, 41–42, 117, 128, 163
Ford, John, 280, 286, 288, 291
Foster, Hal, 31
Fourth World, 137, 151–52
Fox, Gardner, 62–63, 65
Fox Features, 107
Frankenstein, 112
French, Philip, 281, 284, 288, 290
Freud, Sigmund/Freudian, 87, 124–25
Friedman, Thomas, xix

Frightful Four, The, 139
Fritzsche, Peter, 176
Frye, Northrop, 74, 84, 88–90, 98
Fuchs, Wolfgang, 15
Funnies: An American Idiom, The, 98
Funny Pages, 11, 113

Gabrielle (*Xena*), 216–19, 221–22, 224, 228
Gaiman, Neil, 137, 198
Gaines, Max, 54
Gaines, William, 101
Galactus, 144–48
Gandhi, 100
Gartland, Mike, 146–47
Gasoline Alley, 40, 195
Geek, The, 190
Gender, xv–xvi, xviii, 36, 54, 121, 201, 230, 232, 236, 276–77
Generation of Vipers, A, xi
George, Stefan, 38
Gernsback, Hugo, 18
Giant Man, 177
Gibbons, Dave, xvii, 195, 197
Gilgamesh, 13
Giunta, John, 65
Gladiator, 4, 13, 16–22, 23–29, 149
Glyn, Elinor, 16
Godfather, The, 69, 280, 288
Godwin, Frank, 56
Golden Age, The, 197
Goodman, Martin, 148
Gornick, Vivian, 175, 196
Gotham, 65, 68, 91, 94, 109–10, 118, 123, 125, 129–30, 133, 135, 163–64, 170, 177, 181–83, 194, 247, 252
Goulart, Ron, 10, 15
Gould, Chester, 181
Graff, Mel, 15
Grant Morrison: Combining the Worlds of Contemporary Comics, xvi, 69
Gray Seal, 11
Great Comic Book Heroes, The, xix, 4, 30–33, 59, 83, 98, 114, 197
Great Depression, 53, 75, 108
Great Women Superheroes, The, 213
Green Arrow, The/Oliver Queen, xvii, 101, 130, 190, 201, 255–58, 263–64, 266, 267

Green Goblin, 140
Green Hornet, 108, 115, 197, 204
Green Lama, 36
Green Lantern/Green Lantern/Hal Jordan/
    John Stewart/Guy Gardner, xvii, 62, 80,
    101, 107, 114, 127, 175, 196, 201, 255–59,
    263–68, 298–99
Green Lantern Co-Starring Green Arrow, xvii,
    21, 201, 255–58, 263, 266–67
Greene, Sid, 64, 66
Grimm's Fairy Tales, 41
Groth, Gary, 113
Gruenwald, Mark, 153
Gumps, The, 40
Gunning, Tom, 182, 197
Gunsmoke, 91, 95

Haggard, H. Rider, 79
Hammett, Dashiell, 118
Hand of Fire: The Comics Art of Jack Kirby,
    xvi, 136–54
Hank Pym, 264
Happy Hooligan, 40
Harbinger (character), 165
Hardware (character), 271
Hardwire, 271
Harmon, Jim, 58, 98
Harrigan, Pat, 139
Harris, Jack C., 67
Hatfield, Charles, xvi, xix
Haunt of Fear, 114
Haunt of Fears, A, 238
Hawkgirl, 264
Hawkman/Hawkman, 53, 62, 80, 107, 175, 190
Hearst, William Randolph, 173, 184, 185
Hellblazer, 101
Hensleigh, Jonathan, 201, 279
Hercules, 36, 83, 102, 230
Hergé, 195
Herrmann, Bernard, 66
Himes, Chester, 266
Hine, Lewis, 179
Hitler, Adolf, 18, 35, 38, 47
Hlusko, Dana, 219
Hobbes, Thomas, 127, 134
Hoffman, Dustin, 247

Holland, Norman, 89–90, 98
Hollander, Anne, 190–91, 197
Hollywood, 20, 100, 121, 237, 244, 248, 251,
    255, 279–94
Homer, 13
Hood, Raymond, 179
hooks, bell, 218, 222–23, 227, 233, 235–36,
    276–77
Horatio Alger, 35
Horror Comics, xii, 10, 100–101, 114, 250
How to Read Superhero Comics and Why, 75,
    116–35
Hugo Danner, 17–19, 23–29
Hugo Hercules, 7–8
Human Bomb, 190
Human Torch/Johnny Storm, 36, 53, 107,
    190, 211–15
Humor Publishing Company, 22
Hush, 164

Iceman, 175
Icon/Icon/Augustus Freeman IV, 271, 274–76
Image Comics, 201, 274
Incredible Hulk, The/Hulk, 101, 114, 141, 150,
    176, 190, 230, 300
Infantino, Carmine, 63–66
Inhumans, 144, 148
Inness, Sherrie A., 222, 235
Invisible Girl/Invisible Woman/Sue Storm,
    200, 211–15, 264
Invisibles, The, xvii
Iron Man, 106, 141
It's a Bird, xvii

Jack Kirby Collector, The, 147
Jacobs, Will, xix, 70–71
James Bond, 79, 85, 91, 96, 244, 297
Jane Foster, 143
Janson, Klaus, 134
Jean Grey, 236, 264
Jenkins, Henry, 70, 199, 202
Jewett, Robert, xiv, 74–75
Jimmy Corrigan: The Smartest Kid on Earth, xiv
John Carter of Mars, 18
Johns, Geoff, 297
Johnson-Laird, Philip, 159–60, 165

314 INDEX

Joker, 85, 90, 112, 114, 116, 122–24, 140, 177, 182, 189–90, 242, 248, 281, 298
Jones, Gerard, xix, 3–4, 61–63, 66, 70–71
Journal of Graphic Novel and Comics, xv
Journey into Mystery, 114
Jowett, Lorna, 219, 221, 232, 236
Joyce, James, 246
Judge, 56
Judge Dredd, 164, 168, 195
Justice League of America/Justice League of America, 68, 114, 127, 150, 226, 263, 298
Justice Society of America/Justice Society of America, 61–62, 140

Kane, Bob, 61, 63–66, 70, 109, 113, 115, 120, 131
Kane, Gil, 196
Kant, Immanuel, 158
Katsuhiro, Otomo, 176
Katzenjammer Kids, The, 40–41
Kaveney, Roz, xvi
Keaton, Michael, 249
Keen Detective Funnies, 113
Kennedy, Robert F., 256, 299
Kermit the Frog, 254
Kerouac, Jack, 256
Kidd, Chip, 196
Killing Joke, The, 248
King, Martin Luther, 256, 259
Kingdom Come, 9, 127, 167
Kingpin (character), 197
Kirby, Jack, xvi, 65–66, 136–54, 176, 255, 302
Kirk, James T., 74, 82
Klock, Geoff, 75–76
Koerner, William H. D., 7
Komix Illustrated, 62
Koolhaas, Rem, 172, 174, 190, 195–96
Krazy Kat, 195
Kristiansen, Teddy, xvii
Krypton/Kryptonian, 119, 138, 177, 179, 253, 290
Kubert, Joe, 62
Kukkonen, Karin, 76–77
Kung Fu, 230
Kurtzman, Harvey, xvii, 195

Ladd, Alan, 171
Lana Lang, 126, 129

Lang, Fritz, 179
Lassie, 82
Lawrence, John Shelton, xiv, 74–75
Lee, Jim, 69
Lee, Stan, 101, 103, 109, 139–48, 152, 197, 213, 255
Leone, Sergio, 279
Lensmen, 9
Lessing, Gotthold Ephraim, 158
Letterman, David, 124
Lévi-Strauss, Claude, 108, 115, 282
Lewis, C. S., 122
Lewis, Jerry, 250
Lewis, Sinclair, 16, 40
Lex Luthor, 112, 140, 161, 181–82, 184, 190
Lichtenstein, Roy, 85, 244
Li'l Abner, 40, 43
Little Nemo in Slumberland/Little Nemo, 10, 173, 177–78, 195
Little Orphan Annie, 43
Loeb, Jeph, 164, 196
Lois and Clark, 9
Lois Lane, 56, 95, 103, 105, 121, 156, 161, 164, 167, 175, 177
Loki, 140, 143
Lone Ranger, The/The Lone Ranger, 4, 82, 86, 91, 100, 189
Lord of the Rings, The, 230
Lorrah, Jean, 231, 236
Luke Cage, 269
Lupoff, Dick, xix

MacFadden, Bernarr, 18
MacKinnon, Kenneth, 280, 288
MacLean, Alistair, 79
Mad, xvii, 300
Mad Hatter, 123
Magneto, 112, 140–43
Mailer, Norman, 192–93
Majestic Studios, 12
Man and Superman, 18
Man from U.N.C.L.E., The, 96, 244
Man-Bat, 123
Mandrake the Magician, 15, 40, 190
Manhunter, 176
Many Lives of the Batman, The, 134, 237–51

Mark of Zorro, The, 120
Marlowe, Philip, 108
Marschall, Rick, 197
Marston, Elizabeth Holloway, 55
Marston, William Mouton/Charles Moulton, 5, 54–55, 59, 200, 206–8, 216, 232–33, 236
Martian Manhunter, 64
Marvel Comics/Marvel Comics/Marvel universe, xiii, 65, 68, 80, 101–2, 106, 109, 113–15, 118, 134, 136–54, 170, 183, 197, 200, 255, 279–94
Marvel Family, 140
Mary Marvel, 168
Mary Poppins, 82
Masculinity/masculine, 36, 55, 59, 60, 105, 191, 201, 205, 207, 216, 237–51, 269–78, 288
Masked Marvel, 100, 113
Maus, xiv, xvii, xxii, 274, 276
Max Guevara, 200, 217, 219–21, 226–27, 229, 233–34
McCabe, James, 187, 197
McCay, Winsor, 173, 177
McCloud, Scott, xix, 196
McCoy, Leonard, 112
McCue, Greg S., 134
McDuffie, Dwayne, 264, 271
McLuhan, Marshall, xiv, 5, 87
Medhurst, Andy, 200–201
Melly, George, 244–45, 251
Men of Tomorrow: Geeks, Gangsters and the Birth of the Comic Book, 4, 16–22
Mencken, H. L., 4, 16
Mesmer, Olga, 12–13, 15
Metropolis, 109, 161, 170, 178–86, 262
Mighty Mouse, 175
Milestone Comics, 201, 269–78
Millar, Mark, xvii, 167
Miller, Frank, 67, 70, 76, 116–35, 164, 182, 197–98, 249, 251, 263, 296
Mills, Tarpé, 5
Milne, A. A., 56
Milton, John, 74, 84, 86, 90, 93, 98
Miss Fury, 5
Mission Impossible, 84, 91
Mitchell, Margaret, 43
Modesty Blaise, 244

Monitor (character), 165
Moore, Alan, xvi, 67, 76, 109, 116–17, 125, 133, 156, 159, 164–65, 168, 170, 175, 188, 190, 194–98
More Fun Comics, 10–11, 15
Morrison, Grant, xvii, 68, 198
Moses, Robert, 181
Motion Picture Funnies Weekly, 80
Mr. and Mrs., 43
Mr. Fantastic/Reed Richards, 211–15, 264
Mr. Freeze, 123, 237
Mr. Miracle, 190
Mr. X/Mr. X, 186–87, 195, 197
Murray, Will, 12, 15
Mussolini, Benito, 35, 38
Mutt and Jeff, 41
Mysterio, 190
Mystery in Space, 62
Myth/mythology/mythos, xii, xiv, 3, 55, 58, 70, 74, 75, 78, 80, 88–91, 99–100, 104, 106–7, 109, 112, 116, 131, 136–37, 143–44, 148–49, 151–52, 162, 175, 197, 208, 210, 216–17, 227, 229, 265, 279, 281–82, 291, 296
Myth of the American Superhero, The, xiv, 74, 80–83
Mythologies, 115

Nama, Adilifu, xvi, 201
Nancy, 41
Nazis/Nazism, 35, 37–38, 43, 48, 52, 107–8, 135, 204, 212, 256
Ndalianis, Angela, xvi
Negative Zone, 148
Neutrino, The, 168
New Comics, The, 113
New 52, The, 68
New Fun Comics, 10, 15
New York City, 68, 108–13, 118, 145, 172–73, 175, 177–80, 183, 194–97, 252
Newton, Don, 67
Nicholson, Jack, 249
Nick Carter, 35
Nietzsche, Friedrich, xi, 17, 35, 38, 48, 120, 178, 193–94, 198
Nightcrawler, 190
Nightingale, Florence, 57

316 INDEX

Nixon, Richard, 255
Noble, Kathleen D., 232, 236
Noir, 201, 280, 283–84, 288, 291–92, 294
Nolan, Christopher, 69–70
Novelty Press, 80
Nyberg, Amy Kiste, 135

Ods Bodkin, 10
Odysseus, 83
O'Neil, Dennis, xvii, 67–68, 121, 196, 201, 255, 259, 261–63, 266
Ong, Walter, xiv, 5, 74, 76
Outsiders, The, 263
Ozymandias, 112

Palmer, Lorrie, 200–201
Panofsky, Erwin, 163
Paradise Lost, 84, 87–90, 94, 98
Pearson, Roberta E., xvi, 134
Peckinpah, Sam, 279, 290
Peggy Allen, 54
Pekar, Harvey, xv
Penguin (character), 123, 140
Penn, Arthur, 290
Persepolis, xiv
Peter, Harry G., 56
Phantom, The/The Phantom, 11, 15, 41
Phantom Magician, 10, 15
Planetary/Planetary, xvii, 156–57, 162–66
Plastic Man, 38–39, 80, 114, 175, 188, 196
Poe, Edgar Allan, 135, 188
Poison Ivy, 123
Polly and Her Pals, 195
Popeye, 8, 14
Pound, Louise, 42
Presley, Elvis, 250
Price, Vincent, 249
Prince Valiant, 195
Professor Charles Xavier/Professor X, 142–43
Promethea, 159–60, 162–63, 194–95
Psycho, 66
Punisher, The/The Punisher/Frank Castle, 201, 279–94

Raban, Jonathan, 190
Race/racial/racism, 18, 35, 142, 201, 207, 252–68, 269–78

Ralph Dibney, 64
Rambo, 74, 80
Raymond, Alex, 31
Reagan, Ronald/Reaganism, 117–18, 123, 125, 128–30, 135, 248
Red Skull, 140
Reeve, Christopher, 100
Reiss, Jana, 225, 232, 235–36
Reitberger, Reinhold, 15
Reynolds, Richard, xvi, 58, 75–77, 123, 134, 136, 233, 268, 281
Riddler, The, 123
Ringmaster, 190
Ro, Ronin, 148
Road Warrior, The, 182
Robbins, Trina, 5, 213
Roberson, Chris, 153
Robin/Dick Grayson/Jason Todd/Carrie Kelly, 97, 110–13, 117, 120–24, 130, 177, 190–91, 196–97, 239–42, 244–51
Robin Hood, 12, 190
Robinson, James, 194, 198
Robinson, Lillian, 200
Robinson, W. R., 85–86, 98
Rocket's Blast, The, 62
Rollin, Roger B., 73
Romance Comics, xii, xx, 78, 137, 143, 150
Romero, Cesar, 249
Roosevelt, Franklin D., 21, 53, 132, 135
Ross, Alex, 198
Roth, Werner, 142
Rozakis, Bob, 67
Rucka, Greg, 297
Rusty Riley, 56
Ryan, Marie-Laure, 155–56, 167

Sale, Tim, 175–76, 196
Salisbury, Mark, 134
Samson, 102
San Diego Comic Con, 63
Sandman (DC character), 80, 143
Sandman, The (DC series), 276
Sandman, The (Marvel character), 141
Sartre, Jean-Paul, 192
Saturday Evening Post, 33, 34
Saunders, Ben, xii, xvi
Scarecrow (character), 123

INDEX 317

Scarlet Witch, 264
Schatz, Thomas, 281–86, 289
Schrader, Paul, 291–92
Schumacher, Joel, 69
Schwartz, Julius, 61–63, 65–66
Science Fiction, 19, 21
Science Fiction Audiences, 70
Scorsese, Martin, 291
Scott-Heron, Gil, 252–53
Seagal, Steven, 74
Seagle, Steven T., xvii
Secret Identity Crisis: Comic Books and the Unmasking of Cold War America, xvi
Seduction of the Innocent, xix, 5, 46–52, 58, 100, 114, 120, 122, 128, 134, 238–39
Segar, E. C., 8
Sensation Comics, 54, 56–57
Sentinels, 142
Sexuality, 58, 190, 201, 237–51
Shadow, The/The Shadow, 21, 182, 187
Shakespeare, William, 13, 69, 122, 131, 250, 279, 282, 286
Shaw, Bernard, 18, 35
Sheena, 50
Shepard, Ernest H., 56
Sheridan, Martin, xix
Sherlock Holmes, 182
Shock Gibson, 100, 113
Shooter, Jim, 109
Showcase, 114
Shuster, Joe, 4, 10, 12, 15, 17–22, 53, 102, 178–79
Siegel, Jerry, 4, 10, 12, 15, 17–22, 53, 102, 178–79
Silver Surfer, 144–48
Simmel, Georg, 174, 186, 197
Simon, Joe, 143
Simonson, Walt, 176
Simpsons, The, 199
Singer, Marc, xvi, 69
Skrulls, 145, 211, 215
Slam Bradley/Slam Bradley, 11, 15, 102
Slotkin, Richard, 74
Smith, E. E., 83
Smith, Sidney, 40
Smithsonian Book of Comic Book Comics, The, 114
Son of Origin of Marvel Comics, 145

Sontag, Susan, 237, 244, 251
Spark Man, 41
Spectre, The/Jim Corrigan, 175, 190
Speed Comics, 113
Spenser, Edmund, 74, 84–87, 90, 93–98
Spicy Mystery Stories, 12–13
Spider, The, 182
Spider Jerusalem, 185–87
Spider-Man/Spider-Man/Peter Parker, 10, 63, 101, 114, 134, 140–41, 150, 175, 183–84, 197, 219, 227, 234, 281, 293, 297, 302–3
Spiegelman, Art, xv, xvii, 196
Spirit, The/The Spirit/Denny Colt, 4, 80, 187–88
Spock, 74, 82, 112
Sprang, Dick, 124, 131
Squadron Supreme/Squadron Supreme, 127, 178, 197
Star Trek, 84, 112, 265, 268, 297
Star Wars/Star Wars, 130, 170, 279
Starman/Starman/Jack Knight, 170, 194, 196
Static/Static, 271–74
Steinberg, Flo, 66
Steinem, Gloria, 60, 200, 216, 235
Stephanie Brown, 68–69
Steranko, James, xix, 58, 195
Steranko History of Comics, The, 58
Steve Canyon/Steve Canyon, 84–86, 88–89, 93, 95
Steve Trevor, 55–56
Stevenson, Robert Louis, 79
Stewart, Susan, 177–78, 196, 299
Stillman, Whit, 135
Street and Smith, 21, 115
Stuller, Jennifer, 201
Sturm, James, xvii
Sub-Mariner, The/Namor, 53, 80, 100–101, 107, 113, 139, 214
Super Black: American Pop Culture and Black Superheroes, xvi, 201, 252–68
Super Friends, 264
Super Heroes: A Modern Mythology, 58, 99–115, 134, 136, 233, 268, 281
Superboy, 48
Supergirl, 101, 114
Superhero: The Secret Origin of a Genre, 3–4, 7–15

Superheroes! Capes and Crusaders in Comics and Film, xvi
Superman: Red Son, xvii, 167
Superman/Superman/Clark Kent, xvii, 4, 9–12, 15, 20–21, 35–39, 48–49, 54, 56, 61, 63, 74–75, 88, 93, 95, 97, 99–108, 113, 119, 121, 125–30, 133, 137–40, 143, 155–56, 161–62, 164, 167, 171, 175–85, 187, 189–97, 204, 227, 253, 259–61, 270, 274, 277, 290–91, 293, 296–98, 301
Superman at Fifty! The Persistence of a Legend, 114
Superman for All Seasons, 175, 196
Supreme/Supreme, 195, 198
Swamp Thing, 190
Swan, Curt, 196

Tales from the Crypt, 100, 114
Tales of the Unexpected, 143
Target Comics, 80
Tarzan/Tarzan, 18, 22, 37, 40–41, 54, 164, 195, 267
Taubin, Amy, 291
Tawky Tawny, 9
Tenniel, John, 56
Terminal City, 178
Thackeray, William, 17
Thimble Theatre, 8
Thing, The/Ben Grimm, 144, 150, 176, 190, 211–15
Thomas, Roy, 62–63, 142
Thompson, Don, xix
Thompson, Hunter S., 185
Thor/*The Mighty Thor*/Thor/Don Blake, 101, 106, 114, 136–37, 140, 143–44, 148–49
Thrilling Comics, 54
Thunderbirds, 244
Tick, The, 197
Tim Tyler, 40
Time Warner/Warner Brothers, xiii, 20, 68
Timely Comics, 53
Time², 176
Titanium Man, 141
Toland, Gregg, 66
Tom Strong, 156–57, 162, 164–66
Tonto, 91

Top 10, 170
Transmetropolitan, 185–87
Trickster (character), 9
Trotsky, Leon, 18
Tulloch, John, 70
2000AD, 168
Two-Face, 112, 116, 123–24, 189

UKCAC (United Kingdom Comic Art Convention), 63
Ultraman, 161
Understanding Comics: The Invisible Art, xix, 196
Unstable Molecules (Fantastic Four Legends Volume 1), xvii
Uricchio, William, xvi, 134

Varley, Lynn, 134
Vault of Horror, 100, 114
Vaz, Mark Cotta, 240, 250–51
Venom (character), 141
Ventriloquist (character), 123
Vietnam War, The, 84, 255, 261, 279, 281
Vigilante/vigilantism, xxi, 5, 82, 123, 125, 132, 134, 148, 171, 183, 190–91, 201, 217, 242, 250, 279–94
Villains/supervillains, 9, 13, 56, 59, 78, 95–96, 112, 122–26, 131–32, 137, 139–44, 149, 161, 165, 181, 205, 211, 246, 255–56, 271, 273, 279–94
Virginian, The, 82
Vision (character), 264
Vixen (character), 264
Voight, Jon, 247

Wagner, Richard, 43
Waid, Mark, 167, 297
Wallace, Edgar, 111
Wandtke, Terrence R., xvi
Wardrip-Fruin, Noah, 139
Warhol, Andy, 244
Washington, Robert L., 271
Wasp (character), 264
Watcher (character), 144–45
Watchmen, xvii, xxi, 76, 101, 109, 125, 133, 188, 194–95, 197

Watterson, Bill, 177
Waugh, Coulton, xix
Wayne, John, 279–80, 282, 291
Weiner, Robert G., xvi
Weisinger, Mort, 61, 63, 138–39
Welles, Orson, 31
Wells, H. G., 17
Wertham, Fredric, xiv, xix, 5, 58–59, 74, 76, 100, 120, 122, 124, 127–28, 133–34, 237–45, 247, 249–51, 253, 267
West, Adam, 117, 120, 124, 201, 246–47, 249–50
Westerns/Western Comics, 78, 90–95, 100, 164, 200–202, 255, 279–94
Whedon, Joss/Whedonverse, 217–18, 222, 224–26, 230, 233, 235–36
White, David Manning, 98
White Streak, 80
Williams, J. H., III, 159
Williams, Martin, 114
Williamson, Jack, 18
Winnie the Pooh, 56
Wirth, Louis, 195
Witek, Joseph, 196
Wolfman, Marv, 156–57, 161, 163
Wolverine, 190
Woman in Red, 54

Wonder Boy, 37
Wonder Woman/Wonder Woman/Diana Prince, xvii, 5, 36–39, 41, 48, 54–60, 80, 99–101, 107, 113, 127, 155, 175, 200, 203–11, 216–17, 229, 232, 234, 236, 241, 297
Wonder Women, 200, 211–15
Wonderman, 37, 107
Wood, Wallace, xvii
World War II, 32–33, 44, 47, 100, 166, 178, 204, 206, 212
World's Fair Comics, 115, 178
Wright, Frank Lloyd, 180
Wylie, Philip, xi, xxii, 4, 13, 149

Xena: Warrior Princess/Xena, 13, 200, 216–19, 221–22, 224, 227–29, 233–34
Xero, 61
X-Men/X-Men, 101, 114, 134, 140–43, 148–52, 190, 226, 236, 254

Yankee Boy, 36

Zacharek, Stephanie, 232, 236
Zorro, 120, 189, 197
Zot! The Complete Black and White Collection: 1987–1991, xix

www.ingramcontent.com/pod-product-compliance
Lightning Source LLC
Chambersburg PA
CBHW030333240426
43661CB00052B/1622